F027 29

D1481705

Lineberger Memorial
Library

Lutheran Theological Southern Seminary   Columbia, S. C.

THE LOEB CLASSICAL LIBRARY

FOUNDED BY JAMES LOEB

EDITED BY

G. P. GOOLD

PREVIOUS EDITORS

T. E. PAGE   E. CAPPS

W. H. D. ROUSE   L. A. POST

E. H. WARMINGTON

VELLEIUS PATERCULUS

AND

RES GESTAE DIVI AUGUSTI

LCL 152

CONTENTS

BIBLIOGRAPHICAL ADDENDUM
(1992)

Editions

H. Volkmann, *Res Gestae Divi Augusti*, Berlin 1957.

P. A. Brunt and J. M. Moore, *Res Gestae Divi Augusti* (Latin with translation and commentary), Oxford 1967.

A. J. Woodman, *Velleius Paterculus: The Tiberian Narrative (2.94–131)*, (Cambridge Classical Texts and Commentaries 19), Cambridge 1977. Full bibliography.

————*Velleius Paterculus: The Caesarian and Augustan Narrative (2.41–93)*, (Cambridge Classical Texts and Commentaries 25), Cambridge 1983. Full bibliography.

Studies

J. D. Newby, *Numismatic Commentary on the Res Gestae of Augustus*, 1938.

G. V. Sumner, 'The Truth about Velleius Paterculus: Prolegomena,' *Harvard Studies in Classical Philology* 74 (1970) 257–297.

A. J. Woodman, 'Questions of Date, Genre, and Style in Velleius,' *Classical Quarterly* 25 (1975) 272–306.

C. VELLEIUS PATERCULUS

INTRODUCTION

" Dicere enim solebat nullum esse librum tam malum ut
non aliqua parte prodesset."—Pliny, *Ep.* iii. 5. 10, quoting a
saying of his uncle.

VELLEIUS PATERCULUS does not rank among the great
Olympians of classical literature either as stylist or
as historian. But, as Pliny the elder says, no book
is so poor that one cannot get some good out of it,
and there is much in this comparatively neglected
author that is worth reading once, at least in translation. In its aim to include all that is of value and
interest in Greek and Latin literature from the days
of Homer to the Fall of Constantinople the Loeb
Library is performing what is perhaps its most
valuable service in making more generally available
the content of those comparatively unknown authors
who, for stylistic or other reasons, are not to be
reckoned among the great classics or do not deserve
a careful study in the original.

A compendium of Roman history, hastily compiled
by an army officer as a memorial volume to commemorate the elevation to the consulship for the year
A.D. 30 of his friend and fellow-Campanian, Marcus
Vinicius, could hardly be expected to rise to the level
either of great history or great literature. And yet,
taken for what it is, a rapid sketch of some ten

viii

centuries of history, it is, in spite of its many defects, which will duly be pointed out, the most successful and most readable of all the abridgements of Roman history which have come down to us. Abridgements are usually little more than skeletons; but Velleius has succeeded, in spite of the brief compass of his work, in clothing the bones with real flesh, and in endowing his compendium with more than a mere shadow of vitality, thanks to his own enthusiastic interest in the human side of the great characters of history. The work, after the large lacuna in the first book, covers uninterruptedly the period from the battle of Pydna to A.D. 30, a period which practically coincides with that covered by the final 97 books of Livy for which no manuscript has come down to us, and one which is but partially treated in the extant portions of the works of other Roman historians of first rank. It is therefore valuable, if for nothing else, in that it furnishes us with a connected account of this period which is at any rate much more readable than the bare epitomes of Livy. Besides, it has certain excellences of its own in the treatment of special subjects, especially the chapters on literary history, in which the author has a genuine if not very critical interest, the chapters on the Roman colonies, and those on the history of the organization of the Roman provinces, and in some of the character portraits of the great figures of Roman history. Even in the treatment of Tiberius, in spite of its tone of adulation which historians have so generally condemned, we have a document which must be considered along with the famous delineation by Tacitus, as representing the psychological attitude toward the new empire of the group of administrative officers

of the equestrian order who ardently supported it without any of the yearnings felt by the senatorial class for the old régime as it existed in the days before the empire had shorn them of their former governmental powers.

As has already been said, the work is a commemorative volume as well as an historical abridgement, and under this pardonable pretext the author feels free to depart from historical objectivity and give his work a personal note. Thus he honours Vinicius not merely by the dedication, but by addressing him frequently in the vocative case, by bringing the more important dates into chronological relation with his consulship, and by bringing into prominence the ancestors of Vinicius who had played any historical role worthy of consideration. Vinicius, who like the author himself was an official of the administration, would also lend sympathetic ears to his rhapsodic eulogy of his old commander, now the emperor Tiberius, and of his prime minister Sejanus, then in the heyday of his power and the virtual head of the government. In doing the honours, in this commemorative volume, he also takes occasion to mention, as something in which his friend would be interested, the participation of the author's own ancestors in the events which he is narrating, and, when he reaches his own times, like the painters of the Renaissance he sees no harm in introducing himself into the canvas as one of the minor participants in the historical pageant.

To this naïve and innocent egotism we owe all our information in regard to the author and his family, since the sparse references in later literature contribute nothing to our knowledge of either. We

thus learn that he reckoned among his ancestors on his mother's side Decius Magius, a distinguished citizen of Capua who remained loyal to the Romans when Capua went over to Hannibal, and Minatius Magius, who raised a legion and fought on the Roman side in the Social War, for which service he received Roman citizenship ; that his father served in Germany as prefect of horse ; that his father's brother Capito supported Agrippa in his indictment of Cassius for the murder of Caesar ; that his paternal grandfather C. Velleius Paterculus served as *praefectus fabrum* under Pompey, Marcus Brutus, and Tiberius Nero, the father of the emperor ; that he was chosen as one of the judges by Pompey in 55 B.C., and that in 41 B.C. he killed himself because he was physically unable to follow Nero in his flight from Naples. The historian himself, C.[1] Velleius Paterculus, also played the role of loyal officer, seeing service as military tribune in Thrace and Macedonia, and accompanying Caius Caesar in A.D. 1 on his visit to the eastern provinces. While there he was an eyewitness of the conference between Caius and the son of the Parthian king on an island in the Euphrates. Later he served under Tiberius for eight consecutive years, first as prefect of horse and then as *legatus*, participating in his German and Pannonian campaigns. In A.D. 6 he was elected quaestor, and while still quaestor designate he led a body of troops to reinforce Tiberius in Pannonia on the occasion of the great

---

[1] His *praenomen* is uncertain. Priscian calls him Marcus. Publius is the *praenomen* on the title-page of the ed. princeps, probably through an error of Rhenanus in identifying him with P. Velleius of Tac. *Ann.* iii. 39. At the beginning and end of Book I. his *praenomen* is given as C.

mutiny. As quaestor, in A.D. 7, he gave up the privilege of a provincial appointment to become a *legatus* under Tiberius in Pannonia. In the winter of A.D. 7–8 he was one of the *legati* in charge of winter quarters. His brother, Magius Celer Velleianus, was also a *legatus* of Tiberius and distinguished himself in the Dalmatian campaign. Both were decorated with military honours at the triumph of Tiberius in A.D. 13. Both were praetors for the year A.D. 15 and were proud of the distinction of having been the last to be nominated to the praetorship by Augustus and the first to be named by Tiberius. Here the chapter of his military career apparently closes. He does not seem to have risen higher than the praetorship in the fifteen years which intervened between the holding of that office and the consulship of Vinicius, though he may have held provincial appointments. He must have enjoyed some leisure in these years, since he hints at having in preparation a more comprehensive historical work, and his genuine enthusiasm for literature, and his familiarity with the rhetorical studies then so much in vogue, must postulate some time for their development, even though his literary work still shows many marks of the novice.

His compendium[1] is divided into two chronologically unequal parts. The first book, preserved

[1] The title of his work as it appears in the heading of Book I. in the ed. princeps is : *C. Vellei Paterculi historiae Romanae ad M. Vinicium Cos. prius volumen mutilum.* But, as the first part of this book was missing from the Murbach MS., this title may simply be the work of a scribe. Most modern editors have adopted the title : *Vellei Paterculi ad M. Vinicium libri duo.*

in a fragmentary condition,[1] began with the times immediately preceding the fall of Troy, dealt rapidly with the early history of Greece in the first seven chapters, reached the founding of Rome in chapter viii., and ended with the fall of Carthage in 146 B.C. The second book covers the period from the time of the Gracchi to the consulship of Vinicius in A.D. 30, and is on a much fuller and more comprehensive scale, especially from the consulship of Caesar to the end. This greater fulness as he approaches his own times is to be explained partly as a traditional proceeding, and partly because, as he himself says, he had in preparation a more comprehensive work covering the period from the beginning of the Civil War between Caesar and Pompey down to his own day, and in consequence he had a larger amount of material to assimilate. Here and there he checks the rapidity of his narrative to dwell at greater length upon topics in which he has a personal interest, as for example the references to literary history, the two digressions upon the colonies and provinces of Rome, the participation of members of his family in historical events, and his own share in the events of the last fifteen years of the reign of Augustus.

Both the virtues and defects of Velleius as an historical writer can be best explained on the supposition that until the year A.D. 15, when he was about thirty-five years of age, all his time had been absorbed in his military duties, and that it was only in the period of comparative leisure which followed

---

[1] The beginning, containing the title, the dedication to Vinicius, and a page or two of text, is missing. There is also a large lacuna extending from the reign of Romulus to the battle of Pydna.

that he discovered a new hobby in literary and biographical studies. These he approached with all the fresh interest and naïve enthusiasm of the amateur. His outlook is still the uncritical attitude of the dilettante. *Nil admirari* had not become his motto. He is still, at the time of writing what is apparently his maiden book, in the stage of appreciation and admiration, and, while his critical faculties are still untrained he has at any rate not become cynical or *blasé*. He can still find romance in the phenomena of history about which more mature writers had ceased to wonder. In the new rhetorical tendencies of Silver Latin he found a medium well adapted to give expression to his enthusiasm and admiration. As an historian he has not learned to weigh evidence ; he has made no close study of the sources ; [1] in giving his chronological references he unwittingly mixes up the dates of the Catonian and the Varronian eras ; [2] in his haste he overlooks events and is obliged to insert them out of their proper order. In fact his attitude is rather that of the

[1] Apart from Cato and Hortensius Velleius does not specifically mention any of his sources. The others are purely a matter of conjecture. For his purpose he needed a chronological table and a collection of biographies. It is likely that he made use of the abridgement of Atticus and the chronological data of Cornelius Nepos. For the Civil Wars he may have used the work of Messala Corvinus. For the reign of Augustus he probably used the autobiography of that emperor. For the reign of Tiberius he of course drew largely on his own experience. If he used Livy, he at any rate frequently disagrees with him.

[2] The dates, however, in so far as they are given in Roman numerals are often hopelessly corrupt. Consequently the dates which I have given in the notes are those established by students of chronology.

journalist than of the historian. There is little evidence, however, of deliberate falsification. Even his extravagant eulogy of Tiberius for which he has been so severely censured may be explained at least in part as an example of the soldier's uncritical, but loyal and enthusiastic devotion to his old commander, which reflects the attitude toward the emperor of the military and official, as opposed to that of the senatorial class and of the sympathisers with the old republic. At the worst it is an interesting example of court history. His interest in history is biographical rather than strictly historical. He is particularly fond of making portraits of the personages of history, which he does with a considerable degree of success. The second book, in particular, is one long gallery of such portraits which are brought into relation to each other by a slender band of historical data. In fact the book is a sort of illustrated *Who's Who* of Roman history. Nor does he confine himself to the great figures such as the Gracchi, Marius, Sulla, Cicero, Pompey, and Caesar ; he is equally fond of portraying the characters of deuteragonists like Clodius, Curio, Lepidus, and Plancus. Some of these portraits are among his best. While these characterizations tend to destroy historical proportion they add greatly to the human interest.

We have said that Velleius gives the impression of having been an amateur who took to historical writing as a new hobby somewhat late in life. Signs of this are not wanting in his style. It has all the pretentiousness of the novice. He desires to soar before he has completely learned to fly. Writing in an age when rhetoric was the vogue, and contaminated poetical as well as prose writing, he cannot

refrain from bringing in all the rhetorical figures and producing all the rhetorical effects. All the colours of the poet and the rhetorician are applied with lavish hand where he aspires to fine writing : rhetorical questions, exclamations, and even apostrophe ; rhetorical rhythm, laboured antitheses, glittering epigrams, sometimes far-fetched, and excessive hyperbole. For this reason his use of superlatives in his praise of Tiberius has perhaps been taken too seriously. The superlative is used with almost as much frequency in eulogizing other historical personages including Pompey, in spite of the author's ardent imperialism. In fact the superlative had already suffered so much rhetorical abuse [1] that it had come to have little more value than a positive. Furthermore his style is lacking in the clarity, the ease, and the poise of the experienced writer. This is especially the case in the interminable periods which crowd his work. Some of them are veritable labyrinths. The periods of Cicero, no matter what their length, are architectural units ; in Velleius the nucleus of the period is often so overloaded with phrases, clauses, and incidental parentheses that the period bears much more resemblance to a stone almost completely hidden by parasitic barnacles than to a structure developed on a logical and artistic plan. This is partly due to the attempt to condense into a single sentence the content of whole chapters which he finds in his sources. In consequence these periods are the despair of the translator, and there is frequently

---

[1] *e.g.* in Cicero's *De imperio Pompei* the choice between positive and superlative is frequently a mere matter of sonorousness and rhythm.

nothing for it but to break them up into smaller units which can be more readily handled in an uninflected language. And yet, with all his stylistic faults, Velleius is an author whom, as Norden has said in his *Antike Kunst-Prosa*, one reads with interest from beginning to end ; and if readability is the real test this quality carries with it its own apology. Were it not for the difficulty of his intricate periods, his work, by reason of its content, its biographical trend, and its human interest, would be the ideal first reading-book for beginners of Latin. Macaulay, who does not admire his style and condemns his flattery, says : " Velleius seems to me a remarkably good epitomist. I hardly know of any work of which the scale is so small and the subject so extensive," [1] a historian's testimony to the measure of success which he has achieved in the task which he undertook, namely, that of writing a *multum in parvo* of historical condensation.

[1] *The Life and Letters of Lord Macaulay*, by George Otto Trevelyan. Longmans, Green & Co., 1913, vol. i. p. 475.

THE TEXT

THE text of Velleius depends upon a single manuscript
found by Beatus Rhenanus in the Benedictine monastery
of Murbach, in Alsace, in the year 1515. This manuscript
has long since disappeared. Rhenanus in describing it
testifies to the almost hopeless state of corruption of the
text: "so monstrously corrupt that no human ingenuity
could restore all of it"; "I am ready to swear that the
scribe who copied it did not understand a word"; "there
is no portion of it that is not corrupt." Not satisfied with
a copy hastily made by a friend, he resolved to delay
publication until he should have a chance to consult a
better manuscript said to have been found in Milan by
Georgius Merula. Disappointed in this hope, he brought
out the ed. princeps at Basle in 1520. The edition while
still in proof was compared with the Murbach manuscript
by Burer, one of the secretaries of Rhenanus, who also
noted many of its variant readings in an appendix to the
edition. The editio princeps, with Burer's readings
appended, was the sole source of our knowledge of the
text until 1834 when Orelli brought to light in the library
of the Academy at Basle an independent copy of the
Murbach MS. made in 1516 by Bonifacius Amberbach.
From this copy is missing the first fragment of Bk. I.
beginning at *tempestate distractus* ch. 1 and ending with
raptus virginum Sabinarum ch. 8. The absence of this
fragment would seem to indicate either that in 1516 it
had not yet been found or at any rate that it had not yet
been recognized as part of the text of Velleius. Amberbach's copy is of great importance, in conjunction with
the readings of Burer, in enabling the critic to restore

xviii

the original readings of the Murbach ᴍꜱ. But while modern scholarship has made progress in solving its enigmas, the text of Velleius, unless some long-hidden manuscript shall unexpectedly come to light, will always continue to be one of the most corrupt among the surviving texts of classical authors.

The text of the present volume is a composite. While chiefly indebted to the editions of Halm and Ellis, I have frequently followed older editors, particularly in the most corrupt passages, where the interpretations of these scholars seem to be nearer to the tradition of the Murbach manuscript or to the sense demanded by the context. The critical nomenclature given in the sigla is that of Ellis. I have occasionally altered the punctuation, and, for the convenience of the reader, have made more frequent use of the paragraph.

BIBLIOGRAPHY

AMONG the older editions after the ed. princeps (see chapter on text) the following are most frequently mentioned in the notes on the text: J. N. Schegkius, Frankfort, 1589 ; Acidalius, Padua, 1590 ; J. Lipsius, Leyden, 1591, Antwerp, 1627 ; Gruter, Frankfort, 1607 (first systematic division into chapters) ; Riguez, Paris, 1675 (Delphin ed. with word index) ; N. Heinsius, Amsterdam, 1678 ; P. Burman, Leyden, 1719 and 1744. More modern editions are : D. Ruhnken, 2 vols., Leyden, 1779 ; reprinted by Frotscher, Leipzig, 1830–9 ; J. C. H. Krause, Leipzig, 1800 ; N. E. Lemaire, Paris, 1822 ; J. C. Orelli, Leipzig, 1835 ; F. Kritz, Leipzig, 1840. Text editions: Haase, Leipzig, 1840 ; Halm, Leipzig, 1863 and 1875 ; Ellis, Oxford, 1898. An annotated edition in English by Frank E. Rockwood, Boston, 1893, will be found useful for the period of Julius Caesar, Augustus, and Tiberius. There is an English translation by J. S. Watson in Bohn's Classical Library. For a complete bibliography, especially of monographs and periodical literature concerning the numerous special problems which arise in Velleius, see lists in Schanz, *Geschichte der römischen Litteratur.*

SIGLA

A = Amberbach's copy of the lost Codex Murbachensis completed in August 1516, now in the library of the Academy at Basle, A.N. ii. 8.

P = Editio Princeps, printed in 1520.

B = Burer's readings from the Murbach Codex, which are printed at the end of the Ed. Princeps. Halm indicates these readings by the letter M.

C. VELLEI PATERCULI HISTORIAE ROMANAE

AD M. VINICIUM COS.

LIBRI DUO

LIBER PRIOR

1 I. *EPEUS*[1] tempestate distractus a duce suo Nestore
Metapontum condidit. Teucer, non receptus a
patre Telamone ob segnitiam non vindicatae fratris
iniuriae, Cyprum adpulsus cognominem patriae suae
Salamina constituit. Pyrrhus, Achillis filius, Epirum
2 occupavit, Phidippus Ephyram in Thesprotia. At
rex regum Agamemnon tempestate in Cretam
insulam reiectus tres ibi urbes statuit, duas a patriae
nomine, unam a victoriae memoria, Mycenas, Tegeam,
Pergamum.

---

[1] *There is an initial lacuna in the text of considerable extent.
The text, as we have it, begins with* tempestate. *The name of
Epeus was supplied by Lipsius.*

---

[a] The subject of the sentence has been lost in the lacuna.
He was relating the return of the heroes from Troy. From
Justin xx. 2. 1 it is clear that he is here speaking of Epeus,
the builder of the Trojan horse. Justin's statement is as
follows: " Metapontini quoque in templo Minervae ferra-

2

THE ROMAN HISTORY
OF
C. VELLEIUS PATERCULUS

DEDICATED TO M. VINICIUS, CONSUL

BOOK I

I. *Epeus,*[a] separated by a storm from Nestor, his chief, founded Metapontum. Teucer, disowned by his father Telamon because of his laxity in not avenging the wrong done to his brother,[b] was driven to Cyprus and founded Salamis, named after the place of his birth. Pyrrhus, the son of Achilles, established himself in Epirus ; Phidippus[c] in Ephyra in Thesprotia. Agamemnon, king of kings, cast by a tempest upon the island of Crete, founded there three cities, two of which, Mycenae and Tegea, were named after towns in his own country, and the other was called Pergamum in commemoration of his victory.

menta, quibus Epeus, a quo conditi sunt, equum Troianum fabricavit, ostendunt."

[b] Ajax.

[c] Phidippus was one of the minor leaders in the Trojan war. According to Homer, *Il.* ii. 678, he came from the islands of Calydnae off the coast of Caria.

Idem mox scelere patruelis fratris Aegisthi, here-
ditarium exercentis in eum odium, et facinore uxoris
3 oppressus occiditur. Regni potitur Aegisthus per
annos septem. Hunc Orestes matremque socia consiliorum omnium sorore Electra, virilis animi femina,
obtruncat. Factum eius a diis comprobatum spatio
vitae et felicitate imperii apparuit; quippe vixit
annis nonaginta, regnavit septuaginta. Quin[1] se
etiam a Pyrrho Achillis filio virtute vindicavit; nam
quod pactae eius Menelai atque Helenae filiae Her-
miones nuptias occupaverat, Delphis eum interfecit.

4 Per haec tempora Lydus et Tyrrhenus frates cum
regnarent in Lydia, sterilitate frugum compulsi
sortiti sunt, uter cum parte multitudinis patria de-
cederet. Sors Tyrrhenum contigit. Pervectus in
Italiam et loco et incolis et mari nobile ac perpetuum
a se nomen dedit.

Post Orestis interitum filii eius Penthilus et Tisamenus regnavere triennio.

1 II. Tum fere anno octogesimo post Troiam captam,
centesimo et vicesimo quam Hercules ad deos excesserat, Pelopis progenies, quae omni hoc tempore
pulsis Heraclidis Peloponnesi imperium obtinuerat,
ab Herculis progenie expellitur. Duces recuperandi

---

[1] quin *Wopkens*; qui P.

---

[a] That is: Tyrrhenia, Tyrrhenians, and Tyrrhenian
Sea.

[b] The traditional date for the fall of Troy was 1183 B.C.
according to the chronology of Eratosthenes; according to
that of Callimachus it was 1127 B.C. But many other dates
are given. See H. Fynes Clinton, *Epitome of the Chronology
of Greece*, Oxford, 1851.

Agamemnon was soon afterwards struck down and slain by the infamous crime of Aegisthus, his cousin, who still kept up against him the feud of his house, and by the wicked act of his wife. Aegisthus maintained possession of the kingdom for seven years. Orestes slew Aegisthus and his own mother, seconded in all his plans by his sister Electra, a woman with the courage of a man. That his deed had the approval of the gods was made clear by the length of his life and the felicity of his reign, since he lived ninety years and reigned seventy. Furthermore, he also took revenge upon Pyrrhus the son of Achilles in fair fight, for he slew him at Delphi because he had forestalled him in marrying Hermione, the daughter of Menelaus and Helen who had been pledged to himself.

About this time two brothers, Lydus and Tyrrhenus, were joint kings in Lydia. Hard pressed by the unproductiveness of their crops, they drew lots to see which should leave his country with part of the population. The lot fell upon Tyrrhenus. He sailed to Italy, and from him the place wherein he settled, its inhabitants, and the sea received their famous and their lasting names.[a]

After the death of Orestes his sons Penthilus and Tisamenus reigned for three years.

II. About eighty years after the capture of Troy,[b] and a hundred and twenty after Hercules had departed to the gods, the descendants of Pelops, who, during all this time had held sway in the Peloponnesus after they had driven out the descendants of Hercules, were again in turn driven out by them. The leaders in the recovery of the

5

imperii fuere Temenus, Cresphontes, Aristodemus, quorum abavus fuerat.

Eodem fere tempore Athenae sub regibus esse desierunt, quarum ultimus rex fuit Codrus, Melanthi filius, vir non praetereundus. Quippe cum Lacedaemonii gravi bello Atticos premerent respondissetque Pythius, quorum dux ab hoste esset occisus, eos futuros superiores, deposita veste regia pastoralem cultum induit, immixtusque castris hostium, de industria rixam ciens, imprudenter interemptus

2 est. Codrum cum morte aeterna gloria, Atheniensis secuta victoria est. Quis eum non miretur, qui iis artibus mortem quaesierit, quibus ab ignavis vita quaeri solet ? Huius filius Medon primus archon Athenis fuit. Ab hoc posteri apud Atticos dicti Medontidae, sed hic insequentesque archontes usque ad Charopem, dum viverent, eum honorem usurpabant. Peloponnesii digredientes finibus Atticis Megara, mediam Corintho Athenisque urbem, condidere.

3 Ea tempestate et Tyria classis, plurimum pollens mari, in ultimo Hispaniae tractu, in extremo[1] nostri orbis termino, in insula circumfusa Oceano, perexiguo a continenti divisa freto, Gadis condidit. Ab iisdem post paucos annos in Africa Utica condita est.

Exclusi ab Heraclidis Orestis liberi iactatique cum

---

[1] in extremo *P* ; in *bracketed by Ruhnken.*

---

[a] The death of Codrus, according to the chronology of Eusebius, is placed in 1068 B.C.

[b] Not all his successors but only his immediate followers, thirteen in number.

[c] According to Eusebius the period of the life archons was 1068–753 B.C.

sovereignty were Temenus, Cresphontes, and Aristodemus, the great-great-grandsons of Hercules.

It was about this time [a] that Athens ceased to be governed by kings. The last king of Athens was Codrus the son of Melanthus, a man whose story cannot be passed over. Athens was hard pressed in war by the Lacedaemonians, and the Pythian oracle had given the response that the side whose general should be killed by the enemy would be victorious. Codrus, therefore, laying aside his kingly robes and donning the garb of a shepherd, made his way into the camp of the enemy, deliberately provoked a quarrel, and was slain without being recognized. By his death Codrus gained immortal fame, and the Athenians the victory. Who could withhold admiration from the man who sought death by the selfsame artifice by which cowards seek life? His son Medon was the first archon at Athens. It was after him that the archons who followed him [b] were called Medontidae among the people of Attica. Medon and all the succeeding archons until Charops continued to hold that office for life. [c] The Peloponnesians, when they withdrew from Attic territory, founded Megara, a city midway between Corinth and Athens.

About this time, also, the fleet of Tyre, which controlled the sea, founded in the farthest district of Spain, on the remotest confines of our world, the city of Cadiz, on an island in the ocean separated from the mainland by a very narrow strait. The Tyrians a few years later also founded Utica in Africa.

The sons of Orestes, expelled by the Heraclidae, were driven about by many vicissitudes and by

7

variis casibus tum saevitia maris quinto decimo anno
sedem cepere circa Lesbum insulam.

1 III. Tum Graecia maximis concussa est motibus.
Achaei ex Laconica pulsi eas occupavere sedes, quas
nunc obtinent; Pelasgi Athenas commigravere,
acerque belli iuvenis nomine Thessalus, natione
Thesprotius, cum magna civium manu eam regionem
armis occupavit, quae nunc ab eius nomine Thessalia
appellatur, ante Myrmidonum vocitata civitas.

2 Quo nomine mirari convenit eos, qui Iliaca com-
ponentes tempora de ea regione ut Thessalia com-
memorant. Quod cum alii faciant, tragici frequentis-
sime faciunt, quibus minime id concedendum est;
nihil enim ex persona poetae, sed omnia sub eorum,
qui illo tempore vixerunt, disserunt.[1] Quod si quis
a Thessalo Herculis filio eos appellatos Thessalos
dicet, reddenda erit ei ratio, cur numquam ante
hunc insequentem Thessalum ea gens id nominis
usurpaverit.

3 Paulo ante Aletes, sextus ab Hercule, Hippotis
filius, Corinthum, quae antea fuerat Ephyre, claustra
Peloponnesi continentem, in Isthmo condidit. Neque
est quod miremur ab Homero nominari Corinthum;
nam ex persona poetae et hanc urbem et quasdam
Ionum colonias iis nominibus appellat, quibus voca-
bantur aetate eius, multo post Ilium captum conditae.

[1] disserunt *Orelli*; dixerunt *P.*

---

[a] *Iliad* ii. 570, xiii. 664.

raging storms at sea, and, in the fifteenth year, finally settled on and about the island of Lesbos.

III. Greece was then shaken by mighty disturbances. The Achaeans, driven from Laconia, established themselves in those localities which they occupy to-day. The Pelasgians migrated to Athens, and a warlike youth named Thessalus, of the race of the Thesprotians, with a great force of his fellow-countrymen took armed possession of that region, which, after his name, is now called Thessaly. Hitherto it had been called the state of the Myrmidones.

On this account, one has a right to be surprised that writers who deal with the times of the Trojan war speak of this region as Thessaly. This is a common practice, but especially among the tragic poets, for whom less allowance should be made; for the poets do not speak in person, but entirely through the mouths of characters who lived in the time referred to. But if anyone insists that the people were named Thessalians from Thessalus the son of Hercules, he will have to explain why this people never adopted the name until the time of this second Thessalus.

Shortly before these events Aletes, the son of Hippotes, descended from Hercules in the sixth generation, founded upon the isthmus the city of Corinth, the key to the Peloponnesus, on the site of the former Ephyre. There is no need for surprise that Corinth is mentioned by Homer,[a] for it is in his own person as poet that Homer calls this city and some of the Ionian colonies by the names which they bore in his day, although they were founded long after the capture of Troy.

9

1   IV. Athenienses in Euboea Chalcida et[1] Eretriam colonis occupavere, Lacedaemonii in Asia Magnesiam. Nec multo post Chalcidenses orti, ut praediximus, Atticis Hippocle et Megasthene ducibus Cumas in Italia condiderunt. Huius classis corsum esse directum alii columbae antecedentis volatu ferunt, alii nocturno aeris sono, qualis Cerealibus 2 sacris cieri solet. Pars horum civium magno[2] post intervallo Neapolim condidit. Utriusque urbis eximia semper in Romanos fides facit eas nobilitate atque amoenitate sua dignissimas. Sed illis diligentior ritus patrii mansit custodia, Cumanos Osca mutavit vicinia. Vires autem veteres earum urbium hodieque magnitudo ostentat moenium.

3   Subsequenti tempore magna vis Graecae iuventutis abundantia virium sedes quaeritans in Asiam se effudit. Nam et Iones duce Ione profecti Athenis nobilissimam partem regionis maritimae occupavere, quae hodieque appellatur Ionia, urbesque constituere Ephesum, Miletum, Colophona, Prienen, Lebedum, Myuntem, Erythram, Clazomenas, Phocaeam, multasque in Aegaeo atque Icario occupavere insulas, Samum, Chium, Andrum, Tenum, Parum, Delum 4 aliasque ignobiles. Et mox Aeolii eadem profecti Graecia longissimisque acti erroribus non minus

---

[1] et *added by Gelenius.*
[2] magno *P*; non magno *Scriner.*

---

[a] Lubker, *Reallexikon,* places the date in the sixth century.

IV. The Athenians established colonies at Chalcis and Eretria in Euboea, and the Lacedaemonians the colony of Magnesia in Asia. Not long afterwards, the Chalcidians, who, as I have already said, were of Attic origin, founded Cumae in Italy under the leadership of Hippocles and Megasthenes. According to some accounts the voyage of this fleet was guided by the flight of a dove which flew before it ; according to others by the sound at night of a bronze instrument like that which is beaten at the rites of Ceres. At a considerably later period, a portion of the citizens of Cumae founded Naples. The remarkable and unbroken loyalty to the Romans of both these cities makes them well worthy of their repute and of their charming situation. The Neapolitans, however, continued the careful observance of their ancestral customs ; the Cumans, on the other hand, were changed in character by the proximity of their Oscan neighbours. The extent of their walls at the present day serves to reveal the greatness of these cities in the past.

At a slightly later date a great number of young Greeks, seeking new abodes because of an excess of population at home, poured into Asia. The Ionians, setting out from Athens under the leadership of Ion, occupied the best known portion of the sea-coast, which is now called Ionia, and established the cities of Ephesus, Miletus, Colophon, Priene, Lebedus, Myus, Erythra, Clazomenae, and Phocaea, and occupied many islands in the Aegaean and Carian seas, namely, Samos, Chios, Andros, Tenos, Paros, Delos, and other islands of lesser note. Not long afterwards the Aeolians also set out from Greece, and after long wanderings took possession of places

inlustres obtinuerunt locos clarasque urbes condiderunt, Smyrnam, Cymen, Larissam, Myrinam Mytilenenque et alias urbes, quae sunt in Lesbo insula.

1 V. Clarissimum deinde Homeri inluxit ingenium, sine exemplo maximum, qui magnitudine operis et
2 fulgore carminum solus appellari poeta meruit ; in quo hoc maximum est, quod neque ante illum, quem ipse[1] imitaretur, neque post illum, qui eum imitari posset, inventus est. Neque quemquam alium, cuius operis primus auctor fuerit, in eo perfectissimum
3 praeter Homerum et Archilochum reperiemus. Hic longius a temporibus belli, quod composuit, Troici, quam quidam rentur, abfuit ; nam ferme ante annos nongentos quinquaginta floruit, intra mille natus est. Quo nomine non est mirandum, quod saepe illud usurpat οἷοι νῦν βροτοί εἰσιν[2] ; hoc enim ut hominum, ita saeculorum notatur differentia. Quem si quis caecum genitum putat, omnibus sensibus orbus est.

1 VI. Insequenti tempore imperium Asiaticum ab Assyriis, qui id obtinuerant annis mille septuaginta, translatum est ad Medos, abhinc annos ferme
2 octingentos septuaginta.[3] Quippe Sardanapalum eorum regem mollitiis fluentem et nimium felicem malo suo, tertio et tricensimo[4] loco ab Nino et Semira-

---

[1] quem ille *P*.
[2] οἷοι . . . εἰσιν om. *P* ; *supplied by Urbinus.*
[3] DCCLXX *P* ; DCCCLXX *Lipsius.*
[4] trecentesimo *P* ; tricensimo *B*.

---

a Clinton, *op. cit.* p. 146, estimates the period at which Homer flourished as 962–927 B.C.
b "Such as men are nowadays" (*Il.* v. 304, xii. 383, 449).
c Barbarus and Castor, corroborated by Ctesias, place the revolt of the Medes in 843 B.C., which corresponds fairly well with the date here given.

no less illustrious and founded the famous cities of Smyrna, Cyme, Larissa, Myrina, Mytilene, and other cities on the island of Lesbos.

V. Then the brilliant genius of Homer burst upon the world, the greatest beyond compare, who by virtue of the magnitude of his work and the brilliance of his poetry alone deserves the name of poet. His highest claim to greatness is that, before his day, no one was found for him to imitate, nor after his day has one been found to imitate him. Nor shall we find any other poet who achieved perfection in the field in which he was also the pioneer, with the exception of Homer and Archilochus. Homer lived at a period more remote than some people think from the Trojan war of which he wrote ; for he flourished only about nine hundred and fifty years ago, and it is less than a thousand since his birth.[a] It is therefore not surprising that he often uses the expression οἷοι νῦν βροτοί εἰσιν,[b] for by it is denoted the difference, not merely in men, but in ages as well. If any man holds to the view that Homer was born blind, he is himself lacking in all his senses.

VI. In the following age—about eight hundred and seventy years ago [c]—the sovereignty of Asia passed to the Medes from the Assyrians, who had held it for ten hundred and seventy years. Indeed, it was their king Sardanapalus, a man enervated by luxurious living, whose excess of fortune was his undoing. Thirty-third,[d] in direct succession of father

---

[d] Diodorus ii. 21. 25 gives the number of Assyrian kings as thirty, and the length of their dynasty as 1360 years. This figure is considerably greater than the 1070 years given by Velleius, and would place the beginning of the dynasty in 2203–2204 B.C.

mide, qui Babylona condiderant, natum, ita ut semper successor regni paterni foret filius, Arbaces Medus imperio vitaque privavit.

3 Ea aetate clarissimus Grai nominis Lycurgus Lacedaemonius, vir generis regii, fuit severissimarum iustissimarumque legum auctor et disciplinae convenientissimae viris,[1] cuius quam diu Sparta diligens fuit, excelsissime floruit.

4 Hoc tractu temporum ante annos quinque et sexaginta quam urbs Romana conderetur, ab Elissa Tyria, quam quidam Dido autumant, Carthago con-

5 ditur. Circa quod tempus Caranus, vir generis regii, undecimus[2] ab Hercule, profectus Argis regnum Macedoniae occupavit; a quo Magnus Alexander cum fuerit septimus decimus, iure materni generis

6 Achille auctore, paterni Hercule gloriatus est. [Aemilius Sura de annis populi Romani : Assyrii principes omnium gentium rerum potiti sunt, deinde Medi, postea Persae, deinde Macedones ; exinde duobus regibus Philippo et Antiocho, qui a Macedonibus oriundi erant, haud multo post Carthaginem subactam devictis summa imperii ad populum Romanum pervenit. Inter hoc tempus et initium regis Nini Assyriorum, qui princeps rerum potitus est,[3] intersunt anni MDCCCCXCV.][4]

1 VII. Huius temporis aequalis Hesiodus fuit, circa

1 viris *Lipsius* ; vir *P.*
2 undecimus *Wesseling* ; sextus decimus *P.*
3 potitus est] potitus *P.*
4 Aemilius Sura . . . intersunt anni MDCCCCXCV] *Delbenius first recognized that this passage was a gloss.*

---

a The date, according to Timaeus, was 813–814 B.C.
b The overthrow of Carthage took place in 146 B.C. The date of the founding of the Assyrian kingdom, based on

and son, from Ninus and Semiramis, who had founded Babylon, he was deprived alike of his empire and of his life by Arbaces the Mede.

At this time lived Lycurgus the Lacedaemonian, one of the most illustrious personages of Greece, a man of royal descent, the author of legislation most severe and most just, and of a discipline excellently adapted for the making of men. As long as Sparta followed it, she flourished in the highest degree.

In this period, sixty-five years before the founding of Rome, Carthage was established [a] by the Tyrian Elissa, by some authors called Dido. About this time also Caranus, a man of royal race, eleventh in descent from Hercules, set out from Argos and seized the kingship of Macedonia. From him Alexander the Great was descended in the seventeenth generation, and could boast that, on his mother's side, he was descended from Achilles, and, on his father's side, from Hercules. [Aemilius Sura says in his book on the chronology of Rome : " The Assyrians were the first of all races to hold world power, then the Medes, and after them the Persians, and then the Macedonians. Then through the defeat of Kings Philip and Antiochus, of Macedonian origin, following closely upon the overthrow of Carthage, the world power passed to the Roman people. Between this time and the beginning of the reign of Ninus king of the Assyrians, who was the first to hold world power, lies an interval of nineteen hundred and ninety-five years." [b]]

VII. To this period belonged Hesiod, separated

Diodorus, is 2203–2204 B.C. The interval, according to this calculation, is 2058 years.

centum et viginti annos distinctus ab Homeri aetate, vir perelegantis ingenii et mollissima dulcedine carminum memorabilis, otii quietisque cupidissimus, ut tempore tanto viro, ita operis auctoritate proximus. Qui vitavit, ne in id quod Homerus incideret, patriamque et parentes testatus est, sed patriam, quia multatus ab ea erat, contumeliosissime.

2 Dum in externis moror, incidi in rem domesticam maximique[1] erroris et multum discrepantem auctorum opinionibus : nam quidam huius temporis tractu aiunt a Tuscis Capuam Nolamque conditam ante annos fere octingentos et triginta. Quibus equidem 3 adsenserim : sed M. Cato quantum differt ! Qui dicat Capuam ab eisdem Tuscis conditam ac subinde Nolam; stetisse autem Capuam, antequam a Romanis 4 caperetur, annis circiter ducentis et sexaginta. Quod si ita est, cum sint a Capua capta anni ducenti et quadraginta, ut condita est, anni sunt fere quingenti. Ego, pace diligentiae Catonis dixerim, vix crediderim tam mature tantam urbem crevisse, floruisse, concidisse, resurrexisse.

1 VIII. Clarissimum deinde omnium ludicrum certamen et ad excitandam corporis animique virtutem efficacissimum Olympiorum initium habuit, auctorem Iphitum Elium. Is eos ludos mercatumque instituit

---

[1] maximique *Rhenanus*; maximeque *P.*

---

[a] Clinton, *op. cit.* p. 146, gives the period at which Hesiod flourished as 859-824 B.C. Porphyry gives the interval between him and Homer as one hundred years.

[b] The fact that Capua was a city of the plain shows that its Etruscan foundation dates from the time when the Etruscan power was supreme in Campania, *i.e. circa* 600 B.C., and supports Cato's statement. It is not unlikely, however, that the foundation was on the site of a previous Oscan settlement.

from the age of Homer by about one hundred and twenty years.[a] A man of an exquisite taste, famous for the soft charm of his poems, and an ardent lover of peace and quiet, he ranks next to Homer, not only in point of time, but also in the reverence in which his work is held. Avoiding the mistake which Homer made, he has indeed told us of his country and parents, but of his country, at whose hands he had suffered punishment, he speaks in the most disparaging terms.

While dwelling on the history of foreign countries, I now come to an event pertaining to our own, one in which there has been much error, and in which the views of the authorities show great discrepancy. For some maintain that about this time, eight hundred and thirty years ago, Capua and Nola were founded by the Etruscans. With these I myself am inclined to agree, but the opinion of Marcus Cato is vastly different. He admits that Capua, and afterwards Nola, were founded by the Etruscans, but maintains that Capua had been in existence for only about two hundred and sixty years before its capture by the Romans. If this is so, as it is but two hundred and forty years since Capua was taken, it is but five hundred years since it was founded. For my own part, with all due regard for Cato's accuracy, I can scarcely believe that the city could have had such growth, such prosperity, or could have fallen and risen again, in so short a space of time.[b]

VIII. Soon afterward the Olympic games, the most celebrated of all contests in sports, and one which was most effective in developing the qualities both of body and mind, had their beginning under the auspices of Iphitus, king of Elis. He instituted

ante annos, quam tu, M. Vinici, consulatum inires,
2 DCCCXXIII. Hoc sacrum eodem loco instituisse fertur
abhinc annos ferme mille ducentos quinquaginta
Atreus, cum Pelopi patri funebres ludos faceret, quo
quidem in ludicro omnisque[1] generis certaminum
Hercules victor extitit.

3 Tum Athenis perpetui archontes esse desierunt,
cum fuisset ultimus Alcmaeon, coeperuntque in
denos annos creari. Quae consuetudo in annos
septuaginta mansit ac deinde annuis commissa est
magistratibus res publica. Ex iis, qui denis annis
praefuerunt, primus fuit Charops, ultimus Eryxias,
ex annuis primus Creon.

4 Sexta olympiade post duo et viginti annos quam
prima constituta fuerat, Romulus, Martis filius, ultus
iniurias avi Romam urbem Parilibus in Palatio condidit. A quo tempore ad vos consules anni sunt
septingenti octoginta unus[2] ; id actum post Troiam
5 captam annis quadringentis triginta septem. Id
gessit Romulus adiutus legionibus Latini[3] avi sui ;
libenter enim iis, qui ita prodiderunt, accesserim,
cum aliter firmare urbem novam tam vicinis Veienti-
bus aliisque Etruscis ac Sabinis cum imbelli et

---

[1] omnisque *P* ; omnis *Gelenius* ; cuiusque *Gurlitt.*
[2] D.CCC.LXXX.L *P* ; *corrected by Laurentius.*
[3] Latini *Orelli* ; Latinis *Lipsius* ; his *P.*

---

[a] Later chronology reckoned the Olympiads from 776 B.C.,
but the games were in existence long before that date.

[b] The legendary connexion of the games with Pelops
indicates that they were of pre-Dorian origin. The cult of
Hercules was a later Dorian importation.

[c] The administration of Athens by decennial archons
began in 752–751 B.C. The annual archons begin in 683–682
B.C., with Creon as the first.

[d] 753 B.C., according to the Varronian era ; 751, according

18

the games and the concourse eight hundred and twenty-three years [a] before your consulship, Marcus Vinicius. There is a tradition that Atreus began this sacred observance in the same place about twelve hundred and fifty years ago, when he held the funeral games in honour of his father Pelops [b] and that at this celebration Hercules was the victor in every class of contest.

It was about this time [c] that the archons at Athens ceased to hold their office for life. Alcmaeon was the last of the life archons. The archons now began to be elected for terms of ten years. This custom continued for seventy years, then the government was entrusted to magistrates elected annually. Charops was the first and Eryxias the last of those who held the office for ten years, and Creon was the first of the annual archons.

In the sixth Olympiad,[d] two and twenty years after the first establishment of the Olympic games, Romulus the son of Mars, after avenging the wrongs of his grandfather, founded the city of Rome on the Palatine on the day of the festival of the Parilia. From this time to your consulship seven hundred and eighty-one years have elapsed. This event took place four hundred and thirty-seven years after the capture of Troy. In the founding of Rome Romulus was assisted by the troops of his grandfather Latinus. I am glad to range myself with those who have expressed this view, since with the Veientines and other Etruscans, as well as the Sabines, in such close proximity, he could scarcely have established his

to the Catonian. Velleius sometimes follows the Catonian, but in this case the Catonian date would fall in the Seventh Olympiad.

pastorali manu vix potuerit, quamquam eam[1] asylo
6 facto inter duos lucos auxit. Hic centum homines
electos appellatosque patres instar habuit consilii
publici. Hanc originem nomen patriciorum habet.
Raptus virginum Sabinarum * * *[2]

Nec minus clarus ea tempestate fuit Miltiadis
filius Cimon.

1   IX. * * *[3] quam timuerat hostis, expetit. Nam
biennio adeo varia fortuna cum consulibus conflixerat,
ut plerumque superior fuerit[4] magnamque partem
2 Graeciae in societatem suam perduceret. Quin
Rhodii quoque, fidelissimi antea Romanis, tum dubia
fide speculati fortunam proniores regis partibus
fuisse visi sunt ; et rex Eumenes in eo bello medius
fuit animo, neque fratris initiis neque suae respondit
3 consuetudini. Tum senatus populusque Romanus
L. Aemilium Paulum, qui et praetor et consul
triumphaverat, virum in tantum laudandum, in
quantum intellegi virtus potest, consulem creavit,[5]

---

[1] eam *Heinsius* ; iam *P.*
[2] *Here begins a great lacuna in the text. The missing
chapters covered 582 years of Roman History from the founding of the city to the war with Perses. The fragment* Nec . . .
Cimon *appended to the present chapter is preserved in
Priscian vi.* 63.
[3] *Haase has completed the sentence as follows:* quorum
iniuriarum populus Romanus poenam tardius quam timuerat
hostis expetit (expetiit). *But this is nothing more than an
interesting conjecture, and the subject of* expetit *must remain
in doubt.*
[4] fuerit *P* ; fuit *AB.*   [5] consulem creavit *om. A.*

---

[a] See note on text.
[b] The subject of *expetit* is lacking.   It is not certain

new city with an unwarlike band of shepherds, even though he increased their numbers by opening an asylum between the two hills. As a council to assist him in administering affairs of state he had one hundred chosen men called *patres*. This is the origin of the name *patricians*. The rape of the Sabine maidens . . .[a]

Nor at this time was Cimon, the son of Miltiades, less famous.

IX. . . . than the enemy had feared.[b] For two years Perses [c] had kept up the struggle with the consuls with such varying fortune that he generally had the advantage in these conflicts, and succeeded in winning over a large part of Greece to ally itself with his cause. Even the Rhodians, who in the past had been most loyal to the Romans, were now wavering in their fidelity, and, watching his success, seemed inclined to join the king's side. In this war King Eumenes [d] maintained a neutral attitude, neither following the initiative of his brother nor his own established custom. Then the senate and the Roman people chose as consul Lucius Aemilius Paulus, who had previously triumphed, both in his praetorship and in his consulship, a man worthy of the highest praise that can be associated with valour.

whether *expetit* is the correct reading, and, if it is, the tense is uncertain. In view of these uncertainties I have refrained from translating it.

[c] In 171 B.C. the Romans had declared war on Perses, King of Macedonia. The Roman commanders thus far had been P. Licinius Crassus, consul for 171 ; A. Hostilius Mancinus, consul for 170 ; and Q. Marcius Philippus, consul for 169.

[d] Eumenes II., King of Pergamum, 197–159 B.C., the eldest son of Attalus I.

filium eius Pauli, qui ad Cannas quam tergiversanter
perniciosam rei publicae pugnam inierat, tam fortiter
4 in ea mortem obierat.   Is Persam ingenti proelio
apud urbem nomine Pydnam in Macedonia fusum
fugatumque castris exuit deletisque eius copiis
destitutum omni spe coëgit e Macedonia profugere,
quam ille linquens in insulam Samothraciam perfugit[1]
5 templique se religioni supplicem credidit.   Ad eum
Cn. Octavius praetor, qui classi praeerat, pervenit
et ratione magis quam vi persuasit, ut se Romanorum
fidei committeret.   Ita Paulus maximum nobilissi-
mumque regem in triumpho duxit.

Quo anno et Octavii praetoris navalis et Anicii
regem Illyriorum Gentium ante currum agentis[2]
6 triumphi fuere celebres.   Quam sit adsidua eminentis
fortunae comes invidia altissimisque adhaereat, etiam
hoc colligi potest, quod cum Anicii Octaviique
triumphum nemo interpellaret, fuere, qui Pauli
impedire obniterentur.   Cuius tantum priores excessit vel magnitudine regis Persei vel specie simula-
crorum vel modo pecuniae, ut bis miliens centiens
sestertium aerario intulerit is, et[3] omnium ante actorum comparationem amplitudine vicerit.

---

[1] perfugit *Crusius*; profugit *AP*.
[2] agentis *Gelenius*; agentium *AP*.
[3] ut b. m. centies ѕн (*sic*) aerario contulerit his et *AP*,
corrected by Schoepfer who was followed by Thomas;   cum
bis m. . . . . aerario intulisset *Halm*.

---

[a] Lucius Aemilius Paulus, consul in 216 with Gaius
Terentius Varro.   His policy had been that of wearing
Hannibal out by avoiding battle.   His more hot-headed
colleague, in command for the day, joined battle with
Hannibal at Cannae, and the Romans suffered the most
disastrous defeat of the war.
[b] 168 B.C.

He was a son of the Paulus [a] who had met death at
Cannae with a fortitude only equalled by his
reluctance to begin a battle so disastrous to the
republic. Paulus defeated Perses in a great battle
at a city in Macedonia named Pydna,[b] put him to
rout, despoiled his camp, destroyed his forces, and
compelled him in his desperate plight to flee from
Macedonia. Abandoning his country, Perses took
refuge in the island of Samothrace, as a suppliant
entrusting himself to the inviolability of the temple.
There Gnaeus Octavius, the praetor in command of
the fleet, reached him and persuaded him by argument
rather than force to give himself up to the good
faith of the Romans. Thus Paulus led in triumph
the greatest and the most illustrious of kings.[c]

In this year two other triumphs were celebrated :
that of Octavius, the praetor in charge of the fleet,
and that of Anicius, who drove before his triumphal
chariot Gentius, King of the Illyrians. How insepar-
able a companion of great success is jealousy, and
how she attaches herself to the most eminent,
may be gathered from this fact : although no one
raised objections to the triumphs of Octavius and
Anicius, there were those who tried to place
obstacles in the way of that of Paulus. His
triumph so far exceeded all former ones, whether
in the greatness of King Perses himself, or in the
display of statues and the amount of money borne
in the procession, that Paulus contributed to the
treasury two hundred million sesterces, and by
reason of this vast sum eclipsed all previous triumphs
by comparison.

[c] The triumph of Paulus took place in 167. Perses was
kept a prisoner at Alba Fucensis where he subsequently died.

VELLEIUS PATERCULUS

1 **X. Per idem** tempus, cum Antiochus Epiphanes, qui Athenis Olympieum inchoavit, tum rex[1] Syriae, Ptolemaeum puerum Alexandriae obsideret, missus est ad eum legatus M. Popilius Laenas, qui iuberet
2 incepto desistere. Mandataque exposuit et[2] regem deliberaturum se dicentem circumscripsit virgula iussitque prius responsum reddere, quam egrederetur finito harenae circulo. Sic cogitationem[3] regiam Romana disiecit constantia oboeditumque imperio.
3 Lucio autem Paulo Macedonicae[4] victoriae compoti quattuor filii fuere ; ex iis duos natu maiores, unum P. Scipioni P. Africani filio, nihil ex paterna maiestate praeter speciem nominis vigoremque eloquentiae retinenti, in adoptionem dederat, alterum Fabio Maximo. Duos minores natu praetextatos,
4 quo tempore victoriam adeptus est, habuit. Is cum in contione extra urbem more maiorum ante triumphi diem ordinem actorum suorum commemoraret, deos immortalis precatus est, ut, si quis eorum invideret operibus ac fortunae suae, in ipsum potius saevirent[5]
5 quam in rem publicam. Quae vox veluti oraculo emissa magna parte eum spoliavit sanguinis sui ; nam alterum ex suis, quos in familia retinuerat, liberis ante paucos triumphi, alterum post pauciores amisit dies.
6 Aspera circa haec tempora censura Fulvii Flacci et Postumii Albini fuit : quippe Fulvii censoris frater,

[1] tum (cum *A*) regem *AP*.
[2] et *P* ; ut *A*.
[3] cogitationem] cunctationem *Acidalius*.
[4] Macedonicae *Ruhnken* ; magnae *AP*.
[5] saevirent *P* ; saeviret *A*.

---

[a] Ptolemy VI. Philometor.

X. About this time Antiochus Epiphanes, king of Syria—the Antiochus who began the Olympieum at Athens—was besieging Ptolemaeus, the boy king,[a] at Alexandria. Marcus Popilius Laenas was dispatched on an embassy to order him to desist. He delivered his message, and when the king replied that he would think the matter over, Popilius drew a circle around the king with his staff and told him that he must give his answer before he stepped out of the circle in the sand. In this way the firmness of the Roman cut short the king's deliberations, and the order was obeyed.

Now Lucius Paulus, who won the victory in Macedonia, had four sons. The two oldest he had given by adoption, the one to Publius Scipio, the son of Africanus, who resembled his great father in nothing except in name and in his vigorous eloquence; the other to Fabius Maximus. The two younger at the time of his victory had not yet assumed the toga of manhood. On the day before his triumph, when, in accordance with ancient custom, he was rendering an account of his acts before an assembly of the people outside the city walls,[b] he prayed to the gods that if any of them envied his achievements or his fortune they should vent their wrath upon himself rather than upon the state. This utterance, as though prophetic, deprived him of a great part of his family, for a few days before his triumph he lost one of the two sons whom he had kept in his household, and the other a still shorter time after it.

About this time occurred the censorship[c] of Fulvius Flaccus and Postumius Albinus famed for its severity.

[b] A triumphant general was obliged to wait outside the walls until the day of his triumph.   [a] 174 B.C.

et quidem consors, Cn. Fulvius senatu motus est ab iis censoribus.

1 XI. Post victum captumque Persen, qui quadriennio post in libera custodia Albae decessit, Pseudophilippus a mendacio simulatae originis appellatus, qui se Philippum regiaeque stirpis ferebat, cum esset ultimae, armis occupata Macedonia, adsumptis[1] regni insignibus brevi temeritatis poenas dedit;

2 quippe Q. Metellus praetor, cui ex virtute Macedonici nomen inditum erat,[2] praeclara victoria ipsum gentemque superavit, et immani etiam Achaeos rebellare incipientis fudit acie.

3 Hic est Metellus Macedonicus, qui porticus, quae fuerunt circumdatae duabus aedibus sine inscriptione positis, quae nunc Octaviae porticibus ambiuntur, fecerat, quique hanc turmam statuarum equestrium, quae frontem aedium spectant, hodieque maximum

4 ornamentum eius loci, ex Macedonia detulit. Cuius turmae hanc causam referunt, Magnum Alexandrum impetrasse a Lysippo, singulari talium auctore operum, ut eorum equitum, qui ex ipsius turma apud Granicum flumen ceciderant, expressa similitudine figurarum faceret statuas et ipsius quoque iis interponeret.

5 Hic idem primus omnium Romae aedem ex marmore in iis ipsis monumentis molitus huius[3] vel magnificentiae vel luxuriae princeps fuit. Vix ullius

---

[1] adsumptis *is Burer's conjecture*; adsumpti *AP*.
[2] inditum erat *AP*; erat *was bracketed by Gelenius*.
[3] huius *added by Ruhnken*.

---

a 148 B.C.

Even Gnaeus Fulvius, who was the brother of the censor and co-heir with him in his estate, was expelled from the senate by these censors.

XI. After the defeat and capture of Perses, who four years later died at Alba as a prisoner on parole, a pseudo-Philippus, so called by reason of his false claim that he was a Philip and of royal race, though he was actually of the lowest birth, took armed possession of Macedonia, assumed the insignia of royalty, but soon paid the penalty for his temerity. For Quintus Metellus the praetor, who received the cognomen of Macedonicus by virtue of his valour in this war, defeated him and the Macedonians in a celebrated victory.[a] He also defeated in a great battle the Achaeans who had begun an uprising against Rome.

This is the Metellus Macedonicus who had previously built the portico about the two temples without inscriptions which are now surrounded by the portico of Octavia, and who brought from Macedonia the group of equestrian statues which stand facing the temples, and, even at the present time, are the chief ornament of the place. Tradition hands down the following story of the origin of the group : that Alexander the Great prevailed upon Lysippus, a sculptor unexcelled in works of this sort, to make portrait-statues of the horsemen in his own squadron who had fallen at the river Granicus, and to place his own statue among them.

This same Metellus was the first of all to build a temple of marble, which he erected in the midst of these very monuments, thereby becoming the pioneer in this form of munificence, or shall we call it luxury ? One will scarcely find a man of any race,

27

gentis aetatis ordinis hominem inveneris, cuius feli-
6 citatem fortunae Metelli compares. Nam praeter
excellentis triumphos honoresque amplissimos et
principale in re publica fastigium extentumque vitae
spatium et acris innocentisque pro re publica cum
inimicis contentiones quattuor filios sustulit, omnis
adultae aetatis vidit, omnis reliquit superstites et
7 honoratissimos. Mortui eius lectum pro rostris sus-
tulerunt quattuor filii, unus consularis et censorius,
alter consularis, tertius consul, quartus candidatus
consulatus, quem honorem adeptus est. Hoc est
nimirum magis feliciter de vita migrare quam mori.
1 XII. Universa deinde instincta[1] in bellum Achaia,
cuius pars magna, ut praediximus, eiusdem Metelli
Macedonici virtute armisque fracta[2] erat, maxime
Corinthiis in arma cum gravibus etiam in Romanos
contumeliis instigantibus, destinatus ei bello gerendo
consul L. Mummius.
2 Et sub idem tempus, magis quia volebant Romani,
quidquid de Carthaginiensibus diceretur[3] credere
quam quia credenda adferebantur, statuit senatus
3 Carthaginem exscindere.[4] Ita eodem tempore P.
Scipio Aemilianus, vir avitis P. Africani paternisque

---

[1] deinde ut praediximus instincta *AP ; Madvig placed* ut
praed. *after* magna.

[2] cuius pars . . . fracta *Aldus*; cum pars . . . tracta *AP.*

[3] diceretur *AB*; dicebatur *P. Burer states that* ba *was
added in the Murbach* MS. *in a later hand.*

[4] excidere *AP.*

or any age, or any rank, whose happy fortune is comparable with that of Metellus. For, not to mention his surpassing triumphs, the great honours which he held, his supreme position in the state, the length of his life, and the bitter struggles on behalf of the state which he waged with his enemies without damage to his reputation, he reared four sons, saw them all reach man's estate, left them all surviving him and held in the highest honour. These four sons bore the bier of their dead father to its place in front of the rostra; one was an ex-consul and ex-censor, the second an ex-consul, the third was actually consul, and the fourth was then a candidate for the consulship, an office which he duly held. This is assuredly not to die, but rather to pass happily out of life.

XII. Thereafter all Achaia was aroused to war though the greater part of it had been crushed, as I have already said, by the valour and arms of this same Metellus Macedonicus. The Corinthians, in particular, were the instigators of it, going so far as to heap grave insults upon the Romans, and Mummius, the consul, was appointed to take charge of the war there.

About the same time the senate resolved to destroy Carthage, rather because the Romans were ready to believe any rumour concerning the Carthaginians, than because the reports were credible. Accordingly at this same time Scipio Aemilianus was elected consul, though but a candidate for the aedileship. He was a man whose virtues resembled those of his grandfather, Publius Africanus, and of his father Lucius Paulus (he was, as has been already said, the son

29

VELLEIUS PATERCULUS

L. Pauli virtutibus simillimus, omnibus belli ac togae dotibus ingeniique ac studiorum eminentissimus saeculi sui, qui nihil in vita nisi laudandum aut fecit aut dixit ac sensit, quem Paulo genitum, adoptatum a Scipione Africani filio diximus, aedilitatem petens
4 consul creatus est. Bellum Carthagini iam ante biennium a prioribus consulibus inlatum maiore vi intulit (cum ante in Hispania murali corona, in Africa obsidionali donatus esset, in Hispania vero etiam ex provocatione, ipse modicus virium, inmanis magni-
5 tudinis hostem interemisset) eamque urbem magis invidia imperii quam ullius eius temporis noxiae invisam Romano nomini funditus sustulit fecitque suae virtutis monimentum, quod fuerat avi eius clementiae. Carthago diruta est, cum stetisset annis sexcentis septuaginta duobus,[1] abhinc annos centum septuaginta tris[2] Cn. Cornelio Lentulo L. Mummio
6 consulibus. Hunc finem habuit Romani imperii Carthago aemula, cum qua bellare maiores nostri coepere Claudio et Fulvio consulibus ante annos ducentos nonaginta duos,[3] quam tu, M. Vinici, consulatum inires. Ita per annos centum et viginti[4] aut bellum inter eos populos aut belli praeparatio
7 aut infida pax fuit. Neque se Roma iam terrarum orbi superato securam speravit fore, si nomen usquam stantis maneret Carthaginis ; adeo odium certaminibus ortum ultra metum durat et ne in victis quidem

[1] DCLXXII *Iani* ; DCLXVII *P* ; DCLXVI *A*.
[2] CLXXIII *Kritz* ; CLXXVII *B* ; CCLXXVII *AP*.
[3] CCXCII *Laurent.* ; CCXCVI *AP*.   [4] CXX *Iani* ; CXV *AP*.

---

[a] The *corona muralis*, given for the storming of a wall, was of gold with embattled ornaments.
[b] A crown or garland presented to a general by the army which he had saved from a siege, or from a disgraceful surrender. It was woven of grasses collected on the spot.

of Paulus, and had been adopted by the son of Publius Scipio)—endowed with all the qualities essential to a good soldier and a good citizen, the most eminent man of his day both in native ability and acquired knowledge, who in his whole life was guilty of no act, word, or thought that was not praiseworthy. He had already received in Spain the mural crown,[a] and in Africa the *corona obsidionalis*[b] for his bravery, and while in Spain he had challenged and slain an enemy of great stature though himself a man of but ordinary physical strength. The war against Carthage begun by the consuls two years previously he now waged with greater vigour, and destroyed to its foundations the city which was hateful to the Roman name more because of jealousy of its power than because of any offence at that time. He made Carthage a monument to his valour —a city which had been a monument to his grandfather's clemency.[c] Carthage, after standing for six hundred and seventy-two years, was destroyed in the consulship of Gnaeus Cornelius Lentulus and Lucius Mummius,[d] one hundred and seventy-three years from the present date. This was the end of Carthage, the rival of the power of Rome, with whom our ancestors began the conflict in the consulship of Claudius and Fulvius[e] two hundred and ninety-two years before you entered upon your consulship, Marcus Vinicius. Thus for one hundred and twenty years there existed between these two people either war, or preparations for war or a treacherous peace. Even after Rome had conquered the world she could not hope for security so long as the name of Carthage remained

[c] Scipio the elder had spared it after the battle of Zama.
[d] 146 B.C.   [e] 264 B.C.

deponitur neque ante invisum esse desinit quam esse
desiit.

1 XIII. Ante triennium quam Carthago deleretur,
M. Cato, perpetuus diruendae eius auctor, L. Cen-
sorino M'. Manilio consulibus mortem obiit. Eodem
anno, quo Carthago concidit, L.[1] Mummius Corinthum post annos nongentos quinquaginta duos,
quam ab Alete Hippotis filio erat condita, funditus
2 eruit. Uterque imperator devictae a se gentis
nomine honoratus, alter Africanus, alter appellatus
est Achaicus ; nec quisquam ex novis hominibus
prior Mummio cognomen virtute partum vindicavit.
3 Diversi imperatoribus mores, diversa fuere studia :
quippe Scipio tam elegans liberalium studiorum
omnisque doctrinae et auctor et admirator fuit, ut
Polybium Panaetiumque, praecellentes ingenio viros,
domi militiaeque secum habuerit. Neque enim quisquam hoc Scipione elegantius intervalla negotiorum
otio dispunxit semperque aut belli aut pacis serviit
artibus : semper inter arma ac studia versatus aut
corpus periculis aut animum disciplinis exercuit.
4 Mummius tam rudis fuit, ut capta Corintho cum
maximorum artificum perfectas manibus tabulas ac
statuas in Italiam portandas locaret, iuberet praedici
conducentibus, si eas perdidissent, novas eos red-

---

[1] L. *Rhenanus* ; a *B* ; A *AP*.

[a] 146 B.C.
[b] A man who was the first of his family to hold a curule
office was called a *novus homo* or " new man."

32

as of a city still standing : to such an extent does
hatred begotten of conflict outlast the fear which
caused it ; it is not laid aside even when the foe is
vanquished nor does the object of it cease to be
hated until it has ceased to be.

XIII. Cato, the constant advocate of her destruction, died three years before the fall of Carthage, in
the consulship of Lucius Censorinus and Manius
Manilius. In the same year in which Carthage fell
Lucius Mummius destroyed Corinth ^a to her very
foundations, nine hundred and fifty-two years after
her founding by Aletes, son of Hippos. The two
conquerors were honoured by the names of the
conquered races. The one was surnamed Africanus,
the other Achaicus. Before Mummius no *new man* ^b
earned for himself a cognomen won by military
glory.

The two commanders differed in their characters
as in their tastes. Scipio was a cultivated patron
and admirer of liberal studies and of every form of
learning, and kept constantly with him, at home and
in the field, two men of eminent genius, Polybius
and Panaetius. No one ever relieved the duties of
active life by a more refined use of his intervals
of leisure than Scipio, or was more constant in
his devotion to the arts either of war or peace.
Ever engaged in the pursuit of arms or his studies,
he was either training his body by exposing it to
dangers or his mind by learning. Mummius was
so uncultivated that when, after the capture of
Corinth, he was contracting for the transportation
to Italy of pictures and statues by the hands of the
greatest artists, he gave instructions that the
contractors should be warned that if they lost them,

33

5 dituros. Non tamen puto dubites, Vinici, quin magis pro re publica fuerit manere adhuc rudem Corinthiorum intellectum quam in tantum ea intellegi, et quin hac prudentia illa imprudentia decori publico fuerit convenientior.

1 XIV. Cum facilius cuiusque rei in unam contracta species quam divisa temporibus oculis animisque inhaereat, statui priorem huius voluminis posterioremque partem non inutili rerum notitia in artum contracta distinguere atque huic loco inserere, quae quoque tempore post Romam a Gallis captam deducta sit colonia iussu senatus : nam militarium et causae et auctores ex ipsarum praefulgent nomine. Huic rei per idem tempus civitates propagatas auctumque Romanum nomen communione iuris haud intempestive subtexturi videmur.

2 Post septem annos quam Galli urbem ceperant,[1] Sutrium deducta colonia est et post annum Setia novemque interiectis annis Nepe, deinde interpositis duobus et triginta Aricini[2] in civitatem recepti.

3 Abhinc annos autem trecentos et sexaginta[3] Sp. Postumio Veturio Calvino consulibus Campanis data est civitas partique Samnitium sine suffragio, et eodem

---

[1] ceperant *Madvig* ; ceperunt *AP.*
[2] Aricini et *A* ; *Orelli supposes that one or more names have dropped out.*
[3] ccclx *Laurent.* ; cccl *AP.*

ᵃ I am inclined to think that Velleius had in mind the fad for collecting Corinthian bronze referred to in Petronius, ch. 50. It is possible that he even means this in *Corinthiorum*, in which case he is in error. For the sentiment *cf.* Plutarch, *Marcellus*, ch. 27.

they would have to replace them by new ones. Yet
I do not think, Vinicius, that you would hesitate to
concede that it would have been more useful to the
state for the appreciation of Corinthian works of art
to have remained uncultivated to the present day,
than that they should be appreciated to the extent
to which they now are, and that the ignorance of
those days was more conducive to the public weal
than our present artistic knowledge.[a]

XIV. Inasmuch as related facts make more
impression upon the mind and eye when grouped
together than when they are given separately in
their chronological sequence, I have decided to
separate the first part of this work from the second
by a useful summary, and to insert in this place an
account, with the date, of each colony founded by
order of the senate since the capture of Rome by
the Gauls ; for, in the case of the military colonies,
their very names reveal their origins and their
founders. And it will perhaps not seem out of place,
if, in this connexion, we weave into our history
the various extensions of the citizenship and the
growth of the Roman name through granting to
others a share in its privileges.

Seven years after the capture of the city by the
Gauls a colony was founded at Sutrium, another a
year later at Setia, and another after an interval of
nine years at Nepe. Thirty-two years later the
Aricians were admitted to the citizenship. Three
hundred and sixty years from the present date, in
the consulship of Spurius Postumius and Veturius
Calvinus, the citizenship without the right of voting
was given to the Campanians and a portion of the
Samnites, and in the same year a colony was

anno Cales deducta colonia. Interiecto deinde
triennio Fundani et Formiani in civitatem recepti,
4 eo ipso anno, quo Alexandria condita est. In-
sequentibusque consulibus a Sp. Postumio Philone
Publilio censoribus Acerranis data civitas. Et post
triennium Tarracina[1] deducta colonia interpositoque
quadriennio Luceria ac deinde interiecto triennio
Suessa Aurunca et Saticula, Interamnaque post bien-
5 nium. Decem deinde hoc munere anni vacaverunt :
tunc Sora atque Alba deductae coloniae et Carseoli
6 post biennium. At Q. Fabio quintum[2] Decio Mure
quartum consulibus, quo anno Pyrrhus regnare
coepit, Sinuessam Minturnasque missi coloni, post
quadriennium Venusiam : interiectoque biennio M'.
Curio et Rufino Cornelio consulibus Sabinis sine
suffragio data civitas : id actum ante annos ferme tre-
7 centos et viginti. At Cosam[3] et Paestum abhinc annos
ferme trecentos Fabio Dorsone et Claudio Canina
consulibus, interiectoque[4] quinquennio Sempronio
Sopho et Appio Caeci filio consulibus Ariminum et[5]
Beneventum coloni missi et suffragii ferendi ius
8 Sabinis datum. At initio primi belli Punici Firmum
et Castrum colonis occupata, et post annum Aesernia
postque septem et decem[6] annos Aefulum et Alsium
Fregenaeque post[7] biennium proximoque anno Tor-

---

[1] Tarracina *Lipsius* ; Tarracinam *AP*.
[2] ad quintum fabioque *AP*.
[3] Cosa *BA* ; Cossa *P*.
[4] interiectoque *Madvig* ; interiecto *AP*.
[5] et *omitted in P*.
[6] XVII *Aldus* ; XXII *AP*.
[7] post *Gelenius* ; anno post *AP*.

---

a 334 B.C.	*b* 332 B.C.	*c* 295 B.C.
d 290 B.C.	*e* 270 B.C.	*f* 266 B.C.

established at Cales.[a]   Then, after an interval of
three years, the people of Fundi and of Formiae
were admitted to the citizenship, in the very year
of the founding of Alexandria.   In the following
year the citizenship was granted to the inhabitants
of Acerra by the censors Spurius Postumius and Philo
Publilius.[b]   Three years later a colony was established
at Tarracina, four years afterwards another at
Luceria; others three years later at Suessa Aurunca
and Saticula, and another two years after these
at Interamna.   After that the work of colonization
was suspended for ten years.   Then the colonies of
Sora and Alba were founded, and two years later
that of Carseoli.   But in the fifth consulship of
Quintus Fabius, and the fourth of Decius Mus,[c] the
year in which King Pyrrhus began his reign, colonists
were sent to Minturnae and Sinuessa, and four years
afterwards to Venusia.   After an interval of two
years the citizenship without the right of suffrage
was given to the Sabines in the consulship of Manius
Curius and Rufinus Cornelius.[d]   This event took
place three hundred and twenty years ago.   In the
consulship of Fabius Dorso and Claudius Canina,
three hundred years before the present date,
colonies were established[e] at Cosa and Paestum.
After an interval of five years, in the consulship of
Sempronius Sophus[f] and Appius, the son of Appius
the Blind, colonists were sent to Ariminum and
Beneventum and the right of suffrage was granted
to the Sabines.   At the outbreak of the First Punic
War Firmum and Castrum were occupied by colonies,
a year later Aesernia, Aefulum and Alsium seventeen
years later, and Fregenae two years afterward.
Brundisium was established in the next year in the

quato Sempronioque consulibus Brundisium et post
triennium Spoletium, quo anno Floralium ludorum
factum est initium.   Postque biennium deducta[1]
Valentia et sub adventum in Italiam Hannibalis
Cremona atque Placentia.

1   XV. Deinde neque dum Hannibal in Italia moratur,
neque proximis post excessum eius annis vacavit
Romanis colonias condere, cum esset in bello con-
quirendus potius miles quam dimittendus et post
bellum vires refovendae magis quam spargendae.
2 Cn. autem Manlio Volsone et Fulvio Nobiliore consulibus Bononia deducta colonia abhinc annos ferme
ducentos septendecim, et post quadriennium Pisaurum ac Potentia interiectoque triennio Aquileia et
3 Gravisca et post quadriennium Luca.   Eodem temporum tractu, quamquam apud quosdam ambigitur,
Puteolos Salernumque et Buxentum missi coloni,
Auximum autem in Picenum abhinc annos ferme
centum octoginta quinque,[2] ante triennium quam
Cassius censor a Lupercali in Palatium versus theatrum facere instituit, cui in eo moliendo[3] eximia
civitatis severitas et consul Scipio restitere, quod
ego inter clarissima publicae voluntatis argumenta
4 numeraverim.   Cassio autem Longino et Sextio
Calvino, qui Sallues apud aquas, quae ab eo Sextiae
appellantur, devicit, consulibus Fabrateria deducta
est abhinc annos ferme centum quinquaginta tris.[4]

[1] ducta *AP*.   [2] clxxxv *Burman*; clxxxvii *AP*.
[3] in eo moliendo *Salmasius*; in demoliendo *AP*.
[4] cliii *Krause*; clvii *AP*; clii *Lips*.

[a] 245 b.c.   [b] 244 b.c.   [c] 124 b.c.

consulship of Torquatus and Sempronius,[a] Spoletium three years afterwards in the year in which the Floralia were instituted. Two years afterwards a colony was established at Valentia, and Cremona and Placentia were established just before Hannibal's arrival in Italy.

XV. Thereafter, during Hannibal's stay in Italy, and in the next few years subsequent to his departure, the Romans had no leisure for the founding of colonies, since, while the war lasted, they had to find soldiers, rather than muster them out, and, after it was over, the strength of the city needed to be revived and concentrated rather than to be dispersed. But, about two hundred and seventeen years ago, in the consulship of Manlius Volso and Fulvius Nobilior,[b] a colony was established at Bononia, others four years later at Pisaurum and Potentia, others three years later still at Aquileia and Gravisca, and another four years afterwards at Luca. About the same time, although the date is questioned by some, colonists were sent to Puteoli, Salernum, and Buxentum, and to Auximum in Picenum, one hundred and eighty-five years ago, three years before Cassius the censor began the building of a theatre beginning at the Lupercal and facing the Palatine. But the remarkable austerity of the state and Scipio the consul successfully opposed him in its building, an incident which I regard as one of the clearest indications of the attitude of the people of that time. In the consulship of Cassius Longinus and Sextius Calvinus[c]—the Sextius who defeated the Sallues at the waters which are called Aquae Sextiae from his name—Fabrateria was founded about one hundred and fifty-three years

Et post annum Scolacium Minervium, Tarentum Neptunia, Carthagoque in Africa, prima, ut prae-
5 diximus, extra Italiam colonia condita est. De Dertona ambigitur, Narbo autem Martius in Gallia Porcio Marcioque consulibus abhinc annos circiter centum quadraginta sex[1] deducta colonia est. Post duodeviginti[2] annos in Bagiennis Eporedia Mario sextum[3] Valerioque Flacco consulibus. Neque facile memoriae mandaverim quae, nisi militaris, post hoc tempus deducta sit.

1 XVI. Cum haec particula operis velut formam pro-positi excesserit, quamquam intellego mihi in hac tam praecipiti festinatione, quae me rotae pronive gurgitis ac verticis modo nusquam patitur consistere, paene magis necessaria praetereunda quam super-vacua[4] amplectenda, nequeo tamen temperare mihi, quin rem saepe agitatam animo meo neque ad
2 liquidum ratione perductam signem stilo. Quis enim abunde mirari potest, quod eminentissima cuiusque professionis ingenia in eandem[5] formam et in idem artati temporis congruere[6] spatium, et quemad-modum clausa capso[7] aliove[8] saepto diversi generis animalia nihilo minus separata alienis in unum quodque[9] corpus congregantur, ita cuiusque clari operis capacia ingenia in similitudine et temporum et profectuum semet ipsa ab aliis separaverunt.

[1] cxlvi Lipsius; cliii AP.   [2] xviii Aldus; xxiii AP.
   [3] sextum Cludius; sexiens (-es) BAP.
 [4] supervacua P; supervania A; supervacanea Orelli.
       [5] in eam AP.
   [6] congruere Heinsius; congruens AP.
        [7] capso BA; capsa P.
     [8] alioue Lipsius; alioque AP.
      [9] quodque Heinsius; quoque AP.

[a] 118 B.C.   [b] 100 B.C.

before the present date, and in the next year
Scolacium Minervium, Tarentum Neptunia, and
Carthage in Africa—the first colony founded outside
of Italy, as already stated. In regard to Dertona
the date is in question. A colony was established at
Narbo Martius in Gaul about one hundred and
forty-six years ago in the consulship of Porcius
and Marcius.[a] Eighteen years later Eporedia was
founded in the country of the Bagienni in the consulship of Marius, then consul for the sixth time,[b] and
Valerius Flaccus.

It would be difficult to mention any colony founded
after this date, except the military colonies.

XVI. Although this portion of my work has already,
as it were, outgrown my plan, and although I am
aware that in my headlong haste—which, just like a
revolving wheel or a down-rushing and eddying
stream, never suffers me to stop—I am almost
obliged to omit matters of essential importance
rather than to include unessential details, yet I
cannot refrain from noting a subject which has often
occupied my thoughts but has never been clearly
reasoned out. For who can marvel sufficiently
that the most distinguished minds in each branch
of human achievement have happened to adopt
the same form of effort, and to have fallen within
the same narrow space of time ? Just as animals
of different species when shut in the same pen
or other enclosure still segregate themselves from
those which are not of their kind, and gather
together each in its own group, so the minds that
have had the capacity for distinguished achievement
of each kind have set themselves apart from the
rest by doing like things in the same period of

41

3 Una neque multorum annorum spatio divisa aetas
per divini spiritus viros, Aeschylum Sophoclen
Euripiden, inlustravit tragoediam[1]; una priscam
illam et veterem sub Cratino Aristophaneque et Eu-
polide comoediam; ac novam comicam[2] Menander[3]
aequalesque eius[4] aetatis magis quam operis Philemo
ac Diphilus et invenere intra paucissimos annos
4 neque imitandam reliquere. Philosophorum quoque
ingenia Socratico ore defluentia omnium, quos paulo
ante enumeravimus, quanto post Platonis Aristotelis-
5 que mortem floruere spatio? Quid ante Isocratem,
quid post eius auditores eorumque discipulos clarum
in oratoribus fuit? Adeo quidem[5] artatum angustiis
temporum, ut nemo memoria dignus alter ab altero
videri nequiverint.

1   XVII. Neque hoc in Graecis quam in Romanis
evenit magis. Nam nisi aspera ac rudia repetas et
inventi laudanda nomine, in Accio circaque eum[6]
Romana tragoedia est; dulcesque Latini leporis
facetiae per Caecilium Terentiumque et Afranium
2 subpari aetate nituerunt. Historicos etiam,[7] ut
Livium quoque priorum aetati adstruas, praeter
Catonem et quosdam veteres et obscuros minus

---

[1] tragoediam *Burman*; tragoedias *AP*.
[2] novam comicam *AP*, *defended by Thomas*; novam
comoediam *Gruner*.
[3] Menander *A*; Menandrus *P*.
[4] *Madvig inserts* non *after* eius.
[5] adeo quidem *AP*; adeo id quidem *Haase*.
[6] cum *is Burer's conjecture*; eorum *AP*.
[7] etiam *Vossius*; et *AP*.

---

[a] As they do not occur in the extant portion of the work
we must assume that they were mentioned in the portion
which has been lost.

[b] He is here referring to comedy. One wonders why the
name of Plautus is omitted from the list. Has the name of

time. A single epoch, and that only of a few years'
duration, gave lustre to tragedy through three men
of divine inspiration, Aeschylus, Sophocles, and
Euripides. So, with Comedy, a single age brought to
perfection that early form, the Old Comedy, through
the agency of Cratinus, Aristophanes, and Eupolis;
while Menander, and Philemon and Diphilus, his
equals in age rather than in performance, within the
space of a very few years invented the New Comedy
and left it to defy imitation. The great philosophers,
too, who received their inspiration from the lips of
Socrates—their names we gave a moment ago[a]—
how long did they flourish after the death of Plato
and of Aristotle ? What distinction was there in
oratory before Isocrates, or after the time of his
disciples and in turn of their pupils ? So crowded
were they into a brief epoch that there were no two
worthy of mention who could not have seen each
other.

XVII. This phenomenon occurred among the
Romans as well as among the Greeks. For, unless
one goes back to the rough and crude beginnings,
and to men whose sole claim to praise is that they
were the pioneers, Roman tragedy centres in and
about Accius ; and the sweet pleasantry of Latin
humour[b] reached its zenith in practically the same
age under Caecilius, Terentius, and Afranius. In
the case of the historians also, if one adds Livy to
the period of the older writers, a single epoch,
comprised within the limits of eighty years, produced
them all, with the exception of Cato and some of the

Plautus dropped out of the text or in Velleius following the
Augustan tradition expressed by Horace in the *Ars Poetica*
270 ?

43

octoginta annis circumdatum aevum tulit, ut nec
poëtarum in antiquius citeriusve processit ubertas.
3 At oratio ac vis forensis perfectumque prosae eloquentiae decus, ut idem separetur Cato (pace P.
Crassi Scipionisque et Laelii et Gracchorum et Fannii
et Servii Galbae dixerim) ita universa sub principe
operis sui erupit Tullio, ut delectari ante eum paucis-
simis, mirari vero neminem possis nisi aut ab illo
4 visum aut qui illum viderit. Hoc idem evenisse
grammaticis, plastis, pictoribus, scalptoribus quisquis
temporum institerit notis, reperiet, eminentiam[1]
cuiusque operis artissimis temporum claustris circumdatam.
5 Huius ergo recedentis in suum quodque saeculum[2]
ingeniorum similitudinis congregantisque se et in
studium par et in emolumentum causas cum saepe[3]
requiro, numquam reperio, quas esse veras confidam,
sed fortasse veri similes, inter quas has maxime.
6 Alit aemulatio ingenia, et nunc invidia, nunc admiratio
imitationem accendit, naturaque quod summo studio
petitum est, ascendit in summum difficilisque in
perfecto mora est, naturaliterque quod procedere
7 non potest, recedit. Et ut primo ad consequendos
quos priores ducimus[4] accendimur, ita ubi aut prae-
teriri aut aequari eos posse desperavimus, studium
cum spe senescit, et quod adsequi non potest, sequi

---

[1] reperiet et eminentiam P; reperiet eminentia AB.
[2] recedentis in suum quodque saeculum] *I have here
adopted the reading of Madvig for this tortured passage.
For the readings of ABP and the various conjectures see
Ellis.*
[3] saepe *Madvig*; semper AP.   [4] quo priores ducimur A.

old and obscure authors. Likewise the period which was productive of poets does not go back to an earlier date or continue to a later. Take oratory and the forensic art at its best, the perfected splendour of eloquence in prose, if we again except Cato—and this I say with due respect to Publius Crassus, Scipio, Laelius, the Gracchi, Fannius, and Servius Galba— eloquence, I say, in all its branches burst into flower under Cicero, its chief exponent, so that there are few before his day whom one can read with pleasure, and none whom one can admire, except men who had either seen Cicero or had been seen by him. One will also find, if he follows up the dates closely, that the same thing holds true of the grammarians, the workers in clay, the painters, the sculptors, and that pre-eminence in each phase of art is confined within the narrowest limits of time.

Though I frequently search for the reasons why men of similar talents occur exclusively in certain epochs and not only flock to one pursuit but also attain like success, I can never find any of whose truth I am certain, though I do find some which perhaps seem likely, and particularly the following. Genius is fostered by emulation, and it is now envy, now admiration, which enkindles imitation, and, in the nature of things, that which is cultivated with the highest zeal advances to the highest perfection ; but it is difficult to continue at the point of perfection, and naturally that which cannot advance must recede. And as in the beginning we are fired with the ambition to overtake those whom we regard as leaders, so when we have despaired of being able either to surpass or even to equal them, our zeal wanes with our hope ; it ceases to follow what it

desinit et velut occupatam relinquens materiam
quaerit novam, praeteritoque eo, in quo eminere
non possumus, aliquid, in quo nitamur, conquirimus,
sequiturque ut frequens ac mobilis transitus maximum
perfecti operis impedimentum sit.

1   XVIII. Transit admiratio ab condicione[1] temporum
et ad urbium.   Una urbs Attica pluribus omnis[2]
eloquentiae quam universa Graecia operibus usque[3]
floruit adeo ut corpora gentis illius separata sint in
alias civitates, ingenia vero solis Atheniensium

2 muris clausa existimes.   Neque hoc ego magis
miratus sim quam neminem Argivum Thebanum
Lacedaemonium oratorem aut dum vixit auctoritate aut post mortem memoria dignum existimatum.

3 Quae urbes eximiae alias[4] talium studiorum fuere
steriles, nisi Thebas unum os Pindari inluminaret:
nam Alcmana Lacones falso sibi vindicant.

LIBER POSTERIOR

1   I. Potentiae Romanorum prior Scipio viam aperue-
rat, luxuriae posterior aperuit : quippe remoto Carthaginis metu sublataque imperii aemula non gradu,
sed praecipiti cursu a virtute descitum, ad vitia

[1] ab condicione *Schegk* ; ad conditionem *AP*.
[2] pluribus omnis *Froelich* ; pluribus annis *AP* ; pluribus
auctoribus *Halm.*
[3] operibus usque *Ellis after Acidalius* ; operibusque *AP*.
For other conjectures see Ellis, p. 19.
[4] eximiae alias *Faehse and Haupt* ; et initalia *AB*, om. *P* ;
et in alia *Halm.*

---

[a] Publius Cornelius Scipio Africanus the elder had
brought the Second Punic War to a close by defeating the
Carthaginians at Zama in 202 B.C.   The younger Scipio had
destroyed Carthage in 146.

cannot overtake, and abandoning the old field as though pre-empted, it seeks a new one. Passing over that in which we cannot be pre-eminent, we seek for some new object of our effort. It follows that the greatest obstacle in the way of perfection in any work is our fickle way of passing on at frequent intervals to something else.

XVIII. From the part played by epochs our wonder and admiration next passes to that played by individual cities. A single city of Attica blossomed with more masterpieces of every kind of eloquence than all the rest of Greece together—to such a degree, in fact, that one would think that although the bodies of the Greek race were distributed among the other states, their intellects were confined within the walls of Athens alone. Nor have I more reason for wonder at this than that not a single Argive or Theban or Lacedaemonian was esteemed worthy, as an orator, of commanding influence while he lived, or of being remembered after his death. These cities, otherwise distinguished, were barren of such literary pursuits with the single exception of the lustre which the voice of Pindar gave to Thebes ; for, in the case of Alcman, the claim which the Laconians lay to him is spurious.

BOOK II

I. The first of the Scipios opened the way for the world power of the Romans ; the second opened the way for luxury.[a] For, when Rome was freed of the fear of Carthage, and her rival in empire was out of her way, the path of virtue was abandoned for that of corruption, not gradually, but in headlong

transcursum ; vetus disciplina deserta, nova inducta ;
in somnum a vigiliis, ab armis ad voluptates, a negotiis
2 in otium conversa civitas. Tum Scipio Nasica in
Capitolio porticus, tum, quas praediximus, Metellus,
tum in circo Cn. Octavius multo amoenissimam moliti
sunt, publicamque magnificentiam secuta privata
luxuria est.

3 Triste deinde et contumeliosum bellum in Hispania
duce latronum Viriatho secutum est : quod ita varia
fortuna gestum est, ut saepius Romanorum gereretur
adversa. Sed interempto Viriatho fraude magis
quam virtute Servilii Caepionis Numantinum gravius
4 exarsit. Haec urbs numquam plura quam decem
milia[1] propriae iuventutis armavit, sed vel ferocia
ingenii vel inscitia nostrorum ducum vel fortunae
indulgentia cum alios duces, tum Pompeium magni
nominis virum ad turpissima deduxit foedera (hic
primus e Pompeis consul fuit), nec minus turpia
5 ac detestabilia Mancinum Hostilium consulem. Sed
Pompeium gratia impunitum habuit, Mancinum
verecundia poenam[2] non recusando perduxit huc, ut
per fetialis nudus ac post tergum religatis manibus
dederetur hostibus. Quem illi recipere se negaverunt,

---

[1] nunquam x̄. plura quam propriae *AP, corrected by Aldus.*
[2] poenam *Halm* ; quippe *AP.*

---

[a] The war with Viriathus had already begun in 148 B.C.
It ended in 140 by the treacherous murder of Viriathus.

[b] Quintus Pompeius was consul in 141 B.C. In the next
year he was forced to make the treaty with the enemy which
the senate refused to ratify.

[c] Caius Hostilius Mancinus was consul in 137 B.C. The
treaty with the Numantines was made in 136.

[d] These priests were charged with the duty of maintaining
the forms of international relationship and officiated at the
making of treaties.

course. The older discipline was discarded to give place to the new. The state passed from vigilance to slumber, from the pursuit of arms to the pursuit of pleasure, from activity to idleness. It was at this time that there were built, on the Capitol, the porticoes of Scipio Nasica, the porticoes of Metellus already mentioned, and, in the Circus, the portico of Gnaeus Octavius, the most splendid of them all ; and private luxury soon followed public extravagance.

Then followed a war that was disastrous and disgraceful to the Romans, the war in Spain with Viriathus,[a] a guerilla chief. The fortunes of this war during its progress shifted constantly and were, more frequently than not, adverse to the Romans. On the death of Viriathus through the perfidy rather than the valour of Servilius Caepio, there broke out in Numantia a war that was more serious still. Numantia city was never able to arm more than ten thousand men of its own ; but, whether it was owing to her native valour, or to the inexperience of our soldiers, or to the mere kindness of fortune, she compelled first other generals, and then Pompey, a man of great name (he was the first of his family to hold the consulship[b]) to sign disgraceful treaties, and forced Mancinus Hostilius[c] to terms no less base and hateful. Pompey, however, escaped punishment through his influence. As for Mancinus his sense of shame, in that he did not try to evade the consequences, caused him to be delivered to the enemy by the fetial priests,[d] naked, and with his hands bound behind his back. The Numantines, however, refused to receive him, following the example of the Samnites at an earlier day at

49

sicut quondam Caudini fecerant,[1] dicentes publicam violationem fidei non debere unius lui sanguine.

1 II. Inmanem deditio Mancini civitatis movit dissensionem. Quippe Tiberius Gracchus, Tiberii Gracchi clarissimi atque eminentissimi viri filius, P. Africani ex filia nepos, quo quaestore et auctore id foedus ictum erat, nunc graviter ferens aliquid a se pactum[2] infirmari, nunc similis vel iudicii vel poenae metuens discrimen, tribunus pl. creatus, vir alioqui vita innocentissimus, ingenio florentissimus, 2 proposito sanctissimus, tantis denique adornatus virtutibus, quantas perfecta et natura et industria mortalis condicio recipit, P. Mucio Scaevola L. Calpurnio consulibus abhinc annos centum sexaginta duos descivit a bonis, pollicitusque toti Italiae civita- 3 tem, simul etiam promulgatis agrariis legibus, omnibus statim[3] concupiscentibus, summa imis miscuit et in praeruptum atque anceps periculum adduxit rem publicam. Octavioque collegae pro bono publico stanti imperium abrogavit, triumviros agris dividendis colonisque deducendis creavit se socerumque suum, consularem Appium, et Gaium fratrem admodum iuvenem.

1 III. Tum P. Scipio Nasica, eius qui optimus vir a senatu iudicatus erat, nepos, eius qui censor porticus

---

[1] fecerant *Heinsius*; fecerunt *AP*.
[2] pactum *Kreyssig*; factum *AP*.
[3] statum *P*; statim *Gelenius*; factum *A*; ista tum *Haupt*.

---

[a] In the year 321 B.C. the consuls Titus Veturius Calvinus and Spurius Postumius were trapped by the Samnites in the Caudine pass and were forced to agree to terms which were subsequently repudiated by the senate.　　　　[b] 133 B.C.

[c] Publius Cornelius Scipio Nasica, consul in 191 B.C. Livy states that in 204 B.C., although he was not yet of sufficient age to obtain the quaestorship, he was nevertheless

Caudium,^a saying that a national breach of faith should not be atoned for by the blood of one man.

II. The surrender of Mancinus aroused in the state a quarrel of vast proportions. Tiberius Gracchus, the son of Tiberius Gracchus, an illustrious and an eminent citizen, and the grandson, on his mother's side, of Scipio Africanus, had been quaestor in the army of Mancinus and had negotiated the treaty. Indignant, on the one hand, that any of his acts should be disavowed, and fearing the danger of a like trial or a like punishment, he had himself elected tribune of the people. He was a man of otherwise blameless life, of brilliant intellect, of upright intentions, and, in a word, endowed with the highest virtues of which a man is capable when favoured by nature and by training. In the consulship of Publius Mucius Scaevola and Lucius Calpurnius^b (one hundred and sixty-two years ago), he split with the party of the nobles, promised the citizenship to all Italy, and at the same time, by proposing agrarian laws which all immediately desired to see in operation, turned the state topsyturvy, and brought it into a position of critical and extreme danger. He abrogated the power of his colleague Octavius, who defended the interests of the state, and appointed a commission of three to assign lands and to found colonies, consisting of himself, his father-in-law the ex-consul Appius, and his brother Gaius, then a very young man.

III. At this crisis Publius Scipio Nasica appeared. He was the grandson of the Scipio^c who had been adjudged by the senate the best citizen of

adjudged by the senate to be the best citizen in the state and, as such, was designated to receive the statue of the Great Mother when it was brought to Rome.

in Capitolio fecerat, filius, pronepos autem Cn.
Scipionis, celeberrimi viri P. Africani patrui, privatusque et togatus, cum esset consobrinus Ti. Gracchi,
patriam cognationi praeferens et quidquid publice
salutare non esset, privatim alienum existimans (ob
eas virtutes primus omnium absens pontifex maximus
factus est), circumdata laevo brachio togae lacinia
ex superiore parte Capitolii summis gradibus insistens
hortatus est, qui salvam vellent rem publicam, se
2 sequerentur.   Tum optimates, senatus atque equestris ordinis pars melior et maior, et intacta perniciosis
consiliis plebs inruere in Gracchum stantem in area
cum catervis suis et concientem paene totius Italiae
frequentiam.   Is fugiens decurrensque clivo Capi-
tolino, fragmine subsellii ictus vitam, quam gloriosis-
3 sime degere potuerat, immatura morte finivit.   Hoc
initium in urbe Roma civilis sanguinis gladiorumque
impunitatis fuit.   Inde ius vi obrutum potentiorque
habitus prior, discordiaeque civium antea condicionibus sanari solitae ferro diiudicatae bellaque non
causis inita, sed prout eorum merces fuit.   Quod
4 haut mirum est : non enim ibi consistunt exempla,
52

the state, the son of the Scipio who, as censor, had built the porticoes on the Capitol, and great-grandson of Gnaeus Scipio, that illustrious man who was the paternal uncle of Publius Scipio Africanus. Although he was a cousin of Tiberius Gracchus, he set his country before all ties of blood, choosing to regard as contrary to his private interests everything that was not for the public weal, a quality which earned for him the distinction of being the first man to be elected pontifex maximus *in absentia*. He held no public office at this time and was clad in the toga. Wrapping the fold of his toga about his left forearm he stationed himself on the topmost steps of the Capitol and summoned all those who wished for the safety of the state to follow him. Then the optimates, the senate, the larger and better part of the equestrian order, and those of the plebs who were not yet infected by pernicious theories rushed upon Gracchus as he stood with his bands in the area of the Capitol and was haranguing a throng assembled from almost every part of Italy. As Gracchus fled, and was running down the steps which led from the Capitol, he was struck by the fragment of a bench, and ended by an untimely death the life which he might have made a glorious one. This was the beginning in Rome of civil bloodshed, and of the licence of the sword. From this time on right was crushed by might, the most powerful now took precedence in the state, the disputes of the citizens which were once healed by amicable agreements were now settled by arms, and wars were now begun not for good cause but for what profit there was in them. Nor is this to be wondered at ; for precedents do not stop where

unde coeperunt, sed quamlibet in tenuem recepta
tramitem latissime evagandi sibi viam faciunt, et
ubi semel recto deerratum est, in praeceps pervenitur,
nec quisquam sibi putat turpe, quod alii fuit fruc-
tuosum.

1 IV. Interim, dum haec in Italia geruntur, Aristonicus, qui[1] mortuo rege Attalo, a quo Asia populo
Romano hereditate relicta erat, sicut relicta postea
est a Nicomede Bithynia, mentitus regiae stirpis
originem armis eam occupaverat, is victus a M.
Perpenna ductusque in triumpho, set a M'. Aquilio,
capite poenas dedit, cum initio belli Crassum Mu-
cianum, virum iuris scientissimum, decedentem ex
Asia proconsulem interemisset.

2 At[2] P. Scipio Africanus Aemilianus, qui Carthaginem deleverat, post tot acceptas circa Numantiam
clades creatus iterum consul missusque in Hispaniam
fortunae virtutique expertae in Africa respondit in
Hispania, et intra annum ac tris menses, quam eo
venerat, circumdatam operibus Numantiam excisam-
3 que aequavit solo. Nec quisquam ullius gentis
hominum ante eum clariore urbium excidio nomen
suum perpetuae commendavit memoriae : quippe
excisa Carthagine ac Numantia ab alterius nos metu,
4 alterius vindicavit contumeliis. Hic, eum interro-
gante tribuno Carbone, quid de Ti. Gracchi caede

---

[1] qui *is bracketed by Gelenius, but may be the result of careless writing.*   [2] At *Vossius* ; et *P.*

---

they begin, but, however narrow the path upon which they enter, they create for themselves a highway whereon they may wander with the utmost latitude ; and when once the path of right is abandoned, men are hurried into wrong in headlong haste, nor does anyone think a course is base for himself which has proven profitable to others.

IV. While these events were taking place in Italy King Attalus had died,[a] bequeathing Asia in his will to the Roman people, as Bithynia was later bequeathed to them by Nicomedes, and Aristonicus, falsely claiming to be a scion of the royal house, had forcibly seized the province. Aristonicus was subdued by Marcus Perpenna and was later led in triumph, but by Manius Aquilius. He paid with his life the penalty for having put to death at the very outset of the war the celebrated jurist Crassus Mucianus, proconsul of Asia, as he was leaving his province.

After all the defeats experienced at Numantia, Publius Scipio Africanus Aemilianus, the destroyer of Carthage, was a second time elected consul[b] and then dispatched to Spain, where he confirmed the reputation for good fortune and for valour which he had earned in Africa. Within a year and three months after his arrival in Spain he surrounded Numantia with his siege works, destroyed the city and levelled it to the ground.[c] No man of any nationality before his day had immortalized his name by a more illustrious feat of destroying cities · for by the destruction of Carthage and Numantia he liberated us, in the one case from fear, in the other from a reproach upon our name. This same Scipio, when asked by Carbo the tribune what he thought about the killing of Tiberius Gracchus,

sentiret, respondit, si is occupandae rei publicae
animum habuisset, iure caesum. Et cum omnis
contio adclamasset, hostium, inquit, armatorum
totiens clamore non territus, qui possum vestro
5 moveri, quorum noverca est Italia ? Reversus in
urbem intra breve tempus, M'. Aquilio C. Sempronio consulibus abhinc annos centum et sexaginta,[1]
post duos consulatus duosque triumphos et bis
excisos terrores rei publicae mane in lectulo repertus
est mortuus, ita ut quaedam elisarum faucium in
6 cervice reperirentur notae. De tanti viri morte
nulla habita est quaestio eiusque corpus velato
capite elatum est, cuius opera super totum terrarum
orbem Roma extulerat caput. Seu fatalem, ut
plures, seu conflatam insidiis, ut aliqui prodidere
memoriae, mortem obiit, vitam certe dignissimam
egit, quae nullius ad id temporis praeterquam avito
fulgore vinceretur. Decessit anno ferme sexto et
7 quinquagesimo : de quo si quis ambiget, recurrat
ad priorem consulatum eius, in quem creatus est
anno octavo et tricesimo[2] : ita dubitare desinet.
1 V. Ante tempus excisae Numantiae praeclara in
Hispania militia D. Bruti fuit, qui penetratis omnibus
Hispaniae gentibus ingenti vi hominum urbiumque

---

[1] CLX *Laurent.* ; CL *AP* ; CLVII *Kritz.*
[2] XXXVIII *Puteanus* ; XXXVI *AP.*

---

[a] 129 B.C.
[b] There was nothing unusual about wrapping up the head
of a corpse (*cf.* Aurelius Victor 58 " obvoluto capite elatus
est)." Velleius is apparently striving for the verbal effect,
somewhat forced it is true, of the contrast between *velato
capite . . . extulerat caput.*

replied that he had been justly slain if his purpose had been to seize the government. When the whole assembly cried out at this utterance he said, " How can I, who have so many times heard the battle shout of the enemy without feeling fear, be disturbed by the shouts of men like you, to whom Italy is only a stepmother?" A short time after Scipio's return to Rome, in the consulship of Manius Aquilius and Gaius Sempronius [a]—one hundred and sixty years ago—this man who had held two consulships, had celebrated two triumphs, and had twice destroyed cities which had brought terror to his country, was found in the morning dead in his bed with marks as though of strangulation upon his throat. Great man though he was, no inquest was held concerning the manner of his death, and with covered head [b] was borne to the grave the body of him whose services had enabled Rome to lift her head above the whole world. Whether his death was due to natural causes as most people think, or was the result of a plot, as some historians state, the life he lived was at any rate so crowded with honours that up to this time it was surpassed in brilliance by none, excepting only his grandsire.[c] He died in his fifty-sixth year. If anyone questions this let him call to mind his first consulship, to which he was elected in his thirty-eighth year, and he will cease to doubt.

V. In Spain, even before the destruction of Numantia, Decimus Brutus had conducted a brilliant campaign in which he penetrated to all the peoples of the country, took a great number of men and

[a] Publius Cornelius Scipio Africanus, the victor of Zama.

potitus numero, aditis quae vix audita erant, Gallaeci cognomen meruit.

2 Et ante eum paucis annis tam severum illius Q. Macedonici in his gentibus imperium fuit, ut, cum urbem Contrebiam nomine in Hispania oppugnaret, pulsas praecipiti loco quinque cohortes legionarias

3 eodem protinus subire iuberet, facientibusque omnibus in procinctu testamenta, velut ad certam mortem eundum foret, non deterritus proposito,[1] quem moriturum miserat militem victorem recepit : tantum effecit mixtus timori pudor spesque desperatione quaesita. Hic virtute ac severitate facti, at Fabius Aemilianus Pauli exemplo disciplina in Hispania fuit clarissimus.

1 VI. Decem deinde interpositis annis, qui Ti. Gracchum, idem Gaium fratrem eius occupavit furor, tam virtutibus eius omnibus quam huic errori similem, ingenio etiam eloquentiaque longe praestantiorem.

2 Qui cum summa quiete animi civitatis princeps esse posset, vel vindicandae fraternae mortis gratia vel praemuniendae regalis potentiae eiusdem exempli tribunatum ingressus, longe maiora et acriora petens[2] dabat civitatem omnibus Italicis, extendebat eam

3 paene usque Alpis, dividebat agros, vetabat quem-

---

[1] perseverantia ducis *followed* proposito *in P. It was bracketed by Davis as a marginal gloss which had crept into the text.*   [2] petens *Ruhnken;* re petens *AP.*

---

[a] The cognomen was given for his partial subjugation of the Gallaeci, a people in western Hispania Tarraconensis inhabiting what is now Galicia and part of Portugal.

[b] 123 B.C.

cities and, by extending his operations to regions which hitherto had scarcely been heard of, earned for himself the cognomen of Gallaecus.ᵃ

A few years before in this same country Quintus Macedonicus had exercised command as general with a discipline of remarkable rigour. For instance, in an assault upon a Spanish town called Contrebia he ordered five legionary cohorts, which had been driven down from a steep escarpment, forthwith to march up it again. Though the soldiers were making their wills on the battlefield, as though they were about to march to certain death, he was not deterred, but afterwards received the men, whom he sent forth to die, back in camp victorious. Such was the effect of shame mingled with fear, and of a hope born of despair. Macedonicus won renown in Spain by the uncompromising bravery of this exploit; Fabius Aemilianus, following the example of Paulus on the other hand, by the severity of his discipline.

VI. After an interval of ten years the same madness which had possessed Tiberius Gracchus now seized upon his brother Gaius, who resembled him in his general virtues as well as in his mistaken ambition, but far surpassed him in ability and eloquence. Gaius might have been the first man in the state had he held his spirit in repose; but, whether it was with the object of avenging his brother's death or of paving the way for kingly power, he followed the precedent which Tiberius had set and entered upon the career of a tribune.ᵇ His aims, however, were far more ambitious and drastic. He was for giving the citizenship to all Italians, extending it almost to the Alps, distributing the public domain, limiting the holdings of each citizen

quam civem plus quingentis iugeribus habere,
quod aliquando lege Licinia cautum erat, nova
constituebat portoria, novis coloniis replebat provincias, iudicia a senatu transferebat ad equites,
frumentum plebi dari instituerat ; nihil immotum,
nihil tranquillum, nihil quietum, nihil[1] denique in
eodem statu relinquebat ; quin alterum etiam con-
tinuavit tribunatum.

4 Hunc L. Opimius consul, qui praetor Fregellas
exciderat, persecutus armis unaque Fulvium Flaccum,
consularem ac triumphalem virum, aeque prava
cupientem, quem C. Gracchus in locum Tiberii fratris
triumvirum nominaverat,[2] eumque[3] socium regalis
5 adsumpserat potentiae, morte adfecit. Id unum
nefarie ab Opimio proditum, quod capitis non dicam
Gracchi, sed civis Romani pretium se daturum idque
6 auro repensurum proposuit. Flaccus in Aventino
armatos[4] ac pugnam ciens cum filio maiore iugulatus
est ; Gracchus profugiens, cum iam comprehen-
deretur ab iis, quos Opimius miserat, cervicem
Euporo servo praebuit, qui non segnius se ipse
interemit, quam domino succurrerat. Quo die singularis Pomponii equitis Romani in Gracchum fides
fuit, qui more Coclitis sustentatis in ponte hostibus

---

[1] nihil *inserted by Haase.*
[2] nominaverat] *Halm conjectured* nomine, re autem.
[3] eum *AP*; eumque *Gelenius.*
[4] armatos *Gelenius*; armatus *AP.*

---

a This limitation of the amount of *ager publicus* which
an individual might hold was one of the many *rogationes*
proposed by the tribune C. Licinius Stolo in 375 B.C. and
finally carried in 365, after ten years of constant struggle
with the patricians.

b 121 B.C.

to five hundred acres as had once been provided by the Licinian law,[a] establishing new customs duties, filling the provinces with new colonies, transferring the judicial powers from the senate to the equites, and began the practice of distributing grain to the people. He left nothing undisturbed, nothing untouched, nothing unmolested, nothing, in short, as it had been. Furthermore he continued the exercise of his office for a second term.

The consul, Lucius Opimius, who, as praetor, had destroyed Fregellae, hunted down Gracchus with armed men and put him to death,[b] slaying with him Fulvius Flaccus, a man who, though now entertaining the same distorted ambitions, had held the consulship and had won a triumph. Gaius had named Flaccus triumvir in the place of his brother Tiberius and had made him his partner in his plans for assuming kingly power. The conduct of Opimius was execrable in this one respect, that he had proposed a reward to be paid for the head, I will not say of a Gracchus, but of a Roman citizen, and had promised to pay it in gold. Flaccus, together with his elder son, was slain upon the Aventine while summoning to battle his armed supporters. Gracchus, in his flight, when on the point of being apprehended by the emissaries of Opimius, offered his neck to the sword of his slave Euporus. Euporus then slew himself with the same promptness with which he had given assistance to his master. On the same day Pomponius, a Roman knight, gave remarkable proof of his fidelity to Gracchus ; for, after holding back his enemies upon the bridge, as Cocles[c]

[a] This is the famous Horatius who defended the bridge single-handed against the army of Porsenna.

7 eius, gladio se transfixit. Ut Ti. Gracchi antea
corpus, ita Gai mira crudelitate victorum in Tiberim
deiectum est.

1 VII. Hunc Ti. Gracchi liberi, P. Scipionis Africani
nepotes, viva adhuc matre Cornelia, Africani filia,
viri optimis ingeniis male usi, vitae mortisque habuere
exitum : qui si civilem dignitatis concupissent
modum, quidquid tumultuando adipisci gestierunt,
quietis obtulisset res publica.

2 Huic atrocitati adiectum scelus unicum. Quippe
iuvenis specie excellens necdum duodevicesimum
transgressus annum immunisque delictorum pater-
norum, Fulvii Flacci filius, quem pater legatum de
condicionibus miserat, ab Opimio interemptus est.
Quem cum haruspex Tuscus amicus flentem in
vincula duci vidisset, quin tu hoc potius, inquit,
facis ? Protinusque inliso capite in postem lapideum
ianuae carceris effusoque cerebro expiravit.

3 Crudelesque mox quaestiones in amicos clientes-
que Gracchorum habitae sunt. Sed Opimium, virum
alioqui sanctum et gravem, damnatum postea
iudicio publico memoria istius saevitiae nulla civilis

4 prosecuta est misericordia. Eadem Rupilium Popi-
liumque, qui consules asperrime in Tiberii Gracchi

---

* Consuls 132 B.C.

had done of yore, he threw himself upon his sword.
The body of Gaius, like that of Tiberius before him,
was thrown into the Tiber by the victors, with the
same strange lack of humanity.

VII. Such were the lives and such the deaths of
the sons of Tiberius Gracchus, and the grandsons of
Publius Scipio Africanus, and their mother
Cornelia, the daughter of Africanus, still lived to
witness their end. An ill use they made of their
excellent talents. Had they but coveted such
honours as citizens might lawfully receive, the state
would have conferred upon them through peaceful
means all that they sought to obtain by unlawful
agitations.

To this atrocity was added a crime without
precedent. The son of Fulvius Flaccus, a youth of
rare beauty who had not yet passed his eighteenth
year and was in no way involved in the acts of
his father, when sent by his father as an envoy
to ask for terms, was put to death by Opimius.
An Etruscan soothsayer, who was his friend, seeing
him dragged weeping to prison, said to him, " Why
not rather do as I do ? " At these words he
forthwith dashed out his brains against the stone
portal of the prison and thus ended his life.

Severe investigations, directed against the friends
and followers of the Gracchi, followed. But when
Opimius, who during the rest of his career had been
a man of sterling and upright character, was afterwards condemned by public trial, his conviction
aroused no sympathy on the part of the citizens
because of the recollection of his cruelty in this
instance. Rupilius and Popilius,[a] who, as consuls,
had prosecuted the friends of Tiberius Gracchus with

amicos saevierant, postea iudiciorum publicorum
merito oppressit invidia.

Rei tantae parum ad notitiam pertinens inter-
5 ponetur.[1] Hic est Opimius, a quo consule celeberrimum Opimiani vini nomen ; quod iam nullum esse
spatio annorum colligi potest, cum ab eo sint ad
te, M. Vinici, consulem anni centum et quinquaginta.

6 Factum Opimii, quod[2] inimicitiarum quaesita erat
ultio, minor secuta auctoritas, et visa ultio privato
odio magis quam publicae vindictae data.

7 In legibus[3] Gracchi inter perniciosissima numerarim,[4] quod extra Italiam colonias posuit. Id
maiores, cum viderent tanto potentiorem Tyro
Carthaginem, Massiliam Phocaea, Syracusas Corintho,
Cyzicum ac Byzantium Mileto, genitali solo, dili-
genter vitaverant et civis Romanos ad censendum
8 ex provinciis in Italiam revocaverant. Prima autem
extra Italiam colonia Carthago condita est. Subinde Porcio Marcioque consulibus deducta colonia
Narbo Martius.

1 VIII. Mandetur deinde memoriae severitas iudiciorum. Quippe C. Cato consularis, M. Catonis nepos,
Africani sororis filius, repetundarum ex Macedonia

[1] interponetur *AP* ; interponatur *Heinsius.*

[2] quod *AP* ; quo *Hensius and Bentley.*

[3] *The passage from* In legibus *to* condita est, § 8, *is found
in AP before* Mors Drusi *in chap. xv. In that context, as
the text now stands, the passage is out of place. Cludius
transferred it to its present position. It may, however, be a
fragment of a chapter comparing the legislative activities of
Drusus with those of Gracchus, the first part of which is now
lost.* [4] numerarim *A* ; numeraverim *P.*

---

[a] The colony at Carthage was founded 122 B.C. under the
name *Colonia Iunonia.*

[b] 118 B.C. It was on the site of the modern Narbonne, to
which it gave its name.

the utmost severity, deservedly met at a later date with the same mark of popular disapproval at their public trials.

I shall insert here a matter hardly relevant to these important events. It was this same Opimius from whose consulship the famous Opimian wine received its name. That none of this wine is now in existence can be inferred from the lapse of time, since it is one hundred and fifty years, Marcus Vinicius, from his consulship to yours.

The conduct of Opimius met with a greater degree of disapproval because it was a case of seeking revenge in a private feud, and this act of revenge was regarded as having been committed rather in satisfaction of a personal animosity than in defence of the rights of the state.

In the legislation of Gracchus I should regard as the most pernicious his planting of colonies outside of Italy. This policy the Romans of the older time had carefully avoided; for they saw how much more powerful Carthage had been than Tyre, Massilia than Phocaea, Syracuse than Corinth, Cyzicus and Byzantium than Miletus, —all these colonies, in short, than their mother cities—and had summoned all Roman citizens from the provinces back to Italy that they might be enrolled upon the census lists. The first colony to be founded outside of Italy was Carthage.[a] Shortly afterwards the colony of Narbo Martius was founded, in the consulship of Porcius and Marcius.[b]

VIII. I must next record the severity of the law courts in condemning for extortion in Macedonia Gaius Cato, an ex-consul, the grandson of Marcus Cato, and son of the sister of Africanus, though the

65

damnatus est, cum lis eius HS. quattuor milibus
aestimaretur : adeo illi viri magis voluntatem
peccandi intuebantur quam modum, factaque ad
consilium dirigebant et quid, non in quantum
admissum foret, aestimabant.

2 Circa eadem tempora M. C.[1] Metelli fratres uno
die triumphaverunt. Non minus clarum exemplum
et adhuc unicum Fulvii Flacci, eius qui Capuam
ceperat, filiorum, sed alterius in adoptionem dati, in
collegio consulatus fuit ; adoptivus in Acidini Manlii
familiam datus. Nam censura Metellorum patrue-
lium, non germanorum fratrum fuit, quod solis
contigerat Scipionibus.

3 Tum Cimbri et Teutoni transcendere Rhenum,
multis mox nostris suisque cladibus nobiles. Per
eadem tempora clarus eius Minucii, qui porticus,
quae hodieque celebres sunt, molitus est, ex Scor-
discis triumphus fuit.

1 IX. Eodem tractu temporum nituerunt oratores
Scipio Aemilianus Laeliusque, Ser. Galba, duo
Gracchi, C. Fannius, Carbo Papirius ; nec praetereundus Metellus Numidicus et Scaurus, et ante
2 omnes L. Crassus et M. Antonius : quorum aetati
ingeniisque successere C. Caesar Strabo, P. Sulpicius ; nam Q. Mucius iuris scientia quam proprie
eloquentiae nomine celebrior fuit.

---

[1] M. C. *Voss*; M. *AP*; *Aldus proposed* duo.

[a] Something less than £40, if the text is correct.

[b] 179 B.C.

[c] What Velleius probably had in mind was the aedileship
in 213 B.C. of Publius and Marcus Scipio, referred to by
Polybius x. 4. Hence some editors have supposed that
aedilibus or *in aedilitate* have dropped out of the text; but
this is hardly necessary. The author is thinking simply of
brothers who were colleagues in office. [d] 108 B.C.

claim against him amounted to but four thousand sesterces.[a] But the judges of that day looked rather at the purpose of the culprit than at the measure of the wrong, applying to actions the criterion of intention and weighing the character of the sin and not the extent of it.

About the same time the two brothers Marcus and Gaius Metellus celebrated their triumphs on one and the same day. A coincidence equally celebrated which still remains unique, was the conjunction in the consulship[b] of the sons of Fulvius Flaccus, the general who had conquered Capua, but one of these sons, however, had passed by adoption into the family of Acidinus Manlius. As regards the joint censorship of the two Metelli, they were cousins, not brothers, a coincidence which had happened to the family of the Scipios alone.[c]

At this time the Cimbri and Teutons crossed the Rhine. These peoples were soon to become famous by reason of the disasters which they inflicted upon us and we upon them. About the same time[d] took place the famous triumph over the Scordisci of Minucius, the builder of the porticoes which are famous even in our own day.

IX. At this same period flourished the illustrious orators Scipio Aemilianus and Laelius, Sergius Galba, the two Gracchi, Gaius Fannius, and Carbo Papirius. In this list we must not pass over the names of Metellus Numidicus and Scaurus, and above all of Lucius Crassus and Marcus Antonius. They were followed in time as well as in talents by Gaius Caesar Strabo and Publius Sulpicius. As for Quintus Mucius, he was more famous for his knowledge of jurisprudence than, strictly speaking, for eloquence.

3 Clara etiam per idem aevi spatium fuere ingenia in togatis Afranii, in tragoediis Pacuvii atque Accii, usque in Graecorum ingeniorum comparationem evecti,[1] magnumque inter hos ipsos facientis operi suo locum, adeo quidem, ut in illis limae, in hoc paene **4** plus videatur fuisse sanguinis,[2] celebre et Lucilii nomen fuit, qui sub P. Africano Numantino bello eques militaverat. Quo quidem tempore iuvenes adhuc Iugurtha ac Marius sub eodem Africano militantes in iisdem castris didicere, quae postea in contrariis **5** facerent. Historiarum auctor iam tum Sisenna erat iuvenis, sed opus belli civilis Sullanique post aliquot **6** annos ab eo seniore editum est. Vetustior Sisenna fuit Caelius, aequalis Sisennae Rutilius Claudiusque Quadrigarius et Valerius Antias. Sane non ignoremus eadem aetate fuisse Pomponium sensibus celebrem, verbis rudem et novitate inventi a se operis commendabilem.

1 X. Prosequamur nota severitatem censorum Cassii Longini Caepionisque, qui abhinc annos centum quinquaginta tris[3] Lepidum Aemilium augurem, quod sex milibus HS. aedes conduxisset, adesse iusserunt. At nunc si quis tanti habitet, vix ut senator agnoscitur : adeo natura a rectis in prava,

---

[1] evecti *Gelenius*; evectis *B*; eius aetatis *A*; eius aetatis *P*.

[2] *I have substituted a comma after* sanguinis *for Halm's period, making* Lucilii *the substantive with which* facientis *agrees. Heinsius supplies* Enni *after* locum.

[3] CLIII *Kritz*; CLVII *AP*.

---

[a] He is referring to the Jugurthine War.

[b] The *Fabulae Atellanae* or *Atellan Farce.* While not the inventor he may have been the first to give these farces literary form.

In the same epoch other men of talent were illustrious : Afranius in the writing of native comedy, in tragedy Pacuvius and Accius, a man who rose into competition even with the genius of the Greeks, and made a great place for his own work among theirs, with this distinction, however, that, while they seemed to have more polish, Accius seemed to possess more real blood. The name of Lucilius was also celebrated ; he had served as a knight in the Numantine war under Publius Africanus. At the same time, Jugurtha and Marius, both still young men, and serving under the same Africanus, received in the same camp the military training which they were later destined to employ in opposing camps.[a] At this time Sisenna, the author of the Histories, was still a young man. His works on the Civil Wars and the Wars of Sulla were published several years later, when he was a relatively old man. Caelius was earlier than Sisenna, while Rutilius, Claudius Quadrigarius and Valerius Antias were his contemporaries. Let us not forget that at this period lived Pomponius, famed for his subject matter, though untutored in style, and noteworthy for the new kind of composition which he invented.[b]

X. Let us now go on to note the severity of the censors Cassius Longinus and Caepio,[c] who summoned before them the augur Lepidus Aemilius for renting a house at six thousand sesterces.[d] This was a hundred and fifty-three years ago. Nowadays, if any one takes a residence at so low a rate he is scarcely recognized as a senator. Thus does nature pass from the normal to the perverted, from that

[c] Censors in 125 B.C.
[d] A little more than £50.

a pravis in vitia,[1] a vitiis in praecipitia pervenitur.

2 Eodem tractu temporum et Domitii ex Arvernis
et Fabii ex Allobrogibus victoria fuit nobilis ; Fabio
Pauli nepoti ex victoria cognomen Allobrogico
inditum. Notetur Domitiae familiae peculiaris quaedam et ut clarissima, ita artata numero felicitas.
Septem ante hunc nobilissimae simplicitatis iuvenem,
Cn. Domitium, fuere, singuli[2] omnes[3] parentibus geniti,
sed omnes ad consulatum sacerdotiaque, ad triumphi
autem paene omnes pervenerunt insignia.

1 XI. Bellum deinde Iugurthinum gestum est per
Q. Metellum nulli secundum saeculi sui. Huius
legatus fuit C. Marius, quem praediximus, natus
agresti[4] loco, hirtus atque horridus vitaque sanctus,
quantum bello optimus, tantum pace pessimus,
immodicus gloriae, insatiabilis, impotens semperque
2 inquietus. Hic per publicanos aliosque in Africa
negotiantis criminatus Metelli lentitudinem, tra-
hentis iam in tertium annum bellum, et naturalem
nobilitatis superbiam morandique in imperiis cupiditatem effecit, ut, cum commeatu petito Romam
venisset, consul crearetur bellique paene patrati a
Metello, qui bis Iugurtham acie fuderat, summa

---

[1] prava . . . vitia *thus transposed by Sterk* ; a rectis in
vitia a (*om. A*) vitiis in prava a pravis *AP.*
[2] singuli *Lipsius and Madvig* ; singulis *AP.*
[3] omnes *Pluygers* ; omnino *AP.*
[4] agresti *Voss* ; equestri *AP.*

---

to the vicious, and from the vicious to the abyss of extravagance.

At the same period[a] took place the notable victory of Domitius over the Arverni, and of Fabius over the Allobroges. Fabius, who was the grandson of Paulus, received the cognomen of Allobrogicus in commemoration of his victory. I must also note the strange fortune which distinguished the family of the Domitii, the more remarkable in view of the limited number of the family. Before the present Gnaeus Domitius, a man of notable simplicity of life, there have been seven Domitii, all only sons, but they all attained to the consulate and priesthoods and almost all to the distinction of a triumph.

XI. Then followed the Jugurthan war waged under the generalship[b] of Quintus Metellus, a man inferior to no one of his time. His second in command was Gaius Marius, whom we have already mentioned, a man of rustic birth, rough and uncouth, and austere in his life, as excellent a general as he was an evil influence in time of peace, a man of unbounded ambition, insatiable, without self-control, and always an element of unrest. Through the agency of the tax-gatherers and others who were engaged in business in Africa he criticized the delays of Metellus, who was now dragging on the war into its third year, charging him with the haughtiness characteristic of the nobility and with the desire to maintain himself in military commands. Having obtained a furlough he went to Rome, where he succeeded in procuring his election as consul and had the chief command of the war placed in his own hands,[c] although the war had already been practically ended by Metellus, who had twice defeated Jugurtha in battle. The

committeretur sibi. Metelli tamen et triumphus
fuit clarissimus et meritum ex virtute[1] ei cognomen
3 Numidici inditum. Ut paulo ante Domitiae familiae,
ita Caeciliae notanda claritudo est. Quippe intra
duodecim ferme annos huius temporis consules fuere
Metelli aut censores aut triumpharunt amplius
duodecies, ut appareat, quemadmodum urbium im-
periorumque, ita gentium nunc florere fortunam,
nunc senescere, nunc interire.

1 XII. At C. Marius L. Sullam iam tunc ut praecaventibus fatis copulatum sibi quaestorem habuit
et per eum missum ad regem Bocchum Iugurtha
rege abhinc annos ferme centum triginta quattuor[2]
potitus est ; designatusque iterum consul in urbem
reversus secundi consulatus initio Kal. Ianuariis
2 eum in triumpho duxit. Effusa, ut praediximus,
immanis vis Germanarum gentium, quibus nomen
Cimbris ac Teutonis erat, cum Caepionem Man-
liumque consules et ante Carbonem Silanumque
fudissent fugassentque in Galliis et exuissent exercitu,
Scaurumque Aurelium consularem et alios celeberrimi
nominis viros trucidassent, populus Romanus non
alium repellendis tantis hostibus magis idoneum
3 imperatorem quam Marium est ratus Tum multi-
plicati consulatus eius. Tertius in apparatu belli
consumptus ; quo anno Cn. Domitius tribunus plebis
legem tulit, ut sacerdotes, quos antea conlegae

---

[1] meritum et (*om. P*) virtutique *AP*.
[2] cxxxiiii *Aldus* ; cxxxviii *AP*.

---

a Praecaventibus fatis is variously interpreted. Krause
takes it to mean that the fates were seeking to guard against
the future rivalry and discord of these two men ; Kritz,
wrongly, I think, that the fates were warning Marius in
advance that Sulla was destined to be his successful
opponent.   *b* 104 B.C.   *c* Bk. ii. ch. 8.   *d* 105 B.C.

triumph of Metellus was none the less brilliant, and
the cognomen of Numidicus earned by his valour was
bestowed upon him. As I commented, a short time
ago, on the glory of the family of the Domitii, let me
now comment upon that of the Caecilii. Within the
compass of about twelve years during this period, the
Metelli were distinguished by consulships, censorships, or triumph more than twelve times. Thus it
is clear that, as in the case of cities and empires, so
the fortunes of families flourish, wane, and pass away.

XII. Gaius Marius, even at this time, had Lucius
Sulla associated with him as quaestor, as though the
fates were trying to avoid subsequent events.[a] He
sent Sulla to King Bocchus and through him gained
possession of Jugurtha, about one hundred and thirty-
four years before the present time. He returned to
the city as consul designate for the second time,
and on the kalends of January,[b] at the inauguration
of his second consulship, he led Jugurtha in triumph.
Since, as has already[c] been stated, an immense horde
of the German races called the Cimbri and the
Teutons had defeated and routed the Consuls Caepio
and Manlius[d] in Gaul, as before them Carbo[e]
and Silanus,[f] and had scattered their armies, and
had put to death Scaurus Aurelius an ex-consul,
and other men of renown, the Roman people was
of the opinion that no general was better qualified
to repel these mighty enemies than Marius. His
consulships then followed each other in succession.
The third was consumed in preparation for this war.
In this year[g] Gnaeus Domitius, the tribune of the
people, passed a law that the priests, who had
previously been chosen by their colleagues, should

• 113 B.C.   ſ 109 B.C.   ɡ 104 B.C.

4 sufficiebant, populus crearet. Quarto trans Alpis circa
Aquas Sextias cum Teutonis conflixit, amplius centum quinquaginta milia hostium priore ac postero
die ab eo trucidata[1] gensque excisa Teutonum.
5 Quinto citra Alpis in campis, quibus nomen erat
Raudiis, ipse consul et proconsul Q. Lutatius Catulus
fortunatissimo decertavere proelio ; caesa aut capta
amplius centum milia[2] hominum.   Hac victoria
videtur meruisse Marius, ne eius nati rem publicam
6 paeniteret, ac mala bonis repensasse.   Sextus consulatus veluti praemium ei meritorum datus.   Non
tamen huius consulatus fraudetur gloria, quo Servilii
Glauciae Saturninique Apulei furorem continuatis
honoribus rem publicam lacerantium et gladiis
quoque et caede comitia discutientium, consul armis
compescuit hominesque exitiabilis in Hostilia curia
morte multavit.
1 XIII. Deinde interiectis paucis annis tribunatum
iniit M. Livius Drusus, vir nobilissimus, eloquentis-
simus, sanctissimus, meliore in omnia ingenio animo-
2 que quam fortuna usus.   Qui cum senatui priscum
restituere cuperet decus et iudicia ab equitibus ad
eum transferre ordinem (quippe eam potestatem
nacti equites Gracchanis legibus cum in multos
clarissimos atque innocentissimos viros saevissent,

---

[1] trucidata *Ruhnken* ; trucidatis *AP*.
[2] $\overline{c}$ *AP* ; $\overline{cc}$ *Puteanus and Lipsius*.

---

[a] 102 B.C.   [b] 101 B.C.   [c] 100 B.C.
[d] Saturninus was elected tribune for the third time ;
Glaucia was praetor and desired the consulship.
[e] 91 B.C.   [f] See ch. vi.

now be elected by the people. In his fourth consulship[a] Marius met the Teutons in battle beyond the Alps in the vicinity of Aquae Sextiae. More than a hundred and fifty thousand of the enemy were slain by him on that day and the day after, and the race of the Teutons was exterminated. In his fifth consulship[b] the consul himself and the proconsul Quintus Lutatius Catulus fought a most successful battle on this side of the Alps on the plain called the Raudian Plain. More than a hundred thousand of the enemy were taken or slain. By this victory Marius seems to have earned some claim upon his country that it should not regret his birth and to have counterbalanced his bad by his good deeds. A sixth consulship[c] was given him in the light of a reward for his services. He must not, however, be deprived of the glory of this consulship, for during this term as consul he restrained by arms the mad acts of Servilius Glaucia and Saturninus Apuleius who were shattering the constitution by continuing in office,[d] and were breaking up the elections with armed violence and bloodshed, and caused these dangerous men to be put to death in the Curia Hostilia.

XIII. After an interval of a few years Marcus Livius Drusus entered the tribunate,[e] a man of noble birth, of eloquent tongue and of upright life ; but in all his acts, his success was not in keeping with his talents or his good intentions. It was his aim to restore to the senate its ancient prestige, and again to transfer the law courts to that order from the knights. The knights had acquired this prerogative through the legislation of Gracchus,[f] and had treated with severity many noted men who were quite

tum P. Rutilium, virum non saeculi sui, sed omnis
aevi optimum, interrogatum lege repetundarum
maximo cum gemitu civitatis damnaverant), in iis
ipsis, quae pro senatu moliebatur, senatum habuit
adversarium non intellegentem, si qua de plebis
commodis ab eo agerentur, veluti inescandae in-
liciendaeque multitudinis causa fieri, ut minoribus
3 perceptis maiora permitteret. Denique ea fortuna
Drusi fuit, ut malefacta collegarum quam quaevis[1]
optime ab ipso cogitata senatus probaret magis, et
honorem, qui ab eo deferebatur, sperneret, iniurias,
quae ab illis intendebantur, aequo animo reciperet,
et huius summae gloriae invideret, illorum modicam[2]
ferret.

1   XIV. Tum conversus Drusi animus, quando bene
incepta male cedebant, ad dandam civitatem Italiae.
Quod cum moliens revertisset e foro, immensa illa
et incondita, quae eum semper comitabatur, cinctus
multitudine in area domus suae cultello percussus,
qui adfixus lateri eius relictus est, intra paucas horas
2 decessit. Sed cum ultimum redderet spiritum, intuens circumstantium maerentiumque frequentiam,
effudit vocem convenientissimam conscientiae suae :
ecquandone, inquit, propinqui amicique, similem
mei civem habebit res publica ? Hunc finem clarissimus iuvenis vitae habuit : cuius morum minime
3 omittatur argumentum. Cum aedificaret domum in

---

[1] quam quaevis *Froelich*; quamvis *A*; eius quam
Ruhnken followed by Halm.
[2] modicam *AP*; inmodicam *Halm.*

innocent, and, in particular, had brought to trial on a charge of extortion and had condemned, to the great sorrow of all the citizens, Publius Rutilius, one of the best men not only of his age, but of all time. But in these very measures which Livius undertook on behalf of the senate he had an opponent in the senate itself, which failed to see that the proposals he also urged in the interest of the plebs were made as a bait and a sop to the populace, that they might, by receiving lesser concessions, permit the passage of more important measures. In the end it was the misfortune of Drusus to find that the senate gave more approval to the evil measures of his colleagues than to his own plans, however excellent, and that it spurned the dignity which he would confer upon it only to accept tamely the real slights levelled against it by the others, tolerating the mediocrity of his colleagues while it looked with jealous eyes upon his own distinction.

XIV. Since his excellent programme had fared so badly, Drusus turned his attention to granting the citizenship to the Italians. While he was engaged in this effort, and was returning from the forum surrounded by the large and unorganized crowd which always attended him, he was stabbed in the area before his house and died in a few hours, the assassin leaving the weapon in his side. As he breathed his last and gazed at the throng of those who stood weeping about him, he uttered the words, most expressive of his own feelings: "O my relatives and friends, will my country ever have another citizen like me?" Thus ended the life of this illustrious man. One index of his character should not be passed over. When he was building

Palatio in eo loco, ubi est quae quondam Ciceronis,
mox Censorini fuit, nunc Statilii Sisennae est, pro-
mitteretque ei architectus, ita se eam aedificaturum,
ut liber a conspectu immunisque ab omnibus arbitris[1]
esset neque quisquam in eam despicere posset, tu
vero, inquit, si quid in te artis est, ita compone
domum meam, ut, quidquid agam, ab omnibus per-
spici possit.[2]

1 XV. Mors Drusi iam pridem tumescens bellum
excitavit Italicum ; quippe L. Caesare et P. Rutilio
consulibus abhinc annos centum viginti, universa
Italia, cum id malum ab Asculanis ortum esset
(quippe Servilium praetorem Fonteiumque legatum
occiderant) ac deinde a Marsis exceptum in omnis
penetrasset regiones, arma adversus Romanos cepit.
2 Quorum ut fortuna atrox, ita causa fuit iustissima :
petebant enim eam civitatem, cuius imperium armis
tuebantur : per omnis annos atque omnia bella
duplici numero se militum equitumque fungi neque
in eius civitatis ius recipi, quae per eos in id ipsum
pervenisset fastigium, per quod homines eiusdem
et gentis et sanguinis ut externos alienosque fastidire
posset.

3 Id bellum amplius trecenta milia iuventutis Italicae
abstulit.   Clarissimi autem imperatores fuerunt
Romani eo bello Cn. Pompeius, Cn. Pompei Magni
pater, C. Marius, de quo praediximus, L. Sulla

---

[1] arbitris *B*, *om.* *A* ; hominibus *P*, et *A above the line.*
[2] *Here followed the paragraph* In legibus . . . condita est
*which has been transferred, after Cludius, to the end of
Ch. vii. as better fitting the context there.   It may, however,
have been the conclusion of a passage in which Velleius compared
the legislation of Livius Drusus with that of Gaius Gracchus,
the first portion of which is now lost.*

his house on the Palatine on the site where now
stands the house which once belonged to Cicero,
and later to Censorinus, and which now belongs to
Statilius Sisenna, the architect offered to build it
in such a way that he would be free from the public
gaze, safe from all espionage, and that no one could
look down into it. Livius replied, " If you possess
the skill you must build my house in such a way
that whatever I do shall be seen by all."

XV. The long smouldering fires of an Italian war
were now fanned into flame by the death of Drusus.
One hundred and twenty years ago,[a] in the consulship of Lucius Caesar and Publius Rutilius, all Italy
took up arms against the Romans. The rebellion
began with the people of Asculum, who had put to
death the praetor Servilius and Fonteius, his deputy ;
it was then taken up by the Marsi, and from them
it made its ways into all the districts of Italy. The
fortune of the Italians was as cruel as their cause was
just ; for they were seeking citizenship in the state
whose power they were defending by their arms ;
every year and in every war they were furnishing a
double number of men, both of cavalry and of
infantry, and yet were not admitted to the rights
of citizens in the state which, through their efforts,
had reached so high a position that it could look
down upon men of the same race and blood as
foreigners and aliens.

This war carried off more than three hundred
thousand of the youth of Italy. On the Roman
side in this war the most illustrious commanders
were Gnaeus Pompeius, father of Pompey the
Great, Gaius Marius, already mentioned, Lucius

anno ante praetura functus, Q. Metellus, Numidici
filius, qui meritum cognomen Pii consecutus erat:
4 quippe expulsum civitate a L. Saturnino tribuno
plebis, quod solus in leges eius iurare noluerat, pietate sua, auctoritate senatus, consensu rei publicae[1]
restituit patrem. Nec triumphis honoribusque quam
aut causa exilii aut exilio aut reditu clarior fuit
Numidicus.

1 XVI. Italicorum autem fuerunt celeberrimi duces
Silo Popaedius, Herius Asinius, Insteius Cato, C.
Pontidius, Telesinus Pontius, Marius Egnatius,
2 Papius Mutilus. Neque ego verecundia domestici
sanguinis gloriae quidquam, dum verum refero,
subtraham: quippe multum Minatii Magii, atavi
mei, Aeculanensis, tribuendum est memoriae, qui
nepos Decii Magii, Campanorum principis, celeberrimi et fidelissimi viri, tantam hoc bello Romanis
fidem praestitit, ut cum legione, quam ipse in Hirpinis conscripserat, Herculaneum simul cum T. Didio
caperet, Pompeios cum L. Sulla oppugnaret Comp-
3 samque[2] occuparet: cuius de virtutibus cum alii, tum
maxime dilucide Q.[3] Hortensius in annalibus suis
rettulit. Cuius illi pietati plenam populus Romanus
gratiam rettulit ipsum viritim civitate donando, duos

---

[1] rei publicae *AP*; populi Romani *Puteanus.*
[2] Compsamque *Voss*; Cosamque *AP.*
[3] dilucideque Q. *P*; dilucideq. que *A, corrected by Lipsius.*

---

[a] *Pius* here means " dutiful towards his father."

Sulla, who in the previous year had filled the praetorship, and Quintus Metellus, son of Metellus Numidicus, who had deservedly received the cognomen of Pius,[a] for when his father had been exiled from the state by Lucius Saturninus, the tribune of the people, because he alone refused to observe the laws which the tribune had made, the son had effected his restoration through his own devotion, aided by the authority of the senate and the unanimous sentiment of the whole state. Numidicus earned no greater renown by his triumphs and public honours than he earned by the cause of his exile, his exile, and the manner of his return.

XVI. On the Italian side the most celebrated generals were Silo Popaedius, Herius Asinius, Insteius Cato, Gaius Pontidius, Telesinus Pontius, Marius Ignatius, and Papius Mutilus ; nor ought I, through excess of modesty, to deprive my own kin of glory, especially when that which I record is the truth ; for much credit is due the memory of my great-grandfather Minatius Magius of Aeculanum, grandson of Decius Magius, leader of the Campanians, of proven loyalty and distinction. Such fidelity did Minatius display towards the Romans in this war that, with a legion which he himself had enrolled among the Hirpini, he took Herculaneum in conjunction with Titus Didius, was associated with Lucius Sulla in the siege of Pompeii, and occupied Compsa. Several historians have recorded his services, but the most extensive and clearest testimony is that of Quintus Hortensius in his *Annals*. The Romans abundantly repaid his loyal zeal by a special grant of the citizenship to himself,

filios eius creando praetores, cum seni adhuc crea-
rentur.

4   Tam varia atque atrox fortuna Italici belli fuit,
ut per biennium continuum[1] duo Romani consules,
Rutilius ac deinde Cato Porcius, ab hostibus occi-
derentur, exercitus populi Romani multis in locis
funderentur, utque ad saga iretur diuque in eo habitu
maneretur. Caput imperii sui Corfinium legerant
atque appellarant Italicam. Paulatim deinde recipiendo in civitatem, qui arma aut non ceperant aut
deposuerant maturius, vires refectae sunt, Pompeio
Sullaque et Mario fluentem procumbentemque rem
populi Romani[2] restituentibus.

1   XVII. Finito ex maxima parte, nisi quae Nolani
belli manebant reliquiae, Italico bello, quo quidem
Romani victis adflictisque ipsi exarmati quam integri[3]
universis civitatem dare maluerunt, consulatum
inierunt Q. Pompeius et L. Cornelius Sulla, vir qui
neque ad finem victoriae satis laudari neque post
2   victoriam abunde vituperari potest. Hic natus
familia nobili, sextus a Cornelio Rufino, qui bello
Pyrrhi inter celeberrimos fuerat duces, cum familiae
eius claritudo intermissa esset, diu ita se gessit, ut
nullam petendi consulatum cogitationem habere

---

[1] continuum *Gelenius*; continuo *AP*.
[2] rem populi Romani *Laurent.*; rem P.R. *BA*; remp. *P*.
[3] integri *Heinsius*; integris *AP*.

---

[a] The number was increased from four to six in 198 B.C.
It was increased to eight by Sulla.

[b] The *sagum* or military cloak symbolized **war** as the
toga symbolized peace.

[c] *i.e.* before the war began. What Velleius had in mind
in using *maluerunt* is a little vague. The original
"choice" lay between granting the citizenship and war.
They chose the latter alternative. After the war was
over they granted to their enemies in defeat the citizenship

and by making his sons praetors at a time when the number elected was still confined to six.[a]

So bitter was this Italian war, and such its vicissitudes, that in two successive years two Roman consuls, first Rutilius and subsequently Cato Porcius, were slain by the enemy, the armies of the Roman people were routed in many places, and the Romans were compelled to resort to military dress[b] and to remain long in that garb. The Italians chose Corfinium as their capital, and named it Italica. Then little by little the strength of the Romans was recruited by admitting to the citizenship those who had not taken arms or had not been slow to lay them down again, and Pompeius, Sulla, and Marius restored the tottering power of the Roman people.

XVII. Except for the remnants of hostility which lingered at Nola the Italian war was now in large measure ended, the Romans, themselves exhausted, consenting to grant the citizenship individually to the conquered and humbled states in preference to giving it to them as a body when their own strength was still unimpaired.[c] This was the year in which Quintus Pompeius and Lucius Cornelius Sulla[d] entered upon the consulship. Sulla was a man to whom, up to the conclusion of his career of victory, sufficient praise can hardly be given, and for whom, after his victory, no condemnation can be adequate. He was sprung of a noble family, the sixth in descent from the Cornelius Rufinus who had been one of the famous generals in the war with Pyrrhus. As the renown of his family had waned, Sulla acted for a long while as though he had no thought of seeking the consul-

which they might have conferred in the beginning and so avoided the war.   [d] 88 B.C.

3 videretur : deinde post praeturam inlustratus bello
Italico et ante in Gallia legatione sub Mario, qua[1]
eminentissimos duces hostium fuderat, ex successu
animum sumpsit petensque consulatum paene omnium
civium suffragiis factus est ; sed eum honorem unde-
quinquagesimo aetatis suae anno adsecutus est.

1 XVIII. Per ea tempora Mithridates, Ponticus rex,
vir neque silendus neque dicendus sine cura, bello
acerrimus, virtute eximius, aliquando fortuna, semper
animo maximus, consiliis dux, miles manu, odio in
Romanos Hannibal, occupata Asia necatisque in ea
omnibus civibus Romanis, quos quidem eadem die
2 atque hora redditis civitatibus litteris ingenti cum
pollicitatione praemiorum interimi iusserat, quo
3 tempore neque fortitudine adversus Mithridatem
neque fide in Romanos quisquam Rhodiis par fuit
(horum fidem Mytilenaeorum perfidia inluminavit,
qui M'.[2] Aquilium aliosque Mithridati vinctos tradi-
derunt, quibus libertas in unius Theophanis gratiam
postea a Pompeio restituta est), cum terribilis Italiae
quoque videretur imminere, sorte obvenit Sullae
Asia provincia.

4 Is egressus urbe cum circa Nolam moraretur

---

[1] qua *Gelenius* ; quae *AP.*
[2] M' *Ruhnken* ; M. *AP.*

---

a 88 B.C.

ship. Then, after his praetorship, having earned distinction not only in the Italian war but also, even before that, in Gaul, where he was second in command to Marius, and had routed the most eminent leaders of the enemy, encouraged by his successes, he became a candidate for the consulship and was elected by an almost unanimous vote of the citizens. But this honour did not come to him until the forty-ninth year of his age.

XVIII. It was about this time[a] that Mithridates, king of Pontus, seized Asia and put to death all Roman citizens in it. He was a man about whom one cannot speak except with concern nor yet pass by in silence; he was ever eager for war, of exceptional bravery, always great in spirit and sometimes in achievement, in strategy a general, in bodily prowess a soldier, in hatred to the Romans a Hannibal. He had sent messages to the various cities of Asia in which he had held out great promises of reward, ordering that all Romans should be massacred on the same day and hour throughout the province. In this crisis none equalled the Rhodians either in courageous opposition to Mithridates or in loyalty to the Romans. Their fidelity gained lustre from the perfidy of the people of Mytilene, who handed Manius Aquilius and other Romans over to Mithridates in chains. The Mytilenians subsequently had their liberty restored by Pompey solely in consideration of his friendship for Theophanes. When Mithridates was now regarded as a formidable menace to Italy herself, the province of Asia fell to the lot of Sulla, as proconsul.

Sulla departed from the city, but was still lingering in the vicinity of Nola, since that city, as though

(quippe ea urbs pertinacissime arma retinebat exercituque Romano obsidebatur, velut paeniteret eius fidei, quam omnium sanctissimam bello praestiterat 5 Punico), P. Sulpicius tribunus plebis, disertus, acer, opibus gratia amicitiis vigore ingenii atque animi celeberrimus, cum antea rectissima voluntate apud populum maxumam quaesisset dignitatem, quasi pigeret eum virtutum suarum et bene consulta ei 6 male cederent, subito pravus et praeceps se[1] C. Mario post septuagesimum annum omnia imperia et omnis provincias concupiscenti addixit legemque ad populum tulit, qua Sullae imperium abrogaretur, C. Mario bellum decerneretur Mithridaticum, aliasque leges perniciosas et exitiabiles neque tolerandas liberae civitati tulit. Quin etiam Q. Pompei consulis filium eundemque Sullae generum per emissarios factionis suae interfecit.

1 XIX Tum Sulla contracto exercitu ad urbem rediit eamque armis occupavit, duodecim auctores novarum pessimarumque rerum, inter quos Marium cum filio et P. Sulpicio, urbe exturbavit ac lege lata exules fecit. Sulpicium etiam[2] adsecuti equites in Laurentinis paludibus iugulavere, caputque eius erectum et ostentatum pro rostris velut omen inminentis 2 proscriptionis fuit. Marius post sextum consula-

---

[1] se *addidit Puteanus.*
[2] etiam *bracketed by Orelli and Cornelissen.*

a 88 B.C.

regretting its exceptional loyalty so sacredly maintained in the Punic war, still persisted in maintaining armed resistance to Rome and was being besieged by a Roman army. While he was still there Publius Sulpicius, tribune of the people, a man of eloquence and energy, who had earned distinction by his wealth, his influence, his friendships, and by the vigour of his native ability and his courage, and had previously won great influence with the people by honourable means, now, as if regretting his virtues, and discovering that an honourable course of conduct brought him only disappointment, made a sudden plunge into evil ways, and attached himself to Marius, who, though he had passed his seventieth year, still coveted every position of power and every province. Along with other pieces of pernicious and baleful legislation intolerable in a free state, he proposed a bill to the assembly of the people abrogating Sulla's command, and entrusting the Mithridatic war to Gaius Marius. He even went so far as to cause, through emissaries of his faction, the assassination of a man who was not only son of Quintus Pompeius the consul but also son-in-law of Sulla.

XIX. Thereupon Sulla assembled his army, returned to the city, took armed possession of it, drove from the city the twelve persons responsible for these revolutionary and vicious measures—among them Marius, his son, and Publius Sulpicius—and caused them by formal decree *a* to be declared exiles. Sulpicius was overtaken by horsemen and slain in the Laurentine marshes, and his head was raised aloft and exhibited on the front of the rostra as a presage of the impending proscription. Marius,

tum annumque[1] septuagesimum nudus ac limo obrutus, oculis tantummodo ac naribus eminentibus, extractus arundineto circa paludem Maricae, in quam se fugiens consectantis Sullae equites abdiderat, iniecto in collum loro in carcerem Minturnensium
3 iussu duumviri[a] perductus est. Ad quem interficiendum missus cum gladio servus publicus natione Germanus, qui forte ab imperatore eo bello Cimbrico captus erat, ut agnovit Marium, magno eiulatu expromens[2] indignationem casus tanti viri abiecto
4 gladio profugit e carcere. Tum cives, ab hoste misereri paulo ante principis viri docti, instructum eum viatico conlataque veste in navem imposuerunt. At ille adsecutus circa insulam Aenariam filium cursum in Africam direxit inopemque vitam in tugurio ruinarum Carthaginiensium toleravit, cum Marius aspiciens Carthaginem, illa intuens Marium, alter alteri possent esse solacio.

1 XX. Hoc primum anno sanguine consulis Romani militis imbutae manus sunt ; quippe Q. Pompeius, collega Sullae, ab exercitu[3] Cn. Pompei proconsulis seditione, sed quam dux creaverat, interfectus est.

2 Non erat Mario Sulpicioque Cinna temperatior. Itaque cum ita civitas Italiae data esset, ut in octo tribus contribuerentur novi cives, ne potentia eorum

___

[1] annumque *Voss* ; annoque *AP*.

[2] expromens *Acidalius and Madvig* ; expromenti *BP* ; exprimenti *A*.

[3] ab exercitu *A* ; ad exercitum *P* ; *Burer was in doubt whether the reading should be* ab *or* ad.

___

[a] *Duumvir* was the title of the chief official in the Roman colonies.   Like the consuls in Rome there were two of them.

who had held six consulships and was now more
than seventy years of age, was dragged, naked and
covered with mud, his eyes and nostrils alone
showing above the water, from a reed-bed near the
marsh of Marica, where he had taken refuge when
pursued by the cavalry of Sulla. A rope was
cast about his neck and he was led to the prison
of Minturnae on the order of its *duumvir*.ᵃ A public
slave of German nationality was sent with a sword
to put him to death. It happened that this man had
been taken a prisoner by Marius when he was
commander in the war against the Cimbri; when
he recognized Marius, giving utterance with loud
outcry to his indignation at the plight of this great
man, he threw away his sword and fled from the
prison. Then the citizens, taught by a foreign
enemy to pity one who had so short a time before
been the first man in the state, furnished Marius
with money, brought clothing to cover him, and
put him on board a ship. Marius, overtaking his
son near Aenaria, steered his course for Africa, where
he endured a life of poverty in a hut amid the ruins
of Carthage. There Marius, as he gazed upon
Carthage, and Carthage as she beheld Marius, might
well have offered consolation the one to the other.

XX. In this year the hands of Roman soldiers
were first stained with the blood of a consul. Quintus
Pompeius, the colleague of Sulla, was slain by the
army of Gnaeus Pompeius the proconsul in a mutiny
which their general himself had stirred up.

Cinna was a man as lacking in restraint as Marius
and Sulpicius. Accordingly, although the citizenship had been given to Italy with the proviso that
the new citizens should be enrolled in but eight

et multitudo veterum civium dignitatem frangeret
plusque possent recepti in beneficium quam auctores
beneficii, Cinna in omnibus tribubus eos se distribu-
turum pollicitus est : quo nomine ingentem totius
3 Italiae frequentiam in urbem acciverat. E qua
pulsus collegae optimatiumque viribus cum in Campaniam tenderet, ex auctoritate senatus consulatus
ei abrogatus est suffectusque in eius locum L. Cornelius Merula flamen dialis. Haec iniuria homine
4 quam exemplo dignior fuit. Tum Cinna corruptis
primo centurionibus ac tribunis, mox etiam spe
largitionis militibus, ab eo exercitu, qui circa Nolam
erat, receptus est. Is cum universus in verba eius
iurasset, retinens insignia consulatus patriae bellum
intulit, fretus ingenti numero novorum civium, e
quorum delectu trecentas amplius cohortes conscrip-
5 serat ac triginta legionum instar impleverat. Opus
erat partibus auctoritate, cuius augendae gratia
C. Marium cum filio de exilio revocavit quique cum
iis pulsi erant.

1   XXI. Dum bellum autem infert patriae Cinna, Cn.
Pompeius, Magni pater, cuius praeclara opera bello
Marsico praecipue circa Picenum agrum, ut prae-
scripsimus, usa erat res publica quique Asculum
ceperat, circa quam urbem, cum in multis aliis
regionibus exercitus dispersi forent, quinque et

---

a 87 B.C.
b The normal strength of a legion was from 5000 to 6000
men. Each legion was divided into ten cohorts.

tribes, so that their power and numbers might not weaken the prestige of the older citizens, and that the beneficiaries might not have greater power than the benefactors, Cinna now promised to distribute them throughout all the tribes. With this object he had brought together into the city a great multitude from all parts of Italy. But he was driven from the city by the united strength of his colleague and the optimates, and set out for Campania. His consulship was abrogated by the authority of the senate and Lucius Cornelius Merula, priest of Jupiter, was chosen consul in his place. This illegal act was more appropriate in the case of Cinna than it was a good precedent. Cinna was then received by the army at Nola, after corrupting first the centurions and tribunes and then even the private soldiers with promises of largesse.[a] When they all had sworn allegiance to him, while still retaining the insignia of the consulate he waged war upon his country, relying upon the enormous number of new citizens, from whom he had levied more than three hundred cohorts, thus raising the number of his troops to the equivalent of thirty legions.[b] But his party lacked the backing of strong men; to remedy this defect he recalled Gaius Marius and his son from exile, and also those who had been banished with them.

XXI. While Cinna was waging war against his country, the conduct of Gnaeus Pompeius, the father of Pompey the Great, was somewhat equivocal. As I have already told, the state had made use of his distinguished services in the Marsian war, particularly in the territory of Picenum; he had taken Asculum, in the vicinity of which, though armies were scattered in other regions also, seventy-five

septuaginta milia civium Romanorum, amplius sexa-
2 ginta Italicorum una die conflixerant, frustratus spe
continuandi consulatus ita se[1] dubium mediumque
partibus praestitit, ut omnia ex proprio usu ageret
temporibusque insidiari videretur, et huc atque illuc,
unde spes maior adfulsisset potentiae, sese[2] exercitum-
3 que deflecteret. Sed ad ultimum magno atrocique
proelio cum Cinna conflixit : cuius commissi patrati-
que sub ipsis moenibus focisque[3] urbis Romanae
pugnantibus spectantibusque quam fuerit eventus
4 exitiabilis, vix verbis exprimi potest. Post hoc cum
utrumque exercitum velut parum bello exhaustum
laceraret pestilentia, Cn. Pompeius decessit.[4] Cuius
interitus voluptas amissorum aut gladio aut morbo
civium paene damno repensata est, populusque
Romanus quam vivo iracundiam debuerat, in corpus
mortui contulit.
5 Seu duae seu tres Pompeiorum fuere familiae,
primus eius nominis ante annos fere centum sexaginta
septem[5] Q. Pompeius cum Cn. Servilio consul fuit.
6 Cinna et Marius haud incruentis utrimque certaminibus editis urbem occupaverunt, sed prior
ingressus Cinna de recipiendo Mario legem tulit.
1 XXII. Mox C. Marius pestifero civibus suis reditu

[1] COS. sulta se _A_.
[2] potentiae sese _Halm_; potentia esse _A_ ; potentiae se _P_.
[3] focisque _Voss_; sociisque _AP_; oculisque _Halm after_ Lipsius.
[4] _Halm marks a lacuna before_ decessit; _Sauppe proposes to supply_ de caelo (_or_ fulmine) tactus.
[5] CLXVII _BA_ ; CLXVIII _P_ ; CLXXII _Laurent_.

thousand Roman citizens and more than sixty
thousand Italians had met in battle on a single day.
Foiled in his hope of a second term in the consulship,
he maintained a doubtful and neutral attitude as
between the two parties, so that he seemed to be
acting entirely in his own interest and to be watching
his chance, turning with his army now to one side
and now to the other, according as each offered a
greater promise for power for himself. In the end,
however, he fought against Cinna in a great and
bloody battle. Words almost fail to express how
disastrous to combatants and spectators alike was
the issue of this battle, which began and ended
beneath the walls and close to the very hearths of
Rome. Shortly after this battle, while pestilence
was ravaging both armies, as though their strength
had not been sapped enough by the war, Gnaeus
Pompeius died. The joy felt at his death almost
counterbalanced the feeling of loss for the citizens
who had perished by sword or pestilence, and the
Roman people vented upon his dead body the hatred
it had owed him while he lived.

Whether there were two families of the Pompeii
or three, the first of that name to be consul was
Quintus Pompeius, who was colleague of Gnaeus
Servilius, about one hundred and sixty-seven years
ago.

Cinna and Marius both seized the city after
conflicts which caused much shedding of blood on
both sides, but Cinna was the first to enter it,
whereupon he proposed a law authorizing the recall
of Marius.

XXII. Then Gaius Marius entered the city, and
his return was fraught with calamity for the citizens.

intravit moenia. Nihil illa victoria fuisset crudelius,
nisi mox Sullana esset secuta ; neque licentia gladiorum in mediocris[1] saevitum, sed excelsissimi quoque
atque eminentissimi[2] civitatis viri variis suppliciorum
2 generibus adfecti. In iis consul Octavius, vir lenis-
simi animi, iussu Cinnae interfectus est. Merula
autem, qui se sub adventum Cinnae consulatu abdi-
caverat, incisis venis superfusoque altaribus sanguine,
quos saepe pro salute rei publicae flamen dialis
precatus erat deos, eos in execrationem Cinnae
partiumque eius tum precatus optime de re publica
3 meritum spiritum reddidit. M. Antonius, princeps
civitatis atque eloquentiae, gladiis militum, quos
ipsos facundia sua moratus erat, iussu Marii Cinnaeque
confossus est. Q. Catulus, et aliarum virtutum et
4 belli Cimbrici gloria, quae illi cum Mario communis
fuerat, celeberrimus, cum ad mortem conquireretur,
conclusit se loco nuper calce harenaque perpolito
inlatoque igni, qui vim odoris excitaret, simul exitiali
hausto spiritu, simul incluso suo mortem magis
voto quam arbitrio inimicorum obiit.

5 Omnia erant praecipitia in re publica, nec tamen
adhuc quisquam inveniebatur, qui bona civis Romani
aut donare auderet aut petere sustineret. Postea
id quoque accessit, ut saevitiae causam avaritia

---

[1] in mediocris] in mediocri *A* ; immediocri *B*; in medio-
creis *P*.

[2] excelsissimi quaque atque eminentissimi *Heinsius* ; excelsissimae quoque a. eminentissimae *AP*.

No victory would ever have exceeded his in cruelty had Sulla's not followed soon afterwards. Nor did the licence of the sword play havoc among the obscure alone ; the highest and most distinguished men in the state were made the victims of many kinds of vengeance. Amongst these Octavius the consul, a man of the mildest temper, was slain by the command of Cinna. Merula, however, who had abdicated his consulship just before the arrival of Cinna, opened his veins and, as his blood drenched the altars, he implored the gods to whom, as priest of Jupiter, he had formerly prayed for safety of the state, to visit their wrath upon Cinna and his party. Thus did he yield up the life which had served the state so well. Marcus Antonius, the foremost statesman and orator of Rome, was struck down, at the order of Marius and Cinna, by the swords of soldiers, though he caused even these to hesitate by the power of his eloquence. Then there was Quintus Catulus, renowned for his virtues in general and for the glory, which he had shared with Marius, of having won the Cimbrian war ; when he was being hunted down for death, he shut himself in a room that had lately been plastered with lime and sand; then he brought fire that it might cause a powerful vapour to issue from the plaster, and by breathing the poisonous air and then holding his breath he died a death according rather with his enemies' wishes than with their judgement.

The whole state was now plunging headlong into ruin ; and yet no one had so far appeared who either dared to offer for pillage the goods of a Roman citizen, or could bring himself to demand them. Later, however, even this extreme was reached, and avarice furnished a motive for ruthlessness ;

praeberet et modus culpae ex pecuniae modo constitueretur et qui fuisset locuples, fieret is nocens,
suique quisque periculi merces foret, nec quidquam
videretur turpe, quod esset quaestuosum.

1   XXIII. Secundum deinde consulatum Cinna et
septimum Marius in priorum dedecus iniit, cuius initio
morbo oppressus decessit, vir in bello hostibus, in
otio civibus infestissimus quietisque impatientissimus.
2 In huius locum suffectus Valerius Flaccus, turpissimae
legis auctor, qua creditoribus quadrantem solvi
iusserat, cuius facti merita eum poena intra bien-
3 nium consecuta est. Dominante in Italia Cinna maior
pars nobilitatis ad Sullam in Achaiam ac deinde post
in Asiam perfugit.

Sulla interim cum Mithridatis praefectis circa
Athenas Boeotiamque et Macedoniam ita dimicavit,
ut et Athenas reciperet et plurimo circa multiplicis
Piraei portus munitiones labore expleto amplius
ducenta milia hostium interficeret nec minus multa
4 caperet. Si quis hoc rebellandi tempus, quo Athenae
oppugnatae a Sulla sunt, imputat Atheniensibus, nimirum veri vetustatisque ignarus est : adeo enim certa
Atheniensium in Romanos fides fuit, ut semper et

---

a That is, his property was divided among those responsible for his death.
  b For this period and its proscriptions see Plutarch, *Life
of Sulla.*   *c* 86 B.C.   *d* 87–86 B.C.

the magnitude of one's crime was determined by the magnitude of his property ; he who possessed riches became a malefactor and was in each case the prize[a] set up for his own murder. In short nothing was regarded as dishonourable that brought profit.[b]

XXIII. Cinna then entered upon his second consulship, and Marius upon his seventh,[c] only to bring dishonour upon his former six. An illness which came upon Marius at the very beginning of his year of office ended the life of this man, who, impatient as he was of tranquillity, was as dangerous to his fellow-citizens in peace as he had been in war to Rome's enemies. In his place was chosen as consul suffectus Valerius Flaccus, the author of a most disgraceful law, by which he had ordained that one-fourth only of a debt should be paid to the creditors, an act for which a well-deserved punishment overtook him within two years. During this time, while Cinna held the reins of power in Italy, a large proportion of the nobles took refuge with Sulla in Achaea, and afterwards in Asia.

In the meantime Sulla fought with the generals of Mithridates at Athens, in Boeotia, and in Macedonia with such success that he recovered Athens, and, after surmounting many difficulties in overcoming the manifold fortifications of Piraeus, slew more than two hundred thousand of the enemy and made prisoners of as many more.[d] If anyone regards this period of rebellion, during which Athens suffered siege at the hands of Sulla, as a breach of good faith on the part of the Athenians, he shows a strange ignorance of the facts of history ; for so constant was the loyalty of the Athenians towards the Romans

97

in omni re, quidquid sincera fide gereretur, id Romani
5 Attica fieri praedicarent. Ceterum tum oppressi
Mithridatis armis homines miserrimae condicionis
cum ab inimicis tenerentur, oppugnabantur ab amicis
et animos extra moenia, corpora necessitati servientes
6 intra muros habebant. Transgressus deinde in Asiam
Sulla parentem ad[1] omnia supplicemque Mithridatem
invenit, quem multatum pecunia ac parte navium
Asia omnibusque aliis provinciis, quas armis occupaverat, decedere coëgit, captivos recepit, in per-
fugas noxiosque animadvertit, paternis, id est
Ponticis finibus contentum esse iussit.

1 XXIV. C. Flavius Fimbria, qui praefectus equitum
ante adventum Sullae Valerium Flaccum consularem
virum interfecerat exercituque occupato imperator
appellatus forti[2] Mithridatem pepulerat proelio, sub
adventu[3] Sullae se ipse interemit, adulescens, quae
2 pessime ausus erat, fortiter executus. Eodem anno
P. Laenas tribunus plebis Sex. Lucilium, qui priore[4]
anno tribunus plebis fuerat, saxo Tarpeio deiecit, et
cum collegae eius, quibus diem dixerat, metu ad
Sullam profugissent, aqua ignique iis interdixit.

[1] ad *Ruhnken*; ante *AP*.
[2] forti *Puteanus*; fonte *AP*; sponte *Halm*.
[3] sub adventu *AP*; sub adventum *Halm*.
[4] qui in priore *AP*.

---

[a] *i.e.* with their Roman besiegers.
[b] The province of Asia, *i.e. Asia Minor.*

that always and invariably, whenever the Romans referred to any act of unqualified loyalty, they called it an example of " Attic faith." But at this time, overwhelmed as they were by the arms of Mithridates, the Athenians were in a most unhappy plight. Held in subjection by their enemies and besieged by their friends, although in obedience to necessity they kept their bodies within the walls, their hearts were outside their fortifications.[a] After the capture of Athens Sulla crossed into Asia, where he found Mithridates submissive to all his demands and in the attitude of a suppliant He compelled him, after paying a fine in money and giving up half his fleet, to evacuate Asia[b] and all the other provinces which he had seized ; he also secured the return of all prisoners, inflicted punishment upon deserters and others who had been in any way culpable, and obliged Mithridates to be satisfied with the boundaries of his inheritance, that is to say, with Pontus.

XXIV. Before the arrival of Sulla, Gaius Flavius Fimbria, prefect of horse, had put to death Valerius Flaccus, a man of consular rank, had taken command of his army, by which he was saluted as *imperator*, and had succeeded in defeating Mithridates in battle. Now, on the eve of Sulla's arrival, he took his own life. He was a young man who, however reprehensible his bold designs might be, at any rate executed them with bravery. In the same year Publius Laenas, tribune of the people, threw Sextus Lucilius, tribune of the previous year, from the Tarpeian rock. When his colleagues, whom he also indicted, fled in fear to Sulla, he had a decree of banishment passed against them.

99

3 Tum Sulla compositis transmarinis rebus, cum ad
eum primum omnium Romanorum legati Parthorum
venissent, et in iis quidam magi ex notis corporis
respondissent caelestem eius vitam et memoriam
futuram, revectus in Italiam haud plura quam triginta
armatorum milia adversum ducenta amplius hostium
4 exposuit Brundusii. Vix quidquam in Sullae operibus clarius duxerim, quam quod cum per triennium
Cinnanae Marianaeque partes Italiam obsiderent,
neque inlaturum se bellum iis dissimulavit nec quod
erat in manibus omisit, existimavitque ante frangen-
dum hostem quam ulciscendum civem, repulsoque
externo metu, ubi quod alienum esset vicisset,
5 superaret[1] quod erat domesticum. Ante adventum
L. Sullae Cinna seditione orta ab exercitu interemptus est, vir dignior, qui arbitrio victorum moreretur
quam iracundia militum. De quo vere dici potest,
ausum esse[2] eum quae nemo auderet bonus, per-
fecisse quae a nullo nisi fortissimo perfici possent,
et fuisse eum in consultando temerarium, in exe-
quendo virum. Carbo nullo suffecto collega solus
toto anno consul fuit.

1 XXV. Putares Sullam venisse in Italiam non belli

[1] superaret *AP* ; *Halm regards as a case of careless writing* ; *Ellis understands* superaret *as having in it an imperative
force.*

[2] ausum esse *Orelli* ; ausum *P* ; aususs *with final* s *subsequently deleted A.*

---

a 83 B.C.

Sulla had now settled affairs across the sea. There came to him ambassadors of the Parthians—he was the first of the Romans to be so honoured—and among them some wise men who, from the marks on his body, foretold that his life and his fame would be worthy of a god. Returning to Italy he landed at Brundisium,[a] having not more than thirty thousand men to face more than two hundred thousand of the enemy. Of all the exploits of Sulla there is nothing that I should consider more noteworthy than that, during the three years in which the party of Marius and Cinna were continuously masters of Italy, he never hid from them his intention to wage war on them, but at the same time he did not interrupt the war which he then had on his hands. He considered that his duty was to crush the enemy before taking vengeance upon citizens, and that after he had repelled the menace of the foreigner and won a victory in this war abroad, he should then prove himself the master in a war at home. Before Sulla's arrival Cinna was slain in a mutiny of his army. He was a man who deserved to die by the sentence of his victorious enemies rather than at the hands of his angry soldiers. Of him one can truly say that he formed daring plans, such as no good citizen would have conceived, and that he accomplished what none but a most resolute man could have accomplished, and that he was foolhardy enough in the formulation of his plans, but in their execution a man. Carbo remained sole consul throughout the year without electing a colleague in the place of Cinna.

XXV. One would think that Sulla had come to Italy, not as the champion of war but as the

vindicem, sed pacis auctorem : tanta cum quiete
exercitum per Calabriam Apuliamque cum singulari
cura frugum, agrorum, hominum, urbium perduxit
in Campaniam temptavitque iustis legibus et aequis
condicionibus bellum componere ; sed iis, quibus
et res[1] pessima et immodica cupiditas erat, non
2 poterat pax placere. Crescebat interim in dies Sullae
exercitus confluentibus ad eum optimo quoque et
sanissimo. Felici deinde circa Capuam eventu Sci-
pionem Norbanumque consules superat, quorum Norbanus acie victus, Scipio ab exercitu suo desertus
3 ac proditus inviolatus a Sulla dimissus est. Adeo
enim Sulla dissimilis fuit bellator ac victor, ut dum
vincit, mitis ac iustissimo[2] lenior, post victoriam audito
fuerit crudelior. Nam et consulem, ut praediximus,
exarmatum Quintumque Sertorium, pro quanti mox
belli facem ! et multos alios, potitus eorum, dimisit
incolumes, credo ut in eodem homine duplicis ac
4 diversissimi animi conspiceretur exemplum. Post[3]
victoriam — namque ascendens[4] montem Tifata cum
C. Norbano concurrerat — Sulla gratis Dianae, cuius
numini regio illa sacrata est, solvit ; aquas salubri-
tate medendisque corporibus nobiles agrosque omnis
addixit deae. Huius gratae religionis memoriam et
inscriptio templi adfixa posti hodieque et tabula
testatur aerea intra aedem.

[1] res *supplied by Ruhnken.*
[2] mitis *supplied by Krause* ; ac iustissimo *AP* ; aequissimo
Halm.
[3] post *Gelenius* ; posuit *AP.*
[4] namque ascendens *Halm* ; qua demendes *AP* ; qua
descendens *Gelenius.*

[a] 83 B.C.   [b] See Chap. XXX.

establisher of peace, so quietly did he lead his army through Calabria and Apulia into Campania, taking unusual care not to inflict damage on crops, fields, men, or cities, and such efforts did he make to end the war on just terms and fair conditions. But peace could not be to the liking of men whose cause was wicked and whose cupidity was unbounded. In the meantime Sulla's army was daily growing, for all the better and saner citizens flocked to his side. By a fortunate issue of events he overcame the consuls Scipio and Norbanus near Capua.[a] Norbanus was defeated in battle, while Scipio, deserted and betrayed by his army, was allowed by Sulla to go unharmed. So different was Sulla the warrior from Sulla the victor that, while his victory was in progress he was mild and more lenient than was reasonable, but after it was won his cruelty was unprecedented. For instance, as we have already said, he disarmed the consul and let him go, and after gaining possession of many leaders including Quintus Sertorius, so soon to become the firebrand of a great war,[b] he dismissed them unharmed. The reason, I suppose, was that we might have a notable example of a double and utterly contradictory personality in one and the same man.

It was while Sulla was ascending Mount Tifata that he had encountered Gaius Norbanus. After his victory over him he paid a vow of gratitude to Diana, to whom that region is sacred, and consecrated to the goddess the waters renowned for their salubrity and power to heal, as well as all the lands in the vicinity. The record of this pleasing act of piety is witnessed to this day by an inscription on the door of the temple, and a bronze tablet within the edifice.

VELLEIUS PATERCULUS

1 XXVI. Deinde consules Carbo tertium et C. Marius, septiens consulis filius, annos natus sex et viginti, vir animi magis quam aevi paterni, multa fortiterque molitus neque usquam inferior nomine suo. Is[1] apud Sacriportum pulsus a Sulla acie Praeneste, quod ante natura munitum praesidiis firmaverat, se exercitumque contulit.

2 Ne quid usquam malis publicis deesset, in qua civitate semper virtutibus certatum erat, certabatur sceleribus, optimusque sibi videbatur, qui fuerat[2] pessimus. Quippe dum ad Sacriportum dimicatur, Damasippus praetor Domitium consularem, Scaevolam[3] Mucium, pontificem maximum et divini humanique iuris auctorem celeberrimum, et C. Carbonem praetorium, consulis fratrem, et Antistium aedilicium velut faventis Sullae partibus in curia 3 Hostilia trucidavit. Non perdat nobilissimi facti gloriam Calpurnia, Bestiae filia, uxor Antistii, quae iugulato, ut praediximus, viro gladio se ipsa transfixit. Quantum huius gloriae famaeque accessit nunc virtute feminae ! nec propria latet.[4]

1 XXVII. At Pontius Telesinus, dux Samnitium, vir domi bellique fortissimus penitusque Romano nomini

---

[1] suo. Is *Orelli*; st'lis *A* (sulis *according to Orelli*); consulis *P*.

[2] fuerat *AP*; foret *Halm*.

[3] Domitium consularem, Scaevolam Mucium *Ruhnken*; Dom. Scaevolam etiam *AP*.

[4] virtute feminae nec propria latet *Thomas*; virtute eminet patria latet *AP*; virtute feminae propria patet *Haupt followed by Halm*.

XXVI. Carbo now became consul for the third time, in conjunction with Gaius Marius, now aged twenty-six, the son of a father who had been seven times consul. He was a man who showed his father's spirit, though not destined to reach his years, who displayed great fortitude in the many enterprises he undertook, and never belied the name. Defeated by Sulla at Sacriportus he retired with his army to Praeneste, which town, thongh already strong by nature, he had strengthened by a garrison.

In order that nothing should be lacking to the calamities of the state, in Rome, a city in which there had already been rivalry in virtues, there was now a rivalry in crimes, and that man now regarded himself as the best citizen who had formerly been the worst. While the battle was being fought at Sacriportus, within the city the praetor Damasippus murdered in the Curia Hostilia, as supposed partisans of Sulla, Domitius, a man of consular rank ; Scaevola Mucius, pontifex maximus and famous author of works on religious and civil law ; Gaius Carbo, a former praetor, and brother of the consul, and Antistius, a former aedile. May Calpurnia, the daughter of Bestia and wife of Antistius, never lose the glory of a noble deed ; for, when her husband was put to death, as I have just said, she pierced her own breast with the sword. What increment has his glory and fame received through this brave act of a woman ! and yet his own name is by no means obscure.

XXVII. While Carbo and Marius were still consuls, one hundred and nine years ago, on the Kalends of November, Pontius Telesinus, a Samnite chief, brave in spirit and in action and hating to the core the

infestissimus, contractis circiter quadraginta milibus
fortissimae pertinacissimaeque in retinendis armis
iuventutis, Carbone ac Mario consulibus abhinc
annos centum et novem[1] Kal. Novembribus ita ad
portam Collinam cum Sulla dimicavit, ut ad summum
2 discrimen et eum et rem publicam perduceret, quae
non maius periculum adiit Hannibalis intra tertium
miliarium castra conspicata, quam eo die, quo cir-
cumvolans ordines exercitus sui Telesinus dictitansque
adesse Romanis ultimum diem vociferabatur eruen-
dam delendamque urbem, adiiciens numquam defu-
turos raptores Italicae libertatis lupos, nisi silva, in
3 quam refugere solerent, esset excisa. Post primam
demum horam noctis et Romana acies respiravit et
hostium cessit. Telesinus postera die semianimis
repertus est, victoris magis quam morientis vultum
praeferens, cuius abscisum caput ferro figi[2] ges-
tarique circa Praeneste Sulla iussit.
4 Tum demum desperatis rebus suis C. Marius
adulescens per cuniculos, qui miro opere fabricati
in diversas agrorum partis ferebant,[3] conatus erumpere, cum foramine e terra emersisset, a dispositis in
5 id ipsum interemptus est. Sunt qui sua manu, sunt
qui concurrentem mutuis ictibus cum minore fratre
Telesini una obsesso et erumpente occubuisse pro-
diderint. Utcumque cecidit, hodieque tanta patris
imagine non obscuratur eius[4] memoria. De quo

[1] cix *Kritz*; xi *BA*; xl *P*.
[2] ferro figi *Madvig*; ferri *AP*.
[3] ferebant *Burman*; fuerunt *AP*; ferunt *Gelenius*.
[4] eius *P*; civis *AB*.

very name of Rome, having collected about him forty thousand of the bravest and most steadfast youth who still persisted in retaining arms, fought with Sulla, near the Colline gate, a battle so critical as to bring both Sulla and the city into the gravest peril. Rome had not faced a greater danger when she saw the camp of Hannibal within the third milestone, than on this day when Telesinus went about from rank to rank exclaiming : " The last day is at hand for the Romans," and in a loud voice exhorted his men to overthrow and destroy their city, adding : " These wolves that made such ravages upon Italian liberty will never vanish until we have cut down the forest that harbours them." It was only after the first hour of the night that the Roman army was able to recover its breath, and the enemy retired. The next day Telesinus was found in a half-dying condition, but with the expression of a conqueror upon his face rather than that of a dying man. Sulla ordered his severed head to be fixed upon a spear point and carried around the walls of Praeneste.

The young Marius, now at last despairing of his cause, endeavoured to make his way out of Praeneste through the tunnels, wrought with great engineering skill, which led into the fields in different directions ; but, on emerging from the exit, he was cut off by men who had been stationed there for that purpose. Some authorities have asserted that he died by his own hand, some that he died in company with the younger brother of Telesinus, who was also besieged and was endeavouring to escape with him, and that each ran upon the other's sword. Whatever the manner of his death, his memory is not obscured even to-day by the great figure of his father. Sulla's

iuvene quid existimaverit Sulla, in promptu est ;
occiso enim demum eo Felicis nomen adsumpsit,
quod quidem usurpasset iustissime, si eundem et
vincendi et vivendi finem habuisset.

6 Oppugnationi autem Praenestis ac Marii praefuerat
Ofella Lucretius, qui cum ante Marianarum fuisset
partium praetor,[1] ad Sullam transfugerat. Felici-
tatem diei, quo Samnitium Telesinique pulsus est
exercitus, Sulla perpetua ludorum circensium honoravit memoria, qui sub eius nomine Sullanae Victoriae
celebrantur.

1 XXVIII. Paulo ante quam Sulla ad Sacriportum
dimicaret, magnificis proeliis partium eius viri
hostium exercitum fuderant, duo Servilii apud
Clusium, Metellus Pius apud Faventiam, M. Lucullus
circa Fidentiam.

2 Videbantur finita belli civilis mala, cum Sullae
crudelitate aucta sunt. Quippe dictator creatus
(cuius honoris usurpatio per annos centum et viginti
intermissa ; nam proximus post annum quam Hannibal Italia excesserat, uti adpareat populum Romanum usum dictatoris haud metu desiderasse tali
quo timuisset potestatem[2]) imperio, quo priores ad
vindicandam maximis periculis rem publicam olim
usi erant,[3] eo in inmodicae crudelitatis licentiam[4]
3 usus est. Primus ille, et utinam ultimus, exemplum
proscriptionis invenit, ut in qua civitate petulantis

[1] praetor *AP*; proditor *Voss*; fautor *Scriner*.
[2] haud . . . potestatem *Ellis*; aut metu desideras tulio
cōtimuis se (Tulio co timuisse *P*) potestatem *AP*; ut in
metu desiderasse ita in otio timuisse potestatem *Halm*.
[3] imperio . . . usi erant *Ruhnken and Gelenius*; imperio
prores (proh res *P*) ad vindicandam (-dum *P*) maximi
periculi spolia musierant *AP*.
[4] eo inmodicae crud. licentia *AP*; *em. Cludius.*

estimate of the young man is manifest; for it was only after he was slain that he took the name of Felix,[a] a name which he would have been completely justified in assuming had his life ended with his victory.

The siege of Marius in Praeneste was directed by Ofella Lucretius, who had been a general on the Marian side but had deserted to Sulla. Sulla commemorated the great good fortune which fell to him on this day by instituting an annual festival of games held in the circus, which are still celebrated as the games of Sulla's victory.

XXVIII. Shortly before Sulla's victory at Sacriportus, several leaders of his party had routed the enemy in successful engagements; the two Servilii at Clusium, Metellus Pius at Faventia, and Marcus Lucullus in the vicinity of Fidentia.

The terrors of the civil war seemed nearly at an end when they received fresh impetus from the cruelty of Sulla. Being made dictator[b] (the office had been obsolete for one hundred and twenty years, and had been last employed in the year after Hannibal's departure from Italy; it is therefore clear that the fear which caused the Roman people to feel the need of a dictator was outweighed by the fear of his excessive power) Sulla now wielded with unbridled cruelty the powers which former dictators had employed only to save their country in times of extreme danger. He was the first to set the precedent for proscription—would that he had been the last! The result was that in the very state in

<hr/>

[a] The "fortunate."
[b] 82 B.C.

convicii iudicium histrioni ex albo[1] redditur, in ea
iugulati civis Romani publice constitueretur auctora-
mentum, plurimumque haberet, qui plurimos interemisset, neque occisi hostis quam civis uberius foret
4 praemium fieretque quisque merces mortis suae. Nec
tantum in eos, qui contra arma tulerant, sed in
multos insontis saevitum. Adiectum etiam, ut bona
proscriptorum venirent exclusique paternis opibus
liberi etiam petendorum honorum iure prohiberentur
simulque, quod indignissimum est, senatorum filii
et onera ordinis sustinerent et iura perderent.

1 XXIX. Sub adventum in Italiam L. Sullae Cn.
Pompeius, eius Cn. Pompei filius, quem magnifi-
centissimas res in consulatu gessisse bello Marsico
praediximus, tris et viginti annos natus, abhinc annos
centum et tredecim[2] privatis ut opibus, ita consiliis
magna ausus magnificeque conata executus, ad
vindicandam restituendamque dignitatem patriae
firmum ex agro Piceno, qui totus paternis eius
2 clientelis refertus erat, contraxit exercitum : cuius
viri magnitudo multorum voluminum instar exigit,
sed operis modus paucis eum narrari iubet.

Fuit hic genitus matre Lucilia stirpis senatoriae,
forma excellens, non ea, qua flos commendatur aetatis,
sed ea[3] dignitate constantiaque, quae[4] in illam con-

---

[1] histrioni ex albo *Gronovius et Mommsen* ; historiarum
(historiarium *P*) ex alto *ABP*.
[2] cx *Kritz.*
[3] sed ea *Burman* ; sed ex *AP*.
[4] quae *added by Aldus.*

---

^a 83 B.C.

which an actor who had been hissed from the stage
has legal redress for wilful abuse, a premium for
the murder of a citizen was now publicly announced;
that the richest man was he who had slain the
greatest number; that the bounty for slaying an
enemy was no greater than that for slaying a citizen;
and that each man became the prize set up for his
own death. Nor was vengeance wreaked upon
those alone who had borne arms against him, but
on many innocents as well. In addition the goods
of the proscribed were sold, and their children were
not only deprived of their fathers' property but were
also debarred from the right of seeking public office,
and to cap the climax of injustice, the sons of senators
were compelled to bear the burdens and yet lose the
rights pertaining to their rank.

XXIX. Just before the arrival of Lucius Sulla in
Italy, Gnaeus Pompeius, the son of the Gnaeus
Pompeius who, as has already been mentioned, won
such brilliant successes in the Marsian war during
his consulship, though but twenty-three years of
age—it was one hundred and thirteen years ago [a]
—on his own initiative and with his own private
funds conceived and brilliantly executed a daring
plan. To avenge his country and restore her dignity
he raised a strong army from the district of Picenum
which was filled with the retainers of his father. To
do justice to the greatness of this man would require
many volumes, but the brief compass of my work
compels me to limit my description to a few words.

On the side of his mother Lucilia he was of
senatorial stock. He was distinguished by a personal
beauty, not of the sort which gives the bloom of
youth its charm, but stately and unchanging, as

veniens amplitudinem fortunamque eum ad ultimum
vitae comitata est diem ; innocentia eximius, sanc-
3 titate praecipuus, eloquentia medius, potentiae, quae
honoris causa ad eum deferretur, non vi[1] ab eo occu-
paretur, cupidissimus, dux bello peritissimus civis
in toga, nisi ubi vereretur ne quem haberet parem,
modestissimus, amicitiarum tenax, in offensis exora-
bilis, in reconcilianda gratia fidelissimus, in acci-
pienda satisfactione facillimus, potentia sua num-
4 quam aut raro ad impotentiam usus, paene omnium
vitiorum expers, nisi numeraretur inter maxima in
civitate libera dominaque gentium indignari, cum
omnes cives iure haberet pares, quemquam aequalem
5 dignitate conspicere. Hic a toga virili adsuetus com-
militio prudentissimi ducis, parentis sui, bonum et
capax recta discendi ingenium singulari rerum
militarium prudentia excoluerat, ut a Sertorio
Metellus laudaretur magis, Pompeius timeretur
validius.[2]

1 XXX. Tum M. Perpenna praetorius, e proscriptis,
gentis clarioris quam animi, Sertorium inter cenam
Oscae interemit Romanisque certam victoriam,
partibus suis excidium, sibi turpissimam mortem
pessimo auctoravit facinore. Metellus et Pompeius

---

[1] ui *Mommsen*; ut *AP.*
[2] *Krause believes that there is a hiatus of some length between this chapter and XXX.*

---

a 72 B.C.
b After the assassination Perpenna took charge of the
army of Sertorius, was defeated by Pompey, and taken
prisoner. He sought to save his life by delivering up to
Pompey the papers of Sertorius implicating many of the
leading men of Rome in a conspiracy to change the constitution of Sulla. Pompey commanded that the papers be
burnt, and that Perpenna be put to death.

befitted the distinction and good fortune of his career, and this beauty attended him to the last day of his life. He was a man of exceptional purity of life, of great uprightness of character, of but moderate oratorical talent, ambitious of such power as might be conferred upon him as a mark of honour, but not that which had to be forcibly usurped. In war a resourceful general, in peace a citizen of temperate conduct except when he feared a rival, constant in his friendships, easily placated when offended, loyal in re-establishing terms of amity, very ready to accept satisfaction, never or at least rarely abusing his power, Pompey was free from almost every fault, unless it be considered one of the greatest of faults for a man to chafe at seeing anyone his equal in dignity in a free state, the mistress of the world, where he should justly regard all citizens as his equals. From the day on which he had assumed the toga he had been trained to military service on the staff of that sagacious general, his father, and by a singular insight into military tactics had so developed his excellent native talent, which showed great capacity to learn what was best, that, while Sertorius bestowed the greater praise upon Metellus, it was Pompey he feared the more strongly.

XXX. Shortly afterwards Marcus Perpenna, an ex-praetor, one of those who had been proscribed, a man more distinguished for his birth than for his character, assassinated Sertorius at Osca at a banquet.[a] By this wicked deed he ensured success to the Romans, and destruction to his own faction, and for himself a death of extreme dishonour.[b] Metellus and Pompey won triumphs for their victories in

113

2 ex Hispaniis triumphaverunt ; sed Pompeius, hoc
quoque triumpho adhuc eques Romanus, ante diem
quam consulatum iniret, curru urbem invectus est.

3 Quem virum quis non miretur per tot extraordinaria
imperia in summum fastigium evectum iniquo tulisse
animo, C. Caesaris absentis[1] in altero consulatu
petendo senatum populumque Romanum rationem
habere : adeo familiare est hominibus omnia sibi
ignoscere, nihil aliis remittere, et invidiam rerum non
ad causam, sed ad voluntatem personasque dirigere.

4 Hoc consulatu Pompeius tribuniciam potestatem restituit, cuius Sulla imaginem sine re[2] reliquerat.

5 Dum Sertorianum bellum in Hispania geritur,
quattuor et sexaginta fugitivi e ludo gladiatorio
Capua profugientes duce Spartaco, raptis ex ea
urbe gladiis, primo Vesuvium montem petiere, mox
crescente in dies multitudine gravibus variisque

6 casibus adfecere Italiam. Quorum numerus in
tantum adulevit, ut qua ultima dimicavere acie,
nonaginta milia[3] hominum se Romano exercitui
opposuerint. Huius patrati gloria penes M. Crassum
fuit, mox rei publicae omnium consensu[4] principem.

---

[1] absentis *add. Krause.*
[2] sine re *Gelenius*; in iure *AP.*
[3] xc milia *Voss*; xl a ccc *AP.*
[4] omnium *P*; omni *A* ; consensu *add. Ellis.*

---

a Extraordinary commands : here may be included the
extraordinary title of proconsul conferred upon him though
but a private citizen in the war against Sertorius ; his extraordinary election to the consulship in which the senate
waived legal age and absence from Rome ; the power of the
imperium maius over the whole Mediterranean to fifty miles
inland from its coasts, conferred in 67 B.C. by the Gabinian
law ; and the extension of this power by the Manilian law
to cover all the fleets and armies in the east and the whole
of Asia as far as Armenia.   *b* 70 B.C.

Spain. Pompey, who even at the time of this triumph was still a Roman knight, entered the city in his triumphal car on the day before his entrance upon his consulate. Who is there who does not feel surprise that this man, who owed his elevation to the highest position in the state to so many extraordinary commands,[a] should have taken it ill that the senate and the Roman people were willing to consider Gaius Caesar as a candidate for the consulship a second time, though suing for it *in absentia*? So common a failing is it for mankind to overlook every irregularity in their own case, but to make no concessions to others, and to let their discontent with conditions be vented upon suspected motives and upon persons instead of the real cause. In this consulship[b] Pompey restored the power of the tribunes, of which Sulla had left the shadow without the substance.[c]

While war was being waged against Sertorius in Spain sixty-four runaway slaves, under the leadership of Spartacus, escaping from a gladiatorial school in Capua, seized swords in that city, and at first took refuge on Mount Vesuvius;[d] then, as their number increased daily, they afflicted Italy with many serious disasters Their number grew to such an extent that in the last battle which they fought they confronted the Roman army with ninety thousand men. The glory of ending this war belongs to Marcus Crassus, who was soon by unanimous consent to be regarded as the first citizen in the state.

[a] *i.e.* by depriving the tribunes of the right of initiating legislation, by reducing the right of *intercessio* to a simple *ius auxilii ferendi* (Cic. *De legg.* iii. 9), and by disqualifying tribunes from holding curule offices.   [d] 73-71 B.C.

1 XXXI. Converterat Cn. Pompei persona totum in
se terrarum orbem et per omnia maior civi[1] habebatur. Qui cum consul perquam laudabiliter iurasset
se in nullam provinciam ex eo magistratu iturum
2 idque servasset, post biennium A. Gabinius tribunus
legem tulit, ut cum belli more, non latrociniorum,
orbem classibus iam, non furtivis expeditionibus
piratae terrerent quasdamque etiam Italiae urbes
diripuissent, Cn. Pompeius ad eos opprimendos mitteretur essetque ei imperium aequum in omnibus
provinciis cum proconsulibus usque ad quinquagesimum miliarium a mari. Quo scito[2] paene totius
3 terrarum orbis imperium uni viro deferebatur ; sed
tamen idem hoc ante septennium[3] in M. Antonii
4 praetura decretum erat. Sed interdum persona ut
exemplo nocet, ita invidiam auget aut levat[4] : in
Antonio homines aequo animo passi erant ; raro
enim invidetur eorum honoribus, quorum vis non
timetur : contra in iis homines extraordinaria refor-
midant, qui ᴜa suo arbitrio aut deposituri aut reten-
turi videntur et modum in voluntate habent. Dis-
suadebant optimates, sed consilia impetu victa sunt.
1 XXXII. Digna est memoria Q. Catuli cum auctoritas tum verecundia. Qui cum dissuadens legem

---

[1] maior civi *Heinsius* ; maiore vi *AP*.
[2] quo scito *Schegk* ; quos c̄ *A* ; quo senatus Cos. *P*.
[3] septennium *Krause* ; biennium *AP*.
[4] leva *A*.

ᵃ 67 B.C.
ᵇ In 74 B.C. Marcus Antonius, the father of the triumvir,
who had held the praetorship the previous year, obtained
through the influence of Cethegus and the consul Cotta the
command of the fleet and the coasts of the Mediterranean
in order to clear the sea of pirates.

XXXI. The personality of Pompey had now turned the eyes of the world upon itself, and in all things he was now regarded as more than a mere citizen. As consul he made the laudable promise, which he also kept, that he would not go from that office to any province. But, two years afterwards, when the pirates were terrifying the world, not as heretofore by furtive marauding expeditions but with fleets of ships in the manner of regular warfare, and had already plundered several cities of Italy, Aulus Gabinius, a tribune, proposed an enactment [a] to the effect that Gnaeus Pompeius should be sent to crush them, and that in all the provinces he should have a power equal with that of the proconsular governors to a distance of fifty miles from the sea. By this decree the command of almost the entire world was being entrusted to one man. Seven years before, it is true, like power had been decreed to Marcus Antonius as praetor.[b] But sometimes the personality of the recipient of such power, just as it renders the precedent more or less dangerous, increases or diminishes its invidiousness. In the case of Antonius people had looked upon his position with no concern. For it is not often that we begrudge honours to those whose power we do not fear. On the other hand men shrink from conferring extraordinary powers upon those who seem likely to retain them or lay them aside only as they themselves choose, and whose inclinations are their only check. The optimates advised against the grant to Pompey, but sane advice succumbed to impulse.

XXXII. The sterling character of Quintus Catulus and his modesty on this occasion are worthy of record. Opposing the law before the assembled

in contione dixisset esse quidem praeclarum virum
Cn. Pompeium, sed nimium iam liberae[1] rei publicae
neque omnia in uno reponenda adiecissetque : " si
quid huic acciderit, quem in eius locum substituetis ? "
subclamavit universa contio, te, Q. Catule. Tum
ille victus consensu omnium et tam honorifico civitatis
2 testimonio e contione discessit. Hic hominis vere-
cundiam, populi iustitiam mirari libet, huius, quod
non ultra contendit, plebis, quod dissuadentem et
adversarium voluntatis suae vero testimonio fraudare
noluit.

3 Per idem tempus Cotta iudicandi munus, quod
C. Gracchus ereptum senatui ad equites, Sulla ab
illis ad senatum transtulerant,[2] aequaliter in utrumque ordinem partitus est ; Otho Roscius lege sua
equitibus in theatro loca restituit.

4 At Cn. Pompeius multis et praeclaris viris in id
bellum adsumptis discriptoque paene in omnis
recessus maris praesidio navium, brevi inexsupera-
bili manu terrarum orbem liberavit praedonesque
saepe multis iam aliis locis[3] victos circa Ciliciam classe
adgressus fudit ac fugavit ; et quo maturius bellum

---

[1] liberae *A* (*an erasure after* ae); liber aeret (aere *P*)
BP.   [2] transtulerat *A*.
[3] praedonesque per multa a multis locis *AP* ; alias ac
multis *Burer*.

---

[a] Otho Roscius, tribune in 67 B.C. The law set apart the
first fourteen rows, next to the Senators, who sat in the
orchestra, for those of equestrian rating. Cicero also speaks
of it as a restoration, but we have no information as to when
the distinction was first made.
118

people he had said that Pompey was without
question a great man, but that he was now becoming
too great for a free republic, and that all powers
ought not to be reposed in one man. "If anything
happens to Pompey," he added, "whom will you
put in his place?" The people shouted with one
accord, "You, Catulus." Then, yielding to the
unanimous desire of the people for the proposed law
and to this honourable tribute of his fellow-citizens,
he left the assembly. At this point one would fain
express admiration for the modesty of the man and
the fairness of the people; in the case of Catulus,
because he ceased his opposition, and, in the case
of the people, because it was unwilling to withhold
from one who was speaking against the measure in
opposition to them this real evidence of their
esteem.

About the same time Cotta divided service.
upon the juries equally between the senatorial and
equestrian orders. Gaius Gracchus had taken this
privilege from the senate and given it to the knights,
while Sulla had again transferred it from the knights
to the senate. Otho Roscius by his law restored to
the knights their places in the theatre.[a]

Meanwhile Gnaeus Pompey enlisted the services
of many illustrious men, distributed detachments
of the fleet to all the recesses of the sea, and
in a short time with an invincible force he freed
the world from the menace of piracy. Near the
Cilician coast he delivered his final attack upon
the pirates, who had already met with frequent
defeats in many other places, and completely routed
them. Then, in order that he might the more
quickly put an end to a war that spread over so wide

5 tam late diffusum conficeret, reliquias eorum contractas in urbibus remotoque mari loco in certa sede
6 constituit. Sunt qui hoc carpant, sed quamquam in
auctore satis rationis est, tamen ratio quemlibet
magnum auctorem faceret ; data enim facultate sine
rapto vivendi rapinis arcuit.

1 XXXIII. Cum esset in fine bellum piraticum et
L. Lucullus, qui ante septem annos ex consulatu
sortitus Asiam Mithridati oppositus erat magnasque
et memorabiles res ibi gesserat, Mithridatem saepe
multis locis fuderat, egregia Cyzicum liberarat
victoria, Tigranem, regum maximum, in Armenia
vicerat ultimamque bello manum paene magis
noluerat imponere quam non potuerat, quia[1] alioqui
per omnia laudabilis et bello paene invictus pecuniae
pellebatur cupidine, idem bellum adhuc adminis-
traret, Manilius tribunus plebis, semper venalis et
alienae minister potentiae, legem tulit, ut bellum
2 Mithridaticum per Cn. Pompeium administraretur.
Accepta ea magnisque certatum inter imperatores
iurgiis, cum Pompeius Lucullo infamiam pecuniae[a],
Lucullus Pompeio interminatam cupiditatem obii-
ceret imperii neuterque ab altero quod arguebat[2]

---

[1] quia *Bothe* ; qui *AP.*
[2] ab altero quod arguebat *Burman* ; ab eo quod argue-
batur *AP.*

---

[a] An allusion to Pompey's cognomen "The Great."
[b] 66 B.C.

an area, he collected the remnants of the pirates and established them in fixed abodes in cities far from the sea. Some criticize him for this; but although the plan is sufficiently recommended by its author, it would have made its author great[a] whoever he might have been; for, by giving the pirates the opportunity to live without brigandage, he restrained them from brigandage.

XXXIII. When the war with the pirates was drawing to a close, Pompey was assigned to the command against Mithridates in place of Lucius Lucullus. Seven years before this, Lucullus, at the conclusion of his consulship, had obtained the pro-consulship of Asia, and had been placed in command against Mithridates.[b] In this post he had performed some great and notable exploits, having defeated Mithridates several times in different regions, freed Cyzicus by a brilliant victory, and conquered Tigranes, the greatest of kings, in Armenia. That he had not put an end to the war was due, one might say, to lack of inclination rather than of ability; for although in all other respects he was a man of laudable character and in war had scarcely ever been defeated, he was a victim to the love of money. He was still engaged in carrying on the same struggle when Manilius, tribune of the people, a man of venal character always, and ready to abet the ambitions of others, proposed a law that Pompey should be given the chief command in the Mithridatic war. The law was passed, and the two commanders began to vie with each other in recriminations, Pompey charging Lucullus with his unsavoury greed for money, and Lucullus taunting Pompey with his unbounded ambition for military power. Neither

121

3 mentitus argui posset. Nam neque Pompeius, ut primum ad rem publicam adgressus est, quemquam omnino[1] parem tulit, et in quibus rebus primus esse debebat, solus esse cupiebat (neque eo viro quisquam aut alia omnia minus aut gloriam magis concupiit, in adpetendis honoribus inmodicus, in gerendis vere-cundissimus, ut qui eos ut libentissime iniret, ita finiret aequo animo, et quod cupisset, arbitrio suo 4 sumeret, alieno deponeret) et Lucullus, summus alioqui vir, profusae huius in aedificiis convictibusque et apparatibus luxuriae primus auctor fuit, quem ob iniectas moles mari et receptum suffossis montibus in terras mare haud infacete Magnus Pompeius Xerxen togatum vocare adsueverat.

1 XXXIV. Per id tempus a Q. Metello Creta insula in populi Romani potestatem redacta est, quae ducibus Panare et Lasthene quattuor et viginti milibus iuvenum coactis, velocitate pernicibus, armo-rum laborumque patientissimis, sagittarum usu cele-berrimis, per triennium Romanos exercitus fati-2 gaverat. Ne[2] ab huius quidem usura gloriae[3] tem-peravit animum Cn. Pompeius, quin[4] victoriae partem conaretur vindicare. Sed et Luculli et Metelli triumphum cum ipsorum singularis virtus,

[1] omnino *Acidalius*; animo *AP*.
[2] ne *add. Gelenius*.
[3] usura gloriae *Rhenanus*; usurae gloria *AP*.
[4] quin *Gelenius*; qui *AP*.

---

[a] Literally, Xerxes in the *toga*. The reference is to Xerxes' bridge across the Hellespont and his canal through the Isthmus at Mount Athos.
[b] As in the case of Lucullus.

could be convicted of falsehood in his charge against
the other. In fact Pompey, from the time when he
first took part in public life, could not brook an
equal at all. In undertakings in which he should
have been merely the first he wished to be the only
one. No one was ever more indifferent to other
things or possessed a greater craving for glory ; he
knew no restraint in his quest for office, though he
was moderate to a degree in the exercise of his
powers. Entering upon each new office with the
utmost eagerness, he would lay them aside with
unconcern, and, although he consulted his own
wishes in attaining what he desired, he yielded to
the wishes of others in resigning it. As for Lucullus,
who was otherwise a great man, he was the first to
set the example for our present lavish extravagance
in building, in banquets, and in furnishings. Because
of the massive piles which he built in the sea, and
of his letting the sea in upon the land by digging
through mountains, Pompey used to call him, and
not without point, the Roman Xerxes.[a]

XXXIV. During the same period the island of Crete
was brought under the sovereignty of the Roman
people by Quintus Metellus. For three years this
island, under the leadership of Panares and Las-
thenes who had collected a force of twenty-four
thousand men, swift in their movements, hardened
to the toils of war, and famous in their use of the
bow, had worn out the Roman armies. Gnaeus
Pompeius could not refrain from coveting some of
this glory also,[b] and sought to claim a share in his
victory. But the triumphs, both of Lucullus and of
Metellus, were rendered popular in the eyes of all
good citizens not only by the distinguished merits

tum etiam invidia Pompei apud optimum quemque
3 fecit favorabilem.

Per haec tempora M. Cicero, qui omnia incre-
menta sua sibi debuit, vir novitatis nobilissimae et ut
vita clarus, ita ingenio maximus, quique[1] effecit, ne
quorum arma viceramus, eorum ingenio vinceremur,
consul Sergii Catilinae Lentulique et Cethegi et
aliorum utriusque ordinis virorum coniurationem
singulari virtute, constantia, vigilia curaque aperuit.[2]
4 Catilina metu consularis imperi urbe pulsus est ;
Lentulus consularis et praetor iterum Cethegusque
et alii clari nominis viri auctore senatu, iussu consulis
in carcere necati sunt.

1 XXXV. Ille senatus dies, quo haec acta sunt, virtutem M. Catonis iam multis in rebus conspicuam
2 atque praenitentem in altissimo culmine locavit.[3]
Hic genitus proavo M. Catone, principe illo familiae
Porciae, homo Virtuti simillimus et per omnia ingenio
diis quam hominibus propior, qui numquam recte
fecit, ut facere videretur, sed quia aliter facere non
potuerat, cuique id solum visum est rationem habere,
quod haberet iustitiam,[4] omnibus humanis vitiis
immunis semper fortunam in sua potestate habuit.
3 Hic tribunus plebis designatus et adhuc admodum
adulescens, cum alii suaderent, ut per municipia

[1] quique *Oudendorp* ; qui *AP*.
[2] aperuit *Gelenius* ; eripuit *AP*.
[3] culmine locavit *Madvig* ; luminavit *AP*.
[4] iustitiam *Gelenius* ; iustitiae *AP*.

---

[a] 63 B.C.
[b] He is referring to the sentiment expressed in the famous
lines of Horace, *Ep.* ii. 1. 156, " Graecia capta ferum victorem
cepit et artes Intulit agresti Latio."

of the two generals themselves but also by the general unpopularity of Pompey.

At this time the conspiracy of Sergius Catiline,[a] Lentulus, Cethegus, and other men of both the equestrian and senatorial orders was detected by the extraordinary courage, firmness, and careful vigilance of the consul Marcus Cicero, a man who owed his elevation wholly to himself, who had ennobled his lowly birth, who was as distinguished in his life as he was great in genius, and who saved us from being vanquished in intellectual accomplishments by those whom we had vanquished in arms.[b] Catiline was driven from the city by fear of the authority of the consul ; Lentulus, a man of consular rank and twice a praetor, Cethegus, and other men of illustrious family were put to death in prison on the order of the consul, supported by the authority of the senate.

XXXV. The meeting of the senate at which this action had been taken raised the character of Marcus Cato, which had already shone forth conspicuously in other matters, to a lofty pinnacle. Descended from Marcus Cato, the first of the Porcian house, who was his great-grandfather, he resembled Virtue herself, and in all his acts he revealed a character nearer to that of gods than of men. He never did a right action solely for the sake of seeming to do the right, but because he could not do otherwise. To him that alone seemed reasonable which was likewise just. Free from all the failings of mankind he always kept fortune subject to his control. At this time, though he was only tribune elect and still quite a young man, while others were urging that Lentulus and the other

Lentulus coniuratique custodirentur, paene inter ultimos interrogatus sententiam, tanta vi animi atque ingenii invectus est in coniurationem, eo ardore oris orationem omnium lenitatem suadentium so-
4 cietate consilii suspectam fecit, sic impendentia ex ruinis incendiisque urbis et commutatione status publici pericula exposuit, ita consulis virtutem amplificavit, ut universus senatus in eius sententiam transiret animadvertendumque in eos, quos praediximus, censeret maiorque pars ordinis eius Ciceronem[1] prosequerentur domum.
5 At Catilina non segnius conata obiit, quam sceleris conandi consilia inierat : quippe fortissime dimicans quem spiritum supplicio debuerat, proelio reddidit.[a]
1 XXXVI. Consulatui Ciceronis non mediocre adiecit decus natus eo anno divus Augustus abhinc annos LXXXII,[2] omnibus omnium gentium viris magnitudine sua inducturus caliginem.[b]
2 Iam paene supervacaneum videri potest eminentium ingeniorum notare tempora. Quis enim ignorat diremptos gradibus aetatis floruisse hoc tempore Ciceronem, Hortensium, anteque[3] Crassum, Cottam, Sulpicium, moxque Brutum, Calidium,[4] Caelium, Calvum et proximum Ciceroni Caesarem eorumque velut alumnos Corvinum ac Pollionem[c]

---

[1] Ciceronem *Hottinger*; Catonem *AP*.
[2] LXXXII *AP*; LXXX *Kritz*; LXXXXII *Aldus*.
[3] anteque *ed. Bipont.*; saneque *AP*.
[4] Cottam *Aldus*; Catonem *AP*.

---

[a] His famous speech is reported in Sallust, *Catiline*, chap. lii.   [b] 63 B.C.
[c] He has now come to Rome's greatest epoch, the Ciceronian and the Augustan ages, sufficiently indicated by the mention of Cicero and Augustus. Hence the emphasis upon *iam*.

126

conspirators should be placed in custody in the Italian towns, Cato,[a] though among the very last to be asked for his opinion, inveighed against the conspiracy with such vigour of spirit and intellect and such earnestness of expression that he caused those who in their speeches had urged leniency to be suspected of complicity in the plot. Such a picture did he present of the dangers which threatened Rome, by the burning and destruction of the city and the subversion of the constitution, and such a eulogy did he give of the consul's firm stand, that the senate as a body changed to the support of his motion and voted the imposition of the death penalty upon the conspirators, and a large number of the senators escorted Cicero to his home.

As for Catiline, he proceeded to carry out his criminal undertaking with as much energy as he had shown in planning it. Fighting with desperate courage, he gave up in battle the life which he had forfeited to the executioner.

XXXVI. No slight prestige is added to the consulship of Cicero by the birth in that year[b]—ninety-two years ago—of the emperor Augustus, who was destined by his greatness to overshadow all men of all races.

It may now[c] seem an almost superfluous task to indicate the period at which men of eminent talent flourished. For who does not know that at this epoch, separated only by differences in their ages, there flourished Cicero and Hortensius; a little earlier Crassus, Cotta, and Sulpicius; a little later Brutus, Calidius, Caelius, Calvus, and Caesar, who ranks next to Cicero; next to them, and, as it were, their pupils, come Corvinus and Pollio Asinius,

Asinium, aemulumque Thucydidis Sallustium, auctoresque carminum Varronem ac Lucretium neque ullo in suscepto carminis sui opere[1] minorem Catullum.

3 Paene stulta est inhaerentium oculis ingeniorum enumeratio, inter quae maxime nostri aevi eminent princeps carminum Vergilius Rabiriusque et consecutus Sallustium Livius Tibullusque et Naso, perfectissimi in forma operis sui ; nam vivorum ut magna admiratio, ita censura difficilis est.

1 XXXVII. Dum haec in urbe Italiaque geruntur, Cn. Pompeius memorabile adversus Mithridaten, qui post Luculli profectionem magnas novi exercitus 2 viris reparaverat, bellum gessit. At rex fusus fugatusque et omnibus exutus copiis Armeniam Tigranemque socer generum[2] petiit,[3] regem eius temporis, nisi qua Luculli armis erat infractus, potentissimum. 3 Simul itaque duos persecutus Pompeius intravit Armeniam. Prior filius Tigranis, sed discors patri, 4 pervenit ad Pompeium ; mox ipse supplex et praesens se regnumque dicioni eius permisit, praefatus neminem alium neque Romanum neque ullius gentis virum futurum fuisse, cuius se societati commissurus foret, quam Cn. Pompeium ; proin omnem sibi vel adversam vel secundam, cuius auctor ille esset, fortunam tolerabilem futuram : non esse turpe ab eo vinci, quem vincere esset nefas, neque inhoneste

---

[1] in suspecti operis sui carmine *AP*; *for the many emendations suggested for this vexed passage see Kritz and Ellis.*

[2] socer generum *Heinsius*; socerum *AP*.

[3] petit *AP*; petiit *Gelenius*.

---

[a] The omission of Horace from this list is as noteworthy as the omission of Plautus from the writers of comedy in Chap. xvii. of Bk. I.

Sallust, the rival of Thucydides, the poets Varro and Lucretius, and Catullus, who ranks second to none in the branch of literature which he undertook. It is almost folly to proceed to enumerate men of talent who are almost beneath our eyes, among whom the most important in our own age are Virgil, the prince of poets, Rabirius, Livy, who follows close upon Sallust, Tibullus, and Naso, each of whom achieved perfection in his own branch of literature.[a] As for living writers, while we admire them greatly, a critical list is difficult to make.

XXXVII. While these occurrences were taking place in the city and in Italy, Gnaeus Pompeius carried on a notable campaign against Mithridates, who after the departure of Lucullus had again prepared a new army of great strength. The king was defeated and routed, and after losing all his forces sought refuge in Armenia with his son-in-law Tigranes, the most powerful king of his day, though his power had been somewhat broken by Lucullus. Pompey accordingly entered Armenia in pursuit of both kings at once. First a son of Tigranes, who was at variance with his father, came to Pompey. Then the king in person, and, in the guise of a suppliant, placed himself and his kingdom under the jurisdiction of Pompey, prefacing this act with the statement that he would not have submitted himself to the alliance of any man but Gnaeus Pompeius, whether Roman or of any other nationality; that he would be ready to bear any condition, favourable or otherwise, upon which Pompey might decide ; that there was no disgrace in being beaten by one whom it would be a sin against the gods to defeat, and that there was no dishonour in sub-

129

aliquem summitti huic, quem fortuna super omnis
5 extulisset. Servatus regi honos imperii, sed multato
ingenti pecunia, quae omnis, sicuti Pompeio moris
erat, redacta in quaestoris potestatem ac publicis
descripta litteris. Syria aliaeque, quas occupaverat,
provinciae ereptae, et aliae restitutae populo Romano,
aliae tum primum in eius potestatem redactae, ut
Syria, quae tum primum facta est stipendiaria. Finis
imperii regii[1] terminatus Armenia.

1 XXXVIII. Haud absurdum videtur propositi operis
regulae paucis percurrere, quae cuiusque ductu gens
ac natio redacta in formulam provinciae stipendiaria
facta[2] sit, ut quae partibus notavimus, facilius[3] simul
universa conspici possint.

2 Primus in Siciliam traiecit exercitum consul
Claudius, set[4] provinciam eam post annos ferme duos
et quinquaginta captis Syracusis fecit Marcellus
Claudius. Primus Africam Regulus nono ferme
anno primi Punici belli aggressus est[5]; sed post
centum et novem[6] annos P. Scipio Aemilianus eruta
Carthagine abhinc annos centum septuaginta[7] tris
Africam in formulam redegit provinciae. Sardinia
inter primum et secundum bellum Punicum ductu
T. Manlii consulis certum recepit imperi iugum.

3 Immane bellicae civitatis argumentum, quod semel

---

[1] regii *Heinsius*; regi *AP*.

[2] stipendiaria facta *Amerbach in marg. et Lipsius*;
stipendia facta *AP*.

[3] notavimus facilius ut quae partibus *AP*; *order changed
by Acidelius and Haase*.

[4] set *Sauppe*; et *AP*.

[5] belli aggressus est *supplied by Halm*.

[6] cviiii *Bipont.*; cciiii *AP*.

[7] clxxiii *Kritz*; clxxxii *AP*.

---

    a 261 b.c.   b 212 b.c.   c 256 b.c.

mitting to one whom fortune had elevated above all others. The king was permitted to retain the honours of royalty, but was compelled to pay a large sum of money, all of which, as was Pompey's practice, was remitted to the quaestor and listed in the public accounts. Syria and the other provinces which Mithridates had seized were wrested from him. Some were restored to the Roman people, and others were then for the first time brought under its sway —Syria, for instance—which first became a tributary province at this time. The sovereignty of the king was now limited to Armenia.

XXXVIII. It does not seem out of keeping with the plan which I have set before me in my work to give a brief synopsis of the races and nations which were reduced to provinces and made tributary to Rome, and by what generals. Thus it will be easier to see at a glance when grouped together, the facts already given in detail.

Claudius the consul was the first to cross into Sicily with an army,[a] but it was only after the capture of Syracuse, fifty years later,[b] that it was converted into a province by Marcellus Claudius. Regulus was the first to invade Africa, in the ninth year of the First Punic war.[c] It was one hundred and nine years later, one hundred and seventy-three years ago, that Publius Scipio Aemilianus destroyed Carthage and reduced Africa to the form of a province.[d] Sardinia finally became subject to the yoke in the interval between the First and Second Punic War,[e] through the agency of Titus Manlius the consul. It is a strong proof of the warlike character of our state that only three times did the

[d] 146 B.C.   [e] 235 B.C.

sub regibus, iterum hoc T. Manlio consule, tertio
Augusto principe certae pacis argumentum Ianus
4 geminus clausus dedit.   In Hispaniam primi omnium
duxere exercitus Cn. et P. Scipiones initio secundi
belli Punici abhinc annos ducentos quinquaginta ;
inde varie possessa et saepe amissa partibus, uni-
5 versa ductu Augusti facta stipendiaria est.   Macedoniam Paulus, Mummius Achaiam, Fulvius Nobilior
subegit Aetoliam, Asiam L. Scipio, Africani frater,
eripuit Antiocho, sed beneficio senatus populique
Romani mox ab Attalis[1] possessam regibus[2] M. Perpenna capto Aristonico fecit tributariam.   Cyprus
6 devicta nullius adsignanda gloriae est[3] ;   quippe
senatus consulto, ministerio Catonis, regis morte,
quam ille conscientia acciverat, facta provincia est.
Creta Metelli ductu longissimae libertatis fine mul-
tata est.   Syria Pontusque Cn. Pompei virtutis
monumenta sunt.

1   XXXIX. Gallias primum a[4] Domitio Fabioque,[5]
nepote Pauli, qui Allobrogicus vocatus est, intratas
cum exercitu, magna mox clade nostra, saepe et
adfectavimus et omisimus.[6]   Sed fulgentissimum C.
Caesaris opus in his conspicitur ;   quippe eius ductu

---

[1] ab Attalis *Gelenius* ; habita lis *AP.*
[2] regibus *P* ; *om. A.*
[3] Cyprus devicta nullius adsignanda gloriae est *Laurent.* ;
Cypro devicta nullis adsignanda gloria est *AP.*
[4] a *add. Aldus.*
[5] Fabioque *Ursinus* ; Fabio *AP.*
[6] omisimus *Heinsius* ; amisimus *AP.*

---

a 218 B.C.   *b* 167 B.C.   *c* 146 B.C.

132

closing of the temple of the double-faced Janus give proof of unbroken peace : once under the kings, a second time in the consulship of the Titus Manlius just mentioned, and a third time in the reign of Augustus. The two Scipios, Gnaeus and Publius, were the first to lead armies into Spain,[a] at the beginning of the Second Punic War, two hundred and fifty years ago ; from that time on we alternately acquired and lost portions of it until under Augustus the whole of it became tributary. Paulus conquered Macedonia,[b] Mummius Achaea,[c] Fulvius Nobilior Aetolia,[d] Lucius Scipio, the brother of Africanus, wrested Asia from Antiochus,[e] but, by the gift of the senate and the Roman people, it soon afterwards passed to the ownership of the Attalids. It was made a tributary province by Marcus Perpenna after the capture of Aristonicus.[f] No credit for the conquest of Cyprus can be assigned to any general, since it was by a decree of the Senate, carried out by Cato, that it became a province [g] on the death of its king, self-inflicted in consciousness of guilt. Crete was punished by Metellus by the termination [h] of the liberty which she had long enjoyed. Syria and Pontus are monuments to the valour of Gnaeus Pompeius.[i]

XXXIX. Domitius and Fabius, son of Paulus, who was surnamed Allobrogicus, first entered the Gauls with an army ; later these provinces cost us much blood in our attempts at conquest alternating with our loss of them. In all these operations the work of Caesar is the most brilliant and most conspicuous. Reduced under his auspices and general-

[d] 189 B.C.	[e] 190 B.C.	[f] 130 B.C.
[g] 57 B.C.	[h] 67 B.C.	[i] 62 B.C.

auspiciisque infractae paene[1] idem, quod totus ter-
2 rarum orbis, in aerarium[2] conferunt stipendium. Ab
eodem facta * * *[3] Numidicus. Ciliciam perdomuit
Isauricus et post bellum Antiochinum Vulso Manlius
Gallograeciam. Bithynia, ut praediximus, testamen-
to Nicomedis relicta hereditaria. Divus Augustus
praeter Hispanias aliasque gentis, quarum titulis
forum eius praenitet, paene idem facta Aegypto
stipendiaria, quantum pater eius Galliis, in aerarium
3 reditus contulit. At Ti. Caesar quam certam Hispanis parendi confessionem extorserat parens, Illyriis
Delmatisque extorsit. Raetiam autem et Vindelicos
ac Noricos Pannoniamque et Scordiscos novas imperio nostro subiunxit provincias. Ut has armis,
ita auctoritate Cappadociam populo Romano fecit
stipendiariam. Sed revertamur ad ordinem.
1 XL. Secuta deinde Cn. Pompei militia, gloriae
laborisne maioris incertum est. Penetratae cum
victoria Media, Albania, Hiberia[4]; deinde flexum
agmen ad eas nationes, quae dextra atque intima
Ponti incolunt, Colchos Heniochosque et Achaeos,
et oppressus auspiciis Pompei, insidiis filii Pharnacis
Mithridates, ultimus omnium iuris sui regum praeter

[1] pene *AP*; plane *vel* plene *Burman.*
[2] in aerarium *Aldus*; ignauum *AP.*
[3] *The lacuna is thus supplied by Haase:* facta [Numidia
provincia, e qua iam olim cognomen virtute partum detulerat
Metellus] Numidicus.
[4] Albani Hiberi (Hideri *A*) ac deinde *AP*; *em. Burman.*

[a] 58–50 B.C.   [b] 46 B.C.
[c] The words in brackets are a translation of Haase's conjecture. See footnote to text.
[d] 78 B.C.   [e] *i.e.* Galatia, 188 B.C.
[f] 74 B.C.   [g] 30 B.C.   [h] 10 B.C.
[i] 16–12 B.C.   [j] A.D. 17.   [k] 66–63 B.C

ship,[a] they pay almost as much tribute into the treasury as the rest of the world. Caesar also made [Numidia a province,[b] from which Metellus had long before won by his valour the cognomen of][c] Numidicus.

Isauricus conquered Cilicia,[d] and Vulso Manlius Gallograecia[e] after the war with Antiochus. Bithynia, as has been already said, was bequeathed to the Romans by the will of Nicomedes.[f] Besides Spain and other countries whose names adorn his Forum, Augustus made Egypt tributary,[g] thereby contributing nearly as much revenue to the treasury as his father had brought to it from the Gauls. Tiberius Caesar extorted from the Illyrians and Dalmatians a definite confession of submission[h] such as that which Augustus had wrested from Spain. He also added to our empire as new provinces Raetia, Vindelicia, Noricum, Pannonia, and the Scordisci These he conquered by arms.[i] Cappadocia he made tributary to the Roman people through the mere prestige of his name.[j] But let us now return to the order of events.

XL. Then followed the military exploits of Gnaeus Pompeius,[k] in regard to which it would be difficult to say whether the glory they earned or the labour they cost was the greater. Media, Albania, and Iberia were invaded with victorious arms. Then he changed the direction of his march to the regions of the interior, to the right of the Black Sea—the Colchians, the Heniochi, and the Achaei. Mithridates was crushed, the last of the independent kings except the rulers of the Parthians, through the treachery of his son Pharnaces, it is true, but during the period of Pompey's command. Then,

2 Parthicos. Tum victor omnium quas adierat gentium
Pompeius suoque et civium voto maior et per omnia
fortunam hominis egressus revertit in Italiam. Cuius
reditum favorabilem opinio fecerat ; quippe plerique
non sine exercitu venturum in urbem adfirmarunt
et libertati publicae staturum arbitrio suo modum.
3 Quo magis hoc homines timuerant, eo gratior civilis
tanti imperatoris reditus fuit : omni quippe Brundusii dimisso exercitu nihil praeter nomen imperatoris
retinens cum privato comitatu, quem semper illi
astare[1] moris fuit, in urbem rediit magnificentissi-
mumque de tot regibus per biduum egit triumphum
longeque maiorem omni ante se inlata pecunia in
aerarium, praeterquam a Paulo, ex manubiis intulit.
4 Absente Cn. Pompeio T. Ampius et T. Labienus
tribuni plebis legem tulerant,[2] ut is ludis circensibus
corona aurea et omni cultu triumphantium uteretur,
scaenicis autem praetexta coronaque aurea. Id ille
non plus quam semel, et hoc sane nimium fuit,
usurpare sustinuit. Huius viri fastigium tantis aucti-
bus fortuna extulit, ut primum ex Africa, iterum ex
Europa, tertio ex Asia triumpharet et, quot partes
terrarum orbis sunt, totidem faceret monumenta

[1] illi astare *Doederlein* ; illi trahere *Ruhnken* ; illi fatare
AP.
[2] tulerant *Acidalius* ; tulerunt *AP.*

---

[a] A general holding the *imperium* had the title *imperator.*
He is here referring to the use of the title in the acclamations of the soldiers after a victory. In this sense it was
considered as the preliminary to a triumph.

after conquering all the races in his path, Pompey returned to Italy, having achieved a greatness which exceeded both his own hopes and those of his fellow-citizens, and having, in all his campaigns, surpassed the fortune of a mere mortal. It was owing to this impression that his return created such favourable comment ; for the majority of his countrymen had insisted that he would not enter the city without his army, and that he would set a limit upon public liberty according to his own caprice. The return of so great a general as an ordinary citizen was all the more welcome because of the apprehensions which had been entertained. For, dismissing his whole army at Brundisium, and retaining none of his former power except the title of *imperator*,[a] he returned to the city with only the retinue which regularly attended him. There he celebrated, for a period of two days, a most magnificent triumph over the many kings whom he had conquered, and from the spoils he contributed to the treasury a far larger sum of money than any other general had ever done except Paulus.

In Pompey's absence the tribunes of the people, Titus Ampius and Titus Labienus, proposed a law that at the games of the circus Pompey should be permitted to wear a golden crown and the full dress of the *triumphator*, and at the theatre the purple-bordered toga and the golden crown. But he forbore to use this honour more than once, and indeed that was itself too often. This man was raised by fortune to the pinnacle of his career by great leaps, first triumphing over Africa, then over Europe, then over Asia, and the three divisions of the world thus became so many monuments of

victoriae suae. Numquam eminentia invidia carent.

5 Itaque et Lucullus et Metellus Creticus memor
tamen acceptae iniuriae,[1] non iniuste querens (quippe
ornamentum triumphi eius captivos duces Pompeius
subduxerat) et cum iis pars optimatium refragabatur,
ne aut promissa civitatibus a Pompeio aut bene
meritis praemia ad arbitrium eius persolverentur.

1 XLI. Secutus deinde est consulatus C. Caesaris,[a]
qui scribenti manum iniicit et quamlibet festinantem
in se morari cogit. Hic nobilissima Iuliorum genitus
familia et, quod inter omnis antiquitatis studiosos[2]
constabat, ab Anchise ac Venere deducens genus,
forma omnium civium excellentissimus, vigore animi
acerrimus, munificentia effusissimus, animo super humanam et naturam et fidem evectus, magnitudine
cogitationum, celeritate bellandi, patientia periculorum Magno illi Alexandro, sed sobrio neque iracundo

2 simillimus, qui denique semper et cibo et somno in
vitam, non in voluptatem uteretur, cum fuisset C.
Mario sanguine coniunctissimus atque idem Cinnae
gener, cuius filiam ut repudiaret nullo metu com-
pelli potuit, cum M. Piso consularis Anniam, quae
Cinnae uxor fuerat, in Sullae dimisisset gratiam,

[1] *The order is that of Ellis; in AP* et Metellus Creticus
follows memor . . . iniuriae.
[2] antiquitatis studiosos *Halm*; antiquissimos *AP*.

[a] 59 B.C.

his victory. Greatness is never without envy. Pompey met with opposition from Lucullus and from Metellus Creticus, who did not forget the slight he had received (indeed he had just cause for complaint in that Pompey had robbed him of the captive generals who were to have adorned his triumph), and from a section of the optimates who sought to prevent the fulfilment of Pompey's promises to the various cities and the payment of rewards in accordance with his wishes to those who had been of service to him.

XLI. Then followed the consulship *a* of Gaius Caesar, who now lays hold upon my pen and compels me, whatever my haste, to linger a while upon him. Sprung from the noble family of the Julii, and tracing his descent from Venus and Anchises, a claim conceded by all investigators of antiquity, he surpassed all his fellow-citizens in beauty of person. He was exceedingly keen and vigorous of mind, lavish in his generosity, and possessed a courage exceeding the nature, and even the credence, of man. In the magnitude of his ambitions, in the rapidity of his military operations, and in his endurance of danger, he closely resembled Alexander the Great, but only when Alexander was free from the influence of wine and master of his passions ; for Caesar, in a word, never indulged in food or in sleep except as they ministered, not to pleasure, but to life. To Gaius Marius he was closely related by blood ; he was also the son-in-law of Cinna, whose daughter no consideration of fear would induce him to divorce, whereas Marcus Piso, a man of consular rank, had divorced Annia, who had been the wife of Cinna, in order to win Sulla's favour. Caesar was only about

habuissetque fere duodeviginti annos eo tempore,
quo Sulla rerum potitus est, magis ministris Sullae
adiutoribusque partium quam ipso conquirentibus
eum ad necem mutata veste dissimilemque fortunae
3 suae indutus habitum nocte urbe elapsus est. Idem
postea admodum iuvenis, cum a piratis captus esset,
ita se per[1] omne spatium, quo ab iis retentus est,
apud eos gessit, ut pariter iis terrori venerationique
esset, neque umquam aut nocte aut die (cur enim
quod vel maximum est, si narrari verbis speciosis
non potest, omittatur ?) aut excalcearetur aut dis-
cingeretur, in hoc scilicet, ne si quando aliquid ex
solito variaret, suspectus iis, qui oculis tantummodo
eum custodiebant, foret.

1   XLII. Longum est narrare, quid et quotiens ausus
sit, quanto opere conata eius qui obtinebat Asiam
magistratus populi Romani metu[2] suo destituerit.
Illud referatur documentum tanti mox evasuri viri :
2 quae nox eam diem secuta est, qua publica civitatium
pecunia redemptus est, ita tamen, ut cogeret ante
obsides a piratis civitatibus dari, et privatus et contracta classe[3] tumultuaria invectus in eum locum,
in quo ipsi praedones erant, partem classis fugavit,
partem mersit, aliquot navis multosque mortalis
cepit ; laetusque nocturnae expeditionis triumpho

¹ se per *B* ; semper *AP*.
² metu *Gelenius* ; motu *AP*.
³ et privatus et contracta classe *Scriner* ; contracta classe
et privatus et *AP* ; *Halm adds* manu *after* tumultuaria, *retaining the* MS. *order of the preceding words.*

---

^a Suetonius, *Div. Iulius* 4, associates the adventure with
the pirates with his visit to Rhodes in 76 B.C., whither he
went to study oratory under Molo. Plutarch, *Caes.*, places

eighteen years of age at the time of Sulla's dictatorship ; and when a search was made for him with a view to putting him to death, not, it is true, by Sulla himself, but by his minions and partisans, he escaped from the city at night by assuming a disguise which effectually concealed his rank. Later,[a] but when still quite a young man, he was captured by pirates and so conducted himself during the entire period of his detention as to inspire in them to an equal degree both fear and respect. Neither by day nor by night did he remove his shoes or loosen his girdle—for why should a detail of the greatest significance be omitted merely because it cannot be adorned in imposing language ?—lest the slightest change in his usual garb might cause him to be suspected by his captors, who guarded him only with their eyes.

XLII. It would take too long to tell of his many bold plans for the punishment of the pirates, or how obstinately the timid governor of Asia refused to second them. The following story, however, may be told as a presage of his future greatness. On the night following the day on which his ransom was paid by the cities of Asia—he had, however, compelled the pirates before payment to give hostages to these cities—although he was but a private citizen without authority, and his fleet had been collected on the spur of the moment, he directed his course to the rendezvous of the pirates, put to flight part of their fleet, sank part, and captured several ships and many men. Well satisfied with the success of his night expedition he returned

it earlier, in connexion with his visit to Bithynia in 81–80 B.C.

3 ad suos revectus[1] est, mandatisque custodiae quos
ceperat, in Bithyniam perrexit ad proconsulem
Iuncum[2] (idem enim Asiam eamque obtinebat)[3]
petens, ut auctor fieret sumendi de captivis supplicii :
quod ille se facturum negasset venditurumque captivos dixisset (quippe sequebatur invidia inertiam),
incredibili celeritate revectus ad mare, priusquam
de ea re ulli proconsulis redderentur epistulae,[4]
omnes, quos ceperat, suffixit cruci.

1 XLIII. Idem mox ad sacerdotium ineundum
(quippe absens pontifex factus erat in Cottae consularis locum, cum[5] paene puer a Mario Cinnaque
flamen dialis creatus victoria Sullae, qui omnia ab
iis acta fecerat irrita, amisisset id[6] sacerdotium)
festinans in Italiam, ne conspiceretur a praedonibus
omnia tunc obtinentibus maria et merito iam[7] in-
festis sibi, quattuor scalmorum navem una cum duobus
amicis decemque servis ingressus effusissimum Adria-
2 tici maris traiecit sinum. Quo quidem in cursu conspectus, ut putabat, piratarum navibus cum exuisset
vestem alligassetque pugionem ad femur alterutri
se fortunae parans, mox intellexit frustratum esse
visum suum arborumque ex longinquo ordinem
3 antemnarum praebuisse imaginem.

Reliqua eius acta in urbe, nobilissima Cn. Dola-

---

[1] revectus *Haase* ; reversus *AP*.
[2] Iuncum *Nipperdey* ; Iunium cum *AP*.
[3] idem enim Asiam eam quam obtinebat *AP* ; eamque
Lipsius for eam quam.
[4] epistulae *Burer* ; epistula *ABP*.
[5] cum *added by Lipsius*.
[6] id *Gelenius* ; ad *AP*.
[7] iam] tam *AP*.

---

[a] 74 B.C.

to his friends and, after handing his prisoners into custody, went straight to Bithynia to Juncus, the proconsul—for the same man was governor of Bithynia as well as of Asia—and demanded his sanction for the execution of his captives. When Juncus, whose former inactivity had now given way to jealousy, refused, and said that he would sell the captives as slaves, Caesar returned to the coast with incredible speed and crucified all his prisoners before anyone had had time to receive a dispatch from the consul in regard to the matter.

XLIII. Not long afterwards he was hastening to Italy to enter upon the priestly office of *pontifex maximus* to which he had been elected [a] in his absence in place of the ex-consul Cotta. Indeed, while still little more than a boy he had already been made priest of Jupiter by Marius and Cinna, but all their acts had been annulled in consequence of Sulla's victory, and Caesar had thus lost this priesthood. On the journey just mentioned, wishing to escape the notice of the pirates who then infested all the seas and by this time had good reasons for being hostile to him, he took two friends and ten slaves and embarked in a four-oared boat, and in this way crossed the broad expanse of the Adriatic Sea. During the voyage, sighting, as he thought, some pirate vessels, he removed his outer garments, bound a dagger to his thigh, and prepared himself for any event; but soon he saw that his eyes had deceived him and that the illusion had been caused by a row of trees in the distance which looked like masts and yards.

As for the rest of his acts after his return to the city, they stand in less need of description, since

bellae[1] accusatio et maior civitatis in ea favor, quam reis praestari solet, contentionesque civiles cum Q. Catulo atque aliis eminentissimis viris celeberrimae, et ante praeturam victus in[2] maximi pontificatus petitione Q. Catulus, omnium confessione senatus

4 princeps, et restituta in aedilitate adversante quidem nobilitate monumenta C. Marii, simulque revocati ad ius dignitatis proscriptorum liberi, et praetura quaesturaque mirabili virtute atque industria obita in Hispania (cum esset quaestor sub Vetere Antistio, avo huius Veteris consularis atque pontificis, duorum consularium et sacerdotum patris, viri in tantum boni, in quantum humana simplicitas intellegi potest) quo notiora sunt, minus egent stilo.

1 XLIV. Hoc igitur consule inter eum et Cn. Pompeium et M. Crassum inita potentiae societas, quae urbi orbique terrarum nec minus diverso cuique tempore ipsis exitiabilis fuit. Hoc consilium sequendi

2 Pompeius causam habuerat, ut tandem acta in transmarinis provinciis, quibus, ut praediximus, multi obtrectabant, per Caesarem confirmarentur consulem, Caesar autem, quod animadvertebat se cedendo Pompei gloriae aucturum suam et invidia communis

---

[1] nobilissima Cn. Dolabellae *Haase*; nobilissimaque Dolabellae *AP*.　　　　[2] in *added by Halm*.

---

[a] 77 B.C.　　　[b] 62 B.C.　　　[c] 63 B.C.　　　[d] 65 B.C.
[e] It was not as *praetor* and *quaestor*, but as *propraetor* and *quaestorius* that he served in Spain in 61 B.C. and 67 B.C.
[f] More probably while Consul elect.

they are better known. I refer to his famous
prosecution *a* of Gnaeus Dolabella, to whom the
people showed more favour than is usually exhibited
to men under impeachment; to the well-known
political contests *b* with Quintus Catulus and other
eminent men; to his defeat *c* of Quintus Catulus,
the acknowledged leader of the Senate, for the
office of pontifex maximus, before he himself had
even been praetor; to the restoration in his
aedileship *d* of the monuments of Gaius Marius in
the teeth of the opposition of the nobles; to the
reinstatement of the children of proscribed persons
in the rights pertaining to their rank; and to his
praetorship *e* and quaestorship passed in Spain, in
which he showed wonderful energy and valour. He
was quaestor under Vetus Antistius, the grandfather
of our own Vetus, the consular and pontiff, himself
the father of two sons who have held the consulship
and the priesthood and a man whose excellence
reaches our highest conception of human integrity.

XLIV. But to resume. It was in Caesar's consulship *f* that there was formed between himself,
Gnaeus Pompeius and Marcus Crassus the partnership in political power which proved so baleful to
the city, to the world, and, subsequently at different
periods to each of the triumvirs themselves.
Pompey's motive in the adoption of this policy had
been to secure through Caesar as consul the long
delayed ratification of his acts in the provinces
across the seas, to which, as I have already said,
many still raised objections; Caesar agreed to it
because he realized that in making this concession
to the prestige of Pompey he would increase his
own, and that by throwing on Pompey the odium

potentiae in illum relegata confirmaturum vires suas,
Crassus, ut quem principatum solus adsequi non
poterat, auctoritate Pompei, viribus teneret Caesaris,
3 adfinitas etiam inter Caesarem Pompeiumque contracta nuptiis, quippe Iuliam,[1] filiam C. Caesaris.
Cn. Magnus duxit uxorem.

4 In hoc consulatu Caesar legem tulit, ut ager
Campanus plebei divideretur, suasore legis Pompeio.
Ita circiter viginti milia civium eo deducta et ius
urbis[2] restitutum post annos circiter centum quinquaginta duos quam bello Punico ab Romanis Capua
5 in formam praefecturae redacta erat. Bibulus,
collega Caesaris, cum actiones eius magis vellet
impedire quam posset, maiore parte anni domi se
tenuit. Quo facto dum augere vult invidiam collegae,
auxit potentiam. Tum Caesari decretae in quinquennium Galliae.

1 XLV. Per idem tempus P. Clodius, homo nobilis,
disertus, audax, quique neque[3] dicendi neque faciendi
ullum nisi quem vellet nosset modum, malorum
propositorum executor acerrimus, infamis etiam
sororis stupro et actus incesti reus ob initum inter
religiosissima populi Romani sacra adulterium, cum
graves inimicitias cum M. Cicerone exerceret (quid
enim inter tam dissimiles amicum esse poterat?) et
a patribus ad plebem transisset, legem in tribunatu

[1] Iuliam *added by Orelli.*
[2] urbis *Heinsius*; ab his *AP.*
[3] quique neque *Halm*; qui neque *Vascosanus*; neque
om. AP.

[a] Dressed as a woman he had appeared at the sacred rites
of the Bona Dea, at which only women were allowed to
be present. They were presided over by Caesar's wife,
Pompeia, with whom Clodius was suspected of having an
amour.   [b] 58 B.C.

146

for their joint control he would add to his own power; while Crassus hoped that by the influence of Pompey and the power of Caesar he might achieve a place of pre-eminence in the state which he had not been able to reach single-handed. Furthermore, a tie of marriage was cemented between Caesar and Pompey, in that Pompey now wedded Julia, Caesar's daughter.

In this consulship, Caesar, with Pompey's backing, passed a law authorizing a distribution to the plebs of the public domain in Campania. And so about twenty thousand citizens were established there, and its rights as a city were restored to Capua one hundred and fifty-two years after she had been reduced to a prefecture in the Second Punic War. Bibulus, Caesar's colleague, with the intent rather than the power of hindering Caesar's acts, confined himself to his house for the greater part of the year. By this conduct, whereby he hoped to increase his colleague's unpopularity, he only increased his power. At this time the Gallic provinces were assigned to Caesar for a period of five years.

XLV. About the same time Publius Clodius, a man of noble birth, eloquent and reckless, who recognized no limits either in speech or in act except his own caprice, energetic in the execution of his wicked projects, of ill-repute as the debaucher of his own sister, and accused of adulterous profanation of the most sacred rites of the Roman people,[a] having conceived a violent hatred against Marcus Cicero—for what friendship could there be between men so unlike?—caused himself to be transferred from a patrician into a plebeian family and, as tribune,[b] proposed a law that whoever put to death

147

tulit, qui civem Romanum indemnatum[1] interemisset,
ei aqua et igni interdiceretur : cuius verbis etsi non
2 nominabatur Cicero, tamen solus petebatur.   Ita vir
optime meritus de re publica conservatae patriae
pretium calamitatem exilii tulit.   Non caruerunt
suspicione oppressi Ciceronis Caesar et Pompeius.
Hoc sibi contraxisse videbatur Cicero, quod inter
viginti viros dividendo agro Campano esse noluisset.
3 Idem intra biennium sera Cn. Pompei cura, verum
ut coepit[2] intenta,[3] votisque Italiae ac decretis
senatus, virtute atque actione Annii Milonis tribuni
plebis dignitati patriaeque restitutus est.   Neque
post Numidici exilium aut reditum quisquam aut
expulsus invidiosius aut receptus est laetius.   Cuius
domus quam infeste a Clodio disiecta erat, tam
speciose a senatu restituta est.
4   Idem P. Clodius in tribunatu[4] sub honorificen-
tissimo ministerii titulo M. Catonem a re publica
relegavit : quippe legem tulit, ut is quaestor cum
iure praetorio, adiecto etiam quaestore, mitteretur in
insulam Cyprum ad spoliandum regno Ptolemaeum,
omnibus morum vitiis eam contumeliam meritum.
5 Sed ille sub adventum Catonis vitae suae vim intulit.

[1] indemnatum *Puteanus*; damnatum *AP*.
[2] ut coepit *Gelenius*; et cupit *AP*.
[3] intenta *Wopkens*; interita *AP*.
[4] tribunatu *Heinsius*; senatu *AP*.

---

[a] Literally "Should be forbidden fire and water."
[b] By his suppression, in his consulship, of the conspiracy
of Catiline.
[c] 57 B.C.   [d] 58 B.C.

148

a Roman citizen without trial should be condemned
to exile.[a] Although Cicero was not expressly named
in the wording of the bill, it was aimed at him
alone. And so this man, who had earned by his
great services the gratitude of his country,[b] gained
exile as his reward for saving the state. Caesar and
Pompey were not free from the suspicion of having
had a share in the fall of Cicero. Cicero seemed to
have brought upon himself their resentment by
refusing to be a member of the commission of twenty
charged with the distribution of lands in Campania.
Within two years Cicero was restored[c] to his country
and to his former status, thanks to the interest
of Gnaeus Pompeius—somewhat belated, it is true,
but effective when once exerted—and thanks to
the prayers of Italy, the decrees of the senate, and
the zealous activity of Annius Milo, tribune of the
people. Since the exile and return of Numidicus
no one had been banished amid greater popular
disapproval or welcomed back with greater enthusiasm. As for Cicero's house, the maliciousness
of its destruction by Clodius was now compensated
for by the magnificence of its restoration by the
senate.

Publius Clodius in his tribunate also removed
Marcus Cato from the state,[d] under the pretence
of an honourable mission. For he proposed a law
that Cato should be sent to the island of Cyprus in
the capacity of quaestor, but with the authority of
a praetor and with a quaestor as his subordinate,
with instructions to dethrone Ptolemaeus, who by
reason of his unmitigated viciousness of character
well deserved this humiliation. However, just
before the arrival of Cato, Ptolemy took his own

149

Unde pecuniam longe sperata maiorem Cato Romam retulit. Cuius integritatem laudari nefas est, insolentia paene argui potest, quod una cum consulibus ac senatu effusa civitate obviam, cum per Tiberim subiret navibus, non ante iis egressus est, quam ad eum locum pervenit, ubi erat exponenda pecunia.

1 XLVI. Cum deinde inmanis res vix multis voluminibus explicandas C. Caesar in Gallia gereret[1] nec contentus plurimis ac felicissimis victoriis innumerabilibusque caesis et captis hostium milibus etiam in Britanniam traiecisset exercitum, alterum paene imperio nostro ac suo quaerens orbem, vetus par[2] consulum, Cn. Pompeius et M Crassus, alterum iniere consulatum, qui neque petitus honeste ab iis 2 neque probabiliter gestus est. Caesari lege, quam Pompeius ad populum tulit, prorogatae in idem spatium temporis provinciae, Crasso bellum Parthicum iam[3] animo molienti Syria decreta. Qui vir cetera sanctissimus immunisque voluptatibus neque in pecunia neque in gloria concupiscenda aut modum norat aut capiebat terminum. Hunc proficiscentem 3 in Syriam diris cum ominibus tribuni plebis frustra retinere conati. Quorum execrationes si in ipsum

---

[1] gereret *Stanger*; ageret *AP*.
[2] vetus par *Ursinus*; victus pars *AP*.
[3] iam *Heinsius*; in *AP*.

---

life. Cato brought home from Cyprus a sum of money which greatly exceeded all expectations. To praise Cato's integrity would be sacrilege, but he can almost be charged with eccentricity in the display of it; for, in spite of the fact that all the citizens, headed by the consuls and the senate, poured out of the city to meet him as he ascended the Tiber, he did not disembark and greet them until he arrived at the place where the money was to be put ashore.

XLVI. Meanwhile, in Gaul, Gaius Caesar was carrying on his gigantic task,[a] which could scarcely be covered in many volumes. Not content with his many fortunate victories, and with slaying or taking as prisoners countless thousands of the enemy, he even crossed into Britain, as though seeking to add another world to our empire and to that which he had himself won. Gnaeus Pompeius and Marcus Crassus, who had once before been consuls together, now entered upon their second consulship,[b] which office they not only won by unfair means, but also administered without popular approval. In a law which Pompey proposed in the assembly of the people, Caesar's tenure of office in his provinces was continued for another five years, and Syria was decreed to Crassus, who was now planning to make war upon Parthia. Although Crassus was, in his general character, entirely upright and free from base desires, in his lust for money and his ambition for glory he knew no limits, and accepted no bounds. On his departure for Asia the tribunes of the people made ineffectual efforts to detain him by the announcement of baleful omens. If the curses which they called down upon him had

151

tantummodo valuissent, utile[1] imperatoris damnum
4 salvo exercitu fuisset rei publicae. Transgressum
Euphraten Crassum petentemque Seleuciam circum-
fusus inmanibus copiis equitum rex Orodes una cum
parte maiore Romani exercitus interemit. Reliquias
legionum C. Cassius, atrocissimi mox auctor facinoris,
tum quaestor, conservavit Syriamque adeo in populi
Romani potestate retinuit, ut transgressos in eam
Parthos felici rerum eventu fugaret ac funderet.

1   XLVII. Per haec insequentiaque et quae praediximus tempora amplius quadringenta milia hostium
a C. Caesare caesa sunt, plura capta ; pugnatum
saepe derecta acie, saepe in agminibus, saepe erup-
tionibus, bis penetrata Britannia, novem denique
aestatibus vix ulla non iustissimus triumphus emeri-
tus. Circa Alesiam vero tantae res gestae, quantas
audere vix hominis, perficere paene nullius nisi dei
fuerit.

2   Quarto[2] ferme anno Caesar morabatur in Galliis,
cum medium iam ex invidia potentiae <et viva illa>
male[3] cohaerentis inter Cn. Pompeium et C. Caesarem concordiae pignus Iulia, uxor Magni, decessit :
atque omnia inter destinatos tanto discrimini duces

---

    [1] utile *AP* ; vile *Lipsius.*
    [2] quarto *Laurent.* ; septimo *AP.*
    [3] potentiae et viva illa male *Shipley* ; Ponti et Camiliae
AP ; potentiae male *Lipsius.*

---

        [a] Battle of Carrhae, 53 B.C.
        [b] The assassination of Julius Caesar.
[c] 52 B.C.   Related in Bk. vii. of the Gallic War.   [d] 54 B.C.

affected Crassus alone, the loss of the commander
would not have been without advantage to the
state, had but the army been saved. He had
crossed the Euphrates and was now marching toward
Seleucia when he was surrounded by King Orodes
with his innumerable bands of cavalry and perished
together with the greater part of his army.[a]
Remnants of the legions were saved by Gaius Cassius
—(he was later the perpetrator of a most atrocious
crime,[b] but was at that time quaestor)—who not
only retained Syria in its allegiance to the Roman
people, but succeeded, by a fortunate issue of
events, in defeating and putting to rout the Parthians
when they crossed its borders.

XLVII. During this period, including the years
which immediately followed and those of which
mention has already been made, more than four
hundred thousand of the enemy were slain by Gaius
Caesar and a greater number were taken prisoners.
Many times had he fought in pitched battles, many
times on the march, many times as besieger or
besieged. Twice he penetrated into Britain, and in
all his nine campaigns there was scarcely one which
was not fully deserving of a triumph. His feats
about Alesia[c] were of a kind that a mere man
would scarcely venture to undertake, and scarcely
anyone but a god could carry through.

About the fourth year of Caesar's stay in Gaul
occurred the death of Julia,[d] the wife of Pompey, the
one tie which bound together Pompey and Caesar in
a coalition which, because of each one's jealousy of
the other's power, held together with difficulty even
during her lifetime ; and, as though fortune were
bent upon breaking all the bonds between the two

dirimente fortuna filius quoque parvus Pompei, Iulia
natus, intra breve spatium obiit. Tum in gladios
3 caedesque civium furente ambitu, cuius neque finis
reperiebatur nec modus, tertius consulatus soli Cn.
Pompeio etiam adversantium antea dignitati eius
iudicio delatus est, cuius ille honoris gloria veluti
reconciliatis sibi optimatibus maxime a C. Caesare
alienatus est ; sed eius consulatus omnem vim in
coërcitionem[1] ambitus exercuit.

4 Quo tempore P. Clodius a Milone candidato consulatus exemplo inutili, facto[2] salutari rei publicae
circa Bovillas contracta ex occursu rixa iugulatus
est. Milonem reum non magis invidia facti quam
5 Pompei damnavit voluntas. Quem quidem M. Cato
palam lata absolvit sententia. Qui si maturius
tulisset, non defuissent qui sequerentur exemplum
probarentque eum civem occisum, quo nemo per-
niciosior rei publicae neque bonis inimicior vixerat.

1 XLVIII. Intra breve deinde spatium belli civilis
exarserunt initia, cum iustissimus quisque et a
Caesare et a Pompeio vellet dimitti exercitus ;
quippe Pompeius in secundo consulatu Hispanias
sibi decerni voluerat easque per triennium absens

---

[1] coercitionem *B*; coertionem *AP*; coercitione *Cludius*.
[2] inutili facto *Gelenius*; inutiliter facto *AP*; inutili sed
facto *Gelenius*.

---

[a] " Son " is supported by Livy, *Epit.* 106 and Suet. *Caes.*
26. Dio xxxix. 64 says " daughter."
[b] 52 B.C.   [c] 52 B.C.   [d] 55 B.C.

men destined for so great a conflict, Pompey's little son [a] by Julia also died a short time afterwards. Then, inasmuch as agitation over the elections found vent in armed conflicts and civil bloodshed, which continued indefinitely and without check, Pompey was made consul for the third time,[b] now without a colleague, with the assent even of those who up to that time had opposed him for that office. The tribute paid him by this honour, which seemed to indicate his reconciliation with the optimates, served more than anything else to alienate him from Caesar. Pompey, however, employed his whole power during this consulship in curbing election abuses.

It was at this time that Publius Clodius was slain [c] by Milo, who was a candidate for the consulship, in a quarrel which arose in a chance meeting at Bovillae ; a bad precedent, but in itself a service to the state. Milo was brought to trial and convicted quite as much through the influence of Pompey as on account of the odium aroused by the deed. Cato, it is true, declared for his acquittal in an opinion openly expressed. Had his vote been cast earlier, men would not have been lacking to follow his example and approve the slaying of a citizen as pernicious to the republic and as hostile to all good citizens as any man who had ever lived.

XLVIII. It was not long after this that the first sparks of civil war were kindled. All fair-minded men desired that both Caesar and Pompey should disband their armies. Now Pompey in his second consulship [d] had caused the provinces of Spain to be assigned to him, and though he was actually absent from them, administering the affairs of the city, he continued to

ipse ac praesidens urbi per Afranium et Petreium,
consularem ac praetorium, legatos suos, admini-
strabat et iis, qui a Caesare dimittendos exercitus
contendebant, adsentabatur, iis, qui ab ipso quoque,
2 adversabatur. Qui si ante biennium, quam ad arma
itum est, perfectis muneribus theatri et aliorum
operum, quae ei circumdedit, gravissima temptatus
valetudine decessisset in Campania (quo quidem
tempore universa Italia vota pro salute eius primi[1]
omnium civium suscepit) defuisset fortunae destru-
endi eius locus, et quam apud superos habuerat
magnitudinem, inlibatam detulisset ad inferos.
3 Bello autem civili et tot, quae deinde per continuos
viginti annos consecuta sunt, malıs non alius maiorem
flagrantioremque quam C. Curio tribunus plebis
subiecit facem, vir nobilis, eloquens, audax, suae
alienaeque et fortunae et pudicitiae prodigus, homo
ingeniosissime nequam et facundus malo publico
4 cuius animo [voluptatibus vel libidinibus][2] neque opes
ullae neque cupiditates sufficere possent. Hic primo
pro Pompei partibus, id est, ut tunc habebatur, pro
re publica, mox simulatione contra Pompeium et
Caesarem, sed animo pro Caesare stetit. Id gratis
an accepto centies sestertio[a] fecerit, ut accepimus,
5 in medio relinquemus. Ad ultimum saluberrimas[3]
coalescentis condiciones pacis, quas et Caesar iustis-

---

[1] primi *Vascosanus*; primo *AP*.
[2] voluptatibus vel libidinibus *deleted as a gloss by Gruter.*
[3] et *after* saluberrimas *deleted by Gelenius.*

[a] About £100,000 or $500,000.

govern them for three years through his lieutenants,
Afranius and Petreius, the former of consular
and the latter of praetorian rank ; and while he
agreed with those who insisted that Caesar should
dismiss his army, he was opposed to those who
urged that he should also dismiss his own   Had
Pompey only died two years before the outbreak of
hostilities, after the completion of his theatre and
the other public buildings with which he had
surrounded it, at the time when he was attacked
by a serious illness in Campania and all Italy prayed
for his safety as her foremost citizen, fortune would
have lost the opportunity of overthrowing him and
he would have borne to the grave unimpaired all the
qualities of greatness that had been his in life.   It
was Gaius Curio, however, a tribune of the people,
who, more than anyone else, applied the flaming
torch which kindled the civil war and all the evils
which followed for twenty consecutive years. Curio
was a man of noble birth, eloquent, reckless, prodigal
alike of his own fortune and chastity and of those of
other people, a man of the utmost cleverness in
perversity, who used his gifted tongue for the
subversion of the state.   No wealth and no pleasures
sufficed to satiate his appetites.   He was at first on
the side of Pompey, that is to say, as it was then
regarded, on the side of the republic.   Then he
pretended to be opposed both to Pompey and Caesar,
but in his heart he was for Caesar.   Whether his
conversion was spontaneous or due to a bribe of ten
million sesterces,[a] as is reported, we shall leave un-
determined.   Finally, when a truce was on the point
of being concluded on terms of the most salutary
character, terms which were demanded in a spirit of

157

simo animo postulabat et Pompeius aequo recipiebat, discussit ac rupit, unice cavente Cicerone concordiae publicae.

Harum praeteritarumque rerum ordo cum iustis[1] aliorum voluminibus promatur, tum, uti spero, 6 nostris explicabitur. Nunc proposito operi sua forma reddatur, si prius gratulatus ero Q. Catulo, duobus Lucullis Metelloque et Hortensio, qui, cum sine invidia in re publica floruissent eminuissentque sine periculo, quieta aut certe non praecipitata fatali ante initium bellorum civilium morte functi sunt.

1 XLIX. Lentulo et Marcello consulibus post urbem conditam annis septingentis et tribus,[2] et annos octo et septuaginta ante quam tu, M. Vinici, consulatum inires, bellum civile exarsit. Alterius ducis causa 2 melior videbatur, alterius erat firmior; hic omnia speciosa, illic valentia; Pompeium senatus auctoritas, Caesarem militum armavit fiducia. Consules senatusque causae non[3] Pompeio summam imperii detule-3 runt. Nihil relictum a Caesare, quod servandae pacis causa temptari posset, nihil receptum a Pompeianis, cum alter consul iusto esset ferocior, Lentulus vero salva re publica salvus esse non posset, M. autem Cato moriendum ante, quam ullam condicionem civis

---

[1] iustis *Gelenius*; iustius *AP*.

[2] annis DCCIII *Gelenius*; annis (*AP*) a CC.III *AB*; ACCIII *P*.

[3] non *AP*; nomine *Gronovius*.

ᵃ 49 B.C.

the utmost fair-mindedness by Caesar and accepted by Pompey without protest, it was in the end broken and shattered by Curio in spite of Cicero's extraordinary efforts to preserve harmony in the state.

As to the order of these events, and of those which have been mentioned before, the reader is referred to the special works of other historians, and I myself hope some day to give them in full. But at the present time it will be consistent with the general plan of this briefer narrative if I merely stop to congratulate Quintus Catulus, the two Luculli, Metellus, and Hortensius, who, after flourishing in public life without envy and rising to pre-eminence without danger to themselves, in the course of nature died a peaceful or at least a not untimely death before the outbreak of the civil wars.

XLIX. In the consulship of Lentulus and Marcellus,[a] seven hundred and three years after the founding of the city and seventy-eight years before your consulship, Marcus Vinicius, the civil war burst into flame. The one leader seemed to have the better cause, the other the stronger ; on the one was the appearance, on the other the reality of power ; Pompey was armed with the authority of the senate, Caesar with the devotion of his soldiers. The consuls and the senate conferred the supreme authority not on Pompey but on his cause. No effort was omitted by Caesar that could be tried in the interest of peace, but no offer of his was accepted by the Pompeians. Of the two consuls, one showed more bitterness than was fair, the other, Lentulus, could not save himself from ruin without bringing ruin upon the state, while Marcus Cato insisted that they should fight to the death rather

accipiendam rei publicae contenderet. Vir antiquus et gravis Pompei partes laudaret magis, prudens sequeretur Caesaris, et illa gloriosiora,[1] haec terribiliora duceret.

4 Ut deinde spretis omnibus quae Caesar postulaverat, tantummodo contentus cum una legione titulum retinere provinciae, privatus[2] in urbem veniret et se in petitione consulatus suffragiis populi Romani committeret decrevere, ratus bellandum Caesar cum exercitu Rubiconem transiit. Cn. Pompeius consulesque et maior pars senatus relicta urbe ac deinde Italia transmisere Dyrrachium.

1 L. At Caesar Domitio legionibusque, Corfini quae[3] una cum eo fuerant, potitus, duce aliisque, qui voluerant[4] abire ad Pompeium, sine dilatione dimissis, persecutus Brundusium, ita ut appareret malle integris rebus et condicionibus finire bellum quam opprimere fugientis, cum transgressos reperisset consules, in
2 urbem revertit redditaque ratione consiliorum suorum in senatu et in contione ac miserrimae necessitudinis, cum alienis armis ad arma compulsus esset, Hispanias petere decrevit.

3 Festinationem itineris eius aliquamdiu morata

---

[1] gloriosiora *Cuperus*; gloriosa *AP*.
[2] privatus *Gelenius*; privatusque *AP*.
[3] legionibusque Corfini quae *P*; legionibusque Corfini *AP*.
[4] voluerant *Gelenius*; venerant *AP*.

---

[a] Probably refers to Caesar's offer (App. *B.C.* ii. 32) to be satisfied with Cisalpine Gaul and Illyria, with *two* legions.
[b] Jan. 12 or 13, 49 B.C.

than allow the republic to accept a single dictate
from a mere citizen. The stern Roman of the old-
fashioned type would praise the cause of Pompey, the
politic would follow the lead of Caesar, recognizing
that while there was on the one side greater prestige,
the other was the more formidable.

When at last, rejecting all the demands of Caesar,
who was content to retain the title to the province,[a]
with but a single legion, the senate decreed that he
should enter the city as a private citizen and should
as such, submit himself to the votes of the Roman
people in his candidacy for the consulship, Caesar
concluded that war was inevitable and crossed the
Rubicon [b] with his army. Gnaeus Pompeius, the
consuls, and the majority of the senate abandoned
first the city, then Italy, and crossed the sea to
Dyrrachium.

L. Caesar, on his side, having got into his power
Domitius and the legions that were with him at
Corfinium, immediately released this commander
and all others who so wished, and allowed them to
join Pompey, whom he now followed to Brundisium,
making it clear that he preferred to put an end to
the war while the state was uninjured and negotiation
still possible, rather than to crush his fleeing enemy.
Finding that the consuls had crossed the sea he
returned to the city, and after rendering to the
senate and also to the assembly of the people an
account of his motives and of the deplorable necessity
of his position, in that he had been driven to arms
by others who had themselves resorted to arms, he
resolved to march on Spain.

The rapidity of his march was delayed for some
time by the city of Massilia, which with more

Massilia est, fide melior quam consilio prudentior, intempestive principalium armorum arbitria captans, quibus hi se debent interponere, qui non parentem
4 coёrcere possunt. Exercitus deinde, qui sub Afranio[1] consulari ac Petreio praetorio fuerat, ipsius adventus vigore ac fulgore occupatus se Caesari tradidit; uterque legatorum et quisquis cuiusque ordinis sequi eos voluerat, remissi ad Pompeium.

1 LI. Proximo anno cum Dyrrachium ac vicina ei urbi regio castris Pompei obtineretur,[2] qui accitis ex omnibus transmarinis provinciis legionibus, equitum ac peditum auxiliis, regumque et[3] tetrarcharum simulque dynastarum copiis inmanem exercitum confecerat et mare praesidiis classium, ut rebatur, saepserat, quo minus Caesar legiones posset trans-
2 mittere, sua et celeritate et fortuna C. Caesar usus nihil in mora habuit, quo minus eo quo vellet[4] ipse exercitusque classibus perveniret, et primo paene castris Pompei sua iungeret, mox etiam obsidione munimentisque eum complecteretur. Sed inopia obsidentibus quam obsessis erat gravior. Tum
3 Balbus Cornelius excedente humanam fidem temeritate ingressus castra hostium saepiusque cum Lentulo conlocutus consule, dubitante quanti se venderet, illis incrementis fecit viam, quibus non in Hispania

---

[1] Afranio *Burer*; Africanio *B*; Africano *AP*.
[2] obtineretur *Heinsius*; retinetur *BAP*.
[3] et *added by Gelenius*.
[4] eo quo vellet *Halm*; et cum vellet *AP*.

---

[a] At Ilerda, August, 49 B.C.
[b] 48 B.C.

honesty of intention than with wise discretion assumed
the unseasonable rôle of arbiter between the two
armed leaders, an intervention suited only to those
who are in a position to coerce the combatant
refusing obedience. Next, the army, commanded
by Afranius, an ex-consul, and Petreius, an ex-
praetor, taken off its guard by Caesar's energy and
the lightning speed of his arrival, surrendered [a] to
him. Both the commanders and all others, of whatever rank, who wished to follow them were allowed
to return to Pompey.

LI. The next year [b] found Dyrrachium and its
vicinity occupied by the camp of Pompey, who by
summoning legions from all the provinces beyond
the sea, together with auxiliary troops of foot and
horse, and the forces of kings, tetrarchs, and other
subject rulers, had in this way collected a formidable
army, and had with his fleets established, as he
thought, a successful blockade upon the sea to
prevent Caesar from transporting his legions across
the Adriatic. But Caesar, relying upon his usual
rapidity of action and his famous luck, allowed
nothing to prevent him or his army from crossing
and landing at any port he pleased, and at first
pitched his camp almost touching that of Pompey,
and then proceeded to surround the latter by
entrenchments and siege works. But lack of provi-
sions was a more serious matter to the besiegers than
to the besieged. It was at this time that Balbus
Cornelius, at incredible risk, entered the camp of
the enemy and held several conferences with the
consul Lentulus, whose only doubt was what price
to put upon himself. It was by stages such as this
that Balbus, who was not even the son of a Roman

ex cive[1] natus, sed Hispanus, in triumphum et ponti-
ficatum adsurgeret fieretque ex privato consularis.
Variatum deinde proeliis, sed uno longe magis Pompeianis prospero, quo graviter impulsi sunt Caesaris
milites.

1 LII. Tum Caesar cum exercitu fatalem victoriae
suae Thessaliam petiit. Pompeius, longe diversa
2 aliis suadentibus, quorum plerique hortabantur, ut
in Italiam transmitteret (neque hercules quidquam
partibus illis salubrius fuit), alii, ut bellum traheret,
quod dignatione partium in dies ipsis magis pro-
sperum fieret, usus impetu suo hostem secutus est.

3 Aciem Pharsalicam et illum cruentissimum Romano
nomini diem tantumque utriusque exercitus profusum
sanguinis et conlisa inter se duo rei publicae capita
effossumque alterum Romani imperii lumen et[2] tot
talesque Pompeianarum partium caesos viros non
4 recipit enarranda hic scripturae modus. Illud notandum est : ut primum C. Caesar inclinatam vidit Pom-
peianorum aciem, neque prius neque antiquius quidquam habuit, quam ut in omnes partes, * * * ut[3]
militari verbo ex[4] consuetudine utar, dimitteret. Pro
5 dii immortales, quod huius voluntatis erga Brutum
suae postea vir tam mitis pretium tulit! Nihil in illa

---

[1] in Hispania ex cive *Morgenstern*; Hispaniae Asiae *AP*.

[2] et *added by Halm*.

[3] ut *added by Gelenius*; in omnes partes *AP*; incolumes
partes *Ellis*. *This is a vexed passage, and many conjectures
have been made as to which was the military expression.
Ruhnken supposes a lacuna.*

[4] ex *Lipsius*; et *AP*.

---

[a] Described in Caes. *Bell. Civ.* iii. 62–70.

[b] August 9, 48 B.C.

[c] See note on text. The general sense is supplied from

citizen born in Spain but actually a Spaniard, paved
the way for his later rise to the pontificate and to
a triumph, and from the rank of private citizen to
that of a consul. Conflicts followed, with shifting
fortunes. One [a] of these battles was much more
favourable to the Pompeians, and Caesar's troops
were severely repulsed.

LII. Then Caesar marched with his army into
Thessaly, destined to be the scene of his victory.
Pompey, in spite of the contrary advice of others,
followed his own impulse and set out after the
enemy. Most of his advisers urged him to cross
into Italy—nor indeed was there any course more
expedient for his party—others advised him to
prolong the war, which, by reason of the esteem in
which the party was held, was daily becoming more
favourable to them.

The limits set to a work of this kind will not
permit me to describe in detail the battle of
Pharsalia,[b] that day of carnage so fatal to the Roman
name, when so much blood was shed on either side,
the clash of arms between the two heads of the
state, the extinction of one of the two luminaries of
the Roman world, and the slaughter of so many
noble men on Pompey's side. One detail, however,
I cannot refrain from noting. When Gaius Caesar
saw that Pompey's army was defeated he made it
his first and foremost concern to send out orders to
grant quarter [c]—if I may use the habitual military
expression. Ye immortal gods! What a reward
did this merciful man afterwards receive for his
kindness to Brutus! There is nothing more mar-

the account in Suet. *Caes.* 75 and Appian, *Bellum Civile*
ii. 80.

6 victoria mirabilius, magnificentius, clarius fuit, quam
quod[1] neminem nisi acie consumptum civem patria
desideravit : sed munus misericordiae corrupit per-
tinacia, cum libentius vitam victor iam daret, quam
victi acciperent.

1 LIII. Pompeius profugiens cum duobus Lentulis
consularibus Sextoque filio et Favonio praetorio,
quos comites ei fortuna adgregaverat, aliis, ut
Parthos, aliis, ut Africam peteret, in qua fidelis-
simum partium suarum haberet regem Iubam, suadentibus, Aegyptum petere proposuit memor beneficiorum, quae in patrem eius Ptolemaei, qui tum
puero quam iuveni propior regnabat Alexandriae,
2 contulerat. Sed quis in adversis beneficiorum servat
memoriam ? Aut quis ullam calamitosis deberi putat
gratiam ? Aut quando fortuna non mutat fidem ?
Missi itaque ab rege, qui venientem Cn. Pompeium
(is iam a Mytilenis Corneliam uxorem receptam in
navem fugae comitem habere coeperat) consilio
Theodoti et Achillae exciperent hortarenturque, ut
ex oneraria in eam navem, quae obviam processerat,
transcenderet ; quod cum fecisset, princeps Romani
nominis imperio arbitrioque Aegyptii mancipii C.
Caesare P. Servilio consulibus iugulatus est. Hic
3 post tres consulatus et totidem triumphos domitum-

----

[1] in illa . . . quam quod *Haase*; illa . . . quando *AP*.

---

[a] Caesar, *Bell. Civ.* 104, says it was a "navicula parvula."
[b] 48 B.C.

vellous about that victory, nothing more magnificent, nothing more glorious, than that our country did not mourn the loss of any citizen save those who had fallen in battle. But his offer of clemency was set at nought by the stubbornness of his opponents, since the victor was more ready to grant life than the vanquished to accept it.

LIII. Pompey fled with the two Lentuli, both ex-consuls, his own son Sextus, and Favonius, a former praetor, friends whom chance had gathered about him as his companions. Some advised him to take refuge with the Parthians, others in Africa, where he had in King Juba a most loyal partisan; but, remembering the favours which he had conferred upon the father of Ptolemy, who, though still between boyhood and manhood, was now reigning at Alexandria, he decided to repair to Egypt. But, in adversity who remembers past services? Who considers that any gratitude is due to those who have met disaster? When does change of fortune fail to shift allegiance? Envoys were sent by the king at the instance of Theodotus and Achillas to receive Pompey on his arrival—he was now accompanied in his flight by his wife Cornelia, who had been taken on board at Mytilene —and to urge him to change from the merchant ship to the vessel[a] which had come out to meet him. Having accepted the invitation, the first of the citizens of Rome was stabbed to death by the order and dictation of an Egyptian vassal, the year of his death being the consulship of Gaius Caesar and Publius Servilius.[b] So died in his fifty-eighth year, on the very eve of his birthday, that upright and illustrious man, after holding three consulships,

que terrarum orbem sanctissimi atque praestantis-
simi viri in id evecti, super quod ascendi non potest,
duodesexagesimum annum agentis pridie natalem
ipsius vitae fuit exitus, in tantum in illo viro a se
discordante fortuna, ut cui modo ad victoriam terra
defuerat, deesset ad sepulturam.

4 Quid aliud quam nimium occupatos dixerim, quos
in aetate et tanti et paene nostri saeculi viri fefellit
quinquennium, cum a C. Atilio et Q. Servilio consulibus tam facilis[1] esset annorum digestio ? Quod
adieci, non ut arguerem, sed ne arguerer.

1 LIV. Non fuit maior in Caesarem, quam in Pompeium fuerat, regis eorumque, quorum is auctoritate
regebatur, fides. Quippe cum venientem eum temp-
tassent insidiis ac deinde bello lacessere auderent,
utrique summorum imperatorum,[2] alteri mortuo,[3]
alteri superstiti meritas poenas luere suppliciis.

2 Nusquam erat Pompeius corpore, adhuc ubique
vivebat[4] nomine. Quippe ingens partium eius favor
bellum excitaverat Africum, quod ciebat rex Iuba
et Scipio, vir consularis, ante biennium quam extin-
3 gueretur Pompeius, lectus ab eo socer, eorumque
copias auxerat M. Cato, ingenti cum difficultate
itinerum locorumque inopia perductis ad eos legioni-

---

[1] facilis *Gelenius*; felix (foelix *A*) *AP*.
[2] summorum imperatorum *Mommsen*; summo imperatorum *AP*.
[3] alteri mortuo *Lipsius*.
[4] vivebat *Heinsius*; Iubae *AP*.

168

celebrating three triumphs, conquering the whole world, and attaining to a pinnacle of fame beyond which it is impossible to rise. Such was the inconsistency of fortune in his case, that he who but a short time before had found no more lands to conquer now found none for his burial.

As regards Pompey's age, what excuse, other than that of excessive preoccupation, shall I make for those who have made an error of five years in the age of one who was not only a great man but who almost belongs to our century, especially as it is so easy to reckon from the consulship of Caius Atilius and Quintus Servilius [a] ? I have added this remark not for the sake of criticizing others, but to avoid criticism of myself.

LIV. The loyalty of the king, and of those by whose influence he was controlled, was no greater towards Caesar than it had been toward Pompey. For, upon Caesar's arrival in Egypt, they assailed him with plots and subsequently dared to challenge him in open warfare. By suffering death they paid to both of these great commanders, the living and the dead, a well-deserved atonement.

Pompey the man was no more, but his name still lived everywhere. For the strong support his party had in Africa had stirred up in that country a war in which the moving spirits were King Juba and Scipio, a man of consular rank, whom Pompey had chosen for his father-in-law two years before his death. Their forces were augmented by Marcus Cato, who, in spite of the great difficulty of the march, and the lack of supplies in the regions traversed, succeeded in conducting his legions to

[a] Consuls 106 B.C.

bus. Qui vir cum summum ei a militibus deferretur imperium, honoratiori parere[1] maluit.

1 LV. Admonet promissae brevitatis fides, quanto omnia transcursu dicenda sint. Sequens fortunam suam Caesar pervectus in Africam est, quam occiso C.[2] Curione, Iulianarum duce partium, Pompeiani obtinebant exercitus. Ibi primo varia fortuna, mox 2 pugnavit sua,[3] inclinataeque hostium copiae : nec dissimilis ibi adversus victos quam in priores clementia Caesaris fuit.

Victorem Africani belli Caesarem gravius excepit Hispaniense (nam victus ab eo Pharnaces vix quidquam gloriae eius adstruxit), quod Cn. Pompeius, Magni filius, adulescens impetus ad bella maximi, ingens ac terribile conflaverat, undique ad eum adhuc paterni nominis magnitudinem sequentium 3 ex toto orbe terrarum auxiliis confluentibus. Sua Caesarem in Hispaniam comitata fortuna est, sed nullum umquam atrocius periculosiusque ab eo initum proelium, adeo ut plus quam dubio Marte descenderet equo consistensque ante recedentem suorum aciem, increpata prius fortuna, quod se in eum servasset exitum, denuntiaret militibus vestigio se non recessurum : proinde viderent, quem et quo loco 4 imperatorem deserturi forent. Verecundia magis

---

[1] parere *Burer* ; parare *P* ; parari *A*.
[2] C. *added by Stanger*.
[3] fortuna mox pugnavit sua *Acidalius and Lipsius* ; fortunam expugnavit uia *AP*.

---

[a] Cato had held the praetorship only.
[b] At Thapsus, April 6, 46.
[c] At Zela, in 47 B.C. It is here mentioned out of its proper order.

them. Cato, although offered the supreme command by the soldiers, preferred to take orders from Scipio, his superior in rank.[a]

LV. Fidelity to my promise of brevity reminds me how rapidly I must pass over the details of my narrative. Caesar, following up his success, passed over to Africa, of which the Pompeian armies now held possession since the death of Gaius Curio, the leader there of the Caesarian party. At first his armies were attended by a varying fortune, but later by his usual luck the forces of the enemy were routed.[b] Here again he showed no less clemency toward the vanquished than to those whom he had defeated in the previous war.

Caesar, victorious in Africa, was now confronted by a more serious war in Spain (for the defeat of Pharnaces[c] may be passed over, since it added but little to his renown). This great and formidable war had been stirred up by Gnaeus Pompeius, the son of Pompey the Great, a young man of great energy in war, and reinforcements flowed in from all parts of the world from among those who still followed his father's great name. Caesar's usual fortune followed him to Spain; but no battle in which he ever engaged was more bitterly fought or more dangerous to his cause.[d] Once, indeed, when the fight was now more than doubtful, he leapt from his horse, placed himself before his lines, now beginning to give way, and, after upbraiding fortune for saving him for such an end, announced to his soldiers that he would not retreat a step. He asked them to consider who their commander was and in what a pass they were about to desert him. It was

[d] Battle of Munda, March 17, 45 B.C.

171

quam virtute acies restituta, et a[1] duce quam a
milite fortius. Cn. Pompeius gravis vulnere inventus
inter solitudines avias interemptus est ; Labienum
Varumque acies abstulit.

1 LVI. Caesar omnium victor regressus in urbem,
quod humanam excedat fidem, omnibus, qui contra
se arma tulerant, ignovit, magnificentissimisque[2]
gladiatorii muneris, naumachiae et equitum peditumque, simul elephantorum certaminis spectaculis
epulique per multos dies dati celebratione replevit
2 eam. Quinque egit triumphos : Gallici apparatus
ex citro, Pontici ex acantho, Alexandrini testudine,
Africi ebore, Hispaniensis argento rasili constitit.
Pecunia ex manubiis lata paulo amplius sexiens
miliens sestertium.

3 Neque illi tanto viro et tam clementer omnibus
victoriis suis uso plus quinque mensium principalis
quies contigit. Quippe cum mense Octobri in urbem
revertisset, idibus Martiis, coniurationis auctoribus
Bruto et Cassio, quorum alterum promittendo consulatum non obligaverat, contra differendo Cassium
offenderat, adiectis etiam consiliariis caedis familiaris-
simis omnium et fortuna partium eius in summum
evectis fastigium, D. Bruto et C. Trebonio aliisque
4 clari nominis viris, interemptus est. Cui magnam
invidiam conciliarat M. Antonius, omnibus audendis

---

[1] restituta et a *Orelli*; restitutae C. A. *B*; restitutae
sunt a *AP*.
[2] magnificentissimisque *AB*; que *om. P*; et magnificentissimis *Halm and Ruhnken.*

• The first four in 46 B.C., the Spanish triumph in 45 B.C.
♭ About £5,500,000 or $27,000,000.
• March 15, 44 B.C.

shame rather than valour that restored their wavering line, and the commander showed more courage than his men. Gnaeus Pompeius, badly wounded, was discovered on a pathless waste and put to death. Labienus and Varus met their death in battle.

LVI. Caesar, victorious over all his enemies, returned to the city, and pardoned all who had borne arms against him, an act of generosity almost passing belief. He entertained the city to repletion with the magnificent spectacle of a gladiatorial show, a sham battle of ships, mock battles of cavalry, infantry, and even mounted elephants, and the celebration of a public banquet which was continued through several days. He celebrated five triumphs.[a] The emblems in his Gallic triumph were of citrus wood; in his Pontic of acanthus; in his Alexandrian triumph of tortoise-shell, in his African of ivory, and in his Spanish of polished silver. The money borne in his triumphs, realized from the sale of spoils, amounted to a little more than six hundred million sesterces.[b]

But it was the lot of this great man, who behaved with such clemency in all his victories, that his peaceful enjoyment of supreme power should last but five months. For, returning to the city in October, he was slain on the ides of March.[c] Brutus and Cassius were the leaders of the conspiracy. He had failed to win the former by the promise of the consulship, and had offended the latter by the postponement of his candidacy. There were also in the plot to compass his death some of the most intimate of all his friends, who owed their elevation to the success of his party, namely Decimus Brutus, Gaius Trebonius, and others of illustrious name. Marcus Antonius, his colleague in the consulship,

paratissimus, consulatus collega, inponendo capiti eius
Lupercalibus sedentis pro rostris insigne regium, quod
ab eo ita repulsum erat, ut non offensus[1] videretur.

1   LVII. Laudandum experientia consilium est Pansae atque Hirtii, qui semper praedixerant Caesari
ut principatum armis quaesitum armis teneret.   Ille
dictitans mori se quam timere[2] malle dum clementiam,
quam praestiterat, expectat, incautus ab ingratis
occupatus est, cum quidem plurima ei[3] praesagia atque
2 indicia dii immortales futuri obtulissent periculi.
Nam et haruspices praemonuerant, ut diligentissime
iduum Martiarum caveret diem, et uxor Calpurnia
territa nocturno visu, ut ea die domi subsisteret,
orabat,[4] et libelli coniurationem nuntiantes dati
neque protinus ab eo lecti erant.   Sed profecto
3 ineluctabilis fatorum vis, cuiuscumque fortunam
mutare constituit, consilia corrumpit.

1   LVIII. Quo anno id patravere facinus Brutus et
Cassius praetores erant, D. Brutus consul designatus.
2 hi una cum coniurationis globo, stipati gladiatorum
D. Bruti manu, Capitolium occupavere.   Tum[5] consul
Antonius (quem cum simul interimendum censuisset
Cassius testamentumque Caesaris abolendum, Brutus
repugnaverat dictitans nihil amplius civibus praeter
tyranni—ita enim appellari Caesarem facto eius ex-

---

[1] ita . . . offensus *Rhenanus*; id . . . offensum *AP*.
[2] timere *corrected to* timeri *A*; timere *is more in keeping
with Plut*. Caes. 57 *and Suet*. Div. Iul. 86.
[3] plurima ei *Orelli*; plurimi *BA*; plurima *P*.
[4] orabat *AP*; orarat *Halm*.
[5] tum *Haase*; cum *AP*.

ᵃ Usually of Etruscan origin, who professed ability to
foretell the future from the examination of the entrails of
sacrificial animals.

ever ready for acts of daring, had brought great odium upon Caesar by placing a royal crown upon his head as he sat on the rostra at the Lupercalia. Caesar put the crown from him, but in such a way that he did not seem to be displeased.

LVII. In the light of experience due credit should be given to the counsel of Pansa and Hirtius, who had always warned Caesar that he must hold by arms the position which he had won by arms. But Caesar kept reiterating that he would rather die than live in fear, and while he looked for a return for the clemency he had shown, he was taken off his guard by men devoid of gratitude, although the gods gave many signs and presages of the threatened danger. For the soothsayers[a] had warned him beforehand carefully to beware the Ides of March; his wife Calpurnia, terrified by a dream, kept begging him to remain at home on that day; and notes warning him of the conspiracy were handed him, but he neglected to read them at the time. But verily the power of destiny is inevitable; it confounds the judgement of him whose fortune it has determined to reverse.

LVIII. Brutus and Cassius were praetors, and Decimus Brutus was consul designate in the year in which they perpetrated this deed. These three, with the remainder of the group of conspirators, escorted by a band of gladiators belonging to Decimus Brutus, seized the capitol. Thereupon Antonius, as consul, summoned the senate. Cassius had been in favour of slaying Antony as well as Caesar, and of destroying Caesar's will, but Brutus had opposed him, insisting that citizens ought not to seek the blood of any but the " tyrant "—for to

175

3 pediebat — petendum esse sanguinem) convocato
senatu, cum iam Dolabella, quem substituturus sibi
Caesar designaverat consulem, fasces atque insignia
corripuisset consulis, velut pacis auctor liberos suos
obsides in Capitolium misit fidemque descendendi
4 tuto interfectoribus Caesaris dedit. Et illud decreti
Atheniensium celeberrimi exemplum, relatum a
Cicerone, oblivionis praeteritarum rerum decreto
patrum comprobatum est.

1 LIX. Caesaris deinde testamentum apertum est,
quo C. Octavium, nepotem sororis suae Iuliae,
adoptabat. De cuius origine, etiam si praeveniet,[1]
pauca dicenda sunt. Fuit C. Octavius ut non patricia,
2 ita admodum speciosa equestri genitus familia, gravis,
sanctus, innocens, dives. Hic praetor inter nobilis-
simos viros creatus primo loco, cum ei dignatio Iulia
genitam Atiam conciliasset uxorem, ex eo honore
sortitus Macedoniam appellatusque in ea[2] imperator,
decedens ad petitionem consulatus obiit praetextato
relicto filio. Quem C. Caesar, maior eius avunculus,
3 educatum apud Philippum vitricum dilexit ut suum,
natumque annos duodeviginti Hispaniensis militiae
adsecutum se postea comitem habuit, numquam aut

---

[1] praeveniet *Ellis*; praevenit et *AP*; per se nitet
Burman.
[2] in eam *AP*; *corrected by Gelenius*; ex ea *Ursinus*.

---

a i.e. on his contemplated departure for the Parthian
expedition.
b It may be that Velleius means simply "son" as was
indeed the fact, and that *liberos* is a rhetorical plural like
that in Cic. *Phil.* i. 1. 1. It is clear from *Phil.* i. 13. 31 that
Cicero is referring to but one.
c When the Thirty Tyrants were overthrown and de-
mocracy was restored under Thrasybulus.

call Caesar "tyrant" placed his deed in a better
light. Dolabella, whom Caesar had named for the
consulship, with the intention of putting him in
his own place,[a] had already seized the fasces and
the insignia of that office. Having summoned the
senate, Antonius, acting as the guarantor of peace,
sent his own sons [b] to the capitol as hostages and
thus gave his assurance to the slayers of Caesar that
they might come down in safety. On the motion
of Cicero the famous precedent of the Athenians [c]
granting amnesty for past acts was approved by
decree of the senate.

LIX. Caesar's will was then opened, by which he
adopted Gaius Octavius, the grandson of his sister
Julia. Of the origin of Octavius I must say a few
words, even if the account comes before its proper
place. Gaius Octavius, his father, though not of
patrician birth, was descended from a very prominent
equestrian family, and was himself a man of dignity,
of upright and blameless life, and of great wealth.
Chosen praetor at the head of the poll among a list
of candidates of noble birth, this distinction won
for him a marriage alliance with Atia, a daughter
of Julia. After he had filled the office of praetor,
the province of Macedonia fell to his lot, where he
was honoured with the title of imperator. He was
returning thence to sue for the consulship when he
died on the way, leaving a son still in his early teens.[d]
Though he had been reared in the house of his stepfather, Philippus, Gaius Caesar, his great-uncle, loved
this boy as his own son. At the age of eighteen
Octavius followed Caesar to Spain in his campaign
there, and Caesar kept him with him thereafter as his

[d] Literally "still wearing the praetexta."

alio usum hospitio quam suo aut alio vectum vehiculo,
4 pontificatusque sacerdotio puerum honoravit. Et
patratis bellis civilibus ad erudiendam liberalibus
disciplinis singularis indolem iuvenis Apolloniam eum
in studia miserat, mox belli Getici ac deinde Parthici
5 habiturus commilitonem. Cui ut est nuntiatum de
caede avunculi, cum protinus ex vicinis legionibus
centuriones suam suorumque militum operam ei
pollicerentur neque eam spernendam Salvidienus et
Agrippa dicerent, ille festinans pervenire in urbem
omnem ordinem ac rationem[1] et necis et testamenti
6 Brundusii comperit. Cui adventanti Romam inmanis
amicorum occurrit frequentia, et cum intraret urbem,
solis orbis super caput eius curvatus aequaliter rotun-
datusque in colorem arcus velut coronam[2] tanti mox
viri capiti imponens conspectus est.
1 LX. Non placebat Atiae matri Philippoque vitrico
adiri nomen invidiosae fortunae Caesaris, sed ad-
serebant salutaria rei publicae terrarumque orbis
fata conditorem conservatoremque Romani nominis.
2 Sprevit itaque caelestis animus humana consilia et
cum periculo potius summa quam tuto humilia proposuit sequi maluitque avunculo et Caesari de se
quam vitrico credere,[3] dictitans nefas esse, quo

---

[1] ordinem ac rationem *Muncker*; ordinationem *AP*.
[2] *The passage is corrupt as it stands. The general sense is, however, clear from the following passage in Seneca*, Nat. Quaest. *I. 2. 1;* memoriae proditum est, quo die Divus Augustus . . . intravit, circa solem visum coloris varii circulum, qualis esse in arcu solet; hunc Graeci halo vocant, nos dicere coronam aptissime possimus.
[3] credere *Gelenius*; cedere *AP*.

---

[a] See note on text.

companion, allowing him to share the same roof and ride in the same carriage, and though he was still a boy, honoured him with the pontificate. When the civil war was over, with a view to training his remarkable talents by liberal studies, he sent him to Apollonia to study, with the intention of taking him as his companion in his contemplated wars with the Getae and the Parthians. At the first announcement of his uncle's death, although the centurions of the neighbouring legions at once proffered their own services and those of their men, and Salvidienus and Agrippa advised him to accept the offer, he made such haste to arrive in the city that he was already at Brundisium when he learned the details of the assassination and the terms of his uncle's will. As he approached Rome an enormous crowd of his friends went out to meet him, and at the moment of his entering the city, men saw above his head the orb of the sun with a circle about it, coloured like the rainbow,ᵃ seeming thereby to place a crown upon the head of one destined soon to greatness.

LX. His mother Atia and Philippus his stepfather disliked the thought of his assuming the name of Caesar, whose fortune had aroused such jealousy, but the fates that preside over the welfare of the commonwealth and of the world took into their own keeping the second founder and preserver of the Roman name. His divine soul therefore spurned the counsels of human wisdom, and he determined to pursue the highest goal with danger rather than a lowly estate and safety. He preferred to trust the judgement concerning himself of a great-uncle who was Caesar, rather than that of a stepfather, saying that he had no right to think himself

179

nomine Caesari dignus esset visus, semet ipsum sibi[1]
3 videri indignum. Hunc protinus Antonius consul
superbe excepit (neque is erat contemptus, sed metus)
vixque admisso in Pompeianos hortos loquendi secum
tempus dedit, mox etiam velut insidiis eius petitus
sceleste insimulare coepit, in quo turpiter depre-
4 hensa eius vanitas est. Aperte deinde Antonii ac
Dolabellae consulum ad nefandam dominationem
erupit furor. Sestertium septiens miliens, deposi-
tum a C. Caesare ad aedem Opis, occupatum ab
Antonio, actorum eiusdem insertis falsis civitatibus
inmunitatibusque[2] corrupti commentarii atque omnia
pretio temperata, vendente rem publicam consule.
5 Idem provinciam D. Bruto designato consuli decretam
Galliam occupare statuit, Dolabella transmarinas
decrevit sibi ; interque naturaliter dissimillimos ac
diversa volentis crescebat odium, eoque C. Caesar
iuvenis cotidianis Antonii petebatur insidiis.
1 LXI. Torpebat oppressa dominatione Antonii
civitas. Indignatio et dolor omnibus, vis ad resis-
tendum nulli aderat, cum C. Caesar undevicesimum
annum ingressus, mira ausus ac summa consecutus
privato consilio maiorem senatu pro re publica ani-

---

[1] sibi *added by Lipsius.*
[2] civitatibus inmunitatibusque *Ellis* ; civitatibusque *AP.*

---

[a] From the period of his adoption Octavius is regularly
spoken of as Gaius Caesar, and Julius Caesar, who was
really his great-uncle, as his father.

unworthy of the name of which Caesar had thought
him worthy. On his arrival, Antony, the consul,
received him haughtily—out of fear, however,
rather than contempt—and grudgingly gave him,
after he had secured admission to Pompey's gardens,
a few moments' conversation with himself; and it
was not long before Antony began wickedly to
insinuate that an attempt had been made upon his
life through plots fostered by Octavius. In this
matter, however, the untrustworthiness of the
character of Antony was disclosed, to his discredit.
Later the mad ambition of Antony and Dolabella,
the consuls, for the attainment of an unholy despotism,
burst into view. The seven hundred thousand
sestertia deposited by Gaius Caesar in the temple
of Ops were seized by Antony; the records of his
acts were tampered with by the insertion of forged
grants of citizenship and immunity; and all his
documents were garbled for money considerations,
the consul bartering away the public interests.
Antony resolved to seize the province of Gaul,
which had been assigned by decree to Decimus
Brutus, the consul designate, while Dolabella had the
provinces beyond the sea assigned to himself.
Between men by nature so unlike and with such
different aims there grew up a feeling of hatred,
and in consequence, the young Gaius Caesar was
the object of daily plots on the part of Antony.

LXI. The state languished, oppressed by the
tyranny of Antony. All felt resentment and indignation, but no one had the power to resist, until Gaius
Caesar,[a] who had just entered his nineteenth year,
with marvellous daring and supreme success, showed
by his individual sagacity a courage in the state's

2 mum habuit primumque a Calatia, mox a Casilino
veteranos excivit paternos ; quorum exemplum secuti
alii brevi in formam iusti coiere exercitus. Mox cum
Antonius occurrisset exercitui, quem ex transmarinis
provinciis Brundusium venire iusserat, legio Martia
et quarta cognita et senatus voluntate et tanti iuvenis
indole sublatis signis ad Caesarem se contulerunt.

3 Eum senatus honoratum equestri statua, quae
hodieque in rostris posita aetatem eius scriptura
indicat (qui honor non alii per trecentos annos quam
L. Sullae et Cn. Pompeio et C. Caesari contigerat),
pro praetore una cum consulibus designatis Hirtio
et Pansa bellum cum Antonio gerere iussit. Id[1]

4 ab eo annum agente vicesimum fortissime circa
Mutinam administratum est et D. Brutus obsidione
liberatus. Antonius turpi ac nuda fuga coactus
deserere Italiam, consulum autem alter in acie, alter
post paucos dies ex volnere mortem obiit.

1 LXII. Omnia ante quam fugaretur Antonius
honorifice a senatu in Caesarem exercitumque eius
decreta sunt maxime auctore Cicerone ; sed ut
recessit metus, erupit voluntas protinusque Pom-
2 peianis partibus rediit animus. Bruto Cassioque
provinciae, quas iam ipsi sine ullo senatus consulto

---

[1] id *added by Gelenius.*

---

a March 43 B.C. Pansa was mortally wounded at Forum
Gallorum. Hirtius fell a few days later in an assault upon
Antony's camp.

behalf which exceeded that of the senate. He summoned his father's veterans first from Calatia then from Casilinum ; other veterans followed their example, and in a short time they united to form a regular army. Not long afterwards, when Antony had met the army which he had ordered to assemble at Brundisium from the provinces beyond the sea, two legions, the Martian and the fourth, learning of the feeling of the senate and the spirit shown by this courageous youth, took up their standards and went over to Caesar. The senate honoured him with an equestrian statue, which is still standing upon the rostra and testifies to his years by its inscription. This is an honour which in three hundred years had fallen to the lot of Lucius Sulla, Gnaeus Pompeius, and Gaius Caesar, and to these alone. The senate commissioned him, with the rank of propraetor, to carry on the war against Antony in conjunction with Hirtius and Pansa, the consuls designate. Now in his twentieth year, he conducted the war at Mutina with great bravery, and the siege of Decimus Brutus there was raised. Antony was compelled to abandon Italy in undisguised and disgraceful flight. Of the two consuls, the one died upon the field of battle, and the other of his wound a few days afterwards.[a]

LXII. Before the defeat of Antony the senate, chiefly on the motion of Cicero, passed all manner of resolutions complimentary to Caesar and his army. But, now that their fears had vanished, their real feelings broke through their disguise, and the Pompeian party once more took heart. By vote of the senate, Brutus and Cassius were now confirmed in possession of the provinces which they

occupaverant, decretae, laudati quicumque se iis
exercitus tradidissent, omnia transmarina imperia
3 eorum commissa arbitrio.[1] Quippe M. Brutus et
C. Cassius, nunc metuentes arma Antonii, nunc ad
augendam eius invidiam simulantes se metuere,
testati edictis libenter se vel in perpetuo exilio vic-
turos, dum rei publicae[2] constaret concordia, nec
ullam belli civilis praebituros materiam, plurimum
sibi honoris esse in conscientia facti sui, profecti
urbe atque Italia, intento ac pari[3] animo sine auctoritate publica provincias exercitusque occupaverant et,
ubicumque ipsi essent, praetexentes esse rem publicam, pecunias etiam, quae ex transmarinis provinciis
Romam ab quaestoribus deportabantur, a volentibus
4 acceperant. Quae omnia senatus decretis comprensa
et comprobata sunt et D. Bruto, quod alieno beneficio
viveret, decretus triumphus, Pansae atque Hirtii
5 corpora publica sepultura honorata, Caesaris adeo
nulla habita mentio, ut legati, qui ad exercitum
eius missi erant, iuberentur summoto eo milites
adloqui. Non fuit tam ingratus exercitus, quam
fuerat senatus ; nam cum eam iniuriam dissimulando
Caesar ipse[4] ferret, negavere milites sine imperatore

[1] arbitrio *A* ; imperio *P*.
[2] rei publicae *Gelenius*; resp. *AP*.
[3] ac pari *AP*; ac parato *Burman*.
[4] Caesar ipse *Halm*; Caesari *AP*.

had seized upon their own authority without any
decree of the senate; the armies which had gone
over to them were formally commended; and Brutus
and Cassius were given all authority and jurisdiction
beyond the sea. It is true that these two men had
issued manifestoes—at first in real fear of armed
violence at the hands of Antony, and later to
increase Antony's unpopularity, with the pretence
of fear — manifestos in which they declared that
for the sake of ensuring harmony in the republic
they were even ready to live in perpetual exile, that
they would furnish no grounds for civil war, and that
the consciousness of the service they had rendered
by their act was ample reward. But, when they had
once left Rome and Italy behind them, by deliberate
agreement and without government sanction they
had taken possession of provinces and armies, and
under the pretence that the republic existed wherever
they were, they had gone so far as to receive from
the quaestors, with their own consent, it is true, the
moneys which these men were conveying to Rome
from the provinces across the sea. All these acts
were now included in the decrees of the senate and
formally ratified. Decimus Brutus was voted a
triumph, presumably because, thanks to another's
services, he had escaped with his life. Hirtius and
Pansa were honoured with a public funeral. Of
Caesar not a word was said. The senate even went
so far as to instruct its envoys, who had been sent
to Caesar's army, to confer with the soldiers alone,
without the presence of their general. But the
ingratitude of the senate was not shared by the
army; for, though Caesar himself pretended not
to see the slight, the soldiers refused to listen to

6 suo ulla se audituros mandata. Hoc est illud tempus,
quo Cicero insito amore Pompeianarum partium
Caesarem laudandum et tollendum censebat, cum
aliud diceret, aliud intellegi vellet.

1 LXIII. Interim Antonius fuga transgressus Alpes,
primo per conloquia repulsus a M. Lepido, qui pontifex
maximus in C. Caesaris locum furto creatus decreta
sibi Hispania adhuc in Gallia morabatur, mox saepius
in conspectum veniens militum (cum et Lepido
omnes imperatores forent meliores et multis Antonius,
dum erat sobrius), per aversa castrorum proruto vallo
a[1] militibus receptus est. Qui titulo imperii cedebat

2 Lepido, cum summa virium penes eum foret. Sub
Antonii ingressum in castra Iuventius Laterensis,
vir vita ac morte consentaneus, cum acerrime
suasisset Lepido, ne se cum Antonio hoste iudicato
iungeret, inritus consilii gladio se ipse transfixit.

3 Plancus deinde dubia, id est sua, fide, diu quarum
esset partium secum luctatus ac sibi difficile consentiens, et nunc adiutor D. Bruti designati consulis,
collegae sui, senatuique se litteris venditans, mox
eiusdem proditor, Asinius autem Pollio firmus pro-

---

[1] a *added by Heinsius.*

---

[a] The equivocation is on the verb *tollere* which means, on
the one hand, to "lift up" or "extol," and on the other to
"remove."

186

any orders without the presence of their commander.
It was at this time that Cicero, with his deep-seated
attachment for the Pompeian party, expressed the
opinion, which said one thing and meant another,
to the effect that Caesar " should be commended
and then—elevated." [a]

LXIII. Meanwhile Antony in his flight had crossed
the Alps, and at first made overtures to Marcus
Lepidus which were rejected. Now Lepidus had
surreptitiously been made pontifex in Caesar's place,
and, though the province of Spain had been assigned
to him, was still lingering in Gaul. Later, however,
Antony showed himself several times to the soldiers
of Lepidus, and being, when sober, better than most
commanders, whereas none could be worse than
Lepidus, he was admitted by the soldiers through
a breach which they made in the fortifications in the
rear of the camp. Antony still permitted Lepidus
to hold the nominal command, while he himself held
the real authority. At the time when Antony
entered the camp, Juventius Laterensis, who had
strongly urged Lepidus not to ally himself with
Antony now that he had been declared an enemy of
the state, finding his advice of no avail ran himself
through with his own sword, consistent unto death.
Later Plancus and Pollio both handed over their
armies to Antony. Plancus, with his usual loose
ideas of loyalty, after a long debate with himself as
to which party to follow, and much difficulty in
sticking to his resolutions when formed, now pretended to co-operate with his colleague, Decimus
Brutus, the consul designate, thus seeking to in-
gratiate himself with the senate in his dispatches,
and again betrayed him. But Asinius Pollio, stead-

posito et Iulianis partibus fidus, Pompeianis adversus, uterque exercitus tradidere Antonio.

1   LXIV. D. Brutus desertus primo a Planco, postea etiam insidiis eiusdem petitus, paulatim relinquente eum exercitu fugiens in hospitis cuiusdam nobilis viri, nomine Cameli, domo ab iis, quos miserat Antonius, iugulatus est iustissimasque optime de se merito viro C. Caesari poenas dedit, cuius cum primus 2 omnium amicorum fuisset, interfector fuit et fortunae, ex qua fructum tulerat, invidiam in auctorem relegabat censebatque aequum, quae acceperat a Caesare retinere, Caesarem, qui illa dederat, perire.

3   Haec[1] sunt tempora, quibus M. Tullius continuis actionibus aeternas Antonii memoriae inussit notas, sed hic fulgentissimo et caelesti ore, at tribunus Cannutius canina[2] rabie lacerabat Antonium. Utri- 4 que vindicta libertatis morte stetit ; sed tribuni sanguine commissa proscriptio, Ciceronis velut[3] satiato Antonio paene finita. Lepidus deinde a senatu hostis iudicatus est, ut ante fuerat Antonius.

1   LXV. Tum inter eum Caesaremque et Antonium commercia epistularum et condicionum facta[4] mentio, cum Antonius subinde Caesarem admoneret, quam[5] inimicae ipsi Pompeianae partes forent et in quod iam emersissent fastigium et quanto Ciceronis studio

---

   [1] peristhaec *A* ; peris. Haec *P* ; perire *vel* perisse *Rhenanus in marg.*

   [2] canina *Ruhnken* ; continna *A* ; continua *P*.

   [3] velut *Puteanus* ; vel *AP* ; ut *Halm.*

   [4] facta *Burer* ; iacta *AP.*

   [5] Antonius subinde Caesarem admoneret, et quam *Bipont.*; et subinde . . . quam *AP.*

fast in his resolution, remained loyal to the Julian
party and continued to be an adversary of the
Pompeians.

LXIV. Decimus Brutus, first abandoned by
Plancus, and later actually the object of his plots,
deserted little by little by his army, and now a fugitive,
was slain by the emissaries of Antony in the house
of a noble named Camelus with whom he had taken
refuge. He thus met his just deserts and paid the
penalty of his treason to Gaius Caesar by whom
he had been treated so well. He who had been the
foremost of all Caesar's friends became his assassin,
and while he threw upon Caesar the odious responsibility for the fortune of which he himself had reaped
the benefits, he thought it fair to retain what he
had received at Caesar's hands, and for Caesar, who
had given it all, to perish.

This is the period when Cicero in a series of speeches
branded the memory of Antony for all time to come.
Cicero assailed Antony with his brilliant and god-
given tongue, whereas Cannutius the tribune tore
him to pieces with the ravening of a mad dog. Each
paid with his life for his defence of liberty. The
proscription was ushered in by the slaying of the
tribune; it practically ended with the death of
Cicero, as though Antony were now sated with
blood. Lepidus was now declared by the senate
an enemy of the state, as Antony had been before
him.

LXV. Then began an interchange of letters
between Lepidus, Caesar, and Antony, and terms
of agreement were suggested. Antony reminded
Caesar how hostile to him the Pompeian party was,
to what a height they had now risen, and how

Brutus Cassiusque attollerentur, denuntiaretque se cum Bruto Cassioque, qui iam decem et septem legionum potentes erant, iuncturum vires suas, si Caesar eius aspernaretur concordiam, diceretque plus Caesarem patris quam se amici ultioni debere. Tum[1]

2 inita potentiae societas et hortantibus orantibusque exercitibus inter Antonium etiam et Caesarem facta adfinitas, cum esset privigna Antonii desponsata Caesari. Consulatumque iniit Caesar pridie quam viginti annos impleret decimo Kal. Octobres cum collega Q. Pedio post urbem conditam[2] annis septingentis et novem,[3] ante duos et septuaginta, quam tu, M. Vinici, consulatum inires.

3 Vidit hic annus Ventidium, per quam urbem inter captivos Picentium in triumpho ductus erat, in ea consularem praetextam iungentem praetoria. Idem hic postea triumphavit.

1 LXVI. Furente deinde Antonio simulque Lepido, quorum uterque, ut praediximus, hostes iudicati erant, cum ambo mallent sibi nuntiari, quid passi essent,[4] quam quid meruissent, repugnante Caesare, sed frustra adversus duos, instauratum Sullani

2 exempli malum, proscriptio. Nihil tam indignum illo tempore fuit, quam quod aut Caesar aliquem proscribere coactus est aut ab ullo Cicero proscriptus

---

[1] tum *or* tunc *Buver*; tur *AP*; tum igitur *Halm.*
[2] abhinc *after* conditam *deleted by Gelenius.*
[3] DCCVIIII *Gelenius*; ACCVIIII *AP*; DCCXI *Aldus.*
[4] cum . . . essent] *the passage is clearly corrupt, but as yet no satisfactory emendation has been offered.*

---

[a] 43 B.C.
[b] Consul suffectus in 43 B.C., after Octavianus resigned the office. Ventidius and his mother had been made prisoners in the Social War, and had been led in triumph by

zealously Cicero was extolling Brutus and Cassius. Antony threatened to join forces with Brutus and Cassius, who had now control of seventeen legions, if Caesar rejected this friendly overture, and said that Caesar was under greater obligations to avenge a father than he to avenge a friend. Then began their partnership in political power, and, on the urgent advice and entreaty of the armies, a marriage alliance was also made between Antony and Caesar, in which Antony's stepdaughter was betrothed to Caesar. Caesar, with Quintus Pedius as colleague, entered on the consulship [a] one day before the completion of his twentieth year on the twenty-second of September, seven hundred and nine years after the founding of the city and seventy-two, Marcus Vinicius, before the beginning of your consulship.

This year saw Ventidius [b] joining the robes of the consular office to those of praetor in the very city in which he had been led in triumph among the Picentine captives. He also lived to celebrate a triumph of his own.

LXVI. Then the vengeful resentment of Antony and Lepidus—for each of them had been declared public enemies, as has already been stated, and both preferred to hear accounts of what they had suffered, rather than of what they had deserved, at the hands of the senate—renewed the horror of the Sullan proscription. Caesar protested, but without avail, being but one against two. The climax of the shame of this time was that Caesar should be forced to proscribe any one, or that any one should

Pompeius Strabo in 89 B.C. Ventidius celebrated his own triumph in 38 B.C.

est. Abscisaque scelere Antonii vox publica est,
cum eius salutem nemo defendisset, qui per tot annos
et publicam civitatis et privatam civium defenderat.
3 Nihil tamen egisti, M. Antoni (cogit enim excedere
propositi formam operis erumpens animo ac pectore
indignatio) nihil, inquam, egisti mercedem caele-
stissimi oris et clarissimi capitis abscisi numerando
auctoramentoque funebri ad conservatoris quondam
rei publicae tantique consulis inritando necem.
4 Rapuisti tu M.[1] Ciceroni lucem sollicitam et aetatem
senilem et vitam miseriorem te principe quam sub
te triumviro mortem, famam vero gloriamque fac-
torum atque dictorum adeo non abstulisti, ut auxeris.
5 Vivit vivetque per omnem saeculorum memoriam,
dumque hoc vel forte vel providentia vel utcumque
constitutum rerum naturae corpus, quod ille paene
solus Romanorum animo vidit, ingenio complexus
est, eloquentia inluminavit, manebit incolume,
comitem aevi sui laudem Ciceronis trahet omnisque
posteritas illius in te scripta mirabitur, tuum in eum
factum execrabitur citiusque e mundo genus hominum
quam Ciceronis nomen [2] cedet.
1 LXVII. Huius totius temporis fortunam ne deflere
quidem quisquam satis digne potuit, adeo nemo

---

[1] tu M. *Gelenius*; tum *AP*.
[2] Ciceronis nomen *supplied by Laurent*.

proscribe the name of Cicero. By the crime of Antony, when Cicero was beheaded the voice of the people was severed, nor did anyone raise a hand in defence of the man who for so many years had protected the interests both of the state and of the private citizen. But you accomplished nothing, Mark Antony—for the indignation that surges in my breast compels me to exceed the bounds I have set for my narrative—you accomplished nothing, I say, by offering a reward for the sealing of those divine lips and the severing of that illustrious head, and by encompassing with a death-fee the murder of so great a consul and of the man who once had saved the state. You took from Marcus Cicero a few anxious days, a few senile years, a life which would have been more wretched under your domination than was his death in your triumvirate; but you did not rob him of his fame, the glory of his deeds and words, nay you but enhanced them. He lives and will continue to live in the memory of the ages, and so long as this universe shall endure—this universe which, whether created by chance, or by divine providence, or by whatever cause, he, almost alone of all the Romans, saw with the eye of his mind, grasped with his intellect, illumined with his eloquence—so long shall it be accompanied throughout the ages by the fame of Cicero. All posterity will admire the speeches that he wrote against you, while your deed to him will call forth their execrations, and the race of man shall sooner pass from the world than the name of Cicero be forgotten

LXVII. No one has even been able to deplore the fortunes of this whole period with such tears as the theme deserves, much less can one now describe it

exprimere verbis potest. Id tamen notandum est,
2 fuisse in proscriptos uxorum fidem summam, libertorum médiam, servorum aliquam, filiorum nullam ;
adeo difficilis est hominibus utcumque conceptae
3 spei mora. Ne quid ulli sanctum relinqueretur,
velut[1] in dotem invitamentumque sceleris Antonius
L. Caesarem avunculum, Lepidus Paulum fratrem
proscripserant ; nec Planco gratia defuit ad im-
petrandum, ut frater eius Plancus Plotius pro-
4 scriberetur. Eoque inter iocos militaris, qui currum
Lepidi Plancique secuti erant, inter execrationem
civium usurpabant hunc versum :

De germanis, non de Gallis duo triumphant
consules.

1 LXVIII. Suo praeteritum loco referatur ; neque
enim persona umbram actae rei capit. Dum in acie
Pharsalica acriter[2] de summa rerum Caesar dimicat,
M. Caelius, vir eloquio animoque Curioni simillimus,
sed in utroque perfectior nec minus ingeniose
nequam, cum ne modica quidem solvere ac servari
posset[3] (quippe peior illi res familiaris quam mens
2 erat), in praetura novarum tabularum auctor extitit
nequiitque senatus et consulis auctoritate[4] deterreri ;

---

[1] velut *Gelenius*; vel *AP*; ut *Halm.*
[2] acriter *Haupt*; Africaque *AP.*
[3] ne modica quidem solvere ac servari posset *Ellis*; immodica (in modica *P*) quidem servari posset *AP*; ne
modica quidem re servari posset *Halm.*
[4] et consulis (*after Lipsius*) auctoritate *Cludius*; et
auctoritate COSS. *AP.*

---

[a] *Germanus* means "full-brother" as opposed to half

in words. One thing, however, demands comment, that toward the proscribed their wives showed the greatest loyalty, their freedmen not a little, their slaves some, their sons none. So hard is it for men to brook delays in the realization of their ambitions, whatever they may be. That no sacred tie might escape inviolate, and, as it were, as an inducement and invitation to such atrocities, Antony had Lucius Caesar, his uncle, placed upon the list, and Lepidus his own brother Paulus. Plancus also had sufficient influence to cause his brother Plancus Plotius to be enrolled among the proscribed. And so the troops who followed the triumphal car of Lepidus and Plancus kept repeating among the soldiers' jests, but amid the execrations of the citizens, the following line:

Brothers-*german* our two consuls triumph over, not the *Gauls.*[a]

LXVIII. Let me now relate a matter which I omitted in its proper place, for the person involved does not permit the deed to rest in obscurity. This person is Marcus Caelius, a man closely resembling Curio in eloquence and in spirit, though more than his peer in either, and quite as clever in his worthlessness. Being quite as bankrupt in property as in character and unable to save himself by paying even a reasonable proportion of his debts, he came forward in his praetorship, at the time when Caesar was fighting for the control of affairs on the field of Pharsalus,[b] as the author of a law for the cancellation of debts, nor could he be deterred from his course by the authority of either the senate or the consul,

brother. The same pun is found in Quint. iii. 8. 29 "Germanum Cimber occidit."   48 B.C.

accito etiam Milone Annio, qui non impetrato reditu
Iulianis partibus infestus erat, in urbe seditionem,
in agris haud[1] occulte bellicum tumultum movens,
primo summotus a re publica, mox consularibus
3 armis auctore senatu circa Thurios oppressus est. In[2]
incepto pari similis fortuna Milonis fuit, qui Comp-
sam in Hirpinis oppugnans ictusque lapide cum[3]
P. Clodio, tum patriae, quam armis petebat, poenas
dedit, vir inquies et ultra fortem temerarius.

4 Quatenus autem aliquid ex omissis peto, notetur
immodica et intempestiva libertate usos adversus
C. Caesarem Marullum Epidium Flavumque Caese-
tium tribunos plebis, dum arguunt in eo regni
voluntatem, paene vim dominationis experti. In
5 hoc tamen saepe lacessiti principis ira excessit, ut
censoria potius contentus nota quam animadversione
dictatoria summoveret eos a re publica testaretur-
que esse sibi miserrimum, quod aut natura sua ei
excedendum foret aut minuenda dignitas. Sed ad
ordinem revertendum est.

1 LXIX. Iam et Dolabella in Asia C. Trebonium
consularem, cui succedebat, fraude deceptum Zmyr-
nae occiderat, virum adversus merita Caesaris
ingratissimum participemque caedis eius, a quo
2 ipse in consulare provectus fastigium fuerat; et

---

[1] in agris haud *Mommsen*; haud magis *AP*; at in agris
Lipsius.
[2] in *added by Madvig.*   [3] cum *Orelli*; tum *AP*.

---

[a] For his conviction for the slaying of Clodius see
Chap. XLVII.   [b] 44 B.C.

Calling to his aid Milo Annius,[a] who was hostile to the Caesarian party because he had failed to secure from them his recall, he stirred up a sedition in the city, and openly raised armed bands in the country. He was first banished from the state and was later overcome at Thurii by the army of the consul, on the order of the senate. A like fortune attended a similar attempt by Milo. While besieging Compsa, a city of the Hirpini, he was struck by a stone, and thus the restless man, too reckless to be called brave, paid the penalty he owed to Publius Clodius and to his country, against which he was bearing arms.

While engaged in supplying omissions I should note the intemperate and untimely display of independence shown towards Caesar by Marullus Epidius and Flavus Caesetius, tribunes of the people,[b] who in charging him with the desire for the kingship, came near feeling the effects of his absolute power. Though Caesar was constantly provoked by them, the only outcome of his wrath was that he was satisfied to brand them through the employment of his power as censor, and refrained from punishing them as dictator by banishing them from the state; and he expressed his great regret that he had no alternative but to depart from his customary clemency or suffer loss of dignity. But I must now return to the regular order of my narrative.

LXIX. Meanwhile in Asia, Dolabella, who succeeded Gaius Trebonius as governor, had surprised the latter at Smyrna and put him to death, a man who had showed the basest ingratitude in return for Caesar's kindness, and had shared in the murder of him to whom he owed his advancement

197

C. Cassius acceptis a Statio Murco et Crispo Marcio,
praetoriis viris imperatoribusque, praevalidis in
Syria legionibus, inclusum Dolabellam, qui praeoccu-
pata Asia in Syriam pervenerat, Laodiciae expugnata
ea urbe interfecerat[1] (ita tamen, ut ad ictum[2] servi
sui Dolabella non segniter cervicem daret) et decem
legiones in eo tractu sui iuris fecerat ; et M. Brutus
3 C. Antonio, fratri M. Antonii, in Macedonia Vatinio-
que circa Dyrrachium volentis legiones extorserat
(sed Antonium bello lacessierat, Vatinium dignatione
obruerat, cum et Brutus cuilibet ducum praeferendus
videretur et Vatinius nulli non esset postferendus,
4 in quo deformitas corporis cum turpitudine certabat
ingenii, adeo ut animus eius dignissimo domicilio
inclusus videretur) eratque septem legionibus validus.
5 At[3] lege Pedia, quam consul Pedius collega
Caesaris tulerat, omnibus, qui Caesarem patrem
interfecerant, aqua ignique[4] interdictum erat. Quo
tempore Capito, patruus meus, vir ordinis senatorii,
6 Agrippae subscripsit in C. Cassium. Dumque ea in
Italia geruntur, acri atque prosperrimo bello Cassius
Rhodum, rem inmanis operis, ceperat, Brutus Lycios
devicerat, et inde in Macedoniam exercitus tra-
iecerant, cum per omnia repugnans naturae suae
Cassius etiam Bruti clementiam vinceret. Neque re-

---

[1] interfecerat *Rhenanus* (*or* confecerat) ; fecerat *AP*.
[2] ad ictum *Rhenanus* ; adiectum *AP*.
[3] at *Lipsius* ; et *AP* ; sed *Kreyssig*.
[4] damnatis *after* ignique *deleted by Delbenius*.

to the consulship. Dolabella had already occupied
Asia and had passed over into Syria when Gaius
Cassius, taking over their strong legions from Statius
Murcus and Crispus Marcius, both praetorians who
had been saluted as imperator by their troops, shut
him up in Laodicea and by taking that city had
caused his death; for Dolabella had promptly
offered his neck to the sword of his own slave.
Cassius also gained control of ten legions in that
part of the empire. Marcus Brutus had raised his
strength to seven legions by wresting their troops,
by voluntary transfer of allegiance, from Gaius
Antonius, the brother of Marcus Antonius, in
Macedonia, and from Vatinius in the vicinity of
Dyrrachium. Brutus had been obliged to offer
battle to Antony, but Vatinius he had overwhelmed
by the weight of his own reputation, since Brutus
was preferable to any general, while no man could
rank lower than Vatinius, whose deformity of body
was rivalled to such an extent by the baseness
of his character, that his spirit seemed to be housed
in an abode that was thoroughly worthy of it.

By the Pedian law, proposed by Pedius, Caesar's
colleague in the consulship, a decree of banishment
was passed upon all the assassins of Caesar. At
this time Capito, my uncle, a man of senatorial rank,
assisted Agrippa in securing the condemnation of
Gaius Cassius. While all this was taking place in
Italy, Cassius in a vigorous and successful campaign
had taken Rhodes, an undertaking of great difficulty.
Brutus had meanwhile conquered the Lycians. The
armies of both then crossed into Macedonia, where
Cassius, contrary to his nature, uniformly outdid
even Brutus in clemency. One will hardly find men

199

perias, quos aut pronior fortuna comitata sit aut veluti fatigata maturius destituerit quam Brutum et Cassium.

1 LXX. Tum Caesar et Antonius traiecerunt exercitus in Macedoniam et apud urbem Philippos cum Bruto Cassioque acie concurrerunt. Cornu, cui Brutus praeerat, impulsis hostibus castra Caesaris cepit (nam ipse Caesar, etiamsi infirmissimus valetudine erat, obibat munia ducis, oratus etiam ab Artorio medico, ne in castris remaneret, manifesta denuntiatione quietis territo), id autem, in quo Cassius fuerat, fugatum ac male mulcatum in altiora

2 se[1] receperat loca. Tum Cassius ex sua fortuna eventum collegae aestimans, cum dimisisset evocatum iussissetque nuntiare sibi, quae esset multitudo ac vis hominum, quae ad se tenderet, tardius eo nuntiante, cum in vicino esset agmen cursu ad eum tendentium neque pulvere facies aut signa denotari possent, existimans hostes esse, qui irruerent, lacerna caput circumdedit extentamque cervicem

3 interritus liberto praebuit. Deciderat Cassii caput, cum evocatus advenit nuntians Brutum esse victorem. Qui cum imperatorem prostratum videret, sequar, inquit, eum, quem mea occidit tarditas, et ita in gladium incubuit.

4 Post paucos deinde dies Brutus conflixit cum hostibus et victus acie cum in tumulum nocte ex fuga se recepisset, impetravit a Stratone Aegeate,

---

[1] se *added by Gelenius.*

* 42 B.C.

who were ever attended by a more favourable fortune than Brutus and Cassius, or who were more quickly deserted by her, as though she were weary.

LXX. Then Caesar and Antonius transported their armies to Macedonia, and met Brutus and Cassius in battle *a* near the city of Philippi. The wing under the command of Brutus, after defeating the enemy, captured Caesar's camp; for Caesar was performing his duties as commander although he was in the poorest of health, and had been urged not to remain in camp by Artorius his physician, who had been frightened by a warning which had appeared to him in his sleep. On the other hand, the wing commanded by Cassius had been routed and roughly handled, and had retreated with much loss to higher ground. Then Cassius, judging his colleague's success by his own fortune, sent a veteran with instructions to report to him what was the large force of men which was now bearing down in his direction. As the orderly was slow in reporting, and the force approaching at a run was now close, while their identity and their standards could not be recognized for the dust, imagining that the troops rushing on him were those of the enemy, he covered his head with his military cloak and undismayed presented his neck to the sword of his freedman. The head of Cassius had scarcely fallen when the orderly arrived with the report that Brutus was victorious. But when he saw his commander lying prostrate, he uttered the words, " I shall follow him whose death my tardiness has caused," and fell upon his sword.

A few days later Brutus met the enemy, and was beaten in battle. In retreat he withdrew at nightfall to a hill, and there prevailed upon Strato of Aegaeae,

familiari suo, ut manum morituro commodaret sibi ;
5 reiectoque laevo super caput brachio, cum mucro-
nem gladii eius dextera tenens sinistrae admovisset
mammillae ad eum ipsum locum, qua cor emicat,
impellens se in vulnus uno ictu transfixus expiravit
protinus.

1   LXXI. Messalla,[1] fulgentissimus iuvenis, proximus in illis castris Bruti Cassiique auctoritati, cum
essent qui eum ducem poscerent, servari beneficio
Caesaris maluit quam dubiam spem armorum temptare amplius ; nec aut Caesari quidquam ex victoriis
suis fuit laetius quam servasse Corvinum aut maius
exemplum hominis grati ac pii, quam Corvinus[2] in
Caesarem fuit.   Non aliud bellum cruentius caede
clarissimorum virorum fuit.   Tum Catonis filius
2 cecidit ; eadem Lucullum Hortensiumque, eminen-
tissimorum civium filios, fortuna abstulit ; nam
Varro ad ludibrium moriturus Antonii digna illo ac
vera de exitu eius magna cum libertate ominatus est.
Drusus Livius, Iuliae Augustae pater, et Varus
Quintilius ne temptata quidem hostis misericordia
alter se ipse in tabernaculo interemit, Varus autem
liberti, quem id facere coëgerat, manu, cum se
insignibus honorum velasset, iugulatus est.

1   LXXII. Hunc exitum M. Bruti partium septimum
et tricesimum annum agentis fortuna esse voluit,
incorrupto[3] animo eius in diem, quae illi omnes
2 virtutes unius temeritate facti[4] abstulit.   Fuit autem

---

[1] *Halm supplied* Corvinus *before* Messalla.
[2] Corvinus *AP* ; Corvini *Bothe and Halm.*
[3] incorrupto *Tollius* ; corrupto *AP.*
[4] facti *Rhenanus* ; fecit *AP.*

one of his household, to lend him his hand in his resolve to die. Raising his left arm above his head, and with his right holding the point of Strato's sword he brought it close to the left nipple, at the place where the heart beats, and throwing himself upon the sword he died at once, transfixed by the stroke.

LXXI. Messalla, a young man of brilliant parts, was next in authority to Brutus and Cassius in their camp. Although there were those who urged him to take command, he preferred to owe his safety to the kindness of Caesar than to try once again the doubtful hope of arms. Caesar, on his side, found no greater pleasure in his victories than in granting life to Corvinus, nor was there ever a better example of loyal gratitude than that shown by Corvinus to Caesar. No other war cost the blood of so many illustrious men. In that battle the son of Cato fell ; the same fortune carried off Lucullus and Hortensius, the sons of eminent citizens. Varro, when about to die, in mockery of Antony, with the utmost freedom of speech prophesied for Antony the death he deserved, a prophecy which came true. Drusus Livius, the father of Julia Augusta, and Quintilius Varus, without making any appeal for mercy, ended their lives. Livius died by his own hand in his tent ; Varus first covered himself with the insignia of his offices and then forced his freedman to commit the deed.

LXXII. This was the end reserved by fortune for the party of Marcus Brutus. He was in his thirty-seventh year, and had kept his soul free from corruption until this day, which, through the rashness of a single act, bereft him, together with his life, of all his virtuous qualities. Cassius was as much the

dux Cassius melior, quanto vir Brutus : **e** quibus
Brutum amicum habere malles, inimicum magis
·meres Cassium ; in altero maior vis, in altero
virtus : qui si vicissent, quantum rei publicae interfuit Caesarem potius habere quam Antonium principem, tantum retulisset habere Brutum quam Cassium.

3   Cn. Domitius, pater L. Domitii nuper a nobis visi,
eminentissimae ac nobilissimae simplicitatis viri,
avus huius Cn. Domitii, clarissimi iuvenis, occupatis
navibus cum magno sequentium consilia sua comitatu
fugae fortunaeque se commisit, semet ipso contentus
4 duce partium.   Statius Murcus, qui classi et custodiae
maris praefuerat, cum omni commissa sibi parte
exercitus naviumque Sex. Pompeium, Cn. Magni
filium, qui ex Hispania revertens Siciliam armis
5 occupaverat, petiit.   Ad quem et e Brutianis castris
et ex Italia aliisque terrarum partibus, quos praesenti periculo fortuna subduxerat, proscripti con-
fluebant : quippe nullum habentibus statum quilibet
dux erat idoneus, cum fortuna non electionem daret,
sed[1] perfugium ostenderet exitialemque tempesta-
tem fugientibus statio pro portu foret.

1   LXXIII. Hic adulescens erat studiis rudis, sermone
barbarus, impetu strenuus, manu promptus, cogitatu[2] celer, fide patri dissimillimus, libertorum
suorum libertus servorumque servus, speciosis in-

---

[1] sed *added by Gelenius.*
[2] cogitatu *Scheffer*; cogitator *AP.*

---

better general as Brutus was the better man. Of the two, one would rather have Brutus as a friend, but would stand more in fear of Cassius as an enemy. The one had more vigour, the other more virtue. As it was better for the state to have Caesar rather than Antony as emperor, so, had Brutus and Cassius been the conquerors, it would have been better for it to be ruled by Brutus rather than by Cassius.

Gnaeus Domitius, father of Lucius Domitius our late contemporary,[a] a man of eminent and noble simplicity, and grandfather of Gnaeus Domitius, a young man of distinction in our own day, seized a number of ships, and relying on himself to lead his party, accompanied by a large number of companions who followed his lead, entrusted himself to the fortunes of flight. Statius Murcus, who had had charge of the fleet and the patrolling of the seas, sought Sextus Pompey, son of Pompey the Great, with that portion of the army and of the fleet which had been entrusted to him. Pompey had returned from Spain and seized Sicily. The proscribed whom fortune had spared, at least from immediate peril, now flocked to him from the camp of Brutus, from Italy, and from other parts of the world. For men who had now no legal status any leader would do, since fortune gave them no choice, but held out a place of refuge, and as they fled from the storm of death any shelter served as a harbour.

LXXIII. Sextus was a young man without education, barbarous in his speech, vigorous in initiative, energetic and prompt in action as he was swift in expedients, in loyalty a marked contrast to his father, the freedman of his own freedmen and slave of his own slaves, envying those in high places only

2 videns, ut pareret humillimis. Quem senatus paene totus adhuc e Pompeianis constans partibus post Antonii a Mutina fugam eodem illo tempore, quo Bruto Cassioque transmarinas provincias decreverat, revocatum ex Hispania, ubi adversus eum clarissimum bellum Pollio Asinius praetorius gesserat, in paterna bona restituerat et orae maritimae praefecerat.

3 Is tum, ut praediximus, occupata Sicilia servitia fugitivosque in numerum exercitus sui recipiens magnum modum legionum effecerat perque Menam et Menecraten paternos libertos, praefectos classium, latrociniis ac praedationibus infestato mari ad se exercitumque tuendum rapto utebatur, cum eum non depuderet vindicatum armis ac ductu patris sui mare infestare piraticis sceleribus.

1 LXXIV. Fractis Brutianis Cassianisque partibus Antonius transmarinas obiturus provincias substitit. Caesar in Italiam se recepit eamque longe quam speraverat tumultuosiorem repperit. Quippe L.

2 Antonius consul, vitiorum fratris sui consors, sed virtutum, quae interdum in illo erant, expers, modo apud veteranos criminatus Caesarem, modo eos, qui iussa[1] divisione praediorum nominatisque coloniis agros amiserant, ad arma conciens magnum exercitum conflaverat. Ex altera parte uxor Antonii

---

[1] iussa *Heinsius*; iuste *AP*; iniusta (*or* iniuste) *Lipsius*.

to obey those in the lowest. The senate, which still consisted almost entirely of Pompeians, in the period which followed the flight of Antony from Mutina, and at the very time at which it had assigned to Brutus and Cassius the provinces across the sea, had recalled Sextus from Spain—where Pollio Asinius the praetorian had distinguished himself in his campaigns against him—restored him to his father's property, and had entrusted to him the guarding of the coast. Seizing Sicily, as we have said, and admitting into his army slaves and runaways, he had raised his legions to their full complement. He supported himself and his army on plunder, and through the agency of Menas and Menecrates, his father's freedmen, who were in charge of his fleet, he infested the seas by predatory and piratical expeditions ; nor was he ashamed thus to infest with piracy and its atrocities the sea which had been freed from it by his father's arms and leadership.

LXXIV. After the defeat of the party of Brutus and Cassius, Antony remained behind with the intention of visiting the provinces beyond the sea. Caesar returned to Italy, which he found in a much more troubled condition than he had expected. Lucius Antonius, the consul, who shared the faults of his brother but possessed none of the virtues which he occasionally showed, by making charges against Caesar before the veterans at one moment, and at the next inciting to arms those who had lost their farms when the division of lands was ordered and colonists assigned, had collected a large army.[a] In another quarter Fulvia, the wife of Antony, who

[a] 41 B.C.

Fulvia, nihil muliebre praeter corpus gerens, omnia
3 armis tumultuque miscebat. Haec belli sedem Praeneste ceperat ; Antonius pulsus undique viribus
Caesaris Perusiam se contulerat : Plancus, Antonianarum adiutor partium, spem magis ostenderat auxilii,
4 quam opem ferebat Antonio. Usus Caesar virtute
et fortuna sua Perusiam expugnavit. Antonium
inviolatum dimisit, in Perusinos magis ira militum
quam voluntate saevitum ducis : urbs incensa, cuius
initium incendii princeps eius loci fecit Macedonicus,
qui subiecto rebus ac penatibus suis igni transfixum
se gladio flammae intulit.

1　　LXXV. Per eadem tempora exarserat in Campania bellum, quod professus eorum, qui perdiderant
agros, patrocinium ciebat T. Claudius Nero praetorius et pontifex, Ti. Caesaris pater, magni vir[1]
animi doctissimique[2] et ingenii. Id quoque adventu
Caesaris sepultum atque discussum est.

2　　Quis fortunae mutationes, quis dubios rerum
humanarum casus satis mirari queat ? Quis non
diversa praesentibus contrariaque expectatis aut
3 speret aut timeat ? Livia, nobilissimi et fortissimi
viri Drusi Claudiani filia, genere, probitate, forma
Romanarum eminentissima, quam postea coniugem
Augusti vidimus, quam transgressi ad deos sacer-

---

[1] vir *P* ; viri *BA*.
[2] doctissimique *AP* ; rectissimique *Madvig* ; promptis-
simique *Ruhnken*.

had nothing of the woman in her except her sex, was creating general confusion by armed violence. She had taken Praeneste as her base of operations; Antonius, beaten on all sides by the forces of Caesar, had taken refuge in Perusia; Plancus, who abetted the faction of Antony, offered the hope of assistance, rather than gave actual help. Thanks to his own valour and his usual good fortune, Caesar succeeded in storming Perusia. He released Antonius unharmed; and the cruel treatment of the people of Perusia was due rather to the fury of the soldiery than to the wish of their commander. The city was burned. The fire was begun by Macedonicus, a leading man of the place who, after setting fire to his house and contents, ran himself through with his sword and threw himself into the flames.

LXXV. At the same period war broke out in Campania at the instigation of the ex-praetor and pontiff, Tiberius Claudius Nero, father of Tiberius Caesar, and a man of noble character and high intellectual training, who now came forward as the protector of those who had lost their lands. This war also was quickly extinguished and its embers scattered by the arrival of Caesar.

Who can adequately express his astonishment at the changes of fortune, and the mysterious vicissitudes in human affairs? Who can refrain from hoping for a lot different from that which he now has, or from dreading one that is the opposite of what he expects? Take for example Livia. She, the daughter of the brave and noble Drusus Claudianus, most eminent of Roman women in birth, in sincerity, and in beauty, she, whom we later saw as the wife of Augustus, and as his priestess and daughter

dotem ac filiam, tum fugiens mox futuri sui Caesaris arma ac manus[1] bimum hunc Tiberium Caesarem, vindicem Romani imperii futurumque eiusdem Caesaris filium, gestans sinu, per avia itinerum vitatis militum gladiis uno comitante, quo facilius occultaretur fuga, pervenit ad mare et cum viro Nerone pervecta in Siciliam est.

1 LXXVI. Quod alieno testimonium redderem, eo non fraudabo avum meum. Quippe C. Velleius, honoratissimo inter illos trecentos et sexaginta iudices loco a Cn. Pompeio lectus, eiusdem Marcique Bruti ac Ti. Neronis[2] praefectus fabrum, vir nulli secundus, in Campania digressu Neronis a Neapoli, cuius ob singularem cum eo amicitiam partium adiutor fuerat, gravis iam aetate et corpore cum 2 comes[3] esse non posset, gladio se ipse transfixit.

Inviolatam excedere Italia Caesar passus est[4] Fulviam Plancumque, muliebris fugae comitem. Nam Pollio Asinius cum septem legionibus, diu retenta in potestate Antonii Venetia, magnis speciosisque rebus circa Altinum aliasque eius regionis urbes editis, Antonium petens, vagum adhuc Domitium, quem digressum e Brutianis castris post caedem

---

[1] arma ac manus *Ellis*; arma *A*; arma nus *P*; arma minus *Voss followed by Halm.*

[2] Ti. Neronis *Aldus*; Tironis *A*; Tyronis *P*.

[3] cum comes *Aldus*; comes *B*; cum *AP*.

[4] est *added by Cludius.*

---

[a] By legal adoption.

[b] In Pompey's time the *iudices* were chosen from the senators, knights, and *tribuni aerarii*, in equal proportion.

after his deification, was then a fugitive before the arms and forces of the very Caesar who was soon to be her husband, carrying in her bosom her infant of two years, the present emperor Tiberius Caesar, destined to be the defender of the Roman empire and the son [a] of this same Caesar. Pursuing by-paths that she might avoid the swords of the soldiers, and accompanied by but one attendant, so as the more readily to escape detection in her flight, she finally reached the sea, and with her husband Nero made her escape by ship to Sicily.

LXXVI. I shall not deprive my own grandfather of the honourable mention which I should give to a stranger. Gaius Velleius, chosen to a most honourable position among the three hundred and sixty judges [b] by Gnaeus Pompey, prefect of engineers under Pompey, Marcus Brutus, and Tiberius Nero, and a man second to none, on the departure from Naples of Nero, whose partisan he had been on account of his close friendship, finding himself unable to accompany him on account of his age and infirmities, ran himself through with his sword in Campania.

Caesar allowed Fulvia to depart from Italy unharmed, and with her Plancus who accompanied the woman in her flight. As for Pollio Asinius, after he with his seven legions had long kept Venetia under the control of Antony, and after he had accomplished several brilliant exploits in the vicinity of Altinum and other cities of that region, when he was on his way to join Antony with these legions he won Domitius over to the cause of Antony by his counsel and by the pledge of immunity. Up to this time Domitius, who, as we have already said, had quitted the camp of Brutus after that leader's death and

211

eius praediximus et propriae classis factum ducem,
consiliis suis inlectum[1] ac fide data iunxit Antonio :
3 quo facto, quisquis aequum se praestiterit, sciat non
minus a Pollione in Antonium quam ab Antonio in
Pollionem esse conlatum. Adventus deinde in Italiam
Antonii apparatusque[2] contra eum Caesaris habuit
belli metum, sed pax circa Brundusium composita.
4 Per quae tempora Rufi Salvidieni scelesta consilia
patefacta sunt. Qui natus obscurissimis initiis parum
habebat summa accepisse et proximus a Cn. Pompeio
ipsoque Caesare equestris ordinis consul creatus esse,
nisi in id[3] ascendisset, e quo infra se et Caesarem
videret et rem publicam.
1 LXXVII. Tum expostulante consensu populi,
quem gravis urebat infesto mari annona, cum Pompeio quoque circa Misenum pax inita, qui haud
absurde, cum in navi Caesaremque et Antonium
cena exciperet, dixit in carinis suis se cenam dare,
referens hoc dictum ad loci nomen, in quo paterna
domus ab Antonio possidebatur. In hoc pacis
2 foedere placuit Siciliam Achaiamque Pompeio con-
cedere, in quo tamen animus inquies manere non
potuit. Id unum tantummodo salutare adventu suo
patriae attulit, quod omnibus proscriptis aliisque,
qui ad eum ex diversis causis fugerant, reditum

---

[1] inlectum *Gelenius*; electum *AP*.
[2] apparatusque *Sylburg*; praeparatusque *AP*; paratusque
Gelenius.
[3] in id *Puteanus*; in is *BA* ; simul *P*.

---

[a] 40 B.C.   [b] *i.e.* Octavianus.   [c] 39 B.C.
[d] Carinae, which also means "keels," was a residential
quarter in Rome between the Caelian and Esquiline Hills,
now *S. Pietro in Vincoli.*

had established himself in command of a fleet of his own, had remained at large. In view of this act of Pollio any fair judge will see that he rendered as great a service to Antony as Antony rendered to him. The return of Antony to Italy and Caesar's preparations against him gave rise to fears of war, but a peace was arranged at Brundisium.[a]

It was at this time that the criminal designs of Rufus Salvidienus were revealed. This man, sprung from the most obscure origin, was not satisfied with having received the highest honours in the state, and to have been the first man of equestrian rank after Gnaeus Pompey and Caesar[b] himself to be elected consul, but aspired to mount to a height where he might see both Caesar and the republic at his feet.

LXXVII. Then in response to a unanimous demand on the part of the people, who were now pinched by the high price of grain because the sea was infested by pirates, a peace was arranged[c] with Pompey also, in the neighbourhood of Misenum. Pompey entertained Caesar and Antony at dinner on board his ship, on which occasion he remarked, not without point, that he was giving the dinner on " his own keels," [d] thereby recalling the name of the quarter in which stood his father's house, now in the possession of Antony. By the terms of this treaty it was agreed that Sicily and Achaea should be conceded to Pompey, but his restless soul would not let him abide by the agreement. There was only one benefit which he rendered to his country by attending the conference, namely, the stipulation that all those who had been proscribed, or who for any other reason had taken refuge with him,

213

3 salutemque pactus est : quae res et alios clarissimos viros et Neronem Claudium et M. Silanum Sentiumque Saturninum et Arruntium ac Titium restituit rei publicae. Statium autem Murcum, qui adventu suo classisque celeberrimae vires eius duplicaverat, insimulatum falsis criminationibus, quia talem virum collegam officii Mena et Menecrates fastidierant, Pompeius in Sicilia interfecerat.

1 LXXVIII. Hoc tractu temporum Octaviam, sororem Caesaris, M. Antonius duxit uxorem. Redierat Pompeius in Siciliam, Antonius in transmarinas provincias, quas magnis momentis[1] Labienus, ex Brutianis castris profectus ad Parthos, perducto eorum exercitu in Syriam interfectoque legato Antonii concusserat ; qui virtute et ductu Ventidii una cum Parthorum copiis celeberrimoque iuvenum Pacoro, regis filio, extinctus est.

2 Caesar[2] per haec tempora, ne res disciplinae inimicissima, otium, corrumperet militem, crebris in Illyrico Delmatiaque expeditionibus patientia periculorum bellique experientia durabat exercitum.

3 Eadem tempestate Calvinus Domitius, cum ex consulatu obtineret Hispaniam, gravissimi comparandique antiquis exempli auctor fuit : quippe primi pili

---

[1] molimentis *Ruhnken*; momentis *AP*.
[2] interim *before* Caesar *deleted by Ellis as a gloss.*

---

[a] Statius Murcus had been made prefect of the fleet by Cassius. After the defeat of the republicans at Philippi, he carried his fleet over to Sextus Pompey in Sicily.

should be granted a safe return. Among other illustrious men, Nero Claudius, Marcus Silanus, Sentius Saturninus, Arruntius and Titius were thereby restored to the state. As to Statius Murcus, however, who had doubled Pompey's forces by joining him with his strong fleet,[a] Pompey had already put him to death in Sicily as the result of false accusations which had been brought against him, Menas and Menecrates having expressed a distaste for such a man as their colleague.

LXXVIII. It was during this period that Marcus Antonius espoused Octavia, the sister of Caesar. Pompey had now returned to Sicily, and Antony to the provinces across the sea, which Labienus had thrown into a panic in consequence of the great movements he had set on foot; for he had gone from the camp of Brutus to the Parthians, had led a Parthian army into Syria, and had slain a lieutenant of Antony. Thanks to the courageous generalship of Ventidius, Labienus perished in the battle [b] and with him the forces of the Parthians, including the most distinguished of their young men, Pacorus, son of the Parthian king.

During this time Caesar, wishing to keep his soldiers from being spoiled by idleness, the great enemy of discipline, was making frequent expeditions in Illyricum and Dalmatia and thus hardening his army by endurance of danger and experience in warfare. At this time also Calvinus Domitius, who, after filling the consulship, was now governor of Spain, executed a rigorous act of discipline comparable with the severity of the older days, in that he caused

[b] 38 B.C.

centurionem nomine Vibillium ob turpem ex acie
fugam fusti percussit.

1 LXXIX. Crescente in dies et classe et fama
Pompei Caesar molem belli eius suscipere statuit.
Aedificandis navibus contrahendoque militi ac remigi
navalibusque adsuescendo certaminibus atque exer-
citationibus praefectus est M. Agrippa, virtutis
nobilissimae, labore, vigilia, periculo invictus paren-
dique, sed uni, scientissimus, aliis sane imperandi
cupidus et per omnia extra dilationes positus con-
2 sultisque facta coniungens. Hic in Averno ac Lucrino
lacu speciosissima classe fabricata cotidianis exer-
citationibus militem remigemque ad summam et
militaris et maritimae rei perduxit scientiam. Hac
classi Caesar, cum prius despondente ei Nerone, cui
ante nupta fuerat Liviam, auspicatis rei publicae
ominibus duxisset eam uxorem, Pompeio Siciliaeque
3 bellum intulit. Sed virum humana ope invictum
graviter eo tempore fortuna concussit : quippe longe
maiorem partem classis circa Veliam Palinurique
promontorium adorta vis Africi laceravit ac distulit.
Ea patrando bello mora fuit, quod postea dubia et
4 interdum ancipiti fortuna gestum est. Nam et
classis eodem loco vexata est tempestate, et ut
navali primo proelio apud Mylas ductu Agrippae

---

a This punishment was called *fustuarium* and was inflicted
on Roman soldiers for desertion. When a soldier was condemned, the tribune touched him slightly with a stick, upon
which all the soldiers of the legion fell upon him with sticks
and stones and generally killed him on the spot (Smith,
Dict. Ant.). b 38 B.C.

a chief centurion by the name of Vibillius to be beaten to death[a] for cowardly flight from the line of battle.

LXXIX. As Pompey's fleet was growing daily, and his reputation as well, Caesar resolved to take up the burden of this new war. Marcus Agrippa was charged with constructing the ships, collecting soldiers and rowers, and familiarizing them with naval contests and manœuvres. He was a man of distinguished character, unconquerable by toil, loss of sleep or danger, well disciplined in obedience, but to one man alone, yet eager to command others ; in whatever he did he knew no such thing as delay, but with him action went hand in hand with conception. Building an imposing fleet in lakes Avernus and Lucrinus, by daily drills he brought the soldiers and the oarsmen to a thorough knowledge of fighting on land and at sea. With this fleet Caesar made war on Pompey in Sicily,[b] after he had espoused Livia, who was given to him in marriage by her former husband[c] under circumstances which augured well for the state. But this man, unconquerable by human power, received at this time a heavy blow at the hands of fortune, since the greater part of his fleet was wrecked and scattered in the vicinity of Velia and Cape Palinurus by a violent scirocco. This delayed finishing the war, which, however, was subsequently carried on with shifting and sometimes doubtful fortune. For Caesar's fleet was again buffeted by a storm in the same locality, and although the issue was favourable in the first naval battle, at Mylae, under the leader-

[c] Tiberius Claudius Nero, to whom she had already borne a son, the future Emperor Tiberius.

pugnatum prospere, ita inopinato Pompeianae[1]
classis adventu gravis sub ipsius Caesaris oculis circa
Tauromenium accepta clades ; neque ab ipso periculum abfuit. Legiones, quae cum Cornificio erant,
legato Caesaris, expositae in terram paene a Pom-
5 peio oppressae sunt. Sed ancipitis fortuna temporis
mature[2] virtute correcta : explicatis quippe utriusque
partis classibus paene omnibus exutus navibus Pompeius Asiam fuga petivit iussuque M. Antonii, cuius
opem petierat, dum inter ducem et supplicem
tumultuatur et nunc dignitatem retinet, nunc vitam
6 precatur, a Titio iugulatus est. Cui in tantum duravit
hoc facinore contractum odium, ut mox ludos in
theatro Pompei faciens execratione populi spectaculo, quod praebebat, pelleretur.
1 LXXX. Acciverat gerens contra Pompeium bellum
ex Africa Caesar Lepidum cum duodecim semiplenis
legionibus. Hic vir omnium vanissimus neque ulla
virtute tam longam fortunae indulgentiam meritus
exercitum Pompei, quia propior fuerat, sequentem
non ipsius, sed Caesaris auctoritatem ac fidem, sibi
2 iunxerat inflatusque amplius viginti legionum numero
in id furoris processerat, ut inutilis alienae victoriae[3]
comes, quam diu moratus erat, dissidendo in consiliis
Caesari[4] et semper diversa iis, quae aliis placebant,
dicendo, totam victoriam ut suam interpretabatur

[1] Pompeianae *added by Heinsius.*
[2] mature *Ruhnken* ; matura *AP.*
[3] alienae victoriae *P* ; in alienae victoriae *AB* ; in aliena
victoria *Burer.*
[4] Caesari *Acidalius* ; Caesaris *AP.*

---

[a] Battle of Naulochus, 36 B.C.

ship of Agrippa, a serious defeat was received near Tauromenium beneath the very eyes of Caesar, in consequence of the unexpected arrival of Pompey's fleet, and Caesar's own person was endangered. The legions which were with Cornificius, Caesar's lieutenant, came near being crushed by Pompey as soon as they landed. But fortune's caprice at this critical period was soon amended by bravery in action; when the fleets on both sides had been drawn up for battle,[a] Pompey lost almost all his ships, and fled to Asia, where, wavering between the rôle of general and suppliant, now endeavouring to retain his dignity and now pleading for his life, he was slain by Titius on the orders of Marcus Antonius, whose aid he had sought. The hatred which Titius brought upon himself by this act lasted for a long time ; indeed, afterwards, when he was celebrating games in Pompey's theatre, he was driven amid the execrations of the people from the spectacle which he himself was giving.

LXXX. While engaged in his war with Pompey, Caesar had summoned Lepidus from Africa with twelve legions of half the usual strength. This man, the most fickle of mankind, who had not earned the long-continued kindness of fortune through any qualities of his own, being nearer to the army of Pompey, annexed it to his own, though it was following not his orders but Caesar's, and owned loyalty to him. His numbers now swollen to twenty legions, he went to such lengths of madness that, though but a useless partner in another's victory, a victory which he had long delayed by refusing to agree to Caesar's plans and always insisting upon something different from that which suited others, he claimed the victory as entirely his own and had

3 audebatque[1] denuntiare Caesari, excederet Sicilia.
Non ab Scipionibus aliisque veteribus Romanorum
ducum quidquam ausum patratumque fortius quam
tunc a Caesare. Quippe cum inermis et lacernatus
esset, praeter nomen nihil trahens, ingressus castra
Lepidi, evitatis telis,[2] quae iussu hominis pravissimi
in eum iacta erant, cum lacerna eius perforata esset

4 lancea, aquilam legionis rapere ausus est. Scires,
quid interesset inter duces : armati inermem secuti
sunt decimoque anno quam ad indignissimam[3] vita
sua potentiam pervenerat, Lepidus et a militibus
et a fortuna desertus pulloque velatus amiculo inter
ultimam confluentium ad Caesarem turbam latens
genibus eius advolutus est. Vita rerumque suarum
dominium concessa ei sunt, spoliata, quam tueri non
poterat, dignitas.

1 LXXXI. Subita deinde exercitus seditio, qui
plerumque contemplatus frequentiam suam a disciplina desciscit et, quod cogere se putat posse, rogare
non sustinet, partim severitate, partim liberalitate

2 discussa principis, speciosumque per idem tempus
adiectum supplementum Campanae coloniae * *[4]

[1] interpretabatur audebatque *AP*; interpretaretur audebatque *Gelenius*; interpretaretur auderetque *Ruhnken*.
[2] telis *added by Orelli.*
[3] indignissimam *Ruhnken*; in dissimillimam *AP*.
[4] *Halm suggests to fill the lacuna:* veteranis in agros
deductis qui coloniae.

---

[a] Octavianus was not *princeps* formally until 27 B.C.
[b] The statement of Dio xlix. 14 is the basis for supplying
the missing words : " In this way Caesar calmed the soldiers
temporarily. The money he gave them at once and the
lands not much later. And since what was still held by
the government at the time did not suffice he bought more
in addition, especially considerable from the Campanians
dwelling in Capua since their city needed a number of

the effrontery to order Caesar out of Sicily. The Scipios and the other Roman generals of the olden time never dared or carried out a braver act than did Caesar at this juncture. For although he was unarmed and dressed in his travelling cloak, carrying nothing except his name, he entered the camp of Lepidus, and, avoiding the weapons which were hurled at him by the orders of that scoundrel, though his cloak was pierced by a lance, he had the courage to carry off the eagle of a legion. Then could one know the difference between the two commanders. Though armed, the soldiers followed Caesar who was unarmed, while Lepidus, in the tenth year after arriving at a position of power which his life had done nothing to deserve, now deserted both by his soldiers and by fortune, wrapping himself in a dark cloak and lurking in the rear of the crowd that thronged to Caesar, thus threw himself at Caesar's feet. He was granted his life and the control of his own property, but was shorn of the high position which he had shown himself unable to maintain.

LXXXI. There followed a sudden mutiny of the army ; for it happens not infrequently that when soldiers observe their own numbers they break discipline and do not endure to ask for what they think they can exact. The mutiny was broken up partly by severity, partly by liberality on the part of the emperor,[a] and considerable additions were at the same time made to the Campanian colony [by placing veterans on the lands of that colony][b]

settlers. To them he also gave in return the so-called Julian supply of water, one of their chief sources of pride at all times, and the Gnosian territory from which they still gather harvests." (Tr. by H. B. Foster.)

eius relicti erant publici : pro his longe uberiores reditus duodecies sestertium in Creta insula redditi et aqua promissa, quae hodieque singulare et salubritatis instrumentum[1] et amoenitatis ornamentum est.

3 Insigne coronae classicae, quo nemo umquam Romanorum donatus erat, hoc bello Agrippa singulari virtute meruit. Victor deinde Caesar reversus in urbem contractas emptionibus complures domos per procuratores, quo laxior fieret ipsius, publicis se usibus destinare professus est, templumque Apollinis et circa porticus facturum promisit, quod ab eo singulari exstructum munificentia est.

1 LXXXII. Qua aestate Caesar tam prospere sepelivit in Sicilia bellum,[2] fortuna, in Caesare et in[3] re publica mitis, saeviit[4] ad Orientem. Quippe Antonius cum tredecim legionibus egressus[5] Armeniam ac deinde Mediam et per eas regiones Parthos petens
2 habuit regem eorum obvium. Primoque duas legiones cum omnibus impedimentis tormentisque et Statiano legato amisit, mox saepius ipse cum summo totius exercitus discrimine ea adiit pericula, a[6] quibus servari se posse desperaret,[7] amissaque non minus

---

[1] instrumentum *Cludius*; instar *AP*.

[2] sepelivit in Sicilia bellum *Ruhnken*; libium in Sicilia B̄n (bene *A*) *AP*.

[3] et in *A*; in *P*.

[4] mitis saeviit *Haupt*; militavit *AP*.

[5] egressus *AP*; ingressus *Gelenius*.

[6] a *added by Kreyssig*.

[7] desperaret *Haupt*; desperaverat *AP*.

---

^a At Gnosos. See previous note.

^b About £10,000 or $50,000.

^c *Corona classica* or *navalis* : a chaplet of gold with

which had been left public. Lands in Crete [a] were given in return for these, which yielded a richer revenue of a million two hundred thousand sesterces,[b] and an aqueduct was promised which is to-day a remarkable agency of health as well as an ornament to the landscape.

In this war Agrippa by his remarkable services earned the distinction of a naval crown,[c] with which no Roman had as yet been decorated. Caesar, on his victorious return to the city, made the announcement that he meant to set apart for public use certain houses which he had secured by purchase through his agents in order that there might be a free area about his own residence. He further promised to build a temple of Apollo with a portico about it, a work which he constructed with rare munificence.

LXXXII. In the summer in which Caesar so successfully ended the war in Sicily, fortune, though kind in the case of Caesar and the republic, vented her anger in the east. For Antony with thirteen legions after passing through Armenia and then through Media, in an endeavour to reach Parthia by this route, found himself confronted by their king.[d] First of all he lost two legions with all their baggage and engines, and Statianus his lieutenant; later he himself with the greatest risk to his entire army, on several occasions encountered perils from which he dared not hope that escape was possible. After losing not less than a fourth part of his soldiers,

beaks of ships worked into the design, presented to the admiral who had destroyed a hostile fleet. Agrippa is represented on a bronze medallion wearing such a chaplet.
[d] 36–35 B.C.

quarta parte militum captivi cuiusdam, sed Romani, consilio ac fide servatus est,[1] qui clade Crassiani exercitus captus, cum fortuna non animum mutasset, accessit nocte ad stationem Romanam praedixitque, ne destinatum iter peterent, sed diverso silvestrique 3 pervaderent. Hoc M. Antonio ac tot[2] illis[3] legionibus saluti fuit ; de quibus tamen totoque exercitu haud minus pars quarta, ut praediximus, militum, calonum servitiique desiderata tertia est ; impedimentorum vix ulla superfuit. Hanc tamen Antonius fugam suam, quia vivus exierat, victoriam vocabat. Qui tertia aestate reversus in Armeniam regem eius Artavasden fraude deceptum catenis, sed, ne quid honori deesset, aureis vinxit. Crescente deinde et 4 amoris in Cleopatram incendio et vitiorum, quae semper facultatibus licentiaque et adsentationibus aluntur, magnitudine, bellum patriae inferre constituit, cum ante novum se Liberum Patrem appellari iussisset, cum redimitus hederis crocotaque[4] velatus aurea et thyrsum tenens cothurnisque succinctus curru velut Liber Pater vectus esset Alexandriae.
1 LXXXIII. Inter hunc apparatum belli Plancus, non iudicio recta legendi neque amore rei publicae aut Caesaris, quippe haec semper impugnabat, sed

---

[1] est *added by Orelli.*
[2] ac tot *Salmasius and Lipsius* ; acto *AP.*
[3] illius *Voss* ; illis *AP.*
[4] crocota *Ruhnken* ; corona *AP.*

---

[a] 34 B.C.

he was saved through the fidelity and by the suggestion of a captive, who was nevertheless a Roman. This man had been made prisoner in the disaster to the army of Crassus, but had not changed his allegiance with his fortune. He came by night to a Roman outpost and warned them not to pursue their intended course but to proceed by a detour through the forest. It was this that saved Marcus Antonius and his many legions ; and yet, even so, not less than a fourth part of these soldiers and of his entire army was lost, as we have already stated, and of the camp-followers and slaves a third, while hardly anything of the baggage was saved. Yet Antonius called this flight of his a victory, because he had escaped with his life ! Three summers later [a] he returned to Armenia, obtained possession of the person of Artavasdes its king by deceit, and bound him with chains, which, however, out of regard for the station of his captive, were of gold. Then as his love for Cleopatra became more ardent and his vices grew upon him—for these are always nourished by power and licence and flattery—he resolved to make war upon his country. He had previously given orders that he should be called the new Father Liber, and indeed in a procession at Alexandria he had impersonated Father Liber, his head bound with the ivy wreath, his person enveloped in the saffron robe of gold, holding in his hand the thyrsus, wearing the buskins, and riding in the Bacchic chariot.

LXXXIII. In the midst of these preparations for war Plancus went over to Caesar, not through any conviction that he was choosing the right, nor from any love of the republic or of Caesar, for he was

morbo proditor, cum fuisset humillimus adsentator
reginae et infra servos cliens, cum Antonii librarius,
cum obscenissimarum rerum et auctor et minister,
2 cum in omnia et omnibus venalis, cum caeruleatus
et nudus caputque redimitus arundine et caudam
trahens, genibus innixus Glaucum saltasset in con-
vivio, refrigeratus ab Antonio ob manifestarum
rapinarum indicia transfugit ad Caesarem. Et idem
postea clementiam victoris pro sua virtute interpretabatur, dictitans id probatum a Caesare, cui
ille ignoverat; mox autem hunc avunculum Titius
3 imitatus est. Haud absurde Coponius, vir e praetoriis gravissimus, P. Silii[1] socer, cum recens transfuga
multa ac nefanda Plancus absenti Antonio in senatu
obiceret, multa, inquit, mehercules fecit Antonius
pridie quam tu illum relinqueres.

1 LXXXIV. Caesare deinde et Messala Corvino consulibus debellatum apud Actium, ubi longe ante quam
dimicaretur exploratissima Iulianarum partium fuit
victoria. Vigebat in hac parte miles atque imperator,
in[2] illa marcebant omnia; hinc remiges[3] firmissimi,
illinc inopia adfectissimi; navium haec magnitudo

---

[1] P. Silii *Gelenius*; Patersilii *A*; pater Silii *A*.
[2] in (*before* illa) *added by Vascosanus.*
[3] remiges *Lipsius*; reges *AP*.

---

[a] Clients were *freemen* who were nevertheless dependent
upon the rich or powerful. Velleius' point seems to be that
the only difference between the status of Plancus and that
of the slave is that Plancus was born free.

[b] See note on Chap. LXXIX.

[c] 31 B.C.

always hostile to both, but because treachery was a
disease with him. He had been the most grovelling
flatterer of the queen, a client[a] with less self-respect
than a slave ; he had also been secretary to Antony
and was the author or the abettor of his vilest acts ;
for money he was ready to do all things for all men ;
and at a banquet he had played the role of Glaucus
the Nereid, performing a dance in which his naked
body was painted blue, his head encircled with reeds,
at the same time wearing a fish's tail and crawling
upon his knees. Now, inasmuch as he had been
coldly treated by Antony because of unmistakable
evidence of his venal rapacity, he deserted to Caesar.
Afterwards he even went so far as to interpret the
victor's clemency as a proof of his own merit, claiming that Caesar had approved that which he had
merely pardoned. It was the example of this man,
his uncle, that Titius soon afterwards followed.[b]
The retort of Coponius, who was the father-in-law of
Publius Silius and a dignified praetorian, was not
so far from the mark when he said, as Plancus in
the senate fresh from his desertion was heaping
upon the absent Antony many unspeakable charges,
" By Hercules, Antony must have done a great
many things before *you* left him."

LXXXIV. Then, in the consulship of Caesar and
Messala Corvinus,[c] the decisive battle took place
at Actium. The victory of the Caesarian party was
a certainty long before the battle. On the one side
commander and soldiers alike were full of ardour,
on the other was general dejection ; on the one
side the rowers were strong and sturdy, on the othe
weakened by privations, on the one side ships of
moderate size, not too large for speed, on the other

227

modica nec celeritati adversa, illa specie[1] terribilior ;
hinc ad Antonium nemo, illinc ad Caesarem cotidie
2 aliquis[2] transfugiebat ; rex[3] Amyntas meliora et
utiliora secutus ; nam Dellius[4] exempli sui tenax
ut a[5] Dolabella ad Cassium, a Cassio ad Antonium,
ita ab Antonio transiit[6] ad Caesarem ; virque clarissimus Cn. Domitius, qui solus Antonianarum
partium numquam reginam nisi nomine salutavit,
maximo et praecipiti periculo transmisit ad Caesarem.
Denique in ore atque oculis Antonianae classis per
M. Agrippam Leucas expugnata, Patrae captae,
Corinthus occupata, bis ante ultimum discrimen
classis hostium superata.
1 LXXXV. Advenit deinde maximi discriminis dies,
quo Caesar Antoniusque productis classibus pro
salute alter, in ruinam alter terrarum orbis dimi-
2 cavere. Dextrum navium Iulianarum cornu M.
Lurio commissum, laevum Arruntio, Agrippae omne
classici certaminis arbitrium ; Caesar ei parti destinatus, in quam a fortuna vocaretur, ubique aderat.
Classis Antonii regimen Publicolae Sosioque commissum. At in terra locatum exercitum Taurus Caesaris,
3 Antonii regebat Canidius. Ubi initum certamen est,
omnia in altera parte fuere, dux, remiges, milites,
in altera nihil praeter milites. Prima occupat fugam
Cleopatra. Antonius fugientis reginae quam pug-

---

[1] specie *Gelenius*; specie et *AP*.

[2] aliquis *Heinsius*; aliquid *AB*; aliqui transfugiebant *P*.

[3] *The clause* rex . . . transmisit ad Caesarem *found in*
AP after superata, *at the end of the paragraph, was trans-*
posed to its present position by Haase.

[4] Dellius *Kritz*; de illius *AP*.

[5] exempli sui tenax ut a *Lipsius*; exemplis uitae naxuta
AP.

[6] ad Cassium . . . transiit *supplied by Ruhnken*.

vessels of a size that made them more formidable
in appearance only ; no one was deserting from
Caesar to Antony, while from Antony to Caesar
someone or other was deserting daily ; and King
Amyntas had embraced the better and more
advantageous side. As for Dellius, consistent to
his habit, he now went over from Antony to Caesar
as he had deserted from Dolabella to Cassius and
from Cassius to Antony. The illustrious Gnaeus
Domitius, who was the only one of the party of
Antony who refused to salute the queen except by
name, went over to Caesar at great and imminent
risk to himself. Finally, before the eyes of Antony
and his fleet, Marcus Agrippa had stormed Leucas,
had captured Patrae, had seized Corinth, and before
the final conflict had twice defeated the fleet of the
enemy.

LXXXV. Then came the day of the great conflict,
on which Caesar and Antony led out their fleets and
fought, the one for the safety, the other for the ruin,
of the world. The command of the right wing of
Caesar's fleet was entrusted to Marcus Lurius, of
the left to Arruntius, while Agrippa had full charge
of the entire conflict at sea. Caesar, reserving
himself for that part of the battle to which fortune
might summon him, was present everywhere. The
command of Antony's fleet was entrusted to Publicola
and Sosius. On the land, moreover, the army of
Caesar was commanded by Taurus, that of Antony
by Canidius. When the conflict began, on the
one side was everything—commander, rowers, and
soldiers ; on the other, soldiers alone. Cleopatra
took the initiative in the flight ; Antony chose
to be the companion of the fleeing queen rather

nantis militis sui comes esse maluit, et imperator,
qui in desertores saevire debuerat, desertor exercitus sui factus est. Illis etiam detracto[1] capite in
4 longum fortissime pugnandi duravit constantia et
desperata victoria in mortem dimicabatur. Caesar,
quos ferro poterat interimere, verbis mulcere cupiens
clamitansque et ostendens fugisse Antonium, quae-
5 rebat, pro quo et cum quo pugnarent. At illi cum
diu pro absente dimicassent duce, aegre summissis
armis cessere victoriam, citiusque vitam veniamque
Caesar promisit, quam illis ut eam precarentur per-
suasum est ; fuitque in confesso milites optimi
imperatoris, imperatorem fugacissimi militis func-
6 tum officio, ut dubites, suone[2] an Cleopatrae arbitrio
victoriam temperaturus fuerit, qui ad eius arbitrium
direxerit[3] fugam. Idem locatus in terra fecit exercitus, cum se Canidius praecipiti fuga rapuisset ad
Antonium.

1 LXXXVI. Quid ille dies terrarum orbi praestiterit,
ex quo in quem statum pervenerit fortuna publica,
quis in hoc transcursu tam artati operis exprimere
2 audeat ? Victoria vero fuit clementissima, nec quisquam interemptus est, paucissimi summoti,[4] qui
ne deprecari quidem pro se sustinerent.[5] Ex qua
lenitate ducis colligi potuit, quem aut initio trium-
viratus sui aut in campis Philippiis, si ei[6] licuisset,

---

[1] detracto *Vascosanus*; detrectato *AP*.
[2] ut dubites, suone *Burer*; videbites ne *A*; videbit e
suo *P*.
[3] direxerit *Halm*; direxit *AP*.
[4] paucissimi summoti *Baiter*; paucissimi et hi *AP*.
[5] qui ne deprecari quidem pro se sustinerent *Heinsius*;
qui deprecari quidem pro se non sustinerent *AP*.
[6] si ei *Halm*; sic *A*; si sic *P*; si *Burer*.

than of his fighting soldiers, and the commander whose duty it would have been to deal severely with deserters, now became a deserter from his own army. Even without their chief his men long continued to fight bravely, and despairing of victory they fought to the death. Caesar, desiring to win over by words those whom he might have slain with the sword, kept shouting and pointing out to them that Antony had fled, and kept asking them for whom and with whom they were fighting. But they, after fighting long for their truant commander, reluctantly surrendered their arms and yielded the victory, Caesar having promised them pardon and their lives before they could bring themselves to sue for them. It was evident that the soldiers had played the part of the good commander while the commander had played that of the cowardly soldier, so that one might question whether in case of victory he would have acted according to Cleopatra's will or his own, since it was by her will that he had resorted to flight. The land army likewise surrendered when Canidius had hurried after Antony in precipitate flight.

LXXXVI. Who is there who, in the compass of so brief a work, would attempt to state what blessings this day conferred upon the world, or to describe the change which took place in the fortunes of the state? Great clemency was shown in the victory; no one was put to death, and but few banished who could not bring themselves even to become suppliants. From this display of mercy on the part of the commander it may be inferred how moderate a use Caesar would have made of his victory, had he been allowed to do so, whether at the beginning of his triumvirate or on the plain of

victoriae suae facturus fuerit modum.[1]   At Sosium
L. Arruntii prisca gravitate celeberrimi fides, mox,
diu cum clementia luctatus[2] sua, Caesar servavit
3 incolumem. Non praetereatur Asinii Pollionis factum
et dictum memorabile : namque cum se post Brun-
dusinam pacem continuisset in Italia neque aut
vidisset umquam reginam aut post enervatum amore
eius Antonii animum partibus eius se miscuisset,
rogante Caesare, ut secum ad bellum proficisceretur
Actiacum : mea, inquit, in Antonium maiora merita
sunt, illius in me beneficia notiora ; itaque discrimini vestro me subtraham et ero praeda victoris.

1   LXXXVII. Proximo deinde anno persecutus reginam Antoniumque Alexandream, ultimam bellis
civilibus imposuit manum. Antonius se ipse non
segniter interemit, adeo ut multa desidiae crimina
morte redimeret. At Cleopatra frustratis custodibus
inlata aspide in[3] morsu et sanie eius[4] expers mu-
2 liebris metus spiritum reddidit. Fuitque et fortuna
et clementia Caesaris dignum, quod nemo ex iis,
qui contra eum arma tulerant, ab eo iussuve eius
interemptus est.[5] D. Brutum Antonii interemit
crudelitas. Sextum Pompeium ab eo devictum[6]
idem Antonius, cum dignitatis quoque servandae

[1] modum added by Rhenanus.
[2] diu . . . luctatus AP ; odium . . . eluctatus Madvig
and Halm.
[3] aspide in B ; aspidem A ; aspide P.
[4] et sanie eius Burman ; sanie eius BAP ; eius sane
Acidalius and Halm.
[5] est added by Orelli.
[6] ab eo devictum Acidalius ; ab (ob P) eodem victum
BAP.

Philippi. But, in the case of Sosius, it was the pledged word of Lucius Arruntius, a man famous for his old-time dignity, that saved him; later, Caesar preserved him unharmed, but only after long resisting his general inclination to clemency. The remarkable conduct of Asinius Pollio should not be passed by nor the words which he uttered. For although he had remained in Italy after the peace of Brundisium, and had never seen the queen nor taken any active part in Antony's faction after this leader had become demoralized by his passion for her, when Caesar asked him to go with him to the war at Actium he replied : " My services to Antony are too great, and his kindness to me too well known ; accordingly I shall hold aloof from your quarrel and shall be the prize of the victor."

LXXXVII. The following year Caesar followed Cleopatra and Antony to Alexandria and there put the finishing touch upon the civil wars. Antony promptly ended his life,[a] thus by his death redeeming himself from the many charges of lack of manhood. As for Cleopatra, baffling the vigilance of her guards she caused an asp to be smuggled in to her, and ended her life by its venomous sting untouched by a woman's fears. It was in keeping with Caesar's fortune and his clemency that not one of those who had borne arms against him was put to death by him, or by his order. It was the cruelty of Antony that ended the life of Decimus Brutus. In the case of Sextus Pompey, though Caesar was his conqueror, it was likewise Antony who deprived him of his life, even though he had given his word that he would not degrade

3 dedisset fidem, etiam spiritu privavit. Brutus et
Cassius ante, quam victorum experirentur animum,
voluntaria morte obierunt. Antonii Cleopatraeque
quis fuisset exitus narravimus. Canidius timidius
decessit, quam professioni ei,[1] qua semper usus
erat, congruebat. Ultimus autem ex interfectoribus
Caesaris Parmensis Cassius morte poenas dedit, ut
dederat Trebonius primus.[2]

1 LXXXVIII. Dum ultimam bello Actiaco Alexan-
drinoque Caesar imponit manum, M. Lepidus, iuvenis
forma quam mente melior, Lepidi eius, qui triumvir
fuerat rei publicae constituendae, filius, Iunia Bruti
sorore natus, interficiendi, simul in urbem revertisset,
2 Caesaris consilia inierat. Erat[3] tunc urbis custodiis
praepositus C. Maecenas equestri, sed splendido
genere natus, vir, ubi res vigiliam exigeret, sane
exsomnis, providens atque agendi sciens, simul vero
aliquid ex negotio remitti posset, otio ac mollitiis
paene ultra feminam fluens, non minus Agrippa
Caesari carus, sed minus honoratus—quippe vixit
angusti clavi plene[4] contentus—, nec minora con-
3 sequi potuit, sed non tam concupivit. Hic speculatus est per summam quietem ac dissimulationem
praecipitis consilia iuvenis et mira celeritate nullaque

[1] ei *Cludius*; eius *AP*.
[2] primus *added by Aldus, but before* Trebonius.
[3] erat *added by Madvig*.
[4] paene *A*; pene *P*; *the most satisfactory emendation is
that of Salmasius* angusticlavio plene contentus.

---

[a] His boasts that he did not fear death.
[b] With Antony and Octavian.
[c] As contrasted with the broad purple band of the
senatorial order.

him from his rank. Brutus and Cassius, without waiting to discover the attitude of their conquerors, died voluntary deaths. Of the end of Antony and Cleopatra we have already told. As for Canidius, he showed more fear in the face of death than was consistent with his lifelong utterances.[a] The last of Caesar's assassins to pay the penalty of death was Cassius of Parma, as Trebonius had been the first.

LXXXVIII. While Caesar was engaged in giving the finishing touch to the war at Actium and Alexandria, Marcus Lepidus, a young man whose good looks exceeded his prudence—son of the Lepidus who had been one of the triumvirs[b] for the re-establishment of order in the state and of Junia the sister of Brutus—had formed plans for the assassination of Caesar as soon as he should return to the city. The guards of the city were at that time under the charge of Gaius Maecenas, of equestrian rank, but none the less of illustrious lineage, a man who was literally sleepless when occasion demanded, and quick to foresee what was to be done and skilful in doing it, but when any relaxation was allowed him from business cares would almost outdo a woman in giving himself up to indolence and soft luxury. He was not less loved by Caesar than Agrippa, though he had fewer honours heaped upon him, since he lived thoroughly content with the narrow stripe of the equestrian order.[c] He might have achieved a position no less high than Agrippa, but had not the same ambition for it. Quietly and carefully concealing his activity he unearthed the plans of the hot-headed youth, and by crushing Lepidus with wonderful swiftness and without

cum perturbatione aut rerum aut hominum oppresso
Lepido inmane novi ac resurrecturi belli civilis
restinxit initium. Et ille quidem male consultorum
poenas exsolvit. Aequetur praedictae iam Antistii[1]
Servilia Lepidi uxor, quae vivo igni devorato praematura morte[2] immortalem nominis sui pensavit
memoriam.

1 LXXXIX. Caesar autem reversus in Italiam atque
urbem quo occursu,[3] quo favore hominum omnium
generum,[4] aetatium, ordinum exceptus sit, quae
magnificentia triumphorum eius, quae fuerit mune-
rum, ne in operis quidem[5] iusti materia, nedum huius
tam recisi digne exprimi potest. Nihil deinde optare
2 a dis homines, nihil dii hominibus praestare possunt,
nihil voto concipi, nihil felicitate consummari, quod
non Augustus post reditum in urbem rei publicae
populoque Romano terrarumque orbi repraesen-
3 taverit. Finita vicesimo anno bella civilia, sepulta
externa, revocata pax, sopitus ubique armorum
furor, restituta vis legibus, iudiciis auctoritas, senatui
maiestas, imperium magistratuum ad pristinum
redactum modum, tantummodo octo praetoribus
adlecti duo. Prisca illa et antiqua rei publicae
4 forma revocata. Rediit cultus agris, sacris honos,
securitas hominibus, certa cuique rerum suarum
possessio ; leges emendatae utiliter, latae salubriter ;

1 Antistii *Vossius* ; Antistiae *AP*.
2 praematura morte *Burer* ; praematuram mortem *AB*.
3 quo occursu *Lipsius* ; occursus *AP*.
4 favore omnium hominum aetatium *AP* ; generum *added by Halm*.
5 ne in operis quidem *Gelenius* ; nedum in operis siquidem *AP*.

a Chap. XXVI.

causing disturbance to either men or things he extinguished the portentous beginnings of a new and reviving civil war. Lepidus himself paid the penalty for his ill-advised plot. Servilia his wife must be placed on a parity with the wife of Antistius already mentioned,[a] for by swallowing live coals she compensated for her untimely death by the lasting memory of her name.

LXXXIX. As for Caesar's return to Italy and to Rome—the procession which met him, the enthusiasm of his reception by men of all classes, ages, and ranks, and the magnificence of his triumphs and of the spectacles which he gave—all this it would be impossible adequately to describe even within the compass of a formal history, to say nothing of a work so circumscribed as this. There is nothing that man can desire from the gods, nothing that the gods can grant to a man, nothing that wish can conceive or good fortune bring to pass, which Augustus on his return to the city did not bestow upon the republic, the Roman people, and the world. The civil wars were ended after twenty years, foreign wars suppressed, peace restored, the frenzy of arms everywhere lulled to rest; validity was restored to the laws, authority to the courts, and dignity to the senate ; the power of the magistrates was reduced to its former limits, with the sole exception that two were added to the eight existing praetors. The old traditional form of the republic was restored. Agriculture returned to the fields, respect to religion, to mankind freedom from anxiety, and to each citizen his property rights were now assured ; old laws were usefully emended, and new laws passed for the general good ; the

senatus sine asperitate nec sine severitate lectus.
Principes viri triumphisque et amplissimis honoribus
functi adhortatu principis ad ornandam urbem inlecti
sunt.   Consulatus tantummodo usque ad undecimum
5 quin[1] continuaret Caesar, cum saepe obnitens repug-
nasset, impetrare non[2] potuit : nam dictaturam quam
pertinaciter ei deferebat populus, tam constanter
repulit.   Bella sub imperatore gesta pacatusque
6 victoriis terrarum orbis et tot extra Italiam domique
opera omne aevi sui spatium impensurum ın id
solum opus scriptorem fatigarent[3] : nos memores
professionis universam imaginem principatus eius
oculis animisque subiecimus.
1   XC. Sepultis, ut praediximus, bellis civilibus co-
alescentibusque rei publicae membris, et coaluere[4]
quae tam longa armorum series laceraverat.   Dalmatia, annos[5] viginti et ducentos rebellis, ad certam
confessionem pacata est imperii.   Alpes feris incultisque[6] nationibus celebres perdomitae.   Hispaniae
nunc ipsius praesentia, nunc Agrippae, quem usque
in tertium consulatum et mox collegium tribuniciae
potestatis amicitia principis evexerat, multo varioque
2 Marte pacatae.   In quas provincias cum initio
Scipione et Sempronio Longo consulibus primo anno

---

[1] quin *Madvig* ; quem *AP*.
[2] non *added by Madvig*.
[3] fatigarent *Vossius* ; fatigant *AP*.
[4] et (*or* etiam) coaluere *Bergk* ; et coram aliero *AP*.
[5] annos *added by Orelli*.
[6] incultisque *Heinsius* ; multisque *AP*.

revision of the senate, while not too drastic, was not lacking in severity. The chief men of the state who had won triumphs and had held high office were at the invitation of Augustus induced to adorn the city. In the case of the consulship only, Caesar was not able to have his way, but was obliged to hold that office consecutively until the eleventh time in spite of his frequent efforts to prevent it ; but the dictatorship which the people persistently offered him, he as stubbornly refused. To tell of the wars waged under his command, of the pacification of the world by his victories, of his many works at home and outside of Italy would weary a writer intending to devote his whole life to this one task. As for myself, remembering the proposed scope of my work, I have confined myself to setting before the eyes and minds of my readers a general picture of his principate.

XC. When the civil wars had been extinguished, as we have already told, and the rent limbs of the state itself began to heal, the provinces, also, torn asunder by the long series of wars began to knit together. Dalmatia, in rebellion for one hundred and twenty years, was pacified to the extent of definitely recognizing the sovereignty of Rome. The Alps, filled with wild and barbarous tribes, were subdued. The provinces of Spain were pacified after heavy campaigns conducted with varied success now by Caesar in person, now by Agrippa, whom the friendship of the emperor had raised to a third consulship and soon afterwards to a share in the emperor's tribunician power. Roman armies had been sent into these provinces for the first time in the consulship of Scipio and Sempronius

secundi belli[1] Punici abhinc annos quinquaginta et ducentos Romani exercitus missi essent duce Cn. Scipione, Africani patruo, per annos ducentos in iis multo mutuoque ita certatum est sanguine, ut amissis populi Romani imperatoribus exercitibusque saepe contumelia, nonnumquam etiam periculum 3 Romano inferretur imperio. Illae enim provinciae Scipiones consumpserunt ; illae contumelioso decem[2] annorum bello sub duce Viriatho maiores nostros exercuerunt ; illae terrore Numantini belli populum Romanum concusserunt ; in illis turpe Q. Pompei foedus turpiusque Mancini senatus cum ignominia dediti imperatoris rescidit ; illa tot consulares, tot praetorios absumpsit duces, patrumque aetate in tantum Sertorium armis extulit, ut per quinquennium diiudicari non potuerit, Hispanis Romanisne in armis plus esset roboris et uter populus alteri pariturus 4 foret. Has igitur provincias tam diffusas, tam frequentis, tam feras ad eam pacem abhinc annos ferme quinquaginta perduxit Caesar Augustus, ut quae maximis bellis numquam vacaverant, eae sub C. Antistio ac deinde P. Silio legato ceterisque postea etiam latrociniis vacarent.

1   XCI. Dum pacatur occidens, ab oriente ac rege Parthorum signa Romana, quae Crasso oppresso[3]

---

[1] belli *added by Heinsius.*
[2] X *Lipsius* ; XX *AP.*
[3] oppresso *Gelenius* ; presso *P* ; praesso *A.*

---

a 218 B.C.

Longus,[a] in the first year of the Second Punic war, two hundred and fifty years ago, under the command of Gnaeus Scipio, the uncle of Africanus. For a period of two hundred years the struggle was kept up with so much bloodshed on both sides that the Roman people, by the loss of its commanders and armies, often suffered disgrace, and sometimes its empire was really endangered. These, namely, were the provinces that brought death to the Scipios; that taxed the endurance of our ancestors in the disgraceful ten years' war under Viriathus; that shook the Roman people with the panic of the Numantine war; here occurred the disgraceful surrender of Quintus Pompeius, whose terms the senate disavowed, and the more shameful capitulation of Mancinus, which was also disavowed, and its maker ignominiously handed over to the enemy; it was Spain that destroyed so many commanders who were consulars or praetorians, and which in the days of our fathers raised Sertorius to such a height of power that for a period of five years it was not possible to decide whether there was greater strength in the arms of the Spaniard or the Roman, and which of the two peoples was destined to obey the other. These, then, were the provinces, so extensive, so populous, and so warlike, which Caesar Augustus, about fifty years ago, brought to such a condition of peace, that whereas they had never before been free from serious wars, they were now, under the governorship of Gaius Antistius and then of Publius Silius and of their successors, exempt even from brigandage.

XCI. While the pacification of the west was going on, in the east the Parthian king restored to

Orodes, quae Antonio pulso filius eius Phraates
ceperant, Augusto remissa sunt. Quod cognomen
illi iure[1] Planci sententia consensus universi senatus
2 populique Romani indidit. Erant tamen qui hunc
felicissimum statum odissent: quippe L. Murena
et Fannius Caepio diversis moribus (nam Murena
sine hoc facinore potuit videri bonus, Caepio et ante
hoc erat pessimus) cum iniissent occidendi Caesaris
consilia, oppressi auctoritate publica, quod vi facere
3 voluerant, iure passi sunt. Neque multo post Rufus
Egnatius, per omnia gladiatori quam senatori propior, collecto in aedilitate favore populi, quem extin-
guendis privata familia incendiis in dies auxerat,
in tantum quidem, ut ei praeturam continuaret, mox
etiam consulatum petere ausus, cum esset omni
flagitiorum scelerumque conscientia mersus nec
melior illi res familiaris quam mens foret, adgregatis
simillimis sibi interimere Caesarem statuit, ut quo
salvo salvus esse non poterat, eo sublato moreretur.
4 Quippe ita se mores habent, ut[2] publica quisque ruina
malit occidere quam sua proteri et[3] idem passurus

---

[1] iure *Orelli*; viro *AP*.
[2] ut *added by Burer*.
[3] et *om. A.*

---

[a] Referred to in Chap. XLVI.
[b] 27 B.C.   [c] 22 B.C.   [d] 19 B.C.
242

Augustus the Roman standards which Orodes had taken at the time of Crassus' disaster,[a] and those which his son Phraates had captured on the defeat of Antony. This title of Augustus was deservedly given him [b] on the motion of Plancus with the unanimous acclaim of the entire senate and the Roman people. Yet there were those who did not like this prosperous state of affairs. For example, Lucius Murena and Fannius Caepio had entered into a plot to assassinate Caesar, but were seized by state authority and themselves suffered by law what they had wished to accomplish by violence.[c] They were two men quite diverse in character, for Murena, apart from this act, might have passed as a man of good character, while Caepio, even before this, had been of the worst. Shortly afterwards a similar attempt was made by Rufus Egnatius,[d] a man who in all respects resembled a gladiator rather than a senator. Securing the favour of the people in his aedileship by putting out fires with his own gang of slaves, he increased it daily to such an extent that the people gave him the praetorship immediately after the aedileship. It was not long before he dared to become a candidate for the consulship, but he was overwhelmed by the general knowledge of his shameless deeds and crimes, and the state of his property came to be as desperate as his mind. Therefore, collecting about him men of his own kind, he resolved to assassinate Caesar in order that he might die after getting rid of him whose existence was not compatible with his own. Such men are so constituted that each would prefer to fall in a general cataclysm than to perish alone, and, though suffering the same fate in the end, to be

minus conspici. Neque hic prioribus in occultando felicior fuit, abditusque carceri cum consciis facinoris mortem dignissimam vita sua obiit.

1 XCII. Praeclarum excellentis viri factum C. Sentii Saturnini circa ea tempora consulis[a] ne fraudetur memoria. Aberat[1] ordinandis Asiae Orientisque 2 rebus Caesar, circumferens terrarum orbi praesentia sua pacis suae bona. Tum Sentius, forte et solus et absente Caesare consul, cum alia prisca severitate, summaque constantia, vetere consulum more ac severitate, gessisset, protraxisset publicanorum fraudes, punisset avaritiam, regessisset in aerarium pecunias publicas, tum in comitiis habendis prae- 3 cipuum egit consulem : nam et quaesturam petentes, quos indignos iudicavit, profiteri vetuit, et, cum id facturos se perseverarent, consularem, si in campum[b] 4 descendissent, vindictam minatus est, et Egnatium florentem favore publico sperantemque ut praeturam aedilitati, ita consulatum praeturae se iuncturum, profiteri vetuit, et cum id non obtinuisset, iuravit, etiam si factus esset consul suffragiis populi, tamen 5 se eum non renuntiaturum. Quod ego factum cuilibet veterum consulum gloriae comparandum reor, nisi

---

[1] in *after* aberat *deleted by Krause.*

---

[a] Consul 19 B.C.
[b] Where the elections took place.

less conspicuous in dying. He, however, was not
more successful than the rest in concealing his
designs, and after being thrust into prison with
his fellow conspirators, died the death his life
richly deserved.

XCII. The remarkable conduct of an excellent
man, Gaius Sentius Saturninus, who was consul about
this time,[a] must not be cheated of its due record.
Caesar was absent from the city engaged in regulating
the affairs of Asia and of the orient, and in bringing
to the countries of the world by his personal presence
the blessings of Augustan peace. On this occasion
Sentius, chancing thus to be sole consul with Caesar
absent, adopting the rigorous regime of the older
consuls, pursued a general policy of old-fashioned
severity and great firmness, bringing to light the
fraudulent tricks of the tax-collectors, punishing
their avarice, and getting the public moneys into
the treasury. But it was particularly in holding the
elections that he played the consul. For in the case
of candidates for the quaestorship whom he thought
unworthy, he forbade them to offer their names,
and when they insisted upon doing so, he threatened
them with the exercise of his consular authority if
they came down to the Campus Martius.[b] Egnatius,
who was now at the height of popular favour, and was
expecting to have his consulship follow his praetorship as his praetorship had followed his aedileship, he
forbade to become a candidate, and failing in this, he
swore that, even if Egnatius were elected consul by
the votes of the people, he would refuse to report
his election. This conduct I consider as comparable
with any of the celebrated acts of the consuls of the
olden days. But we are naturally more inclined to

quod naturaliter audita visis laudamus libentius et praesentia invidia, praeterita veneratione prosequimur et his nos obrui, illis instrui credimus.

1 XCIII. Ante triennium fere, quam Egnatianum scelus erumperet, circa Murenae Caepionisque coniurationis tempus, abhinc annos quinquaginta, M. Marcellus, sororis Augusti Octaviae filius, quem homines ita, si quid accidisset Caesari, successorem potentiae eius arbitrabantur futurum, ut tamen id per M. Agrippam securo ei posse contingere non existimarent, magnificentissimo munere aedilitatis edito decessit admodum iuvenis, sane, ut aiunt, ingenuarum virtutum laetusque animi et ingenii fortunae-
2 que, in quam alebatur, capax. Post cuius obitum Agrippa, qui sub specie ministeriorum principalium profectus in Asiam, ut fama loquitur, ob tacitas cum Marcello offensiones praesenti se subduxerat tempori, reversus inde filiam Caesaris Iuliam, quam in matrimonio Marcellus habuerat, duxit uxorem, feminam neque sibi neque rei publicae felicis uteri.

1 XCIV. Hoc tractu temporum Ti. Claudius Nero, quo trimo,[1] ut praediximus, Livia, Drusi Claudiani

---

[1] trimo *Aldus*; primo *AP*.

---

[a] 23 B.C.

[b] Daughter of Augustus and his first wife Scribonia.

[c] The children of Julia and Agrippa were: Julia, who became the wife of Aemilius Paullus, banished by Augustus, her grandfather, to the island of Tremerus for adulterous intercourse with C. Silanus; Agrippina, the wife of Germanicus, banished by Tiberius to the island of Pandateria; Gaius and Lucius, adopted by Augustus, with the intention that they should succeed him (their untimely deaths are narrated in Chap. CII.); and Agrippa Postumus, adopted by Augustus in A.D. 4, but later banished by him to

praise what we have heard than what has occurred before our eyes ; we regard the present with envy, the past with veneration, and believe that we are eclipsed by the former, but derive instruction from the latter.

XCIII. Some three years before the plot of Egnatius was exposed, about the time of the conspiracy of Murena and Caepio, fifty years from the present date, Marcus Marcellus died,[a] the son of Octavia, sister of Augustus, after giving a magnificent spectacle to commemorate his aedileship and while still quite a youth. People thought that, if anything should happen to Caesar, Marcellus would be his successor in power, at the same time believing, however, that this would not fall to his lot without opposition from Marcus Agrippa. He was, we are told, a young man of noble qualities, cheerful in mind and disposition, and equal to the station for which he was being reared. After his death Agrippa, who had set out for Asia on the pretext of commissions from the emperor, but who, according to current gossip, had withdrawn, for the time being, on account of his secret animosity for Marcellus, now returned from Asia and married Julia the daughter of Caesar,[b] who had been the wife of Marcellus, a woman whose many children[c] were to be blessings neither to herself nor to the state.

XCIV. At this period Tiberius Claudius Nero, in his nineteenth year, began his public life as quaestor. I have already told how, when he was three years of age, his mother Livia, the daughter of Drusus Claudianus, had become the wife of Caesar, her

the island of Planasia where he was murdered by a centurion on the succession of Tiberius.

filia, despondente[1] Ti. Nerone, cui ante nupta fuerat,
2 Caesari nupserat, innutritus caelestium praeceptorum
disciplinis, iuvenis genere, forma, celsitudine corporis, optimis studiis maximoque ingenio instructis-
simus, qui protinus quantus est, sperari potuerat
3 visuque praetulerat principem, quaestor undevicesimum annum agens capessere coepit rem publicam
maximamque difficultatem annonae ac rei frumen-
tariae inopiam ita Ostiae atque[2] in urbe mandatu
vitrici moderatus est, ut per id, quod agebat, quantus
4 evasurus esset, eluceret. Nec multo post missus ab
eodem vitrico cum exercitu ad visendas ordinandas-
que, quae sub Oriente sunt, provincias, praecipuis
omnium virtutum experimentis in eo tractu[3] editis,
cum legionibus ingressus Armeniam, redacta ea in
potestatem populi Romani regnum eius Artavasdi
dedit. Quin[4] rex quoque Parthorum tanti nominis
fama territus liberos suos ad Caesarem misit obsides.
1 XCV. Reversum inde Neronem Caesar haud mediocris belli mole[5] experiri statuit, adiutore operis dato
fratre ipsius Druso Claudio, quem intra Caesaris
penates enixa erat Livia. Quippe uterque e diversis[6]
2 partibus Raetos Vindelicosque adgressi, multis urbium
et castellorum oppugnationibus nec non derecta
quoque acie feliciter functi gentes locis tutissimas,

[1] despondente *Gelenius*; respondente *AP*.
[2] ostiae atque *Rhenanus*; ostia eratque *AP*.
[3] tractu *Gelenius*; tractatu *AP*.
[4] quin *Ruhnken*; cuius *AP*.
[5] mole *Heinsius*; molem *P*; morem *A*.
[6] e diversis *Stanger*; divisis *AP*.

^a See Chap. LXXI. 19.

former husband, Tiberius Nero, himself giving her in marriage to him.[a] Nurtured by the teaching of eminent praeceptors, a youth equipped in the highest degree with the advantages of birth, personal beauty, commanding presence, an excellent education combined with native talents, Tiberius gave early promise of becoming the great man he now is, and already by his look revealed the prince. Now, acting on the orders of his stepfather, he so skilfully regulated the difficulties of the grain supply and relieved the scarcity of corn at Ostia and in the city that it was apparent from his execution of this commission how great he was destined to become. Shortly afterwards he was sent by his stepfather with an army to visit the eastern provinces and restore them to order, and in that part of the world gave splendid illustration of all his strong qualities. Entering Armenia with his legions, he brought it once more under the sovereignty of the Roman people, and gave the kingship to Artavasdes. Even the king of the Parthians, awed by the reputation of so great a name, sent his own children as hostages to Caesar.

XCV. On Nero's return Caesar resolved to test his powers in a war of no slight magnitude. In this work he gave him as a collaborator his own brother Drusus Claudius, to whom Livia gave birth when already in the house of Caesar. The two brothers attacked the Raeti and Vindelici from different directions, and after storming many towns and strongholds, as well as engaging successfully in pitched battles, with more danger than real loss to the Roman army, though with much bloodshed on the part of the enemy, they thoroughly subdued

aditu difficillimas, numero frequentes, feritate truces maiore cum periculo quam damno Romani exercitus plurimo cum earum sanguine perdomuerunt.

3 Ante quae tempora censura Planci et Pauli acta inter discordiam neque ipsis honori neque rei publicae usui fuerat,[1] cum alteri vis censoria, alteri vita deesset, Paulus vix posset implere censorem, Plancus timere deberet, nec quidquam obiicere posset adulescentibus aut obiicientes audire, quod non agnosceret senex.

1 XCVI. Mors deinde Agrippae, qui novitatem suam multis rebus nobilitaveret atque in hoc perduxerat, ut et Neronis esset socer, cuiusque liberos nepotes suos divus Augustus praepositis Gai ac Lucii nominibus adoptaverat, admovit propius Neronem Caesari: quippe filia Iulia[2] eius, quae fuerat Agrippae nupta, Neroni nupsit.

2 Subinde bellum Pannonicum, quod inchoatum ab[3] Agrippa, Marco Vinicio, avo tuo consule,[4] magnum atroxque et perquam vicinum imminebat Italiae, per Neronem gestum est. Gentes Pannoniorum Delmatarumque nationes situmque regionum ac flumi-

3 num numerumque et modum virium excelsissimasque et multiplices eo bello victorias tanti imperatoris

[1] fuerat *Orelli*; foret *AP.*
[2] Iulia filia *Haase.*
[3] ab *added by Lipsius.*
[4] consule *Lipsius*; COS. *A*; consulari *Kritz followed by Halm.*

---

[a] 15 B.C.　　　　　　　　　　　　[b] 12 B.C.
[c] Tiberius had married Agrippina, daughter of Agrippa and Pomponia.

these races,[a] protected as they were by the nature
of the country, difficult of access, strong in numbers,
and fiercely warlike.

Before this had occurred the censorship of Plancus
and Paulus, which, exercised as it was with mutual
discord, was little credit to themselves or little
benefit to the state, for the one lacked the force,
the other the character, in keeping with the office ;
Paulus was scarcely capable of filling the censor's office,
while Plancus had only too much reason to fear it,
nor was there any charge which he could make against
young men, or hear others make, of which he, old
though he was, could not recognize himself as guilty.

XCVI. Then occurred the death of Agrippa.[b]
Though a " new man " he had by his many achievements brought distinction upon his obscure birth,
even to the extent of becoming the father-in-law[c]
of Nero[d] ; and his sons, the grandsons of the emperor,
had been adopted by Augustus under the names of
Gaius and Lucius. His death brought Nero closer
to Caesar, since his daughter Julia, who had been
the wife of Agrippa, now married Nero.

Shortly after, the Pannonian war, which had been
begun by Agrippa in the consulate of your grandfather, Marcus Vinicius, was conducted by Nero, a
war which was important and formidable enough,
and on account of its proximity a menace to Italy.
In another place I shall describe the tribes of the
Pannonians and the races of Dalmatians, the situation of their country and its rivers, the number and
extent of their forces, and the many glorious
victories won in the course of this war by this great

[d] Nero is throughout these chapters the later emperor
Tiberius.

251

alio loco explicabimus : hoc opus servet formam
suam. Huius victoriae compos Nero ovans triumphavit.

1 XCVII. Sed dum in hac parte imperii omnia
geruntur prosperrime, accepta in Germania clades
sub legato M. Lollio, homine in omnia pecuniae quam
recte faciendi cupidiore et inter summam vitiorum
dissimulationem vitiosissimo, amissaque legionis quin-
tae aquila vocavit ab urbe in Gallias Caesarem.
2 Cura deinde atque onus Germanici belli delegata
Druso Claudio, fratri Neronis, adulescenti tot tanta-
rumque virtutum, quot et quantas natura mortalis
recipit vel industria perficit.[1] Cuius ingenium utrum
bellicis magis operibus an civilibus suffecerit artibus,
in incerto est : morum certe dulcedo ac suavitas et
3 adversus amicos aequa ac par sui aestimatio inimita-
bilis fuisse dicitur ; nam pulchritudo corporis proxima
fraternae fuit. Sed illum magna ex parte domitorem
Germaniae, plurimo eius gentis variis in locis profuso
sanguine, fatorum iniquitas consulem, agentem annum
4 tricesimum, rapuit. Moles deinde eius belli translata
in Neronem est : quod is sua et virtute et fortuna
administravit peragratusque victor omnis partis
Germaniae sine ullo detrimento commissi exercitus,
quod praecipue huic duci semper curae fuit, sic
perdomuit eam, ut in formam paene stipendiariae

----

[1] perficit *Lipsius*; percipit *AP*.

----

a An ovation was a lesser triumph. This distinction
between ovation and triumph is given by Gell. v. 6.
b 12–9 B.C.

252

commander; my present work must keep to its design. After achieving this victory Nero celebrated an ovation.[a]

XCVII. But while everything was being successfully managed in this quarter of the empire, a disaster received in Germany under Marcus Lollius the legate—he was a man who was ever more eager for money than for honest action, and of vicious habits in spite of his excessive efforts at concealment—and the loss of the eagle of the fifth legion, summoned Caesar from the city to the provinces of Gaul. The burden of responsibility for this war[b] was then entrusted to Drusus Claudius, the brother of Nero, a young man endowed with as many great qualities as men's nature is capable of receiving or application developing. It would be hard to say whether his talents were the better adapted to a military career or the duties of civil life; at any rate, the charm and the sweetness of his character are said to have been inimitable, and also his modest attitude of equality towards his friends. As for his personal beauty, it was second only to that of his brother. But, after accomplishing to a great extent the subjection of Germany, in which much blood of that people was shed on various battle-fields, an unkind fate carried him off during his consulship, in his thirtieth year. The burden of responsibility for this war was then transferred to Nero. He carried it on with his customary valour and good fortune, and after traversing every part of Germany in a victorious campaign, without any loss of the army entrusted to him—for he made this one of his chief concerns — he so subdued the country as to reduce it almost to the status of a tributary

redigeret provinciae. Tum alter triumphus cum altero consulatu ei oblatus est.

1 XCVIII. Dum ea, quae diximus,[1] in Pannonia Germaniaque geruntur, atrox in Thracia bellum ortum, omnibus eius gentis nationibus in arma accensis, L. Pisonis, quem hodieque diligentissimum atque eundem lenissimum securitatis urbanae custodem 2 habemus, virtus compressit (quippe legatus Caesaris triennio cum iis bellavit gentesque ferocissimas plurimo cum earum excidio nunc acie, nunc expugnationibus in pristinum pacis redegit modum) eiusque patratione Asiae securitatem, Macedoniae pacem reddidit. De quo viro hoc omnibus sentiendum ac praedicandum est, esse mores eius vigore ac 3 lenitate mixtissimos et vix quemquam reperiri posse, qui aut otium validius diligat aut facilius sufficiat negotio et magis quae agenda sunt curet sine ulla ostentatione agendi.

1 XCIX. Brevi interiecto spatio Ti. Nero duobus consulatibus totidemque triumphis actis tribuniciae potestatis consortione aequatus Augusto, civium post unum, et hoc, quia volebat, eminentissimus, ducum maximus, fama fortunaque celeberrimus et 2 vere alterum rei publicae lumen et caput, mira quadam et incredibili atque inenarrabili pietate,

---

[1] diximus *A*; praediximus *P*.

province. He then received a second triumph, and a second consulship.

XCVIII. While the events of which we have spoken were taking place in Pannonia and in Germany, a fierce rebellion arose in Thrace, and all its clans were aroused to arms. It was terminated by the valour of Lucius Piso, whom we still have with us to-day as the most vigilant and at the same time the gentlest guardian of the security of the city. As lieutenant of Caesar he fought the Thracians for three years, and by a succession of battles and sieges, with great loss of life to the Thracians, he brought these fiercest of races to their former state of peaceful subjection. By putting an end to this war he restored security to Asia and peace to Macedonia. Of Piso all must think and say that his character is an excellent blend of firmness and gentleness, and that it would be hard to find anyone possessing a stronger love of leisure, or, on the other hand, more capable of action, and of taking the necessary measures without thrusting his activity upon our notice.

XCIX. Soon afterwards Tiberius Nero, who had now held two consulships and celebrated two triumphs ; who had been made the equal of Augustus by sharing with him the tribunician power ; the most eminent of all Roman citizens save one (and that because he wished it so) ; the greatest of generals, attended alike by fame and fortune ; veritably the second luminary and the second head of the state—this man, moved by some strangely incredible and inexpressible feeling of affection for Augustus, sought leave from him who was both his father-in-law and stepfather to rest from the unbroken succession of his labours.[a] The real

cuius causae mox detectae sunt, cum Gaius Caesar sumpsisset iam virilem togam, Lucius item maturus esset viribus,[1] ne fulgor suus orientium iuvenum obstaret initiis, dissimulata causa consilii sui, commeatum ab socero atque eodem vitrico adquiescendi

3 a continuatione laborum petiit. Quis fuerit eo tempore civitatis habitus, qui singulorum animi, quae digredientium a tanto viro omnium lacrimae, quam paene ei patria manum iniecerit, iusto servemus

4 operi : illud etiam in hoc transcursu dicendum est, ita septem annos Rhodi moratum, ut omnes, qui pro consulibus legatique in transmarinas sunt[2] profecti provincias, visendi eius gratia Rhodum deverterint[3] atque eum[4] convenientes semper privato, si illa maiestas privata umquam fuit, fasces suos summiserint fassique sint otium eius honoratius imperio suo.

1 C. Sensit terrarum orbis digressum a custodia Neronem urbis : nam et Parthus desciscens a societate Romana adiecit Armeniae manum et Germania aversis domitoris sui oculis rebellavit.

2 At in urbe eo ipso anno, quo magnificentissimis[5] gladiatorii muneris naumachiaeque spectaculis divus Augustus abhinc annos triginta se et Gallo Caninio consulibus, dedicato Martis templo animos oculosque populi Romani repleverat, foeda dictu memoriaque

---

[1] viribus *Bipont.* ; viris *AP* ; curis *Heinsius.*
[2] sunt *added by Halm.*
[3] Rhodum deverterint *add. Halm.*
[4] atque eum *Halm* ; ad quem *AP.*
[5] magnificentissimis *Cuperus* ; magnificentissimi *AP.*

---

[a] ? B.C.
[b] The Temple of Mars Ultor in the Forum of Augustus.

reasons for this were soon made plain. Inasmuch as Gaius Caesar had already assumed the toga of manhood, and Lucius was reaching maturity, he concealed his reason in order that his own glory might not stand in the way of the young men at the beginning of their careers. I must reserve for my regular history a description of the attitude of the state at this juncture, of the feelings of the individual citizens, of the tears of all at taking leave of such a man, and how nearly the state came to laying upon him its staying hand. Even in this brief epitome I ought to say that his stay of seven years in Rhodes was such that all who departed for the provinces across the sea, whether proconsuls or governors appointed by the emperor, went out of their way to see him at Rhodes, and on meeting him they lowered their fasces to him though he was but a private citizen—if such majesty could ever belong to a private citizen—thereby confessing that his retirement was more worthy of honour than their official position.

C. The whole world felt the departure of Nero from his post as protector of the city. The Parthian, breaking away from his alliance with us, laid hold of Armenia, and Germany revolted when the eyes of its conqueror were no longer upon it.

But in the city, in the very year in which Augustus, then consul with Gallus Caninius [a] (thirty years ago), had sated to repletion the minds and eyes of the Roman people with the magnificent spectacle of a gladiatorial show and a sham naval battle on the occasion of the dedication of the temple of Mars,[b] a calamity broke out in the emperor's own household which is shameful to narrate and dreadful to

3 horrenda in ipsius domo tempestas erupit. Quippe
filia eius Iulia, per omnia tanti parentis ac viri im-
memor, nihil, quod facere aut pati turpiter posset
femina, luxuria libidineve[1] infectum reliquit magni-
tudinemque fortunae suae peccandi licentia metie-
4 batur, quidquid liberet pro licito vindicans. Tum
Iulus[2] Antonius, singulare exemplum clementiae
Caesaris, violator eius domus, ipse sceleris a se
commissi ultor fuit (quem victo eius patre non tantum
incolumitate donaverat, sed sacerdotio, praetura,
consulatu, provinciis honoratum, etiam matrimonio
sororis suae filiae in artissimam adfinitatem receperat),
5 Quintiusque Crispinus, singularem nequitiam super-
cilio truci protegens, et Appius Claudius et Sempronius Gracchus ac Scipio aliique minoris nominis
utriusque ordinis viri, quas[3] cuiuslibet uxore violata
poenas pependissent,[4] pependere, cum Caesaris
filiam et Neronis violassent coniugem. Iulia relegata in insulam patriaeque et parentum subducta
oculis, quam tamen comitata mater Scribonia voluntaria[5] exilii permansit comes.
1 CI. Breve ab hoc intercesserat spatium, cum C.
Caesar ante aliis provinciis ad visendum[6] obitis in
Syriam missus, convento prius Ti. Nerone, cui

[1] libidineve *Halm* ; libidine *AP.*
[2] Iulus *Schegk* ; Iulius *AP.*   [3] quas *Orelli* ; quasi *AP.*
[4] pependissent *A* ; *om. P.*
[5] voluntaria *Lipsius* ; voluntarii *AP.*
[6] ad visendum *Lipsius*; ad sidendum *BA* ; ad sedandum *A.*

---

[a] By committing suicide.
[b] Marcella, daughter of Octavia by her first husband,
C. Marcellus.
[c] Pandataria, off the coast of Campania.
[d] He means Augustus and Livia. Her own mother was
of course Scribonia.

recall. For his daughter Julia, utterly regardless of her great father and her husband, left untried no disgraceful deed untainted with either extravagance or lust of which a woman could be guilty, either as the doer or as the object, and was in the habit of measuring the magnitude of her fortune only in the terms of licence to sin, setting up her own caprice as a law unto itself. Iulus Antonius, who had been a remarkable example of Caesar's clemency, only to become the violator of his household, avenged with his own hand *a* the crime he had committed. After the defeat of Marcus Antonius, his father, Augustus had not only granted him his life, but after honouring him with the priesthood, the praetorship, the consulship, and the governorship of provinces, had admitted him to the closest ties of relationship through a marriage with his sister's daughter.*b* Quintius Crispinus also, who hid his extraordinary depravity behind a stern brow, Appius Claudius, Sempronius Gracchus, Scipio, and other men of both orders but of less illustrious name, suffered the penalty which they would have paid had it been the wife of an ordinary citizen they had debauched instead of the daughter of Caesar and the wife of Nero. Julia was banished to an island *c* and removed from the eyes of her country and her parents,*d* though her mother Scribonia accompanied her and remained with her as a voluntary companion of her exile.

CI. Shortly after this Gaius Caesar, who had previously made a tour of other provinces, but only as a visitor, was dispatched to Syria. On his way he first paid his respects to Tiberius Nero, whom

omnem honorem ut superiori habuit, tam varie se
ibi gessit, ut nec laudaturum magna nec vitupera-
turum mediocris materia deficiat. Cum rege Parthorum, iuvene excelsissimo, in insula[1] quam amnis
Euphrates ambiebat, aequato utriusque partis numero
coiit. Quod spectaculum stantis ex diverso hinc
2 Romani, illinc Parthorum exercitus, cum duo inter
se eminentissima imperiorum et hominum coirent
capita, perquam clarum et memorabile sub initia
3 stipendiorum meorum tribuno militum mihi visere
contigit : quem militiae gradum ante sub patre tuo,
M. Vinici, et P. Silio auspicatus in Thracia Mace-
doniaque, mox Achaia Asiaque et omnibus ad Orientem visis provinciis et ore atque utroque maris
Pontici latere, haud iniucunda tot rerum, locorum,
gentium, urbium recordatione perfruor. Prior Parthus apud Gaium in nostra ripa, posterior hic apud
regem in hostili epulatus est.
1 CII. Quo tempore M. Lollii, quem veluti modera-
torem iuventae filii sui Augustus esse voluerat, per-
fida et plena subdoli ac versuti animi consilia, per
Parthum indicata Caesari, fama vulgavit.[2] Cuius
mors intra paucos dies[3] fortuita an voluntaria fuerit
ignoro. Sed quam hunc decessisse laetati homines,
tam paulo post obiisse Censorinum in iisdem provinciis graviter tulit civitas, virum demerendis homi-

[1] excelsissimo in insula *Gelenius*; excelsissimae insulae
AP.
[2] Caesari fama vulgavit *Lipsius*; Caesaris iam avulgavit
AP.
[3] *after* dies *Halm adds* secuta.

he treated with all honour as his superior. In his province he conducted himself with such versatility as to furnish much material for the panegyrist and not a little for the critic. On an island in the Euphrates, with an equal retinue on each side, Gaius had a meeting with the king of the Parthians, a young man of distinguished presence. This spectacle of the Roman army arrayed on one side, the Parthian on the other, while these two eminent leaders not only of the empires they represented but also of mankind thus met in conference—truly a notable and a memorable sight—it was my fortunate lot to see early in my career as a soldier, when I held the rank of tribune. I had already entered upon this grade of the service under your father, Marcus Vinicius, and Publius Silius in Thrace and Macedonia; later I visited Achaia and Asia and all the eastern provinces, the outlet of the Black Sea and both its coasts, and it is not without feelings of pleasure that I recall the many events, places, peoples, and cities. As for the meeting, first the Parthian dined with Gaius upon the Roman bank, and later Gaius supped with the king on the soil of the enemy.

CII. It was at this time that there were revealed to Caesar, through the Parthian king, the traitorous designs, revealing a crafty and deceitful mind, of Marcus Lollius, whom Augustus had desired to be the adviser of his still youthful son; and gossip spread the report abroad. In regard to his death, which occurred within a few days, I do not know whether it was accidental or voluntary. But the joy which people felt at this death was equalled by the sorrow which the state felt long afterwards at the decease in the same province of Censorinus,

2 nibus genitum. Armeniam deinde Gaius[1] ingressus prima parte introitus prospere rem[2] gessit; mox in conloquio, cui se temere crediderat, circa Artageram graviter a quodam, nomine Adduo, vulneratus, ex eo ut corpus minus habile, ita animum minus utilem 3 rei publicae habere coepit. Nec defuit conversatio hominum vitia eius adsentatione alentium (etenim semper magnae fortunae comes adest adulatio), per quae eo ductus erat, ut in ultimo ac remotissimo terrarum orbis angulo consenescere quam Romam regredi mallet Diu deinde reluctatus[3] invitusque revertens in Italiam in urbe Lyciae (Limyra nominant) morbo obiit, cum ante annum ferme L.[4] Caesar frater eius Hispanias petens Massiliae decessisset.

1 CIII. Sed fortuna, quae subduxerat spem magni nominis, iam tum rei publicae sua praesidia reddiderat: quippe ante utriusque horum obitum patre tuo P. Vinicio consule Ti. Nero reversus Rhodo incredibili laetitia patriam repleverat. Non est diu 2 cunctatus Caesar Augustus; neque enim quaerendus erat quem legeret, sed legendus qui eminebat. 3 Itaque quod post Lucii mortem adhuc Gaio vivo facere voluerat atque[5] vehementer repugnante Nerone erat inhibitus, post utriusque adulescentium obitum facere perseveravit, ut et tribuniciae po-

---

[1] Gaius *added by Krause.*
[2] rem *added by Heinsius.*
[3] diu deinde reluctatus *Ruhnken*; diu de reluctatus *A*; deinde reluctatus *P*.
[4] L. *Gelenius*; quinquagesimum *AP*.
[5] atque *P*; eoque (vel eo quod) *B*; quae eo *A*; adeoque *Heinsius.*

---

[a] A.D. 4.   [b] A.D. 2.

a man born to win the affections of men. Then
Gaius entered Armenia and at first conducted his
campaign with success ; but later, in a parley near
Artagera, to which he rashly entrusted his person,
he was seriously wounded by a man named Adduus,
so that, in consequence, his body became less active,
and his mind of less service to the state. Nor was
there lacking the companionship of persons who
encouraged his defects by flattery — for flattery
always goes hand in hand with high position—as a
result of which he wished to spend his life in a remote
and distant corner of the world rather than return
to Rome. Then, in the act of returning to Italy,
after long resistance and still against his will, he
died [a] in a city of Lycia which they call Limyra, his
brother Lucius having died about a year before [b] at
Massilia on his way to Spain.

CIII. But fortune, which had removed the hope
of the great name of Caesar,[c] had already restored
to the state her real protector ; for the return of
Tiberius Nero from Rhodes in the consulship of
Publius Vinicius, your father, and before the death
of either of these youths, had filled his country with
joy. Caesar Augustus did not long hesitate, for he
had no need to search for one to choose as his
successor but merely to choose the one who
towered above the others. Accordingly, what he
had wished to do after the death of Lucius but
while Gaius was still living, and had been prevented
from doing by the strong opposition of Nero himself,
he now insisted upon carrying out after the death
of both young men, namely, to make Nero his

[c] *i.e.* Gaius and Lucius who were grandsons of Augustus.
Tiberius was merely a step-son.

VELLEIUS PATERCULUS

testatis consortionem Neroni constitueret, multum
quidem eo cum domi tum in senatu recusante, et
eum Aelio Cato C. Sentio consulibus V. Kal. Iulias,
post urbem conditam annis septingentis quinquaginta quattuor, abhinc annos septem et viginti ad-
optaret. Laetitiam illius diei concursumque civitatis
4 et vota paene inserentium caelo manus spemque
conceptam perpetuae securitatis aeternitatisque
Romani imperii vix in illo iusto opere abunde per-
sequi poterimus, nedum hic implere temptemus,
5 contenti[1] id unum dixisse quam ille omnibus faustus[2]
fuerit. Tum refulsit certa spes liberorum parentibus,
viris matrimoniorum, dominis patrimonii, omnibus
hominibus salutis, quietis, pacis, tranquillitatis, adeo
ut nec plus sperari potuerit nec spei responderi
felicius.
1 CIV. Adoptatus eadem die etiam M. Agrippa,
quem post mortem Agrippae Iulia enixa erat, sed
in Neronis adoptione illud adiectum his ipsis Caesaris
2 verbis : hoc, inquit, rei publicae causa facio. Non
diu vindicem custodemque imperii sui morata in
urbe patria protinus in Germaniam misit, ubi ante
triennium sub M. Vinicio, avo tuo, clarissimo viro,
immensum exarserat bellum. Erat id[3] ab eo qui-

---

[1] contenti *added by Rhenanus* ; contenti simus *Burer.*
[2] faustus *added by Halm.*
[3] id *Lipsius* ; et *AP.*

---

[a] A.D. 4.

associate in the tribunician power, in spite of his continued objection both in private and in the senate ; and in the consulship of Aelius Catus and Gaius Sentius,[a] on the twenty-seventh of June, he adopted him, seven hundred and fifty-four years after the founding of the city, and twenty-seven years ago. The rejoicing of that day, the concourse of the citizens, their vows as they stretched their hands almost to the very heavens, and the hopes which they entertained for the perpetual security and the eternal existence of the Roman empire, I shall hardly be able to describe to the full even in my comprehensive work, much less try to do it justice here. I shall simply content myself with stating what a day of good omen it was for all. On that day there sprang up once more in parents the assurance of safety for their children, in husbands for the sanctity of marriage, in owners for the safety of their property, and in all men the assurance of safety, order, peace, and tranquillity ; indeed, it would have been hard to entertain larger hopes, or to have them more happily fulfilled.

CIV. On the same day Marcus Agrippa, to whom Julia had given birth after the death of Agrippa, was also adopted by Augustus ; but, in the case of Nero, an addition was made to the formula of adoption in Caesar's own words : " This I do for reasons of state." His country did not long detain at Rome the champion and the guardian of her empire, but forthwith dispatched him to Germany, where, three years before, an extensive war had broken out in the governorship of that illustrious man, Marcus Vinicius, your grandfather. Vinicius had carried on this war with success in some quarters,

busdam in locis gestum, quibusdam sustentatum feliciter, eoque nomine decreta ei cum speciossisima inscriptione operum ornamenta triumphalia.

3 Hoc tempus me, functum ante tribunatu, castrorum Ti. Caesaris militem fecit : quippe protinus ab adoptione missus cum eo praefectus equitum in Germaniam, successor officii patris mei, caelestissimorum eius operum per annos continuos novem[1] praefectus aut legatus spectator, tum[2] pro captu mediocritatis meae adiutor fui. Neque illi spectaculo, quo fructus sum, simile condicio mortalis recipere videtur mihi, cum per celeberrimam Italiae partem tractumque omnem Galliae provinciarum veterem imperatorem et ante meritis ac virtutibus[3] quam nomine Caesarem revisentes sibi quisque quam 4 illi gratularentur plenius. At vero militum conspectu eius elicitae gaudio lacrimae alacritasque et salutationis nova quaedam exultatio et contingendi manum cupiditas non continentium protinus quin adiicerent, " videmus te, imperator ? Salvum recepimus ? " Ac deinde " ego tecum, imperator, in Armenia, ego in Raetia fui, ego a te in Vindelicis, ego in Pannonia, ego in Germania donatus sum " neque verbis exprimi et fortasse vix mereri fidem potest.

[1] VIIII. *P*; VIII. *A*.
[2] spectator tum *Thomas*; spectatum *A*; spectatus *P*; spectator et *Gelenius followed by Halm.*
[3] virtutibus *Lipsius*; viribus *AP*.

---

[a] Inasmuch as, under the empire, the emperor was technically commander-in-chief, he alone had a legitimate claim to a triumph. After 14 B.C. triumphs were rarely conceded to any but members of the imperial family. But in lieu of a triumph the victorious general was given ti tles bestowed upon the *imperator* of republican times, the permission to wear the triumphal robe and the right to bequeath triumphal statues to his descendants.

and in others had made a successful defence, and on this account there had been decreed to him the ornaments of a triumph *a* with an honorary inscription recording his deeds.

It was at this time that I became a soldier in the camp of Tiberius Caesar, after having previously filled the duties of the tribunate. For, immediately after the adoption of Tiberius, I was sent with him to Germany as prefect of cavalry, succeeding my father in that position, and for nine continuous years as prefect of cavalry or as commander of a legion I was a spectator of his superhuman achievements, and further assisted in them to the extent of my modest ability. I do not think that mortal man will be permitted to behold again a sight like that which I enjoyed, when, throughout the most populous parts of Italy and the full extent of the provinces of Gaul, the people as they beheld once more their old commander, who by virtue of his services had long been a Caesar before he was such in name, congratulated themselves in even heartier terms than they congratulated him. Indeed, words cannot express the feelings of the soldiers at their meeting, and perhaps my account will scarcely be believed—the tears which sprang to their eyes in their joy at the sight of him, their eagerness, their strange transports in saluting him, their longing to touch his hand, and their inability to restrain such cries as " Is it really you that we see, commander? " " Have we received you safely back among us? " " I served with you, general, in Armenia! " " And I in Raetia! " " I received my decoration from you in Vindelicia! " " And I mine in Pannonia! " " And I in Germany! "

VELLEIUS PATERCULUS

1   **CV.** Intrata protinus Germania, subacti Cannine-
fates, Attuarii, Bructeri, recepti Cherusci (gentis eius
Arminius[1] mox nostra clade nobilis),transitus Visurgis,
penetrata ulteriora, cum omnem partem asperrimi
et periculosissimi belli Caesar vindicaret sibi,[2] iis,
quae minoris erant discriminis, Sentium Saturninum,
qui iam[3] legatus patris eius in Germania fuerat,
2 praefecisset, virum multiplicem virtutibus,[4] gnavum,
agilem, providum militariumque officiorum patientem
ac peritum pariter, sed eundem, ubi negotia fecissent
locum otio, liberaliter lauteque eo abutentem, ita
tamen, ut eum splendidum atque hilarem potius
quam luxuriosum aut desidem diceres.   De cuius
viri claro ingenio celebrique consulatu praediximus.
3 Anni eius aestiva usque in mensem Decembrem pro-
ducta inmanis emolumentum fecere victoriae.   Pietas
sua Caesarem paene obstructis[5] hieme Alpibus in
urbem traxit, at tutela[6] imperii eum veris initio re-
duxit in Germaniam, in cuius mediis finibus ad caput
Lupiae[7] fluminis hiberna digrediens princeps locaverat.
1   **CVI.** Pro dii boni, quanti voluminis opera insequenti aestate sub duce Tiberio Caesare gessimus!
Perlustrata armis tota Germania est, victae gentes

---

   [1] gentis eius Arminius *Fr. Jacob*; gentis (-tes *P*) et
inamminus (inamminus *BA*) *AP*.
   [2] sibi *Cludius*; in *AP*.
   [3] iam *Gruner*; tum *AP*.
   [4] multiplicem virtutibus *Raphelengius*; multiplicem in
virtutibus *AP*.
   [5] obstructis *Gelenius*; extructis *AP*.
   [6] at tutela *Lipsius*; ad tutelam *AP*.
   [7] Lupiae *Lipsius*; Iuliae *AP*.

---

      [a] A.D. 4.   [b] Bk. II. Chap. XCII.
   [c] The position of *princeps* before the verb seems to justify
this interpretation in preference to taking it as a substantive.

CV. He at once entered Germany.[a] The Cannine-
fates, the Attuarii, and Bructeri were subdued, the
Cherusci (Arminius, a member of this race, was soon
to become famous for the disaster inflicted upon us)
were again subjugated, the Weser crossed, and the
regions beyond it penetrated. Caesar claimed for
himself every part of the war that was difficult or
dangerous, placing Sentius Saturninus, who had
already served as legate under his father in Germany,
in charge of expeditions of a less dangerous character :
a man many-sided in his virtues, a man of energy
of action, and of foresight, alike able to endure the
duties of a soldier as he was well trained in them,
but who, likewise, when his labours left room for
leisure, made a liberal and elegant use of it, but with
this reservation, that one would call him sumptuous
and jovial rather than extravagant or indolent.
About the distinguished ability of this illustrious
man and his famous consulship I have already
spoken.[b] The prolonging of the campaign of that
year into the month of December increased the
benefits derived from the great victory. Caesar
was drawn to the city by his filial affection, though
the Alps were almost blocked by winter's snows ;
but the defence of the empire brought him at the
beginning of spring back to Germany, where he had
on his departure pitched his winter camp at the
source of the river Lippe, in the very heart of the
country, the first[c] Roman to winter there.

CVI. Ye Heavens, how large a volume could be
filled with the tale of our achievements in the
following summer[d] under the generalship of Tiberius
Caesar ! All Germany was traversed by our armies,

[d] A.D. 5.

paene nominibus incognitae, receptae Cauchorum
nationes : omnis eorum iuventus infinita numero,
immensa corporibus, situ locorum tutissima, traditis
armis una cum ducibus suis saepta fulgenti armato-
que militum nostrorum agmine ante imperatoris
2 procubuit tribunal. Fracti Langobardi, gens etiam
Germana feritate ferocior ; denique quod numquam
antea spe conceptum, nedum opere temptatum erat,
ad quadringentesimum miliarium a Rheno usque ad
flumen Albim, qui Semnonum Hermundurorumque
fines praeterfluit, Romanus cum signis perductus
3 exercitus. Et eadem[1] mira felicitate et cura ducis,
temporum quoque observantia, classis, quae Oceani
circumnavigaverat sinus, ab inaudito atque incognito
ante mari flumine Albi subvecta, cum plurimarum
gentium victoria parta[2] cum abundantissima rerum
omnium copia exercitui Caesarique se iunxit.

1 CVII. Non tempero mihi quin tantae rerum magnitudini hoc, qualecumque est, inseram. Cum citerio-
rem ripam praedicti fluminis castris occupassemus
et ulterior armata hostium virtute[3] fulgeret, sub
omnem motum conatumque[4] nostrarum navium protinus refugientium, unus e barbaris aetate senior,
corpore excellens, dignitate, quantum ostendebat
cultus, eminens, cavatum, ut illis mos est, ex materia

---

[1] eadem *Kritz* ; eodem *AP*.   [2] parta *added by Halm*.
          [3] virtute *A* ; iuventute *P*.
  [4] motum conatumque *Halm* ; motumque *BA* ; motum *P*.

---

[a] If he means simply the North Sea, it had been already
navigated by Drusus but not so far to the eastward.

races were conquered hitherto almost unknown, even
by name ; and the tribes of the Cauchi were again
subjugated. All the flower of their youth, infinite
in number though they were, huge of stature and
protected by the ground they held, surrendered
their arms, and, flanked by a gleaming line of our
soldiers, fell with their generals upon their knees
before the tribunal of the commander. The power
of the Langobardi was broken, a race surpassing
even the Germans in savagery ; and finally—and
this is something which had never before been
entertained even as a hope, much less actually
attempted—a Roman army with its standards was
led four hundred miles beyond the Rhine as far as
the river Elbe, which flows past the territories of
the Semnones and the Hermunduri. And with the
same wonderful combination of careful planning and
good fortune on the part of the general, and a close
watch upon the seasons, the fleet which had skirted
the windings of the sea coast sailed up the Elbe
from a sea hitherto unheard of and unknown,[a] and
after proving victorious over many tribes effected a
junction with Caesar and the army, bringing with
it a great abundance of supplies of all kinds.

CVII. Even in the midst of these great events I
cannot refrain from inserting this little incident. We
were encamped on the nearer bank of the aforesaid
river, while on the farther bank glittered the arms
of the enemies' troops, who showed an inclination
to flee at every movement and manœuvre of our
vessels, when one of the barbarians, advanced in
years, tall of stature, of high rank, to judge by his
dress, embarked in a canoe, made as is usual with

conscendit alveum solusque id navigii genus temperans ad medium processit fluminis et petiit, liceret
2 sibi sine periculo in eam, quam armis tenebamus,
egredi ripam ac videre Caesarem. Data petenti
facultas. Tum adpulso lintre et diu tacitus contemplatus Caesarem, nostra quidem, inquit, furit iuventus, quae cum vestrum numen absentium colat, prae-
sentium potius arma metuit quam sequitur fidem.
Sed ego beneficio ac permissu tuo, Caesar, quos ante
audiebam, hodie vidi deos, nec feliciorem ullum
vitae meae aut optavi aut sensi diem. Impetrato-
que ut manum contingeret, reversus in navicu-
lam, sine fine respectans Caesarem ripae suorum
adpulsus est. Victor omnium gentium locorumque,
3 quos adierat Caesar,[1] incolumi inviolatoque et semel
tantummodo magna cum clade hostium fraude
eorum temptato exercitu in hiberna legiones re-
duxit, eadem qua priore anno festinatione urbem
petens.

1   CVIII. Nihil erat iam in Germania, quod vinci
posset, praeter gentem Marcomannorum, quae Maro-
boduo duce excita sedibus suis atque in interiora
refugiens incinctos Hercynia silva[2] campos incolebat.
2 Nulla festinatio huius viri mentionem transgredi
debet. Maroboduus, genere nobilis, corpore prae-
valens, animo ferox, natione magis quam ratione
barbarus, non tumultuarium neque fortuitum neque

---

[1] cum *after* Caesar *deleted by Herelius.*
[2] Hercinia silva *Heinsius*; Herciniae silvae *AP.*

them of a hollowed log, and guiding this strange craft he advanced alone to the middle of the stream and asked permission to land without harm to himself on the bank occupied by our troops, and to see Caesar. Permission was granted. Then he beached his canoe, and, after gazing upon Caesar for a long time in silence, exclaimed : " Our young men are insane, for though they worship you as divine when absent, when you are present they fear your armies instead of trusting to your protection. But I, by your kind permission, Caesar, have to-day seen the gods of whom I merely used to hear ; and in my life have never hoped for or experienced a happier day." After asking for and receiving permission to touch Caesar's hand, he again entered his canoe. and continued to gaze back upon him until he landed upon his own bank. Victorious over all the nations and countries which he approached, his army safe and unimpaired, having been attacked but once, and that too through deceit on the part of the enemy and with great loss on their side, Caesar led his legions back to winter quarters, and sought the city with the same haste as in the previous year.

CVIII. Nothing remained to be conquered in Germany except the people of the Marcomanni, which, leaving its settlements at the summons of its leader Maroboduus, had retired into the interior and now dwelt in the plains surrounded by the Hercynian forest. No considerations of haste should lead us to pass over this man Maroboduus without mention. A man of noble family, strong in body and courageous in mind, a barbarian by birth but not in intelligence, he achieved among his countrymen no mere chief's position gained as the result of internal

273

mobilem et ex voluntate parentium constantem inter suos occupavit principatum, sed certum imperium vimque regiam complexus animo statuit avocata procul a Romanis gente sua eo progredi, ubi cum propter potentiora arma refugisset, sua faceret potentissima. Occupatis igitur, quos[1] praediximus, locis finitimos omnis aut bello domuit aut condicionibus iuris sui fecit.

1 CIX. Corpus suum custodientium[2] imperium, perpetuis exercitiis paene ad Romanae disciplinae formam redactum, brevi in eminens et nostro quoque imperio timendum perduxit fastigium gerebatque se ita adversus Romanos, ut neque bello nos lacesseret, et si[3] lacesseretur, superesse sibi vim ac 2 voluntatem resistendi ostenderet.[4] Legati, quos mittebat ad Caesares, interdum ut supplicem commendabant, interdum ut pro pari loquebantur. Gentibus hominibusque a nobis desciscentibus erat apud eum perfugium, in[5] totumque ex male dissimulato agebat aemulum ; exercitumque, quem septuaginta milium peditum, quattuor equitum fecerat, adsiduis adversus finitimos bellis exercendo maiori quam, 3 quod habebat, operi praeparabat : eratque etiam eo timendus, quod cum Germaniam ad laevam et in fronte, Pannoniam ad dextram, a tergo sedium suarum haberet Noricos, tamquam in omnes semper venturus

---

[1] quos *P*; quis *BA*.
[2] custodientium *Madvig*; custodia tum *AP*.
[3] lacesseret, at si *added by Rhenanus*.
[4] ostenderet *added by Burman*.
[5] in *added by Acidalius*.

---

[a] The region was that of Bohemia. By "in front" he means "to the north." The "rear" is to the south, the "left" to the west, and the "right" to the east, although Pannonia really lay south-east.

disorders or chance or liable to change and dependent
upon the caprice of his subjects, but, conceiving in
his mind the idea of a definite empire and royal
powers, he resolved to remove his own race far
away from the Romans and to migrate to a place
where, inasmuch as he had fled before the strength
of more powerful arms, he might make his own all
powerful. Accordingly, after occupying the region
we have mentioned, he proceeded to reduce all the
neighbouring races by war, or to bring them under
his sovereignty by treaty.

CIX. The body of guards protecting the kingdom
of Maroboduus, which by constant drill had been
brought almost to the Roman standard of discipline,
soon placed him in a position of power that was
dreaded even by our empire. His policy toward
Rome was to avoid provoking us by war, but at the
same time to let us understand that, if he were
provoked by us he had in reserve the power and the
will to resist. The envoys whom he sent to the
Caesars sometimes commended him to them as a
suppliant and sometimes spoke as though they
represented an equal. Races and individuals who
revolted from us found in him a refuge, and in all
respects, with but little concealment, he played the
part of a rival. His army, which he had brought up
to the number of seventy thousand foot and four
thousand horse, he was steadily preparing, by
exercising it in constant wars against his neighbours,
for some greater task than that which he had in
hand. He was also to be feared on this account, that,
having Germany at the left and in front of his
settlements, Pannonia on the right, and Noricum in
the rear [2] of them, he was dreaded by all as one who

4 ab omnibus timebatur. Nec securam incrementi sui
patiebatur esse Italiam, quippe cum a summis Alpium
iugis, quae finem Italiae terminant, initium eius[1]
finium haud multo plus ducentis milibus passuum
5 abesset. Hunc virum et hanc regionem proximo
anno diversis e partibus Ti. Caesar adgredi statuit.
Sentio Saturnino mandatum, ut per Cattos excisis
continentibus Hercyniae silvis legiones Boiohaemum
(id regioni, quam incolebat Maroboduus, nomen est)
duceret,[2] ipse a Carnunto, qui locus Norici regni
proximus ab hac parte erat, exercitum, qui in
Illyrico merebat, ducere in Marcomannos orsus est.
1   CX. Rumpit interdum, interdum[3] moratur proposita hominum fortuna. Praeparaverat iam hiberna
Caesar ad Danubium admotoque exercitu non plus
quam quinque dierum iter a primis hostium aberat,
2 legionesque quas[4] Saturninum admovere placuerat,
paene aequali divisae intervallo ab hoste intra paucos
dies in praedicto loco cum Caesare se[5] iuncturae erant,
cum universa Pannonia, insolens longae pacis bonis,
adulta viribus, Delmatia omnibusque tractus eius gentibus in societatem adductis consilii,[6] arma corripuit.
3 Tum necessaria gloriosis praeposita neque tutum
visum abdito in interiora exercitu vacuam tam
vicino hosti relinquere Italiam. Gentium nationum-

---

[1] eius *P*; cuius *BA*.
[2] duceret *supplied by Lipsius.*
[3] *The second* interdum *added by Heinsius*; iter dum *AP*.
[4] aberat legionesque quas *supplied by Haupt.*
[5] se *added by Krause.*
[6] consilii *Fröhlich*; constitit *AP*.

---

[a] Pannonian War, A.D. 6–9.

might at any moment descend upon all. Nor did he permit Italy to be free from concern as regards his growing power, since the summits of the Alps which mark her boundary were not more than two hundred miles distant from his boundary line. Such was the man and such the region that Tiberius Caesar resolved to attack from opposite directions in the course of the coming year. Sentius Saturninus had instructions to lead his legions through the country of the Catti into Boiohaemum, for that is the name of the region occupied by Maroboduus, cutting a passage through the Hercynian forest which bounded the region, while from Carnuntum, the nearest point of the kingdom of Noricum in this direction, he himself undertook to lead against the Marcomanni the army which was serving in Illyricum.

CX. Fortune sometimes breaks off completely, sometimes merely delays, the execution of men's plans. Caesar had already arranged his winter quarters on the Danube, and had brought up his army to within five days' march of the advanced posts of the enemy ; and the legions which he had ordered Saturninus to bring up, separated from the enemy by an almost equal distance, were on the point of effecting a junction with Caesar at a predetermined rendezvous within a few days, when all Pannonia, grown arrogant through the blessings of a long peace and now at the maturity of her power, suddenly took up arms,ᵃ bringing Dalmatia and all the races of that region into her alliance. Thereupon glory was sacrificed to necessity ; and it did not seem to Tiberius a safe course to keep his army buried in the interior of the country and thus leave Italy unprotected from an enemy so near at hand. The

277

que, quae rebellaverant, omnis numerus amplius octingentis milibus explebat ; ducenta fere peditum colligebantur armis habilia, equitum novem. Cuius 4 immensae multitudinis, parentis acerrimis ac peritissimis ducibus, pars petere Italiam decreverat iunctam sibi Nauporti ac Tergestis confinio, pars in Macedoniam se effuderat,[1] pars suis sedibus praesidium esse destinaverat. Maxima[2] duobus Batoni- 5 bus[3] ac Pinneti ducibus auctoritas erat.[4] Omnibus autem Pannoniis non disciplinae tantummodo, sed linguae quoque notitia Romanae, plerisque etiam litterarum usus et familiaris animorum[5] erat exercitatio. Itaque hercules nulla umquam natio tam 6 mature consilio belli bellum iunxit ac decreta patravit. Oppressi cives Romani, trucidati negotiatores, magnus vexillariorum numerus ad internecionem ea in regione, quae plurimum ab imperatore aberat, caesus, occupata armis Macedonia, omnia et in omnibus locis igni ferroque vastata. Quin[6] etiam tantus huius belli metus fuit, ut stabilem illum et firmatum[7] tantorum bellorum experientia Caesaris Augusti animum quateret atque terreret.

1 CXI. Habiti itaque dilectus, revocati undique et omnes veterani, viri feminaeque ex censu libertinum

---

[1] se effuderat *Ursinus* ; effugerat *AP*.
[2] maxima *Heinsius* ; proxima *AP*.
[3] duobus Batonibus *AP* ; Batoni *Halm*.
[4] in *after* erat *deleted by Heinsius*.
[5] animorum *AP* ; armorum *Bothe followed by Halm*.
[6] quin *Vascosanus* ; quia *AP*.
[7] firmatum *Burer* ; formatum *BA* ; fortunatum *P*.

full number of the races and tribes which had
rebelled reached a total of more than eight hundred
thousand. About two hundred thousand infantry
trained to arms, and nine thousand cavalry were
being assembled. Of this immense number, which
acted under the orders of energetic and capable
generals, one portion had decided to make Italy its
goal, which was connected with them by the line of
Nauportum and Tergeste, a second had already
poured into Macedonia, while a third had set itself
the task of protecting their own territories. The
chief authority rested with the two Batones and
Pinnes as generals. Now all the Pannonians possessed
not only a knowledge of Roman discipline but also
of the Roman tongue, many also had some measure
of literary culture, and the exercise of the intellect
was not uncommon among them. And so it came
to pass, by Hercules, that no nation ever displayed
such swiftness in following up with war its own
plans for war, and in putting its resolves into execution. Roman citizens were overpowered, traders were
massacred, a considerable detachment of veterans,
stationed in the region which was most remote from
the commander, was exterminated to a man, Macedonia was seized by armed forces, everywhere was
wholesale devastation by fire and sword. Moreover,
such a panic did this war inspire that even the
courage of Caesar Augustus, rendered steady and
firm by experience in so many wars, was shaken
with fear.

CXI. Accordingly levies were held, from every
quarter all the veterans were recalled to the
standards, men and women were compelled, in
proportion to their income, to furnish freedmen as

coactae dare militem. Audita in senatu vox principis, decimo die, ni caveretur, posse hostem in urbis Romae venire conspectum. Senatorum equitumque
2 Romanorum exactae ad id bellum operae, pollicitati.[1] Omnia haec frustra praeparassemus, nisi qui illa regeret fuisset. Itaque ut praesidium ultimum[2] res publica ab Augusto ducem in bellum poposcit Tiberium.
3 Habuit in hoc quoque bello mediocritas nostra speciosi ministerii[3] locum. Finita equestri militia designatus quaestor necdum senator aequatus senatoribus, etiam designatis tribunis plebei, partem exercitus ab urbe traditi ab Augusto perduxi ad
4 filium eius. In quaestura deinde remissa sorte provinciae legatus eiusdem ad eundem missus sum.[4]

Quas nos primo anno acies hostium vidimus! Quantis prudentia ducis opportunitatibus furentes[5] eorum vires universas elusimus,[6] fudimus[7] partibus! Quanto cum temperamento simul civilitatis[8] res auctoritate imperatoria[9] agi vidimus! Qua prudentia hiberna disposita sunt! Quanto opere inclusus custodiis exercitus nostri, ne qua posset erumpere inopsque copiarum et intra se furens viribus hostis elanguesceret!

1 CXII. Felix eventu, forte conatu prima aestate

[1] *Before* pollicitati *Halm supplies* prompte.
[2] ultimum *Lipsius*; militum *AP*.
[3] ministerii *Lipsius*; ministri *AP*.
[4] missus sum *Halm*; missum *A*; missus *P*.
[5] furentes *BAP*; fruentes *Orelli*.
[6] elusimus *suggested by a reviewer in Bibl. phil.* i. 42, eius imus
euasimus *A*; evasimus *P*.   [7] fudimus *added by Haase.*
[8] civilitatis *Madvig after Ruhnken*; utilitatis *AP*.
[9] imperatoria *Madvig*; imperatoris *AP*.

---

a Legatus Augusti: as staff officer appointed by Augustus and attached to the army of Tiberius.

soldiers. Men heard Augustus say in the senate, that, unless precautions were taken, the enemy might appear in sight of Rome within ten days. The services of senators and knights were demanded for this war, and promised. All these our preparations would have been vain had we not had the man to take command. And so, as a final measure of protection, the state demanded from Augustus that Tiberius should conduct the war.

In this war also my modest abilities had an opportunity for glorious service. I was now, at the end of my service in the cavalry, quaestor designate, and though not yet a senator I was placed upon a parity with senators and even tribunes elect, and led from the city to Tiberius a portion of the army which was entrusted to me by Augustus. Then in my quaestorship, giving up my right to have a province allotted me, I was sent to Tiberius as *legatus Augusti*.[a]

What armies of the enemy did we see drawn up for battle in that first year! What opportunities did we avail ourselves of through the foresight of the general to evade their united forces and rout them in separate divisions! With what moderation and kindness did we see all the business of warfare conducted, though under the authority of a military commander! With what judgement did he place our winter camps! How carefully was the enemy so blockaded by the outposts of our army that he could nowhere break through, and that, through lack of supplies and by disaffection within his own ranks, he might gradually be weakened in strength!

CXII. An exploit of Messalinus in the first summer of the war, fortunate in its issue as it was bold in

2 belli Messalini opus mandandum est memoriae. Qui
vir animo etiam quam gente nobilior dignissimusque,[1]
qui et patrem Corvinum habuisset et cognomen suum
Cottae fratri relinqueret, praepositus Illyrico subita
rebellione cum semiplena legione vicesima circum-
datus hostili exercitu amplius viginti milia[2] fudit
fugavitque et ob id ornamentis triumphalibus honoratus est.

3   Ita placebat barbaris numerus suus, ita fiducia
virium, ut ubicumque Caesar esset, nihil in se
reponerent. Pars exercitus eorum, proposita ipsi duci
et ad arbitrium utilitatemque nostram macerata per-
ductaque ad exitiabilem famem, neque instantem
sustinere neque cum[3] facientibus copiam pugnandi
derigentibusque aciem ausa congredi occupato monte

4 Claudio munitione se defendit. At ea pars, quae
obviam se effuderat exercitui, quem A. Caecina et
Silvanus Plautius consulares ex transmarinis adduce-
bant provinciis, circumfusa quinque legionibus nostris
auxiliaribusque et equitatui regio (quippe magnam
Thracum manum iunctus praedictis ducibus Rhoemetalces,[4] Thraciae rex, in adiutorium eius belli
secum trahebat) paene exitiabilem omnibus cladem

5 intulit : fusa[5] regiorum equestris acies, fugatae alae,

---

[1] que *added by Heinsius.*
[2] hostium *after* milia *deleted by Orelli.*
[3] cum *Ruhnken* ; ut *AP.*
[4] Rhoemetalces *Rhenanus* ; Rhomo et Alces *BAP.*
[5] fusa *Voss.* ; fuga *BA* ; fugata *P.*

---

[a] A mountain range in Pannonia near the modern
Warasdin on the river Drave.

undertaking, must here be recorded for posterity. This man, who was even more noble in heart than in birth, and thoroughly worthy of having had Corvinus as his father, and of leaving ·his cognomen to his brother Cotta, was in command in Illyricum, and, at the sudden outbreak of the rebellion, finding himself surrounded by the army of the enemy and supported by only the twentieth legion, and that at but half its normal strength, he routed and put to flight more than twenty thousand, and for this was honoured with the ornaments of a triumph.

The barbarians were so little satisfied with their numbers and had so little confidence in their own strength that they had no faith in themselves where Caesar was. The part of their army which faced the commander himself, worn down according as it suited our pleasure or advantage, and reduced to the verge of destruction by famine, not daring to withstand him when he took the offensive, nor to meet our men when they gave them an opportunity for fighting and drew up their line of battle, occupied the Claudian mountain[a] and defended itself behind fortifications. But the division of their forces which had swarmed out to meet the army which the consulars Aulus Caecina and Silvanus Plautius were bringing up from the provinces across the sea, surrounded five of our legions, together with the troops of our allies and the cavalry of the king (for Rhoemetalces, king of Thrace, in conjunction with the aforesaid generals was bringing with him a large body of Thracians as reinforcements for the war), and inflicted a disaster that came near being fatal to all. The horsemen of the king were routed, the cavalry of the allies put to flight, the cohorts

conversae cohortes sunt, apud signa quoque legionum trepidatum. Sed Romani virtus militis plus eo tempore vindicavit gloriae quam ducibus reliquit, qui multum a more imperatoris sui discrepantes ante in hostem inciderunt, quam per exploratores, ubi hostis esset, cognoscerent. Iam igitur in dubiis 6 rebus semet ipsae legiones adhortatae, iugulatis ab hoste quibusdam tribunis militum, interempto praefecto castrorum praefectisque cohortium, non incruentis centurionibus, e quibus[1] etiam primi ordinis[2] cecidere, invasere hostes nec sustinuisse contenti perrupta eorum acie ex insperato victoriam vindicaverunt.

7 Hoc fere tempore Agrippa, qui eodem die quo Tiberius adoptatus ab avo suo naturali erat et iam ante biennium, qualis esset, apparere coeperat, mira pravitate animi atque ingenii in praecipitia conversus patris atque eiusdem avi sui animum alienavit sibi, moxque crescentibus in dies vitiis dignum furore suo habuit exitum.

1 CXIII. Accipe nunc, M. Vinici, tantum in bello ducem, quantum in pace vides principem. Iunctis exercitibus, quique sub Caesare fuerant quique ad eum venerant, contractisque in una castra decem legionibus, septuaginta amplius cohortibus, decem

[1] e quibus *Boecler* ; qui *P* ; quibus *BA*.
[2] ordinis *Gelenius* ; ordines *AP*.

---

a i.e. Augustus who was his grandfather and adopted father.

turned their backs to the enemy, and the panic
extended even to the standards of the legion. But
in this crisis the valour of the Roman soldier claimed
for itself a greater share of glory than it left to the
generals, who, departing far from the policy of their
commander, had allowed themselves to come into
contact with the enemy before they had learned
through their scouts where the enemy was. At
this critical moment, when some tribunes of the
soldiers had been slain by the enemy, the prefect
of the camp and several prefects of cohorts had been
cut off, a number of centurions had been wounded,
and even some of the centurions of the first rank
had fallen, the legions, shouting encouragement to
each other, fell upon the enemy, and not content with sustaining their onslaught, broke through
their line and wrested a victory from a desperate
plight.

About this time Agrippa, who had been adopted
by his natural grandfather on the same day as
Tiberius, and had already, two years before, begun
to reveal his true character, alienated from himself
the affection of his father and grandfather,[a] falling
into reckless ways by a strange depravity of mind
and disposition ; and soon, as his vices increased
daily, he met the end which his madness deserved.

CXIII. Listen now, Marcus Vinicius, to the proof
that Caesar was no less great in war as a general
than you now see him in peace as an emperor.
When the two armies were united, that is to say
the troops which had served under Caesar and
those which had come to reinforce him, and there
were now gathered together in one camp ten legions,
more than seventy cohorts, fourteen troops of cavalry

alis et[1] pluribus quam decem veteranorum milibus,
ad hoc magno voluntariorum numero frequentique
equite regio, tanto denique exercitu, quantus nullo
umquam loco post bella fuerat civilia, omnes eo
ipso laeti erant maximamque fiduciam victoriae in
2 numero reponebant. At imperator, optimus eorum
quae agebat iudex et utilia speciosis praeferens
quodque semper eum facientem vidi in omnibus
bellis, quae probanda essent, non quae utique pro-
barentur sequens, paucis diebus exercitum, qui
venerat, ad refovendas ex itinere eius vires moratus,
cum eum maiorem, quam ut temperari posset, neque
habilem gubernaculo cerneret, dimittere statuit;
3 prosecutusque longo et perquam laborioso itinere,
cuius difficultas narrari vix potest, ut neque universos
quisquam auderet adgredi et partem digredientium,
suorum quisque metu finium, universi temptare non
possent, remisit eo, unde venerant, et ipse asperrimae
hiemis initio regressus Sisciam legatos, inter quos
ipsi fuimus, partitis praefecit hibernis.
1 CXIV. O rem dictu non eminentem, sed solida
veraque virtute atque utilitate maximam, experientia
suavissimam, humanitate singularem! Per omne

---

[1] X alis et *Laurent.*; XIIII sed *PA*; XIIII alis et
Lipsius.

and more than ten thousand veterans, and in addition a large number of volunteers and the numerous cavalry of the king—in a word a greater army than had ever been assembled in one place since the civil wars—all were finding satisfaction in this fact and reposed their greatest hope of victory in their numbers. But the general, who was the best judge of the course he pursued, preferring efficiency to show, and, as we have so often seen him doing in all his wars, following the course which deserved approval rather than that which was currently approved, after keeping the army which had newly arrived for only a few days in order to allow it to recover from the march, decided to send it away, since he saw that it was too large to be managed and was not well adapted to effective control. And so he sent it back whence it came, escorting it with his own army a long and exceedingly laborious march, whose difficulty can hardly be described. His purpose in this was, on the one hand, that no one might dare to attack his united forces, and, on the other, to prevent the united forces of the enemy from falling upon the departing division, through the apprehension of each nation for its own territory. Then returning himself to Siscia, at the beginning of a very hard winter, he placed his lieutenants, of whom I was one, in charge of the divisions of his winter quarters.

CXIV. And now for a detail which in the telling may lack grandeur, but is most important by reason of the true and substantial personal qualities it reveals and also of its practical service—a thing most pleasant as an experience and remarkable for the kindness it displayed. Throughout the whole

287

belli Germanici Pannonicique tempus nemo e nobis gradumve nostrum aut praecedentibus aut sequentibus imbecillus fuit, cuius salus ac valetudo non ita sustentaretur Caesaris cura, tamquam distractissimus[1] ille tantorum onerum mole huic uni negotio[2]
2 vacaret animus. Erat desiderantibus paratum iunctum vehiculum, lectica eius publicata, cuius usum[3] cum alii tum ego sensi ; iam medici, iam apparatus cibi, iam in hoc solum uni portatum[4] instrumentum balinei nullius non succurrit valetudini ; domus tantum ac domestici deerant, ceterum nihil, quod
3 ab illis aut praestari aut desiderari posset. Adiciam illud, quod, quisquis illis temporibus interfuit, ut alia, quae retuli, agnoscet protinus : solus semper equo vectus est, solus cum iis, quos invitaverat, maiore parte aestivarum expeditionum cenavit sedens ; non sequentibus disciplinam, quatenus exemplo non nocebatur, ignovit ; admonitio frequens, interdum[5] et castigatio, vindicta tamen rarissima,[6] agebatque medium plurima dissimulantis, aliqua inhibentis.[7]
4 Hiems emolumentum patrati belli contulit, sed insequenti aestate omnis Pannonia reliquiis totius

[1] distractissimus *Rhenanus*; distraximus *AP*.
[2] negotio *Gelenius*; genitio *BA*, om. *P*.
[3] usum *added by Lipsius*.
[4] uni portatum *A* ; *after erasing* um, importatum *P* ; una portatum *Orelli followed by Halm*.
[5] interdum *an anonymous scholar* ; inerat *AP*.
[6] tamen rarissima *Halm* ; amarissima *AP*.
[7] dissimulantis . . . inhibentis *AP*; dissimulans . . . inhibens *Acidalius*.

[a] At formal dinners the Romans reclined on couches.

period of the German and Pannonian war there was
not one of us, or of those either above or below our
rank, who fell ill without having his health and
welfare looked after by Caesar with as much
solicitude indeed as though this were the chief
occupation of his mind, preoccupied though he
was by his heavy responsibilities. There was a
horsed vehicle ready for those who needed it, his
own litter was at the disposal of all, and I, among
others, have enjoyed its use. Now his physicians,
now his kitchen, and now his bathing equipment,
brought for this one purpose for himself alone,
ministered to the comfort of all who were sick.
All they lacked was their home and domestic
servants, but nothing else that friends at home
could furnish or desire for them. Let me also add
the following trait, which, like the others I have
described, will be immediately recognized as true
by anyone who participated in that campaign.
Caesar alone of commanders was in the habit of
always travelling in the saddle, and, throughout the
greater portion of the summer campaign, of sitting "
at the table when dining with invited guests. Of
those who did not imitate his own stern discipline
he took no notice, in so far as no harmful precedent
was thereby created. He often admonished, sometimes gave verbal reproof, but rarely punishment,
and pursued the moderate course of pretending in
most cases not to see things, and of administering
only occasionally a reprimand.

The winter brought the reward of our efforts
in the termination of the war, though it was
not until the following summer that all Pannonia
sought peace, the remnants of the war as a whole

belli in Delmatia manentibus pacem petiit. Ferocem illam tot milium iuventutem, paulo ante servitutem minatam Italiae, conferentem arma, quibus usa erat, apud flumen nomine Bathinum prosternentemque se universam genibus imperatoris, Batonemque et Pinnetem excelsissimos duces, captum alterum, alterum[1] a se deditum iustis voluminibus ordine narrabimus, ut spero.

5 Autumno[2] victor in hiberna reducitur exercitus, cuius omnibus copiis a Caesare[3] M. Lepidus praefectus est, vir nomini[4] ac fortunae Caesarum[5] proximus, quem in quantum quisque aut cognoscere aut intellegere potuit, in tantum miratur ac diligit tantorumque nominum, quibus ortus est, ornamentum iudicat.

1 CXV. Caesar ad alteram belli Delmatici molem animum atque arma contulit. In qua regione quali adiutore legatoque fratre meo Magio Celere Velleiano usus sit, ipsius patrisque eius praedicatione testatum est et amplissimorum donorum, quibus triumphans eum Caesar donavit, signat memoria. Initio aestatis

2 Lepidus educto hibernis exercitu per gentis integras immunesque adhuc clade belli et eo feroces ac truces tendens ad Tiberium imperatorem et cum difficultate locorum et cum vi hostium luctatus, magna cum

---

[1] alterum alterum *Rhenanus*; alterum *AP*.
[2] autumno *Gelenius*; autumni *AP*.
[3] a Caesare *Rhenanus*; Caesarem *AP*.
[4] nomini *Acidalius*; nominis *AP*.
[5] Caesarum *Scheffer*; eorum *AP*.

being confined to Dalmatia. In my complete work
I hope to describe in detail how those fierce warriors,
many thousand in number, who had but a short
time before threatened Italy with slavery, now
brought the arms they had used in rebellion and
laid them down, at a river called the Bathinus,
prostrating themselves one and all before the knees
of the commander ; and how of their two supreme
commanders, Bato and Pinnes, the one was made a
prisoner and the other gave himself up.

In the autumn the victorious army was led back
to winter quarters. Caesar gave the chief command
of all the forces to Marcus Lepidus, a man who in
name and in fortune approaches the Caesars, whom
one admires and loves the more in proportion to his
opportunities to know and understand him, and
whom one regards as an ornament to the great
names from whom he springs.

CXV. Caesar then devoted his attention and his
arms to his second task, the war in Dalmatia. What
assistance he had in this quarter from his aide and
lieutenant Magius Celer Velleianus, my brother, is
attested by the words of Tiberius himself and of
his father, and signalized by the record of the high
decorations conferred upon him by Caesar on the
occasion of his triumph. In the beginning of summer
Lepidus led his army out of winter quarters, in an
effort to make his way to Tiberius the commander,
through the midst of races that were as yet unaffected
and untouched by the disasters of war and therefore
still fierce and warlike ; after a struggle in which he
had to contend with the difficulties of the country
as well as the attacks of the enemy, and after
inflicting great loss on those who barred his way,

clade obsistentium excisis agris, exustis aedificiis,
caesis viris, laetus victoria praedaque onustus per-
3 venit ad Caesarem, et ob ea, quae si propriis gessisset
auspiciis, triumphare debuerat, ornamentis triumphalibus consentiente cum iudicio principum voluntate
senatus donatus[1] est.

4 Illa aestas maximi belli consummavit effectus:
quippe Perustae et Desidiates Delmatae, situ locorum
ac montium, ingeniorum ferocia, mira etiam pugnandi scientia et praecipue angustiis saltuum paene
inexpugnabiles, non iam ductu, sed manibus atque
armis ipsius Caesaris tum demum pacati sunt, cum
paene funditus eversi forent.

5 Nihil in hoc tanto bello, nihil in Germania aut
videre maius aut mirari magis potui, quam quod
imperatori numquam adeo ulla opportuna visa est
victoriae occasio, quam damno amissi pensaret
militis semperque visum est gloriosissimum,[2] quod
esset tutissimum, et ante conscientiae quam famae
consultum nec umquam consilia ducis iudicio exercitus, sed exercitus providentia ducis rectus est.

1 CXVI. Magna in bello Delmatico experimenta
virtutis in incultos[3] ac difficilis locos praemissus

---

[1] donatus *added by Rhenanus.*
[2] gloriosissimum *Halm*; gloriosum *AP.*
[3] incultos *Heinsius*; multos *AP.*

by the devastation of fields, burning of houses, and slaying of the inhabitants, he succeeded in reaching Caesar, rejoicing in victory and laden with booty. For these feats, for which, if they had been performed under his own auspices he would properly have received a triumph, he was granted the ornaments of a triumph, the wish of the senate endorsing the recommendation of the Caesars.

This campaign brought the momentous war to a successful conclusion; for the Perustae and Desiadates, Dalmatian tribes, who were almost unconquerable on account of the position of their strongholds in the mountains, their warlike temper, their wonderful knowledge of fighting, and, above all, the narrow passes in which they lived, were then at last pacified, not now under the mere generalship, but by the armed prowess of Caesar himself, and then only when they were almost entirely exterminated.

Nothing in the course of this great war, nothing in the campaigns in Germany, came under my observation that was greater, or that aroused my admiration more, than these traits of its general; no chance of winning a victory ever seemed to him timely, which he would have to purchase by the sacrifice of his soldiers; the safest course was always regarded by him as the best; he consulted his conscience first and then his reputation, and, finally, the plans of the commander were never governed by the opinion of the army, but rather the army by the wisdom of its leader.

CXVI. In the Dalmatian war Germanicus, who had been dispatched in advance of the commander to regions both wild and difficult, gave great proof of

Germanicus dedit ; celebri etiam opera diligenti-
2 que Vibius Postumus vir consularis, praepositus
Delmatiae, ornamenta meruit triumphalia : quem
honorem ante paucos annos Passienus et Cossus,
viri quamquam[1] diversis virtutibus celebres, in Africa
meruerant. Sed Cossus victoriae testimonium etiam
in cognomen filii contulit, adulescentis in omnium
3 virtutum exempla geniti. At Postumi operum L.
Apronius particeps illa quoque militia eos, quos mox
consecutus est, honores excellenti virtute meruit.

Utinam non maioribus experimentis testatum
esset, quantum in omni re fortuna posset ! Sed in
hoc[2] quoque genere abunde agnosci vis eius potest.
Nam et Aelius Lamia,[3] vir antiquissimi moris et
priscam gravitatem semper humanitate temperans,
in Germania Illyricoque et mox in Africa splendi-
dissimis functus ministeriis, non merito, sed materia
4 adipiscendi triumphalia defectus est, et A. Licinius
Nerva Silianus, P. Silii filius, quem virum ne qui
intellexit quidem abunde miratus est, in eo nihil
non optimo civi simplicissimo duci superesse[4] praeferens, inmatura morte[5] et fructu amplissimae principis amicitiae et consummatione evectae in altissi-
mum paternumque fastigium imaginis defectus est.
5 Horum virorum mentioni si quis quaesisse me dicet

[1] quamquam *Halm* ; quibusdem *AP*.
[2] hoc *Gelenius* ; loco *AP*.
[3] Aelius Lamia *Ruhnken* ; etiam *AP*.
[4] in eo nihil . . . superesse *Ellis* ; ne (me *A*) nihil (*om.
P*) optimo civi (civis *A*) . . . perisset *BAP*.
[5] morte *added by Orelli*.

his valour. By his repeated services and careful
vigilance the governor of Dalmatia, Vibius Postumus'
the consular, also earned the ornaments of a triumph.
A few years before this honour had been earned in
Africa by Passienus and Cossus, both celebrated
men, though not alike in merit. Cossus passed on
to his son, a young man born to exhibit every
variety of excellence, a cognomen that still testifies
to his victory. And Lucius Apronius, who shared
in the achievements of Postumus, earned by the
distinguished valour which he displayed in this
campaign also, the honours which he actually won
shortly afterwards.

Would that it had not been demonstrated, by
greater proofs, how mighty an influence fortune
wields in all things ; yet even here her power can
be recognized by abundant examples. For instance,
Aelius Lamia, a man of the older type, who always
tempered his old-fashioned dignity by a spirit of
kindliness, had performed splendid service in Germany and Illyricum, and was soon to do so in Africa,
but failed to receive triumphal honours, not through
any fault of his, but through lack of opportunity ;
and Aulus Licinius Nerva Silianus, the son of Publius
Silius, a man who was not adequately praised even
by the friend who knew him best, when he declared
that there were no qualities which he did not possess
in the highest degree, whether as an excellent
citizen or as an honest commander, through his untimely death failed not only to reap the fruit of his
close friendship with the emperor but also to realize
that lofty conception of his powers which had been
inspired by his father's eminence. If anyone shall
say that I have gone out of my way to mention these

locum, fatentem arguet; neque enim iustus sine mendacio candor apud bonos crimini est.

CXVII. Tantum quod ultimam imposuerat Pannonico ac Delmatico bello Caesar manum, cum intra quinque consummati tanti operis dies funestae ex Germania epistulae nuntium attulere[1] caesi Vari trucidatarumque legionum trium totidemque alarum et sex cohortium, velut in hoc saltem tantummodo indulgente nobis fortuna, ne occupato duce tanta clades inferretur.[2] Sed et causa et persona[3] moram exigit.

2 Varus Quintilius inlustri magis quam nobili ortus familia, vir ingenio mitis, moribus quietus, ut corpore, ita[4] animo immobilior, otio magis castrorum quam bellicae adsuetus militiae, pecuniae vero quam non contemptor, Syria, cui praefuerat, declaravit, quam pauper divitem ingressus dives pauperem 3 reliquit; is cum exercitui, qui erat in Germania, praeesset, concepit esse homines, qui nihil praeter vocem membraque haberent hominum, quique gladiis domari non poterant, posse iure mulceri. Quo pro- 4 posito mediam ingressus Germaniam velut inter viros pacis gaudentes dulcedine iurisdictionibus agendoque pro tribunali ordine trahebat aestiva.[a]

---

[1] nuntium attulere *supplied here by Halm, by other editors after* cohortium.
[2] tanta clades inferretur *supplied by Halm.*
[3] et causa et persona *Orelli*; et causa persona *AP.*
[4] ita *Acidalius*; et *AP.*

[a] A.D. 9.

men, his criticism will meet no denial. In the sight of honest men fair-minded candour without misrepresentation is no crime.

CXVII. Scarcely had Caesar put the finishing touch upon the Pannonian and Dalmatian war, when, within five days of the completion of this task, dispatches from Germany brought the baleful news of the death of Varus,[a] and of the slaughter of three legions, of as many divisions of cavalry, and of six cohorts—as though fortune were granting us this indulgence at least, that such a disaster should not be brought upon us when our commander was occupied by other wars. The cause of this defeat and the personality of the general require of me a brief digression.

Varus Quintilius, descended from a famous rather than a high-born family, was a man of mild character and of a quiet disposition, somewhat slow in mind as he was in body, and more accustomed to the leisure of the camp than to actual service in war. That he was no despiser of money is demonstrated by his governorship of Syria : he entered the rich province a poor man, but left it a rich man and the province poor. When placed in charge of the army in Germany, he entertained the notion that the Germans were a people who were men only in limbs and voice, and that they, who could not be subdued by the sword, could be soothed by the law. With this purpose in mind he entered the heart of Germany as though he were going among a people enjoying the blessings of peace, and sitting on his tribunal he wasted the time of a summer campaign in holding court and observing the proper details of legal procedure.

1 CXVIII. At illi, quod nisi expertus vix credat,[1] in summa feritate versutissimi natumque mendacio genus, simulantes fictas litium series et nunc provocantes alter alterum in iurgia,[2] nunc agentes gratias quod ea Romana iustitia finiret feritasque sua novitate incognitae disciplinae mitesceret et solita armis discerni iure terminarentur, in summam socordiam perduxere Quintilium, usque eo, ut se praetorem urbanum in foro ius dicere, non in mediis Germaniae 2 finibus exercitui praeesse crederet. Tum iuvenis genere nobilis, manu fortis, sensu celer, ultra barbarum promptus ingenio, nomine Arminius, Sigimeri principis gentis eius filius, ardorem animi vultu oculisque praeferens, adsiduus militiae nostrae prioris comes, iure etiam civitatis Romanae decus[3] equestris consecutus[4] gradus, segnitia ducis in occasionem sceleris usus est, haud imprudenter speculatus neminem celerius opprimi, quam qui nihil timeret, et frequentissimum initium esse calamitatis securitatem. 3 Primo igitur paucos, mox pluris in societatem consilii recepti ; opprimi posse Romanos et dicit et persuadet, decretis facta iungit, tempus insidiarum

---

[1] credat *Lipsius*; credebat *AP*.
[2] in iurgia *Madvig*; in iuria *AP*.
[3] Romanae decus *Burman*; Romae eius (ius *P*) *AP*.
[4] consecutus *Heinsius*; consequens *AP*.

CXVIII. But the Germans, who with their great
ferocity combine great craft, to an extent scarcely
credible to one who has had no experience with
them, and are a race to lying born, by trumping up
a series of fictitious lawsuits, now provoking one
another to disputes, and now expressing their
gratitude that Roman justice was settling these
disputes, that their own barbarous nature was being
softened down by this new and hitherto unknown
method, and that quarrels which were usually settled
by arms were now being ended by law, brought
Quintilius to such a complete degree of negligence,
that he came to look upon himself as a city praetor
administering justice in the forum, and not a general
in command of an army in the heart of Germany.
Thereupon appeared a young man of noble birth,
brave in action and alert in mind, possessing an
intelligence quite beyond the ordinary barbarian ;
he was, namely, Arminius, the son of Sigimer, a
prince of that nation, and he showed in his counten-
ance and in his eyes the fire of the mind within.
He had been associated with us constantly on previous
campaigns, had been granted the right of Roman
citizenship, and had even attained the dignity
of equestrian rank. This young man made use of
the negligence of the general as an opportunity for
treachery, sagaciously seeing that no one could be
more quickly overpowered than the man who feared
nothing, and that the most common beginning of
disaster was a sense of security. At first, then, he
admitted but a few, later a large number, to a share
in his design ; he told them, and convinced them too,
that the Romans could be crushed, added execution
to resolve, and named a day for carrying out the

4 constituit. Id Varo per virum eius gentis fidelem clarique nominis, Segesten, indicatur. Postulabat etiam vinciri socios. Sed praevalebant iam[1] fata consiliis omnemque animi eius aciem praestrinxerant[2] : quippe ita se res habet, ut plerumque cuius fortunam mutaturus est[3] deus, consilia corrumpat efficiatque, quod miserrimum est, ut, quod accidit, etiam merito accidisse videatur et casus in culpam transeat. Negat itaque se credere speciemque[4] in se benevolentiae ex merito aestimare profitetur. Nec diutius post primum indicem secundo relictus locus.

1 CXIX. Ordinem atrocissimae calamitatis, qua nulla post Crassi in Parthis damnum in externis gentibus gravior Romanis fuit, iustis voluminibus ut alii, ita nos conabimur exponere : nunc summa deflenda 2 est. Exercitus omnium fortissimus, disciplina, manu experientiaque bellorum inter Romanos milites princeps, marcore ducis, perfidia hostis, iniquitate fortunae circumventus, cum ne pugnandi quidem egrediendive[5] occasio nisi inique, nec in quantum[6] voluerant, data esset immunis, castigatis etiam quibusdam gravi poena, quia Romanis et armis et animis usi fuissent, inclusus silvis, paludibus, insidiis ab eo hoste ad internecionem trucidatus est, quem

---

[1] vinciri socios. sed praevalebant iam *supplied by Ellis from Tac. Ann.* i. 58.
[2] praestrinxerant *Gelenius*; praestrinxerat *AP*.
[3] cuius fortunam mutaturus est *ed. Bipont.*; qui fortunam mutaturus (imitaturus *A*) *AP*.
[4] speciemque *Burman*; spemque *AP*.
[5] egrediendive *Voss.*; egredie͂ (egredie *with* ad *written above the* g *A*, egregie *P*) aut *BAP*.

300

plot. This was disclosed to Varus through Segestes, a loyal man of that race and of illustrious name, who also demanded that the conspirators be put in chains. But fate now dominated the plans of Varus and had blindfolded the eyes of his mind. Indeed, it is usually the case that heaven perverts the judgement of the man whose fortune it means to reverse, and brings it to pass—and this is the wretched part of it—that that which happens by chance seems to be deserved, and accident passes over into culpability. And so Quintilius refused to believe the story, and insisted upon judging the apparent friendship of the Germans toward him by the standard of his merit. And, after this first warning, there was no time left for a second.

CXIX. The details of this terrible calamity, the heaviest that had befallen the Romans on foreign soil since the disaster of Crassus in Parthia, I shall endeavour to set forth, as others have done, in my larger work. Here I can merely lament the disaster as a whole. An army unexcelled in bravery, the first of Roman armies in discipline, in energy, and in experience in the field, through the negligence of its general, the perfidy of the enemy, and the unkindness of fortune was surrounded, nor was as much opportunity as they had wished given to the soldiers either of fighting or of extricating themselves, except against heavy odds; nay, some were even heavily chastised for using the arms and showing the spirit of Romans. Hemmed in by forests and marshes and ambuscades, it was exterminated almost to a man by the very enemy whom it had always

---

[6] occasio nisi inique, nec in quantum *Ellis*; occasionis in quantum *APB*.

ita semper more pecudum trucidaverat, ut vitam
aut mortem eius nunc ira nunc venia temperaret.
3 Duci plus ad moriendum quam ad pugnandum animi
fuit : quippe paterni avitique successor exempli se
ipse transfixit. At e praefectis castrorum duobus
4 quam clarum exemplum L. Eggius, tam turpe
Ceionius prodidit, qui, cum longe maximam partem
absumpsisset acies, auctor deditionis supplicio quam
proelio mori maluit. At Vala Numonius, legatus
Vari, cetera quietus ac probus, diri auctor exempli,
spoliatum equite peditem relinquens fuga cum alis[1]
Rhenum petere ingressus est. Quod factum eius
fortuna ulta est ; non enim desertis superfuit, sed
5 desertor occidit. Vari corpus semiustum hostilis[2]
laceraverat feritas ; caput eius abscisum latumque
ad Maroboduum et ab eo missum ad Caesarem
gentilicii tamen tumuli sepultura honoratum est.
1   CXX. His auditis revolat ad patrem Caesar ; perpetuus patronus Romani imperii adsuetam sibi causam
suscipit.   Mittitur ad Germaniam, Gallias confirmat,
disponit exercitus, praesidia munit et se magnitudine
sua, non fiducia hostis[3] metiens, qui Cimbricam
Teutonicamque militiam Italiae minabatur, ultro
2 Rhenum cum exercitu transgreditur.   Arma infert

[1] equite peditem relinquens fuga cum alis *Gelenius*;
equitem peditem relinquens fugatum (fuga cum *P*) aliis *BAP*.
[2] hostilis *Burer* ; hosti *BA* ; hostium *P*.
[3] hostis *Haupt*; hostium *AP* ; *om. B.*

---

* His father Sextus Quintilius Varus fought on the
side of Brutus and Cassius at Philippi. After the loss of
the battle he was slain, at his own request, by one of his
freedmen, see Bk. II. Chap. LXXI. Information is lacking
concerning his grandfather and the manner of his death.

slaughtered like cattle, whose life or death had depended solely upon the wrath or the pity of the Romans. The general had more courage to die than to fight, for, following the example of his father [a] and grandfather, he ran himself through with his sword. Of the two prefects of the camp, Lucius Eggius furnished a precedent as noble as that of Ceionius was base, who, after the greater part of the army had perished, proposed its surrender, preferring to die by torture at the hands of the enemy than in battle. Vala Numonius, lieutenant of Varus, who, in the rest of his life, had been an inoffensive and an honourable man, also set a fearful example in that he left the infantry unprotected by the cavalry and in flight tried to reach the Rhine with his squadrons of horse. But fortune avenged his act, for he did not survive those whom he had abandoned, but died in the act of deserting them. The body of Varus, partially burned, was mangled by the enemy in their barbarity ; his head was cut off and taken to Maroboduus and was sent by him to Caesar ; but in spite of the disaster it was honoured by burial in the tomb of his family.

CXX. On hearing of this disaster, Caesar flew to his father's side. The constant protector of the Roman empire again took up his accustomed part. Dispatched to Germany, he reassured the provinces of Gaul, distributed his armies, strengthened the garrison towns, and then, measuring himself by the standard of his own greatness, and not by the presumption of an enemy who threatened Italy with a war like that of the Cimbri and Teutones, he took the offensive and crossed the Rhine with his army. He thus made aggressive war upon the

hosti quem arcuisse[1] pater et patria contenti erant;
penetrat interius, aperit limites, vastat agros, urit
domos, fundit obvios maximaque cum gloria, incolumi omnium, quos transduxerat, numero in hiberna
3 revertitur.

Reddatur verum L. Asprenati testimonium, qui
legatus sub avunculo suo Varo militans gnava
virilique opera duarum legionum, quibus praeerat,
exercitum immunem tanta calamitate servavit
matureque ad inferiora hiberna descendendo
vacillantium etiam cis Rhenum sitarum gentium
animos confirmavit. Sunt tamen, qui ut vivos ab
eo vindicatos, ita iugulatorum sub Varo occupata
crediderint patrimonia hereditatemque occisi exer-
4 citus, in quantum voluerit, ab eo aditam. L. etiam
Caedicii praefecti castrorum eorumque, qui una
circumdati Alisone immensis Germanorum copiis
obsidebantur, laudanda virtus est, qui omnibus diffi-
cultatibus superatis, quas inopia rerum intolerabilis,
vis hostium faciebat inexsuperabilis, nec temerario
consilio nec segni providentia usi speculatique oppor-
tunitatem ferro sibi ad suos peperere reditum.
5 Ex quo apparet Varum, sane gravem et bonae voluntatis virum, magis imperatoris defectum consilio
quam virtute destitutum militum se magnificentis-

---

[1] arma infert (hosti *Voss.*) quem arcuisse *Lipsius*; arma
interfecti qui arguisse *AP.*

enemy when his father and his country would have been content to let him hold them in check, he penetrated into the heart of the country, opened up military roads, devastated fields, burned houses, routed those who came against him, and, without loss to the troops with which he had crossed, he returned, covered with glory, to winter quarters.

Due tribute should be paid to Lucius Asprenas, who was serving as lieutenant under Varus his uncle, and who, backed by the brave and energetic support of the two legions under his command, saved his army from this great disaster, and by a quick descent to the quarters of the army in Lower Germany strengthened the allegiance of the races even on the hither side of the Rhine who were beginning to waver. There are those, however, who believed that, though he had saved the lives of the living, he had appropriated to his own use the property of the dead who were slain with Varus, and that inheritances of the slaughtered army were claimed by him at pleasure. The valour of Lucius Caedicius, prefect of the camp, also deserves praise, and of those who, pent up with him at Aliso, were besieged by an immense force of Germans. For, overcoming all their difficulties which want rendered unendurable and the forces of the enemy almost insurmountable, following a design that was carefully considered, and using a vigilance that was ever on the alert, they watched their chance, and with the sword won their way back to their friends. From all this it is evident that Varus, who was, it must be confessed, a man of character and of good intentions, lost his life and his magnificent army more through lack of judgement in the commander than of valour in his

305

6 simumque perdidisse exercitum. Cum in captivos
saeviretur a Germanis, praeclari facinoris auctor fuit
Caldus Caelius, adulescens[1] vetustate familiae suae
dignissimus, qui complexus catenarum, quibus vinctus
erat, seriem, ita illas inlisit capiti suo, ut protinus
pariter sanguinis cerebrique effluvio[2] expiraret.

1 CXXI. Eadem virtus et fortuna subsequenti tempore ingressi Germaniam[3] imperatoris Tiberii fuit,
quae initio fuerat. Qui concussis hostium viribus
classicis peditumque expeditionibus, cum res Galliarum maximae molis accensasque plebis Viennen-
sium dissensiones coërcitione magis quam poena
mollisset,[4] senatus populusque Romanus postulante
patre eius, ut aequum ei ius[5] in omnibus provinciis
exercitibusque esset, quam erat ipsi, decreto complexus est.[6] Etenim absurdum erat non esse sub illo,
2 quae ab illo vindicabantur, et qui ad opem ferendam
primus erat, ad vindicandum honorem non iudicari
parem. In urbem reversus iam pridem debitum,
sed continuatione bellorum dilatum ex Pannoniis
Delmatisque egit triumphum. Cuius magnificentiam
quis miretur in Caesare ? Fortunae vero quis non
3 miretur indulgentiam? Quippe omnis eminentissimos
hostium duces non occisos fama narravit, sed
vinctos triumphus ostendit ; quem mihi[7] fratrique

[1] adulescens *Ruhnken* ; ad *AP.*
[2] effluvio *Lipsius* ; influvio *AP.*
[3] ingressi Germaniam *Bardili* ; ingressa anima (animum
P) *BAP.*
[4] *Rhenanus supplied* et *after* mollisset.
[5] aequum ei ius *Rhenanus* ; equum eius *AP.*
[6] est *Ellis* ; esset *AP.*
[7] mihi *Burer* ; militi *AP.*

soldiers. When the Germans were venting their rage upon their captives, an heroic act was performed by Caldus Caelius, a young man worthy in every way of his long line of ancestors, who, seizing a section of the chain with which he was bound, brought it down with such force upon his own head as to cause his instant death, both his brains and his blood gushing from the wound.

CXXI. Tiberius showed the same valour, and was attended by the same fortune, when he entered Germany on his later campaigns as in his first. After he had broken the force of the enemy by his expeditions on sea and land, had completed his difficult task in Gaul, and had settled by restraint rather than by punishment the dissensions that had broken out among the Viennenses, at the request of his father that he should have in all the provinces and armies a power equal to his own, the senate and Roman people so decreed. For indeed it was incongruous that the provinces which were being defended by him should not be under his jurisdiction, and that he who was foremost in bearing aid should not be considered an equal in the honour to be won. On his return to the city he celebrated the triumph over the Pannonians and Dalmatians, long since due him, but postponed by reason of a succession of wars. Who can be surprised at its magnificence, since it was the triumph of Caesar? Yet who can fail to wonder at the kindness of fortune to him? For the most eminent leaders of the enemy were not slain in battle, that report should tell thereof, but were taken captive, so that in his triumph he exhibited them in chains. It was my lot and that of my brother to participate in this

meo inter praecipuos praecipuisque donis adornatos
viros comitari contigit.

1 CXXII. Quis non inter reliqua, quibus singularis
moderatio Ti. Caesaris elucet atque eminet, hoc
quoque miretur, quod, cum sine ulla dubitatione
septem triumphos meruerit, tribus contentus fuit[1]?
Quis enim dubitare potest, quin ex Armenia recepta
et ex rege praeposito ei,[2] cuius capiti insigne regium
sua manu imposuerat, ordinatisque rebus Orientis
ovans triumphare debuerit, et Vindelicorum Rae-
2 torumque victor curru urbem ingredi? Fractis deinde
post adoptionem continua triennii militia Germaniae
viribus idem illi honor et deferendus et recipiendus
fuerit? Et post cladem sub Varo acceptam, expectato[3] ocius[4] prosperrimo rerum eventu eadem
excisa Germania triumphus summi ducis adornari
debuerit? Sed in hoc viro nescias utrum magis
mireris quod laborum periculorumque semper excessit modum an quod honorum temperavit.

1 CXXIII. Venitur ad tempus, in quo fuit plurimum
metus. Quippe Caesar Augustus cum Germanicum
nepotem suum reliqua belli patraturum misisset in
Germaniam, Tiberium autem filium missurus esset
in Illyricum ad firmanda pace quae bello subegerat,

[1] fuit *Haase*; fuerit *AP*.
[2] praeposito ei *Heinsius*; praepositi (pro- *P*) *BAP*.
[3] expectato *added by Halm*.   [4] ocius *P*; totius *BA*.

triumph among the men of distinguished rank and those who were decorated with distinguished honours.

CXXII. Among the other acts of Tiberius Caesar, wherein his remarkable moderation shines forth conspicuously, who does not wonder at this also, that, although he unquestionably earned seven triumphs, he was satisfied with three? For who can doubt that, when he had recovered Armenia, had placed over it a king upon whose head he had with his own hand set the mark of royalty, and had put in order the affairs of the east, he ought to have received an ovation; and that after his conquest of the Vindelici and the Raeti he should have entered the city as victor in a triumphal chariot? Or that, after his adoption, when he had broken the power of the Germans in three consecutive campaigns, the same honour should have been bestowed upon him and should have been accepted by him? And that, after the disaster received under Varus, when this same Germany was crushed by a course of events which, sooner than was expected, came to a happy issue, the honour of a triumph should have been awarded to this consummate general? But, in the case of this man, one does not know which to admire the more, that in courting toils and danger he went beyond all bounds or that in accepting honours he kept within them.

CXXIII. We now come to the crisis which was awaited with the greatest foreboding. Augustus Caesar had dispatched his grandson Germanicus to Germany to put an end to such traces of the war as still remained, and was on the point of sending his son Tiberius to Illyricum to strengthen by peace the

prosequens eum simulque interfuturus athletarum
certaminis ludicro, quod eius honori sacratum a
Neapolitanis est, processit in Campaniam. Quamquam iam motus imbecillitatis inclinataeque in
deterius principia valetudinis senserat, tamen obni-
tente vi animi prosecutus filium digressusque ab eo
Beneventi ipse Nolam petiit : et ingravescente in
dies valetudine, cum sciret, quis volenti omnia post
se salva remanere accersendus foret, festinanter
revocavit filium ; ille ad patrem patriae expectato
2 revolavit maturius. Tum securum se Augustus prae-
dicans circumfususque amplexibus Tiberii sui, com-
mendans illi sua atque ipsius opera nec quidquam
iam de fine, si fata poscerent, recusans, subrefectus
primo conspectu alloquioque carissimi sibi spiritus,
mox, cum omnem curam fata vincerent, in sua
resolutus initia Pompeio Apuleioque consulibus sep-
tuagesimo et sexto anno animam caelestem caelo
reddidit.

1   CXXIV. Quid tunc homines timuerint, quae
senatus trepidatio, quae populi confusio, quis urbis
metus, in quam arto salutis exitiique fuerimus confinio, neque mihi tam festinanti exprimere vacat
neque cui vacat potest. Id solum voce publica
dixisse satis[1] habeo : cuius orbis ruinam timueramus,

---

[1] satis *added by Ruhnken.*

regions he had subjugated in war. With the double purpose of escorting him on his way, and of being present at an athletic contest which the Neapolitans had established in his honour, he set out for Campania. Although he had already experienced symptoms of growing weakness and of a change in his health for the worse, his strong will resisted his infirmity and he accompanied his son. Parting from him at Beneventum he went to Nola. As his health grew daily worse, and he knew full well for whom he must send if he wished to leave everything secure behind him, he sent in haste for his son to return. Tiberius hurried back and reached the side of the father of his country before he was even expected. Then Augustus, asserting that his mind was now at ease, and, with the arms of his beloved Tiberius about him, commending to him the continuation of their joint work, expressed his readiness to meet the end if the fates should call him. He revived a little at seeing Tiberius and at hearing the voice of one so dear to him, but, ere long, since no care could withstand the fates, in his seventy-sixth year, in the consulship of Pompeius and Apuleius [a] he was resolved into the elements from which he sprang and yielded up to heaven his divine soul.

CXXIV. Of the misgivings of mankind at this time, the trepidation of the senate, the confusion of the people, the fears of the city, of the narrow margin between safety and ruin on which we then found ourselves, I have no time to tell as I hasten on my way, nor could he tell who had the time. Suffice it for me to voice the common utterance: "The world whose ruin we had feared we found

311

eum ne commotum quidem sensimus, tantaque unius
viri maiestas fuit, ut nec pro[1] bonis neque contra
2 malos opus armis foret. Una tamen veluti luctatio
civitatis fuit, pugnantis cum Caesare senatus populique Romani, ut stationi paternae succederet, illius,
ut potius aequalem civem quam eminentem liceret
agere principem. Tandem magis ratione quam
honore victus est, cum quidquid tuendum non sus-
cepisset, periturum videret, solique huic contigit
paene diutius recusare principatum, quam, ut
occuparent eum, alii armis pugnaverant.
3   Post redditum caelo patrem et corpus eius humanis
honoribus, numen divinis honoratum, primum principalium eius operum fuit ordinatio comitiorum,
quam manu sua scriptam divus Augustus reliquerat.
4 Quo tempore mihi fratrique meo, candidatis Caesaris,
proxime a nobilissimis ac sacerdotalibus[2] viris destinari
praetoribus contigit, consecutis quidem,[3] ut neque
post nos quemquam divus Augustus neque ante nos
Caesar commendaret Tiberius.
1   CXXV. Tulit protinus et voti et consilii sui
pretium res publica, neque diu latuit aut quid non
impetrando passuri fuissemus aut quid impetrando

[1] pro *added by Ellis*; *Halm suggests* nec bonis votis.
[2] sacerdotalibus *Scheffer*; sacerdotibus *AP*.
[3] consecutis quidem *Ellis*; consecutisque *A*; consecutis
P.

---

[a] This refers to his official deification. He was given the
title of Divus, a temple was erected in his honour, a special
class of priests was created to conduct the rites, and a special
festival, the Augustalia, was established in his memory.
    [b] *i.e.* among the candidates nominated by Caesar. The
emperor nominated part of the candidates, allowing the
people to nominate the rest, reserving, however, the right
312

not even disturbed, and such was the majesty of one man that there was no need of arms either to defend the good or to restrain the bad." There was, however, in one respect what might be called a struggle in the state, as, namely, the senate and the Roman people wrestled with Caesar to induce him to succeed to the position of his father, while he on his side strove for permission to play the part of a citizen on a parity with the rest rather than that of an emperor over all. At last he was prevailed upon rather by reason than by the honour, since he saw that whatever he did not undertake to protect was likely to perish. He is the only man to whose lot it has fallen to refuse the principate for a longer time, almost, than others had fought to secure it.

After heaven had claimed his father, and human honours had been paid to his body as divine honours were paid to his soul,[a] the first of his tasks as emperor was the regulation of the *comitia*, instructions for which Augustus had left in his own handwriting. On this occasion it was my lot and that of my brother, as Caesar's candidates,[b] to be named for the praetorship immediately after those of noble families and those who had held the priesthoods, and indeed to have had the distinction of being the last to be recommended by Augustus and the first to be named by Tiberius Caesar.

CXXV. The state soon reaped the fruit of its wise course in desiring Tiberius, nor was it long before it was apparent what we should have had to endure had our request been refused, and what of veto in the case of candidates whom he deemed unworthy.

profecissemus. Quippe exercitus, qui in Germania militabat praesentisque Germanici imperio regebatur, simulque legiones, quae in Illyrico erant, rabie quadam et profunda confundendi omnia cupiditate novum ducem, novum statum, novam quaerebant rem publicam ; quin etiam ausi sunt 2 minari daturos se[1] senatui, daturos principi leges ; modum stipendii, finem militiae sibi ipsi constituere conati sunt. Processum etiam in arma ferrumque strictum est et paene in ultima[2] gladiorum erupit impunitas, defuitque, qui contra rem publicam 3 duceret, non qui sequerentur. Sed haec omnia veteris imperatoris maturitas, multa inhibentis, aliqua cum gravitate pollicentis, et[3] inter severam praecipue noxiorum[4] ultionem mitis aliorum castigatio brevi sopiit ac sustulit.

4 Quo quidem tempore ut pleraque non ignave[5] Germanicus, ita Drusus,[6] qui a patre in id ipsum plurimo quidem[7] igne emicans incendium militaris tumultus missus erat, prisca antiquaque severitate usus ancipitia sibi maluit tenere quam exemplo perniciosa, et his ipsis militum gladiis, quibus 5 obsessus erat, obsidentes coërcuit, singulari adiutore in eo negotio usus Iunio Blaeso, viro nescias utiliore in castris an meliore in toga : qui post paucos annos

[1] se *added by Orelli.*
[2] ultima *Voss* ; ultimam *BA* ; ultimum *P.*
[3] et *added by Krause.*
[4] noxiorum *Gronovius* ; nostrorum *AP.*
[5] non ignave *Ellis* ; ignave *P* ; ignovit *Bipont. edition.*
[6] Drusus *Gelenius* ; Brutus *AP.*
[7] in id ipsum plurimo quidem *AP* ; in diversum plurimoque idem *Madvig.*

we had gained in having it granted. For the army serving in Germany, commanded by Germanicus in person, and the legions in Illyricum, seized at the same moment by a form of madness and a deep desire to throw everything into confusion, wanted a new leader, a new order of things, and a new republic. Nay, they even dared to threaten to dictate terms to the senate and to the emperor. They tried to fix for themselves the amount of their pay and their period of service. They even resorted to arms; the sword was drawn; their conviction that they would not be punished came near to breaking out into the worst excesses of arms. All they needed was someone to lead them against the state; there was no lack of followers. But all this disturbance was soon quelled and suppressed by the ripe experience of the veteran commander, who used coercion in many cases, made promises where he could do so with dignity, and by the combination of severe punishment of the most guilty with milder chastisement of the others.

In this crisis, while in many respects the conduct of Germanicus was not lacking in rigour, Drusus employed the severity of the Romans of old. Sent by his father into the very midst of the conflagration, when the flames of mutiny were already bursting forth, he preferred to hold to a course which involved danger to himself than one which might prove a ruinous precedent, and used the very swords of those by whom he had been besieged to coerce his besiegers. In this task he had in Junius Blaesus no ordinary helper, a man whom one does not know whether to consider more useful in the camp or better in the toga. A few years later, as proconsul

proconsul in Africa ornamenta triumphalia cum appellatione imperatoria meruit.

At Hispanias exercitumque in iis cum M. Lepidus, de cuius[1] virtutibus celeberrimaque in Illyrico militia praediximus, cum imperio obtineret, in summa pace et[2] quiete continuit, cum ei pietas rectissima sentiendi et auctoritas quae sentiebat obtinendi superesset. Cuius curam ac fidem Dolabella quoque, vir simplicitatis generosissimae, in maritima parte Illyrici per omnia imitatus est.

1 CXXVI. Horum sedecim annorum opera quis cum ingerantur[3] oculis animisque omnium, partibus[4] eloquatur ? Sacravit parentem suum Caesar non imperio, sed religione, non appellavit eum, sed fecit 2 deum. Revocata in forum fides, summota e foro seditio, ambitio campo, discordia curia, sepultaeque ac situ obsitae[5] iustitia, aequitas, industria civitati redditae ; accessit magistratibus[6] auctoritas, senatui maiestas, iudiciis gravitas ; compressa theatralis seditio, recte faciendi omnibus aut incussa voluntas 3 aut imposita necessitas : honorantur recta, prava puniuntur, suspicit potentem humilis, non timet, antecedit, non contemnit humiliorem potens. Quando annona moderatior, quando pax laetior ? Diffusa in orientis occidentisque tractus et quidquid meridiano

---

[1] in iis . . . cuius *supplied by Madvig.*
[2] et *added by Orelli.*
[3] ingerantur *Ellis* ; insera *BA* ; inserta sint *P.*
[4] partibus *Voss* ; in partibus *AP.*
[5] obsitae *Burer* ; oppositae *BAP.*
[6] magistratibus *Gelenius* ; militibus *AP.*

---

[a] *Pax augusta,* "Augustan peace." The expression, used to characterize the contrast between the tranquillity of his reign and the turmoil of the Civil Wars, which preceded it, had become proverbial.

in Africa, he earned the ornaments of a triumph, with the title of *imperator*.

The two provinces of Spain, however, and the army in them were held in peace and tranquillity, since Marcus Lepidus, of whose virtues and distinguished service in Illyricum I have already spoken, was there in command, and since he had in the highest degree the quality of instinctively knowing the best course and the firmness to hold to his views. On the coast of Illyricum his vigilance and fidelity was emulated in detail by Dolabella, a man of noble-minded candour.

CXXVI. Who would undertake to tell in detail the accomplishments of the past sixteen years, since they are borne in upon the eyes and hearts of all? Caesar deified his father, not by exercise of his imperial authority, but by his attitude of reverence; he did not call him a god, but made him one. Credit has been restored in the forum, strife has been banished from the forum, canvassing for office from the Campus Martius, discord from the senate-house; justice, equity, and industry, long buried in oblivion, have been restored to the state; the magistrates have regained their authority, the senate its majesty, the courts their dignity; rioting in the theatre has been suppressed; all citizens have either been impressed with the wish to do right, or have been forced to do so by necessity. Right is now honoured, evil is punished; the humble man respects the great but does not fear him, the great has precedence over the lowly but does not despise him. When was the price of grain more reasonable, or when were the blessings of peace greater? The *pax augusta,*[a] which has spread to the regions of the east and of the

317

aut septentrione finitur, pax augusta omnis[1] terrarum orbis angulos a latrociniorum metu servat immunes. 4 Fortuita non civium tantummodo, sed urbium damna principis munificentia vindicat. Restitutae urbes Asiae, vindicatae ab iniuriis magistratuum provinciae : honor dignis paratissimus, poena in malos sera, sed aliqua : superatur aequitate gratia, ambitio virtute ; nam facere recte civis suos princeps optimus faciendo docet, cumque sit imperio maximus, exemplo maior est.

1 CXXVII. Raro eminentes viri non magnis adiutoribus ad gubernandam fortunam suam usi sunt, ut duo Scipiones duobus Laeliis, quos per omnia aequaverunt sibi, ut divus Augustus M. Agrippa et proxime[2] ab eo Statilio Tauro, quibus novitas familiae haut obstitit quominus ad multiplicis consulatus triumphosque et complura eveherentur[3] sacerdotia. Etenim magna 2 negotia magnis adiutoribus egent[4] interestque rei publicae quod usu necessarium est,[5] dignitate eminere 3 utilitatemque auctoritate muniri. Sub his exemplis Ti. Caesar Seianum Aelium, principe equestris ordinis patre natum, materno vero genere clarissimas veteresque et insignes honoribus complexum familias, haben-

---

[1] *MSS.* have per *before* omnis.
[2] proxime *Scheffer* ; maxime *AP.*
[3] complura eveherentur *Vascosanus* ; complura enumerentur (complurae numerentur *A*) *BA* ; complura enumerarentur *P.*
[4] *after* egent *the words* neque in parvo paucitas ministeria defecit *are deleted by Halm after Vossius and Boecler.*
[5] est *Ruhnken* ; e *A* ; et *P.*

west and to the bounds of the north and of the
south, preserves every corner of the world safe from
the fear of brigandage. The munificence of the
emperor claims for its province the losses inflicted
by fortune not merely on private citizens, but on
whole cities. The cities of Asia have been restored,
the provinces have been freed from the oppression
of their magistrates. Honour ever awaits the
worthy ; for the wicked punishment is slow but
sure ; fair play has now precedence over influence,
and merit over ambition, for the best of emperors
teaches his citizens to do right by doing it, and
though he is greatest among us in authority, he is
still greater in the example which he sets.

CXXVII. It is but rarely that men of eminence
have failed to employ great men to aid them in direct-
ing their fortune, as the two Scipios employed the
two Laelii, whom in all things they treated as equal
to themselves, or as the deified Augustus employed
Marcus Agrippa, and after him Statilius Taurus. In
the case of these men their lack of lineage was no
obstacle to their elevation to successive consulships,
triumphs, and numerous priesthoods. For great
tasks require great helpers, and it is important to
the state that those who are necessary to her service
should be given prominence in rank, and that their
usefulness should be fortified by official authority.
With these examples before him, Tiberius Caesar
has had and still has as his incomparable associate
in all the burdens of the principate Sejanus Aelius,
son of a father who was among the foremost in the
equestrian order, but connected, on his mother's
side, with old and illustrious families and families
distinguished by public honours, while he had

tem consularis fratres, consobrinos, avunculum,
ipsum vero laboris ac fidei capacissimum, sufficiente
etiam vigori animi compage corporis, singularem
principalium onerum adiutorem in omnia habuit
4 atque habet, virum severitatis laetissimae, hilaritatis
priscae, actu otiosis simillimum, nihil sibi vindican-
tem eoque adsequentem omnia, semperque infra
aliorum aestimationes se metientem, vultu vitaque
tranquillum, animo exsomnem.

1   CXXVIII. In huius virtutum aestimatione iam
pridem iudicia civitatis cum iudiciis principis certant;
neque novus hic mos senatus populique Romani est
putandi, quod optimum sit, esse nobilissimum. Nam et
illi qui ante[1] bellum Punicum abhinc annos trecentos
Ti. Coruncanium, hominem novum, cum aliis omnibus
honoribus tum pontificatu etiam maximo ad principale
extulere fastigium, et qui[2] equestri loco natum Sp.
2 Carvilium et mox M. Catonem, novum etiam Tusculo
urbis inquilinum, Mummiumque Achaicum in consulatus, censuras et triumphos provexere, et qui C.
3 Marium ignotae originis usque ad sextum consulatum
sine dubitatione Romani nominis habuere principem,
et qui M. Tullio[3] tantum tribuere, ut paene
adsentatione sua quibus vellet principatus conciliaret,
quique nihil Asinio Pollioni negaverunt, quod nobilissimis summo cum sudore consequendum foret,

───────

[1] qui ante *Ellis*; antiqui ante *P*; primi ante *A*; antiqui
qui ante *Halm*.
[2] qui *Fröhlich*; eque *A*; *om. P*.
[3] Tullio *Lipsius*; Fulvio *AP*.

───────

[a] Tacitus, *Annals* iv. 1, has a very different description.

brothers, cousins, and an uncle who had reached the
consulship. He himself combined with loyalty to
his master great capacity for labour, and possessed
a well-knit body to match the energy of his mind;
stern but yet gay, cheerful but yet strict; busy, yet
always seeming to be at leisure. He is one who
claims no honours for himself and so acquires all
honours, whose estimate of himself is always below
the estimate of others, calm in expression and in his
life, though his mind is sleeplessly alert.[a]

CXXVIII. In the value set upon the character
of this man, the judgement of the whole state has
long vied with that of the emperor. Nor is it a new
fashion on the part of the senate and the Roman
people to regard as most noble that which is best.
For the Romans who, three centuries ago, in the
days before the Punic war, raised Tiberius
Coruncanius, a " new man," to the first position in
the state, not only bestowing on him all the other
honours but the office of *pontifex maximus* as well;
and those who elevated to consulships, censorships,
and triumphs Spurius Carvilius, though born of
equestrian rank, and soon afterwards Marcus Cato,
though a new man and not a native of the city
but from Tusculum, and Mummius, who triumphed
over Achaia; and those who regarded Gaius Marius,
though of obscure origin, as unquestionably the
first man of the Roman name until his sixth
consulship; and those who yielded such honours to
Marcus Tullius that on his recommendation he
could secure positions of importance almost for anyone he chose; and those who refused no honour
to Asinius Pollio, honours which could only be
earned, even by the noblest, by sweat and toil—

ɔfecto hoc senserunt, in cuiuscumque animo virtus
ɛsset, ei plurimum esse tribuendum. Haec naturalis
empli imitatio ad experiendum Seianum
ᴀesarem, ad iuvanda vero onera principis Seianum
opulit[1] senatumque et populum Romanum eo
ɛrduxit, ut, quod usu optimum intellegit, id in
ᴀtelam securitatis suae libenter advocet.

CXXIX. Sed proposita quasi universa principatus
ı. Caesaris forma[2] singula recenseamus. Qua ille
prudentia Rhascupolim, interemptorem fratris sui
filii Cotyis consortisque eiusdem imperii, Romam[3]
evocavit! Singulari in eo negotio usus opera Flacci
Pomponii consularis viri, nati ad omnia, quae recte
facienda sunt, simplicique virtute merentis semper,
2 numquam[4] captantis gloriam. Cum quanta gravitate
ut senator et iudex, non ut princeps, causam Drusi
Libonis audivit[5]! Quam celeriter ingratum et nova
molientem oppressit! Quibus praeceptis instructum
Germanicum suum imbutumque rudimentis militiae
secum actae domitorem recepit Germaniae! Quibus
iuventam eius exaggeravit honoribus, respondente
cultu triumphi rerum, quas gesserat, magnitudini!

[1] propulit *Acidalius*; protulit *AP*.
[2] forma *added by Rhenanus*.
[3] Romam *Ursinus*; formam *BAP*.
[4] numquam *Orelli*; quam *AP*.
[5] causam Drusi Libonis audivit *Madvig*; et causas pressius
audit *AP*.

---

[a] On the death of Rhoemetalces, King of Thrace,
Augustus divided the kingdom between Cotys, son of
Rhoemetalces, and Rhascupolis, the king's brother. On
the death of Augustus, Rhascupolis had invaded his
nephew's kingdom, and subsequently, on the pretext of an
amicable adjustment, invited him to a conference, seized his
person, and later put him to death. When Tiberius
summoned him to Rome he began to collect an army. He

all these assuredly felt that the highest honours should be paid to the man of merit. It was but the natural following of precedent that impelled Caesar to put Sejanus to the test, and that Sejanus was induced to assist the emperor with his burdens, and that brought the senate and the Roman people to the point where they were ready to summon for the preservation of its security the man whom they regarded as the most useful instrument.

CXXIX. But having set before the reader a sort of general outline of the principate of Caesar, let us now review some of the details. With what sagacity did he draw to Rome Rhascupolis,[a] the slayer of his brother's son Cotys who shared the throne with him; in this transaction Tiberius employed the rare services of Flaccus Pomponius, a consular, and a man born to carry out tasks requiring accurate discrimination, and who by his straightforward character always deserved glory though he never sought it. With what dignity did he listen to the trial of Drusus Libo, not in the capacity of emperor, but as a senator and a judge! How swiftly did he suppress that ingrate in his plot for revolution! How well had Germanicus been trained under his instructions, having so thoroughly learned the rudiments of military science under him that he was later to welcome him home as conqueror of Germany! What honours did he heap upon him, young though he was, making the magnificence of his triumph to correspond to the

---

[a] was enticed into the Roman camp by Pomponius Flaccus, propraetor of Illyria and sent to Rome. He was condemned to exile at Alexandria, where an excuse was found for putting him to death.

3 Quotiens populum congiariis honoravit senatorumque
censum, cum id senatu auctore facere potuit, quam
libenter explevit, ut neque luxuriam invitaret neque
honestam paupertatem pateretur dignitate destitui!
Quanto cum honore Germanicum suum in transmarinas misit provincias! Qua vi consiliorum suorum,
ministro et adiutore usus Druso filio suo, Maroboduum inhaerentem occupati regni finibus, pace
maiestatis eius dixerim, velut serpentem abstrusam
terrae salubribus[1] medicamentis coëgit egredi!
Quam illum ut honorate, sic[2] secure continet!
Quantae molis bellum principe Galliarum ciente
Sacroviro Floroque Iulio mira celeritate ac virtute
compressit, ut ante populus Romanus vicisse se
quam bellare cognosceret nuntiosque periculi victoriae
4 praecederet nuntius! Magni etiam terroris bellum
Africum et cotidiano auctu maius auspiciis consiliisque
eius brevi sepultum est.

1 CXXX. Quanta suo suorumque nomine exstruxit
opera! Quam pia munificentia superque humanam
evecta fidem templum patri molitur! Quam magnifico
animi temperamento Cn. quoque Pompei munera
absumpta igni restituit! Quidquid enim umquam[3]
claritudine eminuit, id veluti cognatum censet
tuendum. Qua liberalitate cum alias, tum proxime

---

[1] consiliorum suorum *after* salubribus *bracketed by Ruhnken.*
[2] sic *Burman*; nec *AP.*
[3] quicquid enim umquam *Haase*; qui quidem quam *AP.*

---

[a] A.D. 21.

greatness of his deeds ! How often did he honour the people with largesses, and how gladly, whenever he could do so with the senate's sanction, did he raise to the required rating the fortunes of senators, but in such a way as not to encourage extravagant living, nor yet to allow senators to lose their rank because of honest poverty ! With what honours did he send his beloved Germanicus to the provinces across the seas ! With what effective diplomacy, carried out through the help and agency of his son Drusus, did he force Maroboduus, who clung to the limits of the territories he had seized as a serpent to his hole, to come forth like the serpent under the spell of his salutary charms—a simile which I use with no disrespect to Caesar. With what honour does he treat him while at the same time he holds him securely ! With what wonderful swiftness and courage did he repress the formidable war, stirred up at the instigation of Sacrovir and Florus Julius,[a] so that the Roman people learned that he had conquered before they knew he was engaged in war, and the news of victory preceded the news of the danger ! The African war also, which caused great consternation and grew more formidable every day, was soon extinguished under his auspices and in accordance with his plans.

CXXX. What public buildings did he construct in his own name or that of his family ! With what pious munificence, exceeding human belief, does he now rear the temple to his father ! With what a magnificent control of personal feeling did he restore the works of Gnaeus Pompey when destroyed by fire ! For a feeling of kinship leads him to protect every famous monument. With what generosity at

325

2 incenso monte Caelio omnis ordinis hominum iacturae patrimonio succurrit suo ! Quanta cum quiete hominum rem perpetui praecipuique timoris, supplementum, sine trepidatione dilectus providet !
3 Si aut natura patitur aut mediocritas recipit hominum, audeo cum deis[1] queri : quid hic meruit, primum ut scelerata Drusus Libo iniret consilia ? Deinde ut Silium Pisonemque tam infestos haberet, quorum[2] alterius dignitatem constituit, auxit alterius ? Ut ad maiora transcendam, quamquam et haec ille duxit[3] maxima, quid, ut iuvenes amitteret filios ? Quid, ut nepotem ex Druso suo ? Dolenda
4 adhuc retulimus : veniendum ad erubescenda est. Quantis hoc triennium, M. Vinici, doloribus laceravit animum eius ! Quam diu abstruso, quod miserrimum est, pectus eius flagravit incendio, quod ex nuru, quod ex nepote dolere, indignari, erubescere coactus est ! Cuius temporis aegritudinem auxit amissa
5 mater, eminentissima et per omnia deis quam hominibus similior femina, cuius potentiam nemo sensit nisi aut levatione periculi aut accessione dignitatis.
1 CXXXI. Voto finiendum volumen est.[4] Iuppiter Capitoline, et auctor ac stator Romani nominis Gradive Mars, perpetuorumque custos Vesta ignium

---

[1] audeo cum deis *Heinsius* ; auro deo cum de his *AP*.
[2] infestos haberet quorum *supplied by Burman.*
[3] duxit *Rhenanus* ; dixit *AP*.
[4] est *Orelli* ; sit *AP*.

---

[a] Agrippina, the wife of Germanicus, adopted son of Tiberius, banished to Pandataria in A.D. 30, where she died, in A.D. 33, of voluntary starvation ; and Nero, the son of Germanicus and Agrippina, who was banished to the island of Pontia.

the time of the recent fire on the Caelian Hill, as well as on other occasions, did he use his private fortune to make good the losses of people of all ranks in life! And the recruiting of the army, a thing ordinarily looked upon with great and constant dread, with what calm on the part of the people does he provide for it, and without any of the usual panic attending conscription! If either nature permits, or man's weak faculties allow, I may dare to make this plaint to the gods : How has this man deserved, in the first place, to have Drusus Libo enter upon a traitorous conspiracy against him, or later to earn the hostility of Silius and Piso, though in the one case he created his rank, and in the other he increased it? Passing on to greater trials—although he regarded these as great enough—how did he deserve the loss of his sons in their prime or of his grandson, the son of Drusus? Thus far I have told of sorrows only, we must now come to the shame. With what pain, Marcus Vinicius, have the past three years rent his heart! With what fire, the more cruel because pent up, was his soul consumed because of the grief, the indignation, and the shame he was forced to suffer through his daughter-in-law and his grandson! ᵃ His sorrow at this time was crowned by the loss of his mother, a woman pre-eminent among women, and who in all things resembled the gods more than mankind, whose power no one felt except for the alleviation of trouble or the promotion of rank.

CXXXI. Let me end my volume with a prayer. O Jupiter Capitolinus, and Mars Gradivus, author and stay of the Roman name, Vesta, guardian of the eternal fire, and all other divinities who have

et quidquid numinum hanc Romani imperii molem in amplissimum terrarum orbis fastigium extulit, vos publica voce obtestor atque precor : custodite, servate, protegite hunc statum, hanc pacem, hunc 2 principem,[1] eique functo longissima statione mortali destinate successores quam serissimos, sed eos, quorum cervices tam fortiter sustinendo terrarum orbis imperio sufficiant, quam huius suffecisse sensimus, consiliaque omnium civium aut pia fovete aut impia opprimite.[2]

[1] hunc principem *added by Lipsius.*
[2] fovete . . . opprimite *supplied by Voss.*

exalted this great empire of Rome to the highest
point yet reached on earth ! On you I call, and to
you I pray in the name of this people : guard,
preserve, protect the present state of things, the
peace which we enjoy, the present emperor, and
when he has filled his post of duty—and may it
be the longest granted to mortals—grant him
successors until the latest time, but successors whose
shoulders may be as capable of sustaining bravely
the empire of the world as we have found his to be :
foster the pious plans of all good citizens and crush
the impious designs of the wicked.

RES GESTAE DIVI AUGUSTI

INTRODUCTION

AMONG extant historical documents there is none that outweighs in importance the account of his stewardship which the Emperor Augustus left among the papers deposited with the Vestal Virgins before his death, preserved to us in a copy chiselled upon the walls of the Temple of Rome and Augustus at Ancyra in Asia Minor, the modern Angora. This copy, known as the Monumentum Ancyranum, has justly been called by Mommsen the "Queen of Inscriptions."

Suetonius, *Augustus*, 101, states that Augustus had deposited with the Vestal Virgins, along with his will, three other documents, all of which were opened and read in the Senate. The first contained instructions for his funeral ; the third, a summarized statement of the condition of the whole empire ; the second, the one with which we are here concerned, contained " a résumé of his acts which he wished to have engraved upon bronze tablets to be set up before his mausoleum." More than forty years before his death Augustus had built this mausoleum on the Tiber at the northern edge of the Campus Martius, in the midst of a small park, which was opened by the Emperor to the public. The mausoleum itself was probably surrounded by an enclosing wall, at the entrance to which, facing the Campus Martius, stood the pillars, or pilasters, on which was engraved the *index rerum gestarum*. The shell of the

mausoleum itself has outlived the centuries and is still standing on the Ripetta, but the bronze tablets have long since disappeared. . The original document, however, was copied on the walls of many of the temples of Augustus throughout the empire, and remains of three copies have come to light in Asia Minor alone. In addition to the Augusteum at Ancyra, inscribed with both the Latin text and a Greek version, there was found another ruined temple at Apollonia with remnants of the same Greek version ; it is fairly certain that the Augusteum at Pergamon had both the Latin and the Greek versions ; and finally at Antioch in Pisidia (Colonia Caesarea) Sir W. M. Ramsay discovered, in 1914, a number of fragments of the Latin text from a fourth copy.[1] But the inscription on the temple of Rome and Augustus at Ancyra is relatively so complete, although marred in places by the scaling of the stone, that it outweighs all the others in importance, and the designation Monumentum Ancyranum has become synonymous with Res Gestae Divi Augusti.

The temple of Rome and Augustus at Ancyra is still in a fair state of preservation. The Latin text is chiselled upon both sides of the inner walls of the pronaos or vestibule. It was arranged in six pages, three of forty-six lines each, on the left as one entered, surmounted by the title, which runs in two and a half lines across the top of all three, and three pages on the right of fifty-four lines each. The arrangement undoubtedly was in general a replica of that of the inscription at Rome. Each line contained on the

[1] Ramsay, "Colonia Caesarea (Pisidian Antioch) in the Augustan Age," *Journal of Roman Studies*, vol. vi., 1916, London, pp. 108-129.

average about sixty letters. The height of the inscription is 2·70 metres on each wall, and the length on each wall is about 4 metres. To mark the paragraphs, the first letter projects beyond the margin, and to indicate periods, a symbol like a figure 7 was used, which is usually, however, printed in the texts as §. On one of the outer walls of the temple was inscribed a Greek translation of the Latin. The fact that several Turkish houses had been built against this wall long made it difficult to read all of the Greek inscription and still more difficult to secure casts.

The Monumentum Ancyranum was first made known to the western world by Buysbecche, a Dutch scholar who was sent, in 1555, by Ferdinand II. on an embassy to the Sultan Soliman at Amasia in Asia Minor. He first read and identified the inscription and published a copy of parts of it. After him the inscription was copied in part by many travellers, but the first faithful and trustworthy copy was made by Georges Perrot and Edmund Guillaume, who had been commissioned by Napoleon III. to explore Asia Minor. They made a facsimile copy, but no casts, of the whole of the Latin, and as much of the Greek as they could get at. Their plates were the basis of Mommsen's edition of the text in 1865, and of that of Bergk in 1873; also of the text in the Corpus Inscriptionum Latinarum. In 1859 the Berlin Academy commissioned Mordtmann to make a cast in papier-mâché, but after visiting the site he reported that the owners of the Turkish houses would not permit his getting at the parts of the Greek inscription which were hidden, and that the making of a cast would still further injure the

inscription itself. In 1882, however, at the suggestion of Mommsen, the Academy commissioned Carl Humann to make a plaster cast. He not only made casts of the Latin inscription, but also of the Greek as well, having persuaded the owners of the houses to allow their walls to be partially torn down for the purpose, and the casts were safely transported to Berlin in the autumn of 1882, where they are now among the treasures of the Museum. Humann's casts have superseded in value all previous copies, except in a few places where the wall had scaled since these earlier copies were made, as, for instance, in page 5, lines 34-48, and page 6, lines 1-6. In 1883, using these casts as a basis, Mommsen published his great critical edition, with a supplement containing heliogravure reproductions from the casts. This edition of Mommsen has become the basis for all subsequent work. There are still passages in which the lacunae in the Latin cannot be supplied with certainty from the Greek translation, either because of lacunae or illegibility in the Greek text, and concerning which subsequent scholars have exercised their ingenuity in conjecture. Some of these conjectures are clearly more probable than Mommsen's, while others raise debatable questions which will never be cleared up until another copy either of the Latin text or the Greek translation is found in one of the many Augustea in Asia Minor.[1]

[1] Sir W. M. Ramsay's work at Colonia Caesarea (Pisidian Antioch) was stopped by the local authorities soon after he began to find fragments of the Latin inscription. When the work of excavation is continued it may be that other fragments will come to light which will clear up a number of the vexed passages. See Ramsay's article in the *Journal of Roman Studies*, vol. vi., 1916.

But for by far the greater portion of the document we have the actual words of Augustus, and for a considerable portion in addition the substance supplied from the Greek or from sure conjecture.

In a style of studied simplicity, and almost telegraphic brevity, with not a word too many or a word too few, and, except for the personal pronoun which is used throughout, with an objectivity worthy of the commentaries of his adopted father, the document sets forth, (1) the honours conferred upon Augustus from time to time by the Senate and the Roman people and the services for which they were conferred, chapters 1-14, (2) the donations which he made from his own personal account to the Republic, to the discharged soldiers, and the Roman plebs ; also the games, shows, and spectacles given to the people at his own expense, chapters 15-24, and (3) an account of his acts in peace and war, chapters 25-35. The title provided by Tiberius includes only the last two, namely, the *Impensae* and the *Res Gestae*, but the first group may easily be reckoned with the third, since the services are there recorded as well as the honours conferred in reward for them. There is no attempt at literary embellishment. The document is almost statistical in its conciseness, and the facts of a long life are allowed to speak for themselves. The superlative is purposely avoided, and there is also an absence of the usual descriptive adjectives and adverbs. Nowhere does the emperor refer by name to any of his public enemies, such as Antony, Brutus and Cassius, Lepidus, or Sextus Pompey. Not even his own name appears in the body of the document, except in the statement that the Senate, out of honour to him, had conferred upon

him the title of Augustus. No mention is made of his father, his mother, or his wife, nor, indeed, of any member of his family, except that he does mention Agrippa, Tiberius, Gaius, and Lucius, when their names were linked with his in public honours and public affairs. In a word, everything of a personal nature is omitted with studied objectivity, and his narration is limited to his relations with the Senate and the Roman people and theirs with him.

For a long time there waged in Germany a controversy as to the purpose and literary classification of the document. Was it intended as a political testament,[1] or a statement of credit and debit in his account with the Roman people,[2] or an account of his stewardship,[3] or an *apologia pro vita sua*,[4] or as an epitaph[5]? Each of these theories had its defenders. If it was intended for an epitaph, Augustus must have contemplated that it would be thrown into epitaph form by his successor, Tiberius, who, in any event, allowed it to stand in the form in which it was written. Mommsen declares against ascribing it to any particular class of composition.[3]

[1] Hirschfeld, *Wiener Studien*, iii. (1881) and vii. (1885); *Wochenschrift für class. Philol,*, 1884; Plew, *Quellenuntersuchungen zur Gesch. des Kaisers Hadrian*, Strassburg, 1890.

[2] Wölfflin, "Epigraphische Beiträge," *S.-B. der Münch. Akad.*, 1886, p. 225, and 1896, p. 162.

[3] Mommsen, von Sybel's *Historische Zeitschrift*, N.F. xxi., 1887.

[4] Cantarelli, "L' Iscrizione di Ancyra," *Bullettino della com. arch. comunale*, iii. ser. 4 (1889), p. 3.

[5] Bormann, *Bemerkungen zum schriftlichen Nachlass des Kaisers Augustus*, Marburger Program, 1884; also "Veranlassung und Zweck des Mon. Anc.," *Verhandl. der 43. Philologen-Versammlung in Köln*, 1895. Supported by Nissen, Schmidt, and Peter.

It is clear that the document was not originally written in A.D. 14, as the last sentence would seem to indicate, but that it was begun much earlier, with later additions from time to time. As to when Augustus wrote his original draft, and what additions were subsequently made, and at what time, there has been much controversy. Some of the details of these problems will be discussed in the historical notes. It is sufficient to say here that it is fairly sure that an early draft of the document was already complete in his twelfth consulship, 2 B.C., and perhaps long before that; that subsequently changes were made in some of the statements as, for instance, in the case of the donations to the city plebs in his twelfth and thirteenth consulships, where the amounts are reckoned in *denarii* and not, as usual, in *sesterces*; that the statement in regard to the subjugation of the German tribes as far as the Elbe, while true at the time at which it was written, was no longer true in A.D. 14, when the last words were added, if, indeed, these were added by Augustus himself; and that the mention of his third census made in A.D. 14 is of course a later addition made either by himself or by Tiberius.

THE TEXT

The Latin text of the *Res Gestae*, as here printed, is based upon that of Mommsen's Second Edition of 1883, supplemented by that of the third edition of the *Monumentum Ancyranum* by Ernst Diehl, Bonn, 1918. Diehl has had the advantage of the

twenty-five years of study which scholars have
devoted to the *Monumentum* since the publication
of Mommsen's second edition and has adopted a
number of readings which better fill the spaces in
the lacunae, or better correspond with the content
of the Greek version. In some of the passages
Mommsen's readings have been retained as against
Diehl, and in a few the conjectures of other scholars
have been adopted as indicated in the notes on the
text. Use has also been made of the fragments
of the Latin text of the *Res Gestae* found by Sir
William Ramsay at Colonia Caesarea (Pisidian
Antioch) in 1914, and published by him in the
Journal of Roman Studies, vol. vi., 1916, pp. 114-134.
These fragments are exceedingly small, but, placed
in position, some of them serve to determine which
of the conjectures of various scholars is the correct
or more probable one.

In the general typography it has seemed best,
for the purposes of the Loeb Library, to follow Diehl
rather than Mommsen. Mommsen's lines, which
correspond to those of the inscription, are too long
for the width of the page of so small a volume. The
ends of the lines in the original monument are here
indicated by a perpendicular line thus, | , and the
beginning of each fifth line, numbered in the margin
5, 10, 15, etc., in the various paragraphs is indicated
by two perpendicular lines thus, ‖ . In the original,
the first letter of each paragraph projects beyond
the margin. To save space, the paragraphs are
here indented according to modern practice. The
lacunae and illegible passages are indicated by
parentheses thus, ( ), and the words which have
been supplied to fill them are, in the case of the

339

Latin text, printed in italics. In the Greek text the parentheses alone are used. In the Latin inscription the long vowels are indicated on the stone, but not always consistently, either by an apex, or in the case of long i, by an elongation of that letter. In printing the Latin text the apex (´) has been used for all vowels whose length is indicated on the stone by either method. The sign § is used to represent a symbol on the stone which resembles sometimes the figure 7, sometimes an open 3.

In printing the Greek text, Diehl has been followed except in a very few passages.

Wherever it has seemed essential, the Latin text has been provided with critical footnotes. These have been omitted for the Greek version, partly for economy of space, and partly because the Greek version is of value chiefly as a subsidiary aid.

THE HISTORICAL NOTES

The interest which the *Monumentum Ancyranum* will have for most readers is chiefly historical. For the benefit of the general reader, and also of the student of history, the translation has been supplemented by historical notes, to amplify or explain the statements of the first emperor, which are throughout characterized by epigraphic brevity. In compiling these notes it has sometimes been exceedingly hard to draw the line between saying too much or too little. Owing to the nature of the document itself, these notes are necessarily much more numerous than is usual in the volumes of the Loeb Classical Library.

BIBLIOGRAPHY

So many articles and comments on the *Monumentum Ancyranum* have appeared, especially since 1861, that a complete bibliography is out of the question here, and the list will have to be limited to the more important books and articles, and particularly to those referred to in the introduction, and the critical and historical notes.

Editions [1]

Corpus Inscriptionum Latinarum, vol. iii., Pars II., pp. 769 ff., Berlin, 1873.

Mommsen, Theodor, *Res Gestae Divi Augusti ex Monumentis Ancyrano et Apolloniensi*, with eleven photogravure plates, Berlin, 1883.

R. Cagnat and G. Lafaye, *Inscriptiones Graecae ad Res Romanas pertinentes* iii., 1, 1902, p. 65 ff.

Ernst Diehl, *Res Gestae Divi Augusti*, third ed., Bonn, 1918.

English Translations

William Fairley, *Monumentum Ancyranum* in *Translations and Reprints from the Original Sources of European History*, Philadelphia, Pa., 1898.

E. S. Shuckburgh, *Augustus*, T. Fisher Unwin, London, pp. 293-301.

Comments on Text

E. Bormann, *Bemerkungen zum schriftlichen Nachlass des Kaisers Augustus*, Marburg, 1884; also, *Verhandlungen der 43. Versammlung deutscher Philologen und Schulmänner in Köln*, Leipzig, 1895, p. 184 ff.

[1] E. G. Hardy, *The Monumentum Ancyranum*, Oxford, Clarendon Press, 1923, appeared after this volume was in page proof, and therefore too late to be used by the translator.

F. Gottakda, *Suetons Verhältnis zu der Denkschrift des Augustus*, Dissertation, Munich, 1904, p. 50 ff.; also *Blätter für das bayerische Gymnasialschulwesen*, 1913, p. 121 ff.

Fr. Haug, *Bursians Jahresberichte über die Fortschritte der Altertumswissenschaft*, lvi., 1888, p. 87 ff.

J. Schmidt, *Philologus*, xliv., 1885, p. 448 ff.; *ib.* xlv., 1886, p. 393 ff.; *ib.* xlvi., 1887, p. 70 ff.

O. Seeck, *Wochenschrift für klassische Philologie*, 1884, col. 1475 ff.

R. Wirtz, *Ergänzungs- und Verbesserungsvorschläge zum Monumentum Ancyranum*, Program, Trier, 1912.

E. Wölfflin, *Sitzungsberichte der kgl. bayer. Akademie der Wissenschaften*, 1886, p. 253 ff.; 1896, p. 160 ff.

Sir **W. M.** Ramsay, " Colonia Caesarea (Pisidian Antioch) in the Augustan Age," *Journal of Roman Studies*, vol. vi., 1916, London, pp. 108-129.

Books and Articles dealing with Literary and Historical Problems

V. Gardthausen, *Augustus und seine Zeit*, i. 1279 ff.; ii. 874 ff., Leipzig, 1904.

M. Schanz, *Römische Litteraturgeschichte*, vol. ii. pt. i. p. 12, Munich, 1911.

M. Besnier, "Récents travaux sur les Res Gestae Divi Augusti," in *Mélanges Cagnat*, p. 119 ff.

Th. Mommsen, von Sybel's *Historische Zeitschrift*, N.F. xxi., 1887, p. 385 ff.; also *Röm. Gesch.* v. 600 ff.; *Journal des Savants*, xii. 176 ff.

A. von Domaszewski, "Untersuchungen zur römischen Kaisergeschichte," *Rheinisches Museum*, lix., 1904, p. 302 ff.

W. Fuerst, *Suetons Verhältnis zu der Denkschrift des Augustus.* Erlangen dissertation, 1904, p. 58.

O. Hirschfeld, "Die kaiserlichen Grabstätten in Rom," *Sitzungsber. der Kgl. preuss. Akad.*, 1886, p. 1154; "Die Abfassungszeit des Regierungsberichtes des Augustus," *ib.*, 1915, p. 423.

INTRODUCTION

E. Kornemann, *Beiträge zur alten Geschichte*, ii., 1902, p. 141 ff.; *ib.* iii., 1903, p. 74 ff.; iv., 1904, p. 88 ff.; v., 1905, p. 317 ff.; *Berliner philologische Wochenschrift*, 1906, col. 120; *Klio*, xiv., 1915, p. 377 ff.

F. Koepp, *Mittheilungen des römisches Instituts*, xix., 1904, p. 51 ff.

F. Marks, " Zur Komposition des Res Gestae des Kaisers Augustus," *Festschrift d. Pädagogiums in Putbus*, 1903.

H. Peter, *Die geschichtliche Litteratur über die römische Kaiserzeit*, i. 453 ff.

G. Sigwart, " Sueton und das Monumentum Ancyranum," *Klio*, x., 1910, p. 394.

P. Viereck, *Sermo Graecus*, Göttingen, 1888, p. 85.

Vulic, *Rivista di storia antica*, xiii., 1909, p. 41 ff.

W. L. Westermann, " The Monument of Ancyra," *American Historical Review*, 17, 1911.

U. Wilcken, *Hermes*, xxxviii., 1903, p. 618 ff.

M. Rostowzew, *Title and Character of the Mon. Anc.* (in Russian), St. Petersburg, 1913.

Chr. Huelsen, *Topographie von Rom*, 1907, p. 620 ff.

E. Norden, *Antike Kunstprosa*, p. 268 ff.

RES GESTAE DIVI AUGUSTI

Rérum[1] gestárum díví Augusti, quibus orbem terra-
(*rum*) ímperio populi Rom. subiécit, § et inpensarum,
quas in rem publicam populumque Ro(*ma*)num fecit,
incísarum in duabus aheneís pílís, quae su(*n*)t Romae
positae, exemplar sub(*i*)ectum.

I   1 Annós undéviginti natus exercitum priváto
consilio et privatá impensá | comparávi, (§) per quem
rem publicam (*do*)minatione factionis oppressam | in

[1] For an explanation of the apices (') and other symbols
such as §, used in printing the text, see Introd. pp. 334, 339 f.

Μεθηρμηνευμέναι ὑπεγράφησαν πράξεις τε καὶ
δωρεαὶ Σεβαστοῦ θεοῦ, ἃς ἀπέλιπεν ἐπὶ ʽΡώμης
ἐνκεχαραγμένας χαλκαῖς στήλαις δυσί.

I   1. Ἐτῶν δεκαε(ν)νέα ὢν τὸ στράτευμα ἐμῆι
γνώμηι καὶ | ἐμοῖς ἀν(αλ)ώμασιν ἡτοί(μασα), δι'
οὗ τὰ κοινὰ πρά|γματα (ἐκ τῆ)ς τ(ῶ)ν συνο(μοσα)-

---

[a] The title *Res Gestae Divi Augusti* is that assigned by
Mommsen.

The superscription, which was engraved in large letters
across the top of the first three columns of the *Mon. Anc.*,
was of course not by Augustus. It was adapted, as is
indicated by the words *incisarum . . . exemplar subiectum*,
from the superscription provided by Tiberius, or some
one acting under his orders, for the bronze pillars before

THE ACTS OF AUGUSTUS

THE MONUMENTUM ANCYRANUM

BELOW is a copy of the acts of the Deified Augustus by which he placed the whole world under the sovereignty of the Roman people, and of the amounts which he expended upon the state and the Roman people, as engraved upon two bronze columns which have been set up in Rome.[a]

1. At the age of nineteen,[b] on my own initiative and at my own expense, I raised an army [c] by means of which I restored liberty [d] to the republic, which

the Mausoleum of Augustus at Rome. Its original form on that monument was probably : Res gestae divl Augusti, quibus orbem terrarum imperio populi Romani subiecit, et impensae quas in rem publicam populumque Romanum fecit.

The Greek superscription reads: " Below is a translation of the acts and donations of the Deified Augustus as left by him inscribed on two bronze columns at Rome."

[b] Octavian was nineteen on September 23, 44 B.C.

[c] During October, by offering a bounty of 500 denarii, he induced Caesar's veterans at Casilinum and Calatia to enlist, and in November the legions named Martia and Quarta repudiated Antony and went over to him. This activity of Octavian, on his own initiative, was ratified by the Senate on December 20, on the motion of Cicero.

[d] In the battle of Mutina, April 43. Augustus may also have had Philippi in mind.

libertátem vindicá(*vi*.   *Quas ob res*[1] *sen*)atus decretís
honor(*ifi*)cís in | ordinem suum m(*e adlegit C. Pansa*
5 *A. Hirti*)o consulibu(*s, c*)on(*sula*)||rem locum s(*ententiae
dicendae simul dans,*[2] *et im*)perium mihi dedit. (§) |
Rés publica n(*e quid detrimenti caperet, me*) pro praetore
simul cum | consulibus pro(*videre iussit.* § *Populus*)
autem eódem anno mé | consulem, cum (*cos. uterque
bello ceci*)disset, et trium virum reí publicae con-
stituend(*ae creavit.*) ||
10   2. Quí parentem meum (*interfecer*)un(*t, eó*)s in
exilium expulí iudiciís legi|timís ultus eórum (*fa*)ci-
n(*us,* § *e*)t posteá bellum inferentís reí publicae | víci
b(*is a*)cie. |

   [1] Quas ob res *Wölfflin*, Ob quae *Mommsen*, Propter quae
Bormann.
   [2] s(*imul dans sententiae ferendae et im*)perium *Mommsen.*

μένων δουλήας | (ἠλευ)θέ(ρωσα.   Ἐφ᾽ o)ἷς ἡ
5 σύνκλητος ἐπαινέσασά || (με ψηφίσμασι) προσ-
κατέλεξε τῆι βουλῆι Γαΐωι Πά(νσ)α | (Αὔλωι
Ἱρτίωι ὑ)π(ά)το(ι)ς, ἐν τῆι τάξει τῶν ὑπατ(ικῶ)ν |
(ἅμα τ)ὸ σ(υμβου)λεύειν δοῦσα, ῥάβδου(ς) τ᾽ ἐμοὶ
ἔδωκεν. | (Περ)ὶ τὰ δημόσια πράγματα μή τι
βλαβῆι, ἐμοὶ με|(τὰ τῶν ὑπά)των προνοεῖν ἐπ-
10 έτρεψεν ἀντὶ στρατηγο(ῦ) || (ὄντι. § Ὁ δ)ὲ
δ(ῆ)μος τῶι αὐτῶι ἐνιαυτῶι, ἀμφοτέρων | (τῶν
ὑπάτων π)ολέμωι πεπτω(κ)ό(τ)ων, ἐμὲ ὕπα|(τον
ἀπέδειξ)εν καὶ τὴν τῶν τριῶν ἀνδρῶν ἔχον|(τα
ἀρχὴν ἐπὶ) τῆι καταστάσει τῶν δ(η)μοσίων πρα|(γ-
μάτων) ε(ἱλ)ατ(ο). ||
15   2. (Τοὺς τὸν πατέρα τὸν ἐμὸν φονεύ)σ(αν)τ(α)ς ἐξ-
ώρισα κρί|(σεσιν ἐνδί)κοις τειμω(ρ)ησάμε(νος) αὐτῶν
τὸ | (ἀσέβημα κ)αὶ (με)τὰ ταῦτα αὐτοὺς πόλεμον
ἐ|(πιφέροντας τῆι πα)τ(ρ)ίδι δὶς ἐνείκησα παρατάξει.|

had been oppressed by the tyranny of a faction.[a]
For which service the senate, with complimentary
resolutions, enrolled me in its order, in the consulship of Gaius Pansa and Aulus Hirtius, giving me
at the same time consular precedence in voting ;
it also gave me the *imperium*.[b] As propraetor it
ordered me, along with the consuls, " to see that
the republic suffered no harm." In the same year,
moreover, as both consuls had fallen in war,[c] the
people elected me consul and a triumvir for settling
the constitution.[d]

2. Those who slew my father[e] I drove into exile,
punishing their deed by due process of law,[f] and
afterwards when they waged war upon the republic
I twice[g] defeated them in battle.

---

[a] By " faction " he means Antony, whom he never
mentions by name.

[b] On January 2, 43 B.C., the Senate decreed that Octavian
should be classed as a *quaestorius* (Dio, xlvi. 29. 41), should be
a member of the Senate (Livy, *Epit.* cxviii.), should have the
consularia ornamenta, and for that reason should give his
opinion along with the consuls (App. *B.C.* iii. 51) ; he was
also given the rank of propraetor with imperium, *i.e.* the
constitutional right to command soldiers.

[c] Pansa died of his wounds, and Hirtius was killed in
action in the operations about Mutina.

[d] Octavian became consul August 19, 43 B.C., after marching his army from Cisalpine Gaul to intimidate the Senate.
On November 27 the appointment of Octavian, Antony,
and Lepidus as triumvirs was brought about by their
arrival in the city with armed forces.

[e] Julius Caesar.

[f] By the *lex Pedia*.

[g] The two battles at Philippi.

3. (*B*)ella terra et mari c(*ivilia exter*)naque tóto in orbe terrarum s(*uscepi*[1]) | victorque omnibus (*veniam* 15 *petentib*)us[2] cívibus peperci. § Éxte(*rnas*) ‖ gentés, quibus túto (*ignosci pot*)ui(*t, co*)nserváre quam excídere m(*alui.* §) | Míllia civium Róma(*norum adacta*) sacrámento meo fuerunt circiter (*quingen*)|ta. § Ex quibus dedú(*xi in coloni*)ás aut remísi in municipia sua stipen(*dis emeri*)|tis millia aliquant(*o plura qu*)am trecenta et iís omnibus agrós a(*dsignavi*[3]) | aut pecuniam pro p(*raemis mil*)itiae[4] dedí. § Naves cépi 20 sescen(*tas praeter*) ‖ eás, si quae minóre(*s quam tri-r*)emes fuerunt. § |

4. (*Bis*) ováns triumpha(*vi, tris egi c*)urulís triumphós

---

[1] s(*uscepi*) Mommsen, s(*aepe gessi*) Bormann.
[2] (*superstitib*)us Mommsen.
[3] a(*dsignavi*) Bormann, a (*me emptos*) Mommsen.
[4] p(*raemis mil*)itiae Bergk and Bormann, p(*raediis a*) me Mommsen.

---

3. (Πολέμους καὶ κατὰ γῆν) καὶ κατὰ θάλασσαν 20 ἐμφυ‖(λίους καὶ ἐξωτικοὺς) ἐν ὅληι τῆι οἰκουμένηι πολ|(λοὺς ἀνεδεξάμην, νεικ)ήσας τε πάντων ἐφεισάμην | (τῶν περιόντων πολειτῶν. Τ)ὰ ἔθνη, οἷς ἀσφαλὲς ἦν συν|(γνώμην ἔχειν, ἔσωσα μ)ᾶλ(λον) 11 ἢ ἐξέκοψα. § Μυριάδες ‖ Ῥωμαίων στρατ(εύ)- σ(ασ)αι ὑπ(ὸ τὸ)ν ὅρκον τὸν ἐμὸν | ἐγένοντ(ο) ἐγγὺς π(εντήκ)ο(ντ)α· (ἐ)ξ ὧν κατή(γ)αγον εἰς | τὰ(ς) ἀπο(ι)κίας ἢ ἀ(πέπεμψα εἰς τὰς) ἰδία(ς πόλεις ἐκ|λυομένας μυριάδας πολλῶι πλείους ἢ τριά- 5 κοντα, ‖ καὶ πάσαις αὐταῖς ἢ ἀγροὺς ἐμέρισα ἢ χρήματα τῆς | στρατείας δωρεὰν ἔδωκα. Ναῦς § δὲ ... εἷλον ἑξα|κοσίας πλὴν τούτων, εἴ τινες ἥσσονες ἐγένοντο ἢ | τριήρεις.)

4. Δὶς ἐ(πὶ κέλητος ἐθριάμβευσα), τρὶς (ἐ)φ'

3. Wars, both civil and foreign, I undertook throughout the world, on sea and land, and when victorious I spared all citizens who sued for pardon.[a] The foreign nations which could with safety be pardoned I preferred to save rather than to destroy. The number of Roman citizens who bound themselves to me by military oath was about 500,000. Of these I settled in colonies or sent back into their own towns, after their term of service, something more than 300,000, and to all I assigned lands, or gave money as a reward for military service.[b] I captured six hundred ships,[c] over and above those which were smaller than triremes.

4. Twice I triumphed with an ovation,[d] thrice I

[a] He is referring in particular to the clemency which he showed after the battle of Actium, for which he received a crown of oak leaves in 27 B.C. *ob cives servatos.*

[b] Of the 300,000 soldiers who received honourable dismissal from the service, 120,000 had been settled in colonies by the year 29 B.C. (see chap. 15); the remaining 180,000 must consequently have been mustered out in the succeeding 42 years of his reign. There were in service at the death of Augustus 25 legions (Tac. *Ann.* iv. 5), or about 150,000 men, exclusive of the praetorian and urban cohorts. Those who were killed in battle or died in service therefore numbered about 50,000.

[c] From Sextus Pompeius at Mylae 30 ships (Appian v. 108), and at Naulochus 283 (*ib.* 108); from Antony at Actium 300 (Plutarch, *Ant.* 68).

[d] " Bis ovans ingressus est urbem, post Philippense (40 B.C.) et rursus post Siculum bellum " (Nov. 13, 36 B.C.), Suet. *Aug.* 22. An ovation was a minor triumph. In this the conqueror entered the city on foot or on horseback instead of in the four-horse chariot, as in the case of the curule triumph.

et appellá(*tus sum viciens*) | (*se*)mel imperátor. (*Cum autem*[1] *plú*)ris triumphos mihi se(*natus decrevisset,*) | (*iis su*)persedi. (§) L(*aurum de fascib*)us[2] deposuí § in Capi(*tolio votis, quae*) | quóque bello nuncu-(*paveram, solu*)tís. § Ob res á (*me aut per legatos*) ||
25 meós auspicís meis terra m(*ariqu*)e pr(*o*)spere gestás qu(*inquagiens et quin*)|quiens decrevit senátus supp(*lica*)ndum esse dís immo(*rtalibus. Dies autem,*) | (*pe*)r quós ex senátús consulto (*s*)upplicátum est, fuere DC(*CCLXXX. In triumphis*) | (*meis*) ducti sunt ante currum m(*e*)um regés aut r(*eg*)um lib(*eri novem. Consul*) | (*fuer*)am terdeciens, c(*u*)m (*scribeb*)a(*m*)

---

[1] deinde *Mommsen*.
[2] l(*aurum de fascib*)us *Wehofer*, I(*tem saepe laur*)us *Mommsen*.

---

10 ἅρματος. Εἰκο||σά(κις καὶ ἅπαξ προσηγορεύθην αὐτο)κράτωρ. Τῆς | (δὲ συγκλήτου ἐμοὶ πλείους θριάμβου)ς ψηφισσ(αμέ|νης, αὐτῶν ἀπηλλάγην (?) καὶ ἀπὸ τῶν ῥάβδ)ων τὴν (δάφνην | κατεθέμην ἐν τῶι Καπιτωλίωι, τὰ)ς εὐχάς, (ἃς ἐν ἑκάσ)|τω(ι τῶι πολέμωι ἐποιησάμην, ἀποδ)ούς. (Διὰ τὰ
15 πράγμα||τα, ἃ ἢ αὐτὸς ἢ διὰ τῶν πρεσβευτῶν τῶν ἐ)μ(ῶν αἰσίοις | οἰωνοῖς καὶ κατὰ γῆν καὶ κατὰ θάλατταν) κατώρθω|σα, π(εντ)ηκοντάκις (καὶ) πεντά(κις ἐψ)ηφίσατο ἡ | σύ(νκλητ)ος θεοῖς δεῖ(ν) θύεσθαι. (Ἡμ)έραι οὖν α|ὗ(τα)ι ἐ(κ συ)ν(κλήτου)
20 δ(ό)γματ(ο)ς ἐγένοντο ὀκτα(κ)όσιαι ἐνενή||(κοντα). Ἐν (τ)οῖς ἐμοῖς (θριάμ)βοις (πρὸ το)ῦ ἐμοῦ ἅρ-| μ(ατος βασι)λεῖς ἢ (βασιλέων παῖ)δες (παρήχθη-σαν | ἐννέα. § (Ὑπάτ)ε(υ)ον τρὶς καὶ δέκ(ατο)ν,
350

celebrated curule triumphs,[a] and was saluted as imperator twenty-one times.[b] Although the Senate decreed me additional triumphs I set them aside. When I had performed the vows which I had undertaken in each war I deposited upon the Capitol the laurels which adorned my fasces.[c] For successful operations on land and sea, conducted either by myself or by my lieutenants under my auspices, the senate on fifty-five occasions decreed that thanks should be rendered to the immortal gods. The days on which such thanks were rendered by decree of the senate numbered 890. In my triumphs there were led before my chariot nine kings or children of kings.[d] At the time of writing these words I had been thirteen

[a] " Curulis triumphos tris egit Delmaticum, Actiacum, Alexandrinum continuo triduo omnes " (Aug. 13, 14, 15 of the year 29), Suet. Aug. 22. "Tres triumphos egit, unum ex Illyrico, alterum ex Achaica victoria, tertium de Cleopatra " (Livy, Epit. 133).

[b] These acclamations as imperator, for military successes, must not be confused with the title of imperator prefixed to the name of Augustus and succeeding emperors. Mommsen gives the list, Res Gestae Divi Augusti, p. 11.

[c] Under the Republic the consul or praetor when starting on an expedition took his vows on the Capitol ; if acclaimed imperator by his troops he decked his fasces with laurel, and on his return deposited the wreath upon the Capitol.

[d] In the three triumphs of the year 29 B.C. the following names are known : Alexander of Emesa, Adiatorix the Galatian prince with his wife and sons, and Alexander and Cleopatra, children of Cleopatra, whose statue was borne in the procession of the Egyptian triumph (Gardthausen, Aug. i. 473).

haec, (*et agebam*[1] *se*)p(*timum et trigensimum annum*) ‖
30 (*tribu*)niciae potestatis. |

5. (*Dictatura*)m et apsent(*i et praesenti a populo et
senatu Romano mihi oblatam*[2]) | (*M. Marce*)llo e(*t*) L.
Ar(*runtio consulibus non accepi. Non recusavi in
summa*) | (*frumenti p*)enuri(*a c*)uratio(*ne*)m an(*nonae,
qu*)am ita ad(*ministravi, ut intra*) | (*paucos die*)s[3] metu
et per(*i*)c(*lo praesenti populu*)m univ(*ersum meis im-*)‖
35 (*pensis liberarem*). § Con(*sulatum tum dat*)um annuum
e(*t perpetuum non*) | (*accepi.*) |

6. (*Consulibus M. Vinucio et Q. Lucretio et postea
P.*) et Cn. L(*entulis et tertium*) | (*Paullo Fabio Maximo*

[1] et agebam *Mommsen*, eramque *Bergk.*
[2] a populo . . . oblatam *Wölfflin*, mihi datam a populo
et senatu *Mommsen.*
[3] intra paucos dies *Wölfflin and Seeck*, paucis diebus
Mommsen.

ὅτε τ(αῦ)τα ἔγραφον, | καὶ ἤμη(ν τρια)κ(οστὸ)ν
καὶ ἕβδομ(ον δημαρχ)ικῆς | ἐξουσίας. ‖

III 5. Αὐτεξούσιόν μοι ἀρχὴν καὶ ἀπόντι καὶ
παρόντι | διδομένην (ὑ)πό ΄. ε τοῦ δήμου καὶ τῆς
συνκλήτου | Μ(άρκ)ωι (Μ)αρκέλλωι καὶ Λευκίωι
5 Ἀρρουντίωι ὑπάτοις ‖ ο(ὐκ ἐδ)εξάμην. § Οὐ
παρητησάμην ἐν τῆι μεγίστηι | (τοῦ) σ(είτ)ου
σπάνει τὴν ἐπιμέλειαν τῆς ἀγορᾶς, ἣν οὕ‖(τως
ἐπετήδευ)σα, ὥστ' ἐν ὀλίγαις ἡμέρα(ις το)ῦ παρόν-
τος | φόβου καὶ κι(νδ)ύνου ταῖς ἐμαῖς δαπάναις
τὸν δῆμον | ἐλευθερῶσα(ι). Ὑπατείαν τέ μοι τότε
10 δι(δ)ομένην καὶ ‖ ἐ(ν)ιαύσιον κα(ὶ δ)ι(ὰ) βίου οὐκ
ἐδεξάμην. |

6. Ὑπάτοις Μάρκωι Οὐινουκίωι καὶ Κοίντωι
Λ(ουκρ)ητ(ίωι) | καὶ μετὰ τα(ῦ)τα Ποπλίωι καὶ
Ναίωι Λέντλοις καὶ | τρίτον Παύλλωι Φαβίωι

times consul, and was in the thirty-seventh year of my tribunician power.[a]

5. The dictatorship[b] offered me by the people and the Roman Senate, in my absence and later when present, in the consulship of Marcus Marcellus and Lucius Arruntius[c] I did not accept. I did not decline at a time of the greatest scarcity of grain the charge of the grain-supply, which I so administered that, within a few days, I freed the entire people, at my own expense, from the fear and danger in which they were.[d] The consulship, either yearly or for life, then offered me I did not accept.

6. In the consulship of Marcus Vinucius and Quintus Lucretius,[e] and afterwards in that of Publius and Gnaeus Lentulus,[f] and a third time in that of Paullus Fabius Maximus and Quintus Tubero,[g]

---

[a] Augustus held his thirteenth consulship in 2 B.C. He held his thirty-seventh *tribunicia potestas* in A.D. 14.

[b] Dio (liv. 4) says in this connexion : " As for the dictatorship, however, he did not accept the office, but went so far as to rend his garments when he found himself unable to restrain the people in any other way either by argument or entreaty ; for, since he was superior to dictators in the power and honours he already possessed, he properly guarded against the jealousy and hatred which the title would arouse " (Cary's trans.). See also Vell. ii. 89. 5.   [c] 22 B.C.

[d] According to Dio (liv. 1) the offer of the dictatorship and the request that Augustus become commissioner of the grain-supply were made at the same time. The crisis was caused by the conjunction of an overflow of the Tiber, a pestilence which interfered with agriculture in Italy, and consequent famine.

[e] 19 B.C.   [f] 18 B.C.   [g] 11 B.C.

et Q. Tuberone senatu populoq)u(*e Romano consen-*)|
(*tientibus*). . . . .

. . . .

. . . .

. . . .

7. . . . . .¹.

(*Princeps senatus fui usque ad eum diem, quo scrip*)seram
45 (*haec,*) ‖ (*per annos quadraginta. Pontifex maximus,*

¹ *The substance of the lacuna in the Latin text is supplied
by the Greek, supplemented by the Greek text of the Fragment
of Apollonia.*

Μαξίμωι καὶ Κοίν(τωι) Του|βέρωνι § τῆς (τε
15 σ)υνκλήτου καὶ τοῦ δήμου τοῦ ‖ Ῥωμαίων ὁμολο-
γ(ο)ύντων, ἵν(α ἐπιμε)λητὴς τῶν τε νόμων καὶ τῶν
τρόπων ἐ(πὶ τῆι με)γίστηι | (ἐξ)ουσ(ίαι μ)ό(νο)ς
χειροτονηθῶι, § ἀρχὴν οὐδε‖μ(ία)ν πα(ρὰ τὰ
πά)τρ(ια) ἔ(θ)η διδομένην ἀνεδε|ξάμην· § ἃ δὲ
20 τότε δι' ἐμοῦ ἡ σύνκλητος οἰ‖κονομεῖσθαι ἐβούλετο,
τῆς δημαρχικῆς ἐξο(υ)|σίας ὢν ἐτέλε(σα. Κ)αὶ
ταύτης αὐτῆς τῆς ἀρχῆς | συνάρχοντα (αὐτ)ὸς
ἀπὸ τῆς συνκλήτου π(εν)τάκις αἰτήσας (ἔλ)αβον. ‖
IV 7. Τριῶν ἀνδρῶν ἐγενόμην δημοσίων πραγ-
μάτων | κατορθωτὴς συνεχέσιν ἔτεσιν δέκα.
§ Πρῶτον | ἀξιώματος τόπον ἔσχον τῆς συνκλήτου
ἄχρι | ταύτης τῆς ἡμέρας, ἧς ταῦτα ἔγραφον, ἐπὶ
5 ἔτη τεσ‖σαράκοντα. § Ἀρχιερεύς, § αὔγουρ,

ᵃ There seems to be a conflict here between the statement
of Augustus and that of Suetonius (*Aug.* 27), who states
that he received the *morum legumque regimen in perpetuum,*
and of Dio (liv. 10. 5) that "he accepted an election . . .
to the position of supervisor of morals for five years." It is
probable that the two writers had in mind the decrees of the

when the Senate and the Roman people unanimously agreed [that I should be elected overseer of laws and morals, without a colleague and with the fullest power, I refused to accept any power offered me which was contrary to the traditions of our ancestors.[a] Those things which at that time the senate wished me to administer I carried out by virtue of my tribunician power. And even in this office I five times received from the senate a colleague at my own request.[b]

7. For ten years in succession I was one of the triumvirs for the re-establishment of the constitution].[c] To the day of writing this I have been *princeps senatus*[d] for forty years. I have been pontifex maximus, augur, a member of the fifteen

Senate offering him the title of *praefectus moribus* and his subsequent legislation, while Augustus has in mind his refusal of a new and extraordinary title, although he carried out the intent by virtue of his tribunician power.

[b] Agrippa for five years in 18 B.C., and again for five years in 13 B.C., Tiberius for five years in 12 B.C., after the death of Agrippa, and again for five years in 6 B.C. His tribunate was apparently twice extended after that, each time for a period of ten years.

[c] Neither the words "ten years" or "in succession" are quite exact. The triumvirate began November 27, 43 B.C. The first quinquennium should have ended at the latest December 31, 38 B.C. The triumvirs functioned *de facto*, but not *de iure*, during the year 37. The formal five-year renewal began January 1, 36 B.C., and should have ended December 31, 32. Their *de facto* tenure was therefore eleven years; their *de iure* tenure was ten, but was not consecutive. See Gardthausen, ii. 175.

[d] Augustus became *princeps senatus* in 28 B.C. In the summer of A.D. 14 he had held the title for forty years not counting fractions. By it he became the ranking Senator with the right of speaking first in debate.

augur, quindecimviru)m sacris (*faciundis,*) | (*septem-
virum epulonum, frater arvalis, sodalis Titius,
fetiali*)s fuí. |

8. Patriciórum numerum auxí consul quintum iussu
populi et senátús. § Sena|tum ter légi. Et[1] In
consulátú sexto cénsum populi conlegá M. Agrippá
égí. § | Lústrum post annum alterum et quadragen-
simum féc(*i*). § Quó lústro cívi|um Románórum
censa sunt capita quadragiens centum millia et
5 sexa||g(*i*)nta tria millia. (§) (*Iteru*)m consulari cum
imperio lústrum | (*s*)ólus féci C. Censorin(*o et C.*)
Asinio cos. § Quó lústro censa sunt | cívium Roma-
nóru(*m capita*) quadragiens centum millia et ducen|ta
triginta tria m(*illia. Tertiu*)m consulári cum imperio

1 Et *deleted by Mommsen.*

§ τῶν δεκαπέντε ἀν|δρῶν τῶν ἱεροποιῶν, § τῶν
ἑπτὰ ἀνδρῶν ἱεροποιῶν, § ἀ(δε)λφὸς ἀρουᾶλις,
§ ἑταῖρος Τίτιος, § φητιᾶλις. |

8. Τῶν (πατ)ρικίων τὸν ἀριθμὸν εὔξησα πέμπτον |
10 ὕπατ(ος ἐπιτ)αγῆι τοῦ τε δήμου καὶ τῆς συνκλή||του.
§ (Τὴν σύ)νκλητον τρὶς ἐπέλεξα. § Ἕκτον
ὕπα|τος τὴν ἀπ(ο)τείμησιν τοῦ δήμου συνάρχον-|
(τ)α ἔχων Μᾶρκον Ἀγρίππαν ἔλαβον, ἥτις ἀπο-|
(τείμη)σις μετὰ (δύο καὶ) τεσσαρακοστὸν ἐνιαυ|τὸν
(σ)υνε(κ)λείσθη. Ἐν ἦι ἀποτειμήσει Ῥωμαίων ||
15 ἐτει(μήσ)α(ντο) κεφαλαὶ τετρακό(σιαι ἑ)ξήκον|τα
μυ(ριάδες καὶ τρισχίλιαι. Δεύτερον ὑ)πατι|κῆι
ἐξ(ουσίαι μόνος Γαΐωι Κηνσωρίνωι καὶ) | Γαΐωι
(Ἀσινίωι ὑπάτοις τὴν ἀποτείμησιν ἔλαβον·) | ἐν
20 (ἧι) ἀπ(οτειμήσει ἐτειμήσαντο Ῥωμαί)||ων τε-
τ(ρακόσιαι εἴκοσι τρεῖς μυριάδες καὶ τ)ρι(σ-)|
χίλιοι. Κ(αὶ τρίτον ὑπατικῆι ἐξουσίαι τὰς ἀπο-)

commissioners for performing sacred rites, one of the seven for sacred feasts, an arval brother, a *sodalis Titius*, a fetial priest.[a]

8. As consul for the fifth time,[b] by order of the people and the senate I increased the number of the patricians. Three times I revised the roll of the senate.[c] In my sixth consulship, with Marcus Agrippa as my colleague, I made a census of the people.[d] I performed the *lustrum* [e] after an interval of forty-one years. In this lustration 4,063,000 Roman citizens were entered on the census roll. A second time,[f] in the consulship of Gaius Censorinus and Gaius Asinius, I again performed the *lustrum* alone, with the consular imperium. In this *lustrum* 4,233,000 Roman citizens were entered on the census roll. A third time, with the consular imperium,

---

[a] Augustus became *pontifex maximus* in 12 B.C., *quindecimvir* between 37 and 34, *augur* in 41 or 40, *septemvir epulonum* before 15, *fetialis* in 32. It is not known when he became a *frater arvalis*, or a *sodalis Titius*. The last three colleges had fallen into abeyance in the last days of the republic and were apparently revived by Augustus.

[b] 29 B.C.

[c] The three revisions of which he speaks apparently correspond to the taking of the census in 28 and 8 B.C., and in A.D. 14, but the Senate was also revised in 18 B.C. and A.D. 4, that is to say, about every ten years. See Gardthausen, ii. 311. The first of these revisions is described by Dio, lii. 42 ; Suet. *Aug.* 35. At that time the Senate had reached the unwieldy number of 1000, and contained many undesirables.   [d] 28 B.C.

[e] The lustrum was the expiatory sacrifice made at the close of the census ; in the sentences which follow it is synonymous with the census. The census had not been taken since 69 B.C. At that time the number of citizens of military age was only 450,000. The enormous increase in the census of 28 B.C. is probably due to the exact enumeration of citizens throughout the empire.   [f] 8 B.C.

lústrum | conlegá Tib. Cae(*sare filio meo*[1] *feci*) § Sex.
10 Pompeio et Sex. Appuleio cos. || Quó lústro ce(*nsa
sunt civium Ro*)mánórum capitum quadragiens |
centum mill(*ia et nongenta tr*)iginta et septem millia.
§ | Legibus novi(*s latis complura*[2] *e*)xempla maiorum
exolescentia | iam ex nost(*ro usu revocavi*[3] *et ipse*)
multárum rér(*um exe*)mpla imi|tanda pos(*teris
tradidi*). ||

15 9. (*Vota pro valetudine mea suscipi*[4] *per cons*)ulés et
sacerdotes qu(*into*) | qu(*oque anno senatus decrevit.
Ex iis*) votís s(*ae*)pe fecerunt vívo | (*me ludos aliquo-
tiens sacerdotu*)m quattuor amplissima collé|(*gia, ali-
quotiens consules. Privati*)m etiam et múnicipatim

[1] meo *not in Mommsen.*
[2] complura, *Ramsay, fills the space better than the* multa *of Mommsen.*   [3] reduxi *Mommsen.*
[4] suscipi *Mommsen, supported by Ramsay. The Greek would seem to demand* suscipere.

τειμή)|σε(ι)ς ἔλα(βο)ν, (ἔχω)ν (συνάρχοντα Τι-
βέριον) | Καίσαρα τὸν υἱόν μο(υ Σέξτωι Πομπηίωι
v καὶ) || Σέξτωι Ἀππουληίωι ὑπάτοις· ἐν ἧι ἀπο-
τειμήσει | ἐτειμήσαντο Ῥωμαίων τετρακόσιαι
ἐνενήκοντα | τρεῖς μυριάδες καὶ ἑπτακισχείλιοι.
§ Εἰσαγαγὼν και|νοὺς νόμους πολλὰ ἤδη τῶν
5 ἀρχαίων ἐθῶν κα||ταλυόμενα διωρθωσάμην καὶ
αὐτὸς πολλῶν | πραγμάτων μείμημα ἐμαυτὸν τοῖς
μετέπει|τα παρέδωκα. |
   9. Εὐχὰς ὑπὲρ τῆς ἐμῆς σωτηρίας ἀναλαμβάνειν |
διὰ τῶν ὑπάτων καὶ ἱερέων καθ᾽ ἑκάστην πεν-||
10 τετηρίδα ἐψηφίσατο ἡ σύγκλητος. Ἐκ τού|των
τῶν εὐχῶν πλειστάκις ἐγένοντο θέαι, | τοτὲ μὲν
ἐκ τῆς συναρχίας τῶν τεσσάρων ἱερέ|ων, τοτὲ δὲ
ὑπὸ τῶν ὑπάτων. Καὶ κατ᾽ ἰδίαν δὲ καὶ | κατὰ

and with my son Tiberius Caesar as my colleague, I performed the *lustrum* in the consulship of Sextus Pompeius and Sextus Apuleius.[a] In this *lustrum* 4,937,000 Roman citizens were entered on the census roll. By the passage of new laws I restored many traditions of our ancestors which were then falling into disuse, and I myself set precedents in many things for posterity to imitate.[b]

9. The senate decreed that every fifth year[c] vows should be undertaken for my health by the consuls and the priests. In fulfilment of these vows games were often held in my lifetime, sometimes by the four chief colleges of priests, sometimes by the consuls.[d] In addition the entire body

---

[a] A.D. 14, three months before the death of Augustus. The gain in the number of citizens in the twenty-two years since the census of 8 B.C. was 704,000.

[b] *Cf.* Suetonius, *Aug.* 34 and 89. Among such laws Suetonius specifically mentions the sumptuary law, the law concerning adultery and chastity, the law concerning bribery, and that concerning the marriage of the orders.

[c] That is to say " every four years."

[d] According to Suetonius, *Aug.* 81, Augustus suffered from chronic ill-health. The divinity invoked in these vows was the Actian Apollo. These games were held for the first time in 28 B.C., and celebrated thereafter at four-year intervals. Dio (liii. 4) states that they were in charge of the following four priesthoods in succession : the pontiffs, the augurs, the *septemviri epulonum*, the *quindecimviri sacris faciundis*.

úniver(*si*) | (*cives uno animo continente*)r¹ apud omnia
₂₀ pulvínária pró vale||(*tudine mea sacrificauerunt.*) |

10. (*Nomen meum senatus consulto inc*)lusum est ín
saliáre carmen et sacrosan|(*ctus ut essem in perpetuum*²
et q)uoa(*d*) víverem, tribúnicia potestás mihí | (*esset,
per legem*³ *sanctum est. Pontif*)ex maximus ne fierem
in víví (*c*)onle|(*gae locum, populo id sace*)rdotium
₂₅ deferente mihi, quod pater meu(*s*) || (*habuerat,*⁴
*recusavi.*⁵   *Cepi id*⁶) sacerdotium aliquod post annós
eó mor|(*tuo demum,*⁷ *qui id tumultus o*)ccasione occu-
paverat (§), cuncta ex Italia | (*ad comitia mea coeunte*

¹ (*cives . . . continente*)r *Wirtz.   Mommsen's* (*cives
sacrificaverunt sempe*)r *did not translate the* ὁμοθυμαδὸν
συνεχῶς *of the Greek.*   ² in perpetuum *Bergk.*
³ per legem *Ramsay, Mon. Ant.,* lege *Mommsen.*
⁴ habuerat *Bormann, confirmed by Ramsay, Mon. Ant.,*
habuit *Mommsen.*
⁵ recusavi *Mommsen, confirmed by Mon. Ant.*
⁶ Cepi id *Mommsen,* Quod *Bormann.*
⁷ demum *Ramsay, Mon. Ant. Bormann had conjectured* suscepi, *but the fragment of the Mon. Ant. shows
that the letter after* mortuo *was not* S *but probably* D.

₁₅ πόλεις σύνπαντες οἱ πολεῖται ὁμοθυμα||δ(ὸν) συν-
εχῶς ἔθυσαν ὑπὲρ τῆς ἐμῆς σω(τ)ηρίας. |

10. Τὸ ὄν(ομ)ά μου συνκλήτου δόγματι ἐν-
περιελή|φθη εἰ(ς) τοὺ)ς σαλίων ὕμνους. Καὶ ἵνα
ἱερὸς ὦι | διὰ (βίο)υ (τ)ε τὴν δημαρχικὴν ἔχωι
ἐξουσίαν, | νό(μωι ἐκ)υρώθη. § Ἀρχιερωσύνην,
₂₀ ἣν ὁ πατήρ || (μ)ου (ἐσχ)ήκει, τοῦ δήμου μοι
καταφέροντος | εἰς τὸν τοῦ ζῶντος τόπον, οὐ
προσεδεξά|μ(η)ν. § (῾Η)ν ἀρχιερατείαν μετά τινας
VI ἐνιαυτοὺς || ἀποθανόντος τοῦ προκατειληφότος
αὐ|τὴν ἐν πολειτικαῖς ταραχαῖς, ἀνείληφα, εἰς |
τὰ ἐμὰ ἀρχαιρέσια ἐξ ὅλης τῆς Ἰταλίας τοσού|του
ᴊᴈᴏ

of citizens with one accord,[a] both individually and by municipalities, performed continued sacrifices for my health at all the couches of the gods.

10. By decree of the senate my name was included in the Salian hymn,[b] and it was enacted by law that my person should be sacred in perpetuity and that so long as I lived I should hold the tribunician power.[c] I declined to be made Pontifex Maximus in succession to a colleague still living, when the people tendered me that priesthood which my father had held. Several years later I accepted that sacred office when he at last was dead who, taking advantage of a time of civil disturbance, had seized it for himself, such a multitude from all Italy

[a] An interesting coin, struck by L. Mescinius Rufus IIIvir, has on the reverse a cippus or altar with the words IMP·CAES·AUGU·COMM·CONS· (Imperatori Caesari Augusto communi consensu), and on the obverse, with initial abbreviations, the following legend: Iovi Optimo Maximo Senatus Populusque Romanus votum susceptum pro salute Imperatoris Caesaris quod per eum respublica in ampliore atque tranquilliore statu est.

[b] Mentioned by Dio, li. 20: "When the letter came concerning the Parthians (29 B.C.), they further arranged that his name should be included in their hymns equally with the gods."

[c] On the overthrow of Lepidus in 36 B.C., the tribunician power was given to Octavian, as it had been to Julius, for life. One of the privileges of the tribunate was that the person of the tribune should be inviolate. In 23 B.C. it was made annual as well as perpetual, and from that time on the years of his principate were reckoned by it.

tanta mu)ltitudine, quanta Romae nun(*q*)uam | (*antea fuisse narratur*[1] §) P. Sulpicio C. Valgio consulibu(*s*) §.|

11. (*Aram Fortunae Reducis*[2] *iuxta ae*)dés Honoris
30 et Virtutis ad portam || (*Capenam pro reditu meo se*)-
nátus consacravit, in qua ponti|(*fices et virgines
Vestales anni*)versárium sacrificium facere | (*iussit eo*[3]
die, quo consulibus Q. Luc)retio et (*M. Vinuci*)o in
urbem ex | (*Syria redi, et diem Augustali*)a ex (*c*)o(*gno-
mine nost*)ro appellavit. |

12. (*Senatus consulto eodem tempor*)e pars (*praetorum*
35 *et tri*)bunorum || (*plebis cum consule Q. Lucret*)io et
princi(*pi*)bus (*viris ob*)viam mihi | mis(*s*)a e(*st in
Campan*)ia(*m, qui*) honos (*ad hoc tempus*) nemini

---

[1] coeunte . . . narratur *is based upon the conjecture of Seeck.*

[2] reduci *Mommsen.*   [3] eo *inserted by Bormann.*

---

5 πλήθους συνεληλυθότος, ὅσον οὐδεὶς || ἔνπροσθεν
ἱστόρησεν ἐπὶ Ῥώμης γεγονέναι Πο|πλίωι Σουλ-
πικίωι καὶ Γαίωι Οὐαλγίωι ὑπάτοις. |

11. Βωμὸν Τύχης Σωτηρίου ὑπὲρ τῆς ἐμῆς
ἐπανόδου | πρὸς τῆι Καπήνηι πύλῃ ἡ σύνκλητος
ἀφιέρωσεν· | πρὸς ὧι τοὺς ἱερεῖς καὶ τὰς ἱερείας
10 ἐνιαύσιον θυ||σίαν ποιεῖν ἐκέλευσεν ἐν ἐκείνῃ τῆι
ἡμέραι, | ἐν ᾗ ὑπάτοις Κοίντωι Λουκρητίωι καὶ
Μάρκωι | Οὐινουκίωι ἐκ Συρίας εἰς Ῥώμην
ἐπανεληλύ|θει(ν), τήν τε ἡμέραν ἐκ τῆς ἡμετέρας
ἐπωνυ|μίας προσηγόρευσεν Αὐγουστάλια. ||

15 12. Δόγματι σ(υ)νκλήτου οἱ τὰς μεγίστας ἀρχὰς
ἄρ|ξαντε(ς σ)ὺν μέρει στρατηγῶν καὶ δημάρχων |
μετὰ ὑπ(ά)του Κοίντου Λουκρητίου ἐπέμφθη|σάν
μοι ὑπαντήσοντες μέχρι Καμπανίας, ἥτις | τειμὴ
362

assembling for my election, in the consulship of Publius Sulpicius and Gaius Valgius, as is never recorded to have been in Rome before.[a]

11. The Senate consecrated in honour of my return an altar to Fortuna Redux at the Porta Capena, near the temple of Honour and Virtue, on which it ordered the pontiffs and the Vestal virgins to perform a yearly sacrifice on the anniversary of the day on which I returned to the city from Syria, in the consulship of Lucius Lucretius and Marcus Vinucius, and named the day, after my cognomen, the Augustalia.[b]

12. At the same time, by decree of the senate, part of the praetors and of the tribunes of the people, together with the consul Quintus Lucretius [c] and the leading men of the state, were sent to Campania to meet me, an honour which up to the

[a] M. Lepidus (like Antony never mentioned by name in the *Mon. Anc.*) had seized upon the office of *pontifex maximus* at Caesar's death, Livy, *Epit.* cxvii. ; Vell. ii. 63. Lepidus died in 13 B.C. and Caesar's election, as we are informed by the *fasti Praenestini*, took place March 6, 12 B.C.

[b] On the return of Augustus in 19 B.C. after settling the affairs of Sicily, Greece, Asia, and Syria, many honours, according to Dio, liv. 10, were decreed to Augustus, but he accepted none except those here mentioned. The Altar of Fortuna Redux was dedicated October 12, and its dedication was celebrated on coins struck in that year. The Porta Capena is the gate by which Augustus entered the city, coming from the south by the Appian Way.

[c] Quintus Lucretius Vespillo was not consul when he started out with the deputation. The year had been one of tumults in the consular comitia and the second consul had not been elected, Dio, liv. 10. One of the purposes of the deputation was to ask Augustus either to accept the consulship, or to name some one to it. His choice fell upon Lucretius, who was one of the delegates.

prae|ter (*m*)e e(*st decretus. Cu*)m ex H(*ispa*)niá
Gal(*liaque, rebus in his p*)rovincís prosp(*e*)|re (*gest*)i(*s*),
R(*omam redi*) Ti. Ne(*r*)one P. Qui(*ntilio consulibu*)s
(§), áram | (*Pacis A*)u(*g*)ust(*ae senatus pro*) redi(*t*)ú
40 meó co(*nsacrari censuit*) ad cam||(*pum Martium, in qua
ma*)gistratús et sác(*erdotes et virgines*) V(*est*)á(*les*) |
(*anniversarium sacrific*)ium facer(*e iussit.*) |

    13. (*Ianum*) Quirin(*um, quem cl*)aussum ess(*e
maiores nostri voluer*)unt, | (*cum p*)er totum i(*mperium
po*)puli Roma(*ni terra marique es*)set parta vic(*torii*)s
pax, cum pr(*ius, quam*) náscerer, (*a condita*) u(*rb*)e
45 bis omnino clausum || (*f*)uisse prodátur m(*emori*)ae,
ter me princi(*pe senat*)us claudendum esse censui(*t*). |

    14. (*Fil*)ios meos, quós iuv(*enes mi*)hi eripuit for-

20 μέχρι τούτου οὐδὲ ἑνὶ εἰ μὴ ἐμοὶ ἐψηφίσ||θη.
§ Ὅτε ἐξ Ἰσπανίας καὶ Γαλατίας, τῶν ἐν ταύ|ταις
ταῖς ἐπαρχείαις πραγμάτων κατὰ τὰς εὐ|χὰς
τελεσθέντων, εἰς Ῥώμην ἐπανῆλθον § | Τιβερίωι
(Νέ)ρωνι καὶ Ποπλίωι Κοιντιλίωι ὑπάτοις, ||
VII βωμὸν Ε(ἰρ)ήνης Σεβαστῆς ὑπὲρ τῆς ἐμῆς ἐπ-|
ανόδου ἀφιερωθῆναι ἐψηφίσατο ἡ σύνκλητος ἐν
πε|δίωι Ἄρεως, πρὸς ὦι τούς τε ἐν ταῖς ἀρχαῖς
καὶ τοὺς | ἱερεῖς τάς τε ἱερείας ἐνιαυσίους θυσίας
ἐκέλευσε ποιεῖν. ||
5 13. Πύλην Ἐννάλιον, ἣν κεκλῖσθαι οἱ πατέρες
ἡμῶν ἠθέ|λησαν εἰρηνευομένης τῆς ὑπὸ Ῥωμαίοις
πάσης γῆς τε | καὶ θαλάσσης, πρὸ μὲν ἐμοῦ, ἐξ
οὗ ἡ πόλις ἐκτίσθη, | τῶι παντὶ αἰῶνι δὶς μόνον
κεκλεῖσθαι ὁμολογεῖ|ται, ἐπὶ δὲ ἐμοῦ ἡγεμόνος
10 τρὶς ἡ σύνκλητος ἐψη||φίσατο κλεισθῆναι. |
    14. Υἱούς μου Γάιον καὶ Λεύκιον Καίσ(α)ρας,

present time has been decreed to no one except myself. When I returned from Spain and Gaul, in the consulship of Tiberius Nero and Publius Quintilius, after successful operations in those provinces, the senate voted in honour of my return the consecration of an altar to Pax Augusta in the Campus Martius, and on this altar it ordered the magistrates and priests and Vestal virgins to make annual sacrifice.[a]

13. Janus Quirinus, which our ancestors ordered to be closed whenever there was peace, secured by victory, throughout the whole domain of the Roman people on land and sea, and which, before my birth is recorded to have been closed but twice in all since the foundation of the city, the senate ordered to be closed thrice while I was princeps.[b]

14. My sons Gaius and Lucius Caesar,[c] whom

---

[a] Augustus was absent for three years in Spain and Gaul, 16 to 13 B.C. The altar was built on the Via Flaminia, by which Augustus returned to the city, and formally dedicated on January 30, 9 B.C. The site was systematically excavated in 1903. For the now famous sculptures see Strong, *Rom. Sculpture*, pp. 39-58.

[b] Tradition records that the Arch of Janus was closed for the first time under Numa. It was closed again after the First Punic War in 235. It was closed by Augustus after the Battle of Actium in 31 B.C., again in 25 B.C. after the Cantabrian war. The year of the third closing of the arch is not known. It stood on the Forum where the Argiletum entered it. See Virg. *Aen.* vii. 607, xii. 198.

[c] Gaius (born in 20 B.C.) and Lucius (born in 17 B.C.), the sons of Agrippa and Julia, the daughter of Augustus. They were adopted by their grandfather in 17 B.C. at the time when Agrippa was associated with Augustus in the *tribunicia potestas*, thus securing the succession. But Agrippa died 12 B.C., Lucius in A.D. 2, and Gaius in A.D. 4.

III *(tuna,)* Gaium et Lucium Caesares ‖ honoris mei
caussá senatus populusque Romanus annum quíntum
et deci|mum agentís consulés designávit, ut (e)um
magistrátum inírent post quin|quennium. Et ex eó
die, quó deducti (s)unt in forum, ut interessent con-
siliís | publicís decrevit sena(t)us. § Equites (a)utem
5 Románi universi principem ‖ iuventútis utrumque
eórum parm(is) et hastís argenteís donátum
ap|pelláverunt. §

15. Plebei Románae viritim ~~HS~~ trecenos numeravi
ex testámento patris | meí, § et nomine meo ~~HS~~
quadringenos ex bellórum manibiís consul | quintum
dedí, iterum autem in consulátú decimo ex (p)atri-
10 monio ‖ meo ~~HS~~ quadringenos congiári viritim per-

οὓς νεανίας ἀ|νήρπασεν ἡ τύχη, εἰς τὴν ἐμὴν
τειμ(ὴ)ν ἥ τ(ε) σύνκλη|τος καὶ ὁ δῆμος τῶν ῾Ρω-
μαίων πεντεκαιδεκαέτεις | ὄντας ὑπάτους ἀπέδειξεν,
15 ἵνα μετὰ πέντε ἔτη ‖ εἰς τὴν ὑπάτων ἀρχὴν εἰσ-
έλθωσιν· καὶ ἀφ' ἧς ἂν | ἡμέ(ρα)ς (εἰς τὴν ἀ)γορὰν
(κατ)αχθ(ῶ)σιν, ἵνα (με)τέχω|σιν τῆς συ(ν)κλήτου
ἐψηφίσατο. § ῾Ιππεῖς δὲ ῾Ρω|μαίων σύν(π)αντες
ἡγεμόνα νεότητος ἑκάτε|ρον αὐτῶν (πρ)οσηγόρευ-
20 σαν, ἀσπίσιν ἀργυρέαις ‖ καὶ δόρασιν (ἐτ)είμησαν. |

15. Δήμωι ῾Ρωμα(ίω)ν κατ' ἄνδρα ἑβδομήκοντα
π(έντ)ε | δηνάρια ἑκάστωι ἠρίθμησα κατὰ δια-|
θήκην τοῦ πατρός μου, καὶ τῶι ἐμῶι ὀνόματι |
ἐκ λαφύρων (π)ο(λέ)μου ἀνὰ ἑκατὸν δηνάρια ‖
VIII πέμπτον ὕπατος ἔδωκα, § πάλιν τε δέ(κατο)ν |
ὑπατεύων ἐκ τ(ῆ)ς ἐμῆς ὑπάρξεως ἀνὰ δηνά|ρια

fortune snatched away from me in their youth, the senate and the Roman people to do me honour made consuls designate, each in his fifteenth year,[a] providing that each should enter upon that office after a period of five years.[b] The senate decreed that from the day on which they were introduced to the forum[c] they should take part in the counsels of state. Moreover, the entire body of Roman knights gave each of them the title of *princeps iuventutis*[a] and presented them with silver shields and spears.

15. To the Roman plebs I paid out three hundred sesterces per man in accordance with the will of my father,[d] and in my own name in my fifth consulship I gave four hundred sesterces apiece from the spoils of war;[e] a second time, moreover, in my tenth consulship I paid out of my own patrimony four

[a] In the year in which they assumed the *toga virilis*, Gaius in 5 B.C. and Lucius in 2 B.C. Augustus assumed the consulship in each of these years in order to introduce them to public life.

[b] Lucius died before reaching the consulship. Gaius was consul A.D. 1.

[c] As their adopted father was *princeps senatus*, so each of his adopted sons was called *princeps iuventutis*, or first among the young men in the class of knights. It seems to have been an honour rather than an official title.

[d] This first donation was in 44 B.C. The amount was $12.00, or £2, 8s. per man, distributed to at least 250,000 people.

[e] In 29 B.C., on the occasion of his triple triumph. The amount was about $16.00, or £3, 6s. per man.

numer(*a*)ví, § et consul | undecimum duodecim
frúmentátiónes frúmento pr(*i*)vatim coémpto | emen-
sus sum, (§) et tribuniciá potestáte duodecimum
quadringenós | nummós tertium viritim dedí. Quae
mea congiaria p(*e*)rvenerunt | ad (*homi*)num millia
15 nunquam minus quinquáginta et ducenta. § || (*T*)ri-
bu(*nic*)iae potestátis duodevicensimum consul xii
trecentís et | vigint(*i*) millibus plebís urbánae sexa-
genós denariós viritim dedí. § | In colon(*i*)s militum
meórum consul quintum ex manibiís viritim | millia
nummum singula dedi ; acceperunt id triumphale
congiárium | in colo(*n*)ís hominum circiter centum
20 et viginti millia. § Consul ter||tium dec(*i*)mum
sexagenós denáriós plebeí, quae tum frúmentum

ἑκατὸν ἠρίθ(μ)ησα, (§) καὶ ἑνδέκατον ὕπατος |
δώδεκα σειτομετρήσεις ἐκ τοῦ ἐμοῦ βίου ἀπ-
5 ε||μέτρησα, (§) καὶ δημαρχικῆς ἐξουσίας τὸ δω-
δέ|κατον ἑκατὸν δηνάρια κατ' ἄνδρα ἔδωκα· αἵ-
τ(ι)|νες ἐμαὶ ἐπιδόσεις οὐδέποτε ἧσσον ἧλθ(ο)ν ε(ἰ)ς
| ἄνδρας μυριάδων εἴκοσι πέντε. Δημα(ρ)χικῆς
ἐ|ξουσίας ὀκτωκαιδέκατον, ὕπατ(ος) δ(ωδέκατον) ||
10 τριάκοντα τρισ(ὶ) μυριάσιν ὄχλου πολειτικ(οῦ
ἑ)ξή|κοντα δηνάρια κατ' ἄνδρα ἔδωκ(α, κα)ὶ
ἀποίκοις στρα|τιωτῶν ἐμῶν πέμπτον ὕπατος ἐ(κ)
λαφύρων κατὰ | ἄνδρα ἀνὰ διακόσια πεντήκοντα
δηνάρια ἔδ(ωκα·) | ἔλαβον ταύτην τὴν δωρεὰν ἐν ταῖς
15 ἀποικίαις ἀν||θρώπων μυριάδες πλ(εῖ)ον δώδε(κα.
Ὕ)πατος τ(ρι)σ|καιδέκατον ἀνὰ ἑξήκοντα δηνάρια

hundred sesterces per man by way of bounty,[a]
and in my eleventh consulship I made twelve
distributions of food from grain bought at my own
expense,[b] and in the twelfth year of my tribunician
power I gave for the third time four hundred sesterces
to each man.[c] These largesses of mine reached a
number of persons never less than two hundred and
fifty thousand.[d] In the eighteenth year of my
tribunician power, as consul for the twelfth time,
I gave to three hundred and twenty thousand of the
city plebs sixty denarii apiece.[e] In the colonies of
my soldiers, as consul for the fifth time, I gave one
thousand sesterces to each man from the spoils of
war ; about one hundred and twenty thousand men
in the colonies received this triumphal largesse.[f]
When consul for the thirteenth time I gave sixty
denarii apiece to the plebs who were then receiving

---

[a] 24 B.C., on his return from the war in Spain. The
amount per man was the same as in 29 B.C.   [b] 23 B.C.

[c] 12 B.C., on the occasion of his assumption of the office
of Pontifex Maximus.

[d] It will be noted that the number of the city plebs is here
a quarter of a million. In the donation of 5 B.C. the number
had reached 320,000. The donation of 2 B.C. is to those
receiving public grain. That this number had been reduced
to 200,000 is attested by Dio, lv. 10. 1.

[e] 5 B.C., on the occasion of introducing Gaius to the
forum. The amount per man is about $9.60, or about
£2 apiece.

[f] 29 B.C. The amount is about $40.00 or £8, 5s.

publicum | accipieba(*t*), dedi ; ea millia hominum
paullo plúra quam ducenta fuerunt. |

16. Pecuniam (*pro*) agrís, quós in consulátú meó
quárto et posteá consulibus | M. Cr(*asso e*)t Cn.
Lentulo augure adsignávi militibus, solví múnicipís.
Ea | (*s*)u(*mma sest*)ertium circiter sexsiens milliens
25 fuit, quam (*p*)ró Italicís || praed(*is*) numeravi, § et
ci(*r*)citer bis mill(*ie*)ns et sescentiens, quod pro agrís |
próvin(*c*)ialibus solví. § Id primus et (*s*)olus omnium,
qui (*d*)edúxerunt | colonias militum in Italiá aut in
provincís, ad memor(*i*)am aetátis | meae feci. Et
postea Ti. Nerone et Cn. Pisone consulibus, (§)
item(*q*)ue C. Antistio | et D. Laelio cos., et C. Calvisio
et L. Pasieno consulibus, et L. Le(*ntulo et*) M. Mes-
30 salla || consulibus, § et L. Cáninio (§) et Q. Fabricio

τῶι σειτομετ(ρου)|μένωι δήμωι ἔδω(κα· οὗτο)ς
ἀρ(ι)θμ(ὸς πλείων εἴκο)|(σ)ι (μυ)ριάδων ὑπῆρχ(ε)ν. |
16. Χρήματα ἐν ὑπατείαι τετάρτηι ἐμῆι κα(ὶ)
20 μετὰ ταῦτα ὑ||πάτοις Μάρκωι Κράσσωι καὶ Ναίωι
Λέντλωι αὔγου|ρι ταῖς πόλεσιν ἠρίθμησα ὑπὲρ
ἀγρῶν, οὓς ἐμέρισα | τοῖς στρατ(ιώ)ταις. Κεφα-
λαίου ἐγένοντο ἐν Ἰταλίαι | μὲν μύριαι π(εντακι)-
σ(χ)ε(ίλιαι μυ)ριάδες, (τῶ)ν (δὲ ἐ)παρ|χειτικῶν
ἀγρῶν (μ)υ(ριάδες ἑξακισχίλ)ιαι πεν(τε κό)σ(ιαι.) ||
ΙΧ Τοῦτο πρῶτος καὶ μόνος ἁπάντων ἐπόησα τῶν
(κατα)γαγόντων ἀποικίας στρατιωτῶν ἐν Ἰτα|λίαι
ἢ ἐν ἐπαρχείαις μέχρι τῆς ἐμῆς ἡλικίας. § Καὶ |
μετέπειτα Τιβερίωι Νέρωνι καὶ Ναίωι Πείσωνι
5 ὑπά||τοις καὶ πάλιν Γαίωι Ἀνθεστίωι καὶ Δέκμωι
Λαι|λίωι ὑπάτοις καὶ Γαίωι Καλουισίωι καὶ Λευ-
κίωι | Πασσιήνωι (ὑ)πάτο(ι)ς (καὶ Λ)ευκίωι Λέντλωι
καὶ Μάρ|κωι Μεσσάλ(αι) ὑπάτοις κ(α)ὶ (Λ)ευκίωι
Κανιν(ί)ωι (κ)αὶ | (Κ)οίντωι Φα(β)ρικίωι ὑπάτοις,

public grain; these were a little more than two hundred thousand persons.[a]

16. To the municipal towns I paid money for the lands which I assigned to soldiers in my own fourth consulship[b] and afterwards in the consulship of Marcus Crassus and Gnaeus Lentulus the augur.[c] The sum which I paid for estates in Italy was about six hundred million sesterces, and the amount which I paid for lands in the provinces was about two hundred and sixty million.[d] I was the first and only one to do this of all those who up to my time settled colonies of soldiers in Italy or in the provinces. And later, in the consulship of Tiberius Nero and Gnaeus Piso, likewise in the consulship of Gaius Antistius and Decimus Laelius, and of Gaius Calvisius and Lucius Pasienus, and of Lucius Lentulus and Marcus Messalla, and of Lucius Caninius and Quintus Fabricius, I paid cash gratuities to the

[a] 2 B.C., on the occasion of introducing Lucius to the forum. $9.60 or £2 per man. The donation to the soldiers breaks the chronological narration of donations to the plebs. This donation therefore looks like a later addition. For a discussion of the problem see Introduction. The total of these donations amounts to something over $27,000,000 or about £5,550,000.

[b] 30 B.C. After Actium he had sent back to Italy a detachment of veterans of his own army and that of Antony. These soldiers mutinied at Brundisium and he was obliged to return from Samos to settle this mutiny, by assigning to the oldest veterans towns in Italy which had favored Antony and by giving money to the rest. Those who were thus dispossessed were in part reimbursed by lands at Dyrrachium and at Philippi and in part by the moneys here referred to. See Dio, li. 3. 4; Suet. *Aug.* 17.

[c] 14 B.C.

[d] $24,000,000 (about £4,980,000), and $10,400,000 (£2,140,000) respectively.

co(*s.*) milit(*ibus, qu*)ós eme|riteis stipendís in sua
municipi(*a dedux*)i,[1] praem(*ia n*)umerato | persolví,
(§) quam in rem seste(*rtium*) q(*uater m*)illien(*s li*)-
b(*ente*)r | impendi. |

17. Quater (*pe*)cuniá meá iuví aerárium, ita ut
35 sestertium míllien(*s*) et || quing(*en*)t(*ien*)s ad eos quí
praerant aerário detulerim. Et M. Lep(*i*)do | et L.
Ar(*r*)unt(*i*)o cos. i(*n*) aerarium militare, quod ex
consilio m(*eo*) | co(*nstitut*)um est, ex (*q*)uo praemia
darentur militibus, qui vicena | (*aut plu*)ra sti(*pendi*)a
emeruissent, (§) ~~HS~~ milliens et septing(*e*)nti|(*ens ex
pa*)t(*rim*)onio (*m*)eo detuli. § ||

40 18. (*Inde ab eo anno, q*)uo Cn. et P. Lentuli c(*on-
s*)ules fuerunt, cum d(*e*)ficerent | (*vecti*)g(*alia, tum*)
centum millibus h(*omi*)num tu(*m pl*)uribus (*mul*)to
  [1] remisi *Mommsen.*

10 στρατιώταις ἀπολυ||ομένοις, οὓς κατήγαγον εἰς τὰς
ἰδίας πόλ(εις), φιλαν|θρώπου ὀνόματι ἔδωκα μ(υ-
ρ)ιάδας ἐγγὺς (μυρία)ς. |

17. Τετρά(κ)ις χρήμ(α)σιν ἐμοῖς (ἀν)έλαβον τὸ
αἰράριον, (εἰς) ὃ | (κ)ατήνενκα (χ)ειλίας (ἐπτ)ακοσίας
πεντήκοντα | μυριάδας. Κ(αὶ) Μ(ά)ρκωι (Λεπίδωι)
15 καὶ Λευκίωι Ἀρρουν||τίωι ὑ(πάτοις ε)ἰς τ(ὸ) στ(ρ)α-
(τιωτ)ικὸν αἰράριον, ὃ τῆι | (ἐμῆι) γ(ν)ώ(μηι) κατέστη,
ἵνα (ἐ)ξ αὐτοῦ αἱ δωρ(ε)αὶ εἰσ|(ἐπειτα τοῖς ἐ)μοῖς
σ(τρατι)ώταις δίδωνται, ο(ἳ εἴκο)|(σι)ν ἐνιαυτο(ὺ)ς
ἢ πλείονας ἐστρατεύσαντο, μ(υ)ρι|άδα(ς) τετρά(κ)ις
20 χειλίας διακοσίας πεντήκοντα || (ἐκ τῆς ἐ)μ(ῆς)
ὑπάρξεως κατήνενκα. |

18. (Ἀπ' ἐκ)είνου τ(ο)ῦ ἐνιαυτοῦ, ἐ(φ') οὗ Ναῖος
καὶ Πόπλιος | (Λ)έντλοι ὕπατοι ἐγένοντο, ὅτε
ὑπέλειπον αἱ δη|(μό)σιαι πρόσοδοι, ἄλλοτε μὲν
δέκα μυριάσιν, ἄλ|(λοτε) δὲ πλείοσιν σειτικὰς καὶ
372

soldiers whom I settled in their own towns at the expiration of their service, and for this purpose I expended four hundred million sesterces as an act of grace.[a]

17. Four times I aided the public treasury with my own money, paying out in this manner to those in charge of the treasury one hundred and fifty million sesterces.[b] And in the consulship of Marcus Lepidus and Lucius Arruntius I contributed one hundred and seventy million sesterces out of my own patrimony to the military treasury, which was established on my advice that from it gratuities might be paid to soldiers who had seen twenty or more years of service.[c]

18. Beginning with the year in which Gnaeus and Publius Lentulus were consuls,[d] whenever taxes were in arrears, I furnished from my own purse and my own patrimony tickets for grain and money,

[a] The years were 7, 6, 4, 3, 2 B.C. The amount is about $16,000,000 (£3,329,000).

[b] Two of these four occasions are known from other evidence. Dio Cassius, liii. 2, mentions that of 28 B.C., and a coin of 16 B.C. (cf. Eckhel, vii. 105) has the inscription, " The Senate and the Roman people to Imperator Caesar because the roads have been paved with money which he contributed to the treasury." The amount is about $6,000,000 (£1,234,000). Up to 28 B.C. the treasury was in charge of the quaestors. From then to 23 B.C. it was in charge of two ex-praetors. From that time until the reign of Claudius two praetors had charge of it.

[c] Augustus founded the *aerarium militare* in A.D. 6. In addition to his own subvention, amounting to $6,809,000 (about £1,400,000), it was also supported by a five per cent tax on inheritance and a one per cent tax on sales. From 13 B.C. the length of service had been 12 years for praetorians and 16 for legionaries. It was now increased to 16 and 20 years respectively.   [d] 18 B.C.

fru|(*mentarias et n*)umma(*riá*)s t(*esseras ex aere*)[1] et
pat(*rimonio*) m(*e*)o | (*dedi*). |

IV   19. Cúriam et continens eí chalcidicum, templum-
que Apollinis in | Palatio cum porticibus, aedem dívi
Iulí, Lupercal, porticum ad cir|cum Fláminium, quam
sum appellári passus ex nómine eius quí pri|órem
eódem in solo fecerat Octaviam, pulvinar ad circum
5 maximum, ‖ aedés in Capitolio Iovis Feretrí et Iovis
Tonantis, (§) aedem Quiriní, § | aedés Minervae § et
Iúnonis Reginae § et Iovis Libertatis in Aventíno,
§ | aedem Larum in summá sacrá viá, § aedem deum

[1] multo . . . aere *Schmidt*. *Mommsen conjectured :*
inlato frumento vel ad nummarios tributus ex agro.

X ἀργυρικὰς συντάξεις ‖ ἐκ τῆς ἐμῆς ὑπάρξεως
ἔδωκα. |

    19. Βουλευτήρ(ιο)ν καὶ τὸ πλησίον αὐτῶι χαλ-
κιδικόν, | ναόν τε Ἀπόλλωνος ἐν Παλατίωι σὺν
στοαῖς, | ναὸν θεοῦ (Ἰ)ουλίου, Πανὸς ἱερόν, στοὰν
5 πρὸς ἱπ‖ποδρόμωι τῶι προσαγορευομένωι Φλα-
μινίωι, ἣν | εἴασα προσαγορεύεσθαι ἐξ ὀνόματος
ἐκείνου Ὀκτα|ουῖαν, ὃ(ς) πρῶτος αὐτὴν ἀνέστησεν,
ναὸν πρὸς τῶι | μεγάλωι ἱπποδρόμωι, (§) ναοὺς ἐν
Καπιτωλίωι | Διὸς Τροπαιοφόρου καὶ Διὸς Βρον-
10 τησίου, ναὸν ‖ Κυρείν(ο)υ, (§) ναοὺς Ἀθηνᾶς καὶ
Ἥρας Βασιλίδος καὶ | Διὸς Ἐλευθερίου ἐν Ἀουεν-
τίνωι, ἡρώων πρὸς τῆι | ἱερᾶι ὁδῶι, θεῶν κατοικι-

sometimes to a hundred thousand persons, sometimes to many more.

19. I built the curia *a* and the Chalcidicum adjoining it, the temple of Apollo on the Palatine with its porticoes,*b* the temple of the deified Julius,*c* the Lupercal,*d* the portico at the Circus Flaminius which I allowed to be called Octavia *e* after the name of him who had constructed an earlier one on the same site, the state box at the Circus Maximus, the temples on the capitol of Jupiter Feretrius *f* and Jupiter Tonans,*g* the temple of Quirinus,*h* the temples of Minerva, of Juno the Queen, and of Jupiter Libertas, on the Aventine,*i* the temple of the Lares at the highest point of the Sacra Via, the temple of the Di Penates on the

a This is the Curia Iulia dedicated in 29 B.C. on the site of the old Curia Hostilia.

b The Temple of Apollo was begun soon after 36 B.C. (Vell. ii. 81) and dedicated 28 B.C.

c At eastern end of the forum, on the site where Caesar's body was burned. Dedicated August 18, 29 B.C.

d Formerly a cave in the rock on the south-west of the Palatine, where the she-wolf was supposed to have suckled the twins. It was now converted into a nymphaeum.

e Near the theatre of Pompey. For the original portico built by Octavius, who defeated the fleet of Perses in 168, see Vell. ii. 1.

f A restoration at the suggestion of Atticus, in 31 B.C., of the chapel near the large temple of Iupiter Optimus Maximus, in which Roman generals hung the arms taken from their enemies slain in single combat.

g Dedicated September 1, 22 B.C., to commemorate his miraculous escape from a bolt of lightning when on his Cantabrian expedition, 26-25 B.C. It was at the entrance to the Area Capitolina.

h On the Quirinal, dedicated in 16 B.C.

i These three temples on the Aventine were restorations of earlier temples.

Penátium in Velia, § | aedem Iuventátis, § aedem
Mátris Magnae in Palátio féci. § |
20. Capitolium et Pompeium theatrum utrumque
10 opus impensá grandí reféci ‖ sine ullá inscriptione
nominis meí. § Rívos aquarum complúribus locís |
vetustáte labentés reféci, (§) et aquam quae Márcia
appellátur duplicavi | fonte novo in rivum eius
inmisso. § Forum Iúlium et basilicam, | quae fuit
inter aedem Castoris et aedem Saturni, (§) coepta
profligata|que opera á patre meó perféci § et eandem
15 basilicam consumptam in‖cendio ampliáto eius solo
sub titulo nominis filiórum m(eorum i)n|cohavi (§) et,
si vivus nón perfecissem, perfici ab heredib(us iussi.) |
Duo et octoginta templa deum in urbe consul sex(tum

δίων ἐν Οὐελίαι, ναὸν Νεό|τητο(ς, να)ὸν Μητρὸς
θεῶν ἐν Παλατίωι ἐπόησα. |
20. Καπιτώλ(ιο)ν καὶ τὸ Πομπηίου θέατρον ἑκά-
15 τερον ‖ τὸ ἔργον ἀναλώμασιν μεγίστοις ἐπεσκεύα-
σα ἄ|νευ ἐπιγραφῆς τοῦ ἐμοῦ ὀνόματος. § Ἀγωγοὺς
ὑ|δάτω(ν ἐν πλεί)στοις τόποις τῆι παλαιότητι
ὀλισ|θάνον(τας ἐπ)εσκεύασα καὶ ὕδωρ τὸ καλού-
μενον | Μάρ(κιον ἐδί)πλωσα πηγὴν νέαν εἰς τὸ
20 ῥεῖθρον ‖ (αὐτοῦ ἐποχετεύσ)ας. (§) Ἀγορὰν Ἰουλίαν
καὶ βασι|(λικὴν τὴν μεταξὺ τ)οῦ τε ναοῦ τῶν
Διοσκό|(ρων καὶ τοῦ Κρόνου κατα)βεβλημένα ἔργα
ὑπὸ τοῦ | (πατρός μου ἐτελείωσα κα)ὶ τὴν αὐτὴν
βασιλικὴν | (καυθεῖσαν ἐπὶ αὐξηθέντι) ἐδάφει αὐτῆς
XI ἐξ ἐπι‖γραφῆς ὀνόματος τῶν ἐμῶν υἱῶν ὑπ(ηρξά-
μη)ν | καὶ εἰ μὴ αὐτὸς τετελειώκ(ο)ι(μι, τ)ελε(ι)ω-
(θῆναι ὑπὸ) | τῶν ἐμῶν κληρονόμων ἐπέταξα. § Δ(ύ)ο
(καὶ ὀγδο)|ήκοντα ναοὺς ἐν τῆι πόλ(ει ἔκτ)ον ὕπ(ατος
376

Velia,[a] the temple of Youth,[b] and the temple of the Great Mother on the Palatine.[c]

20. The Capitolium [d] and the theatre of Pompey,[e] both works involving great expense, I rebuilt without any inscription of my own name. I restored the channels of the aqueducts which in several places were falling into disrepair through age, and doubled the capacity of the aqueduct called the Marcia by turning a new spring into its channel.[f] I completed the Julian Forum [g] and the basilica which was between the temple of Castor and the temple of Saturn, works begun and far advanced by my father, and when the same basilica was destroyed by fire I began its reconstruction on an enlarged site, to be inscribed with the names of my sons, and ordered that in case I should not live to complete it, it should be completed by my heirs.[h] In my sixth consulship,[i] in accordance with a decree

[a] These two temples in the neighbourhood of the later arch of Titus apparently disappeared to make room for the colossal constructions of Hadrian and Constantine.

[b] On the Palatine facing the Circus Maximus, destroyed by fire 16 B.C.

[c] Dedicated in 191 B.C. ; destroyed by fire, 3 A.D.

[d] The temple of Iupiter Optimus Maximus, built according to tradition by Tarquinius Superbus, burned to the ground in 83 ; the rebuilding was begun by Sulla and completed by Catulus in 69 B.C.

[e] The first stone theatre in Rome, built in 55 B.C. It continued to be the most important theatre in the city.

[f] For these restorations of the aqueducts see Frontinus, *De aquis*, 125, translated by Herschel.

[g] Dedicated along with the Basilica Iulia on the occasion of the triumph after the battle of Thapsus.

[h] The basilica was soon destroyed by fire. The rebuilding was begun in 12 B.C. The later name, basilica Gai et Luci, never gained general acceptance.

[i] Augustus was consul for the sixth time in 28 B.C.

ex decreto) | senatus reféci, nullo praetermisso quod
e(*o*) temp(*ore refici debebat.*) | Con(*s*)ul septimum viam
20 Flaminiam a(*b urbe*) Ari(*minum feci et pontes*) ‖ omnes
praeter Mulvium et Minucium. |

21. In privato solo Mártis Vltoris templum(*f*)orum-
que Augustum (*ex mani*)|biís feci. § Theatrum ad
aede[1] Apollinis in solo magná ex parte á p(*r*)i(*v*)atis |
empto féci, quod sub nomine M. Marcell(*i*) generi
mei esset. § Don(*a e*)x | manibiís in Capitolio et in
25 aede dívi Iú(*l*)í et in aede Apollinis et in ae‖de
Vestae et in templo Martis Vltoris consacrávi, § quae
mihi consti|terunt ~~HS~~ circiter milliens. § Aurí
coronárí pondo triginta et quinque millia múnicipiís

[1] aede (*sic*).

5 δόγμα)‖τι συνκ(λ)ήτου ἐπεσκεύασ(α) ο(ὐ)δένα π(ε)ρι-
λ(ιπών, ὃς | ἐκείνωι τῶι χρόνωι ἐπισκευῆς ἐδεῖτο.
§ (Ὕ)πα(τος ἕ)‖βδ(ο)μον ὁδὸν Φ(λαμινίαν ἀπὸ)
Ῥώμης (Ἀρίμινον) | γ(εφ)ύρας τε τὰς ἐν αὐτῆι
πάσας ἔξω δυεῖν τῶν μὴ | ἐπ(ι)δεομένων ἐπ(ι)σκευῆς
ἐπόησα. ‖

10 21. Ἐν ἰδιωτικῶι ἐδάφει Ἄρεως Ἀμύντορος
ἀγοράν τε Σε|βαστὴν ἐκ λαφύρων ἐπόησα. (§)
Θέατρον πρὸς τῶι | Ἀπόλλωνος ναῶι ἐπὶ ἐδάφους
ἐκ πλείστου μέρους ἀγο|ρασθέντος ἀνήγειρα (§) ἐπὶ
ὀνόματος Μαρκέλλου | τοῦ γαμβροῦ μου. Ἀναθέ-
15 ματα ἐκ λαφύρων ἐν Καπι‖τωλίωι καὶ ναῶι Ἰουλίωι
καὶ ναῶι Ἀπόλλωνος | καὶ Ἑστίας καὶ Ἄ(ρεω)ς
ἀφιέρωσα, ἃ ἐμοὶ κατέστη | ἐνγὺς μυριάδω(ν δι)σ-
χε(ι)λίων πεντακ(οσίων.) | Εἰς χρυσοῦν στέφανον
λειτρῶν τρισ(μυρίων) | πεντακισχειλίων καταφερού-
378

of the senate, I rebuilt in the city eighty-two temples of the gods, omitting none which at that time stood in need of repair. As consul for the seventh time [a] I constructed the Via Flaminia from the city to Ariminum, and all the bridges except the Mulvian and the Minucian.[b]

21. On my own ground I built the temple of Mars Ultor and the Augustan Forum from the spoils of war.[c] On ground purchased for the most part from private owners I built the theatre near the temple of Apollo which was to bear the name of my son-in-law Marcus Marcellus.[d] From the spoils of war I consecrated offerings on the Capitol, and in the temple of the divine Julius, and in the temple of Apollo, and in the temple of Vesta, and in the temple of Mars Ultor, which cost me about one hundred million sesterces.[e] In my fifth consulship I remitted thirty-five thousand pounds weight of

[a] 27 B.C.

[b] Now the *Ponte Molle* over the Tiber. The location of the Minucian Bridge is not known. In the Greek version these two bridges are not named but simply referred to as "two bridges not in need of repair."

[c] This temple was vowed before the battle of Philippi, but only completed and dedicated in 2 B.C. Part of the temple still stands, as also part of the surrounding wall of the Forum.

[d] The theatre of Marcellus on the Campus Martius was dedicated May 4, 11 B.C. Marcellus died in 23. Part of the outer wall still stands.

[e] Suet. *Aug.* 30, states that at one single donation he presented to the temple of Iupiter Capitolinus 16,000 pounds of gold (64,000,000 sesterces) and in addition gems and pearls amounting to 50,000,000 sesterces. That such statements were grossly exaggerated is shown by the fact that his total donations, 100,000,000 sesterces ($4,000,000 or £800,000) fell short of the amount reported for this one gift

et colonís Italiae conferentibus ad triumphó(*s*) | meós
quintum consul remisi, et posteá, quotienscumque
imperátor a(*ppe*)l|látus sum, aurum coronárium nón
30 accepi decernentibus municipii(*s*) ‖ et coloni(*s*) aequ(*e*)
beni(*g*)ne adquo antea decreverant. |

22. T(*e*)r munus gladiátorium dedí meo nomine
et quinquens[1] filiórum me(*o*)|rum aut n(*e*)pótum
nomine ; quibus muneribus depugnaverunt homi-|
nu(*m*) ci(*rc*)iter decem millia. (§) Bis (*at*)hletarum
undique accitorum | spec(*ta*)c(*lum po*)pulo pra(*ebui*
35 *meo*) nómine et tertium nepo(*tis*) meí no‖mine.
§ L(*u*)dos fecí m(*eo no*)m(*ine*) quater, (§) aliorum
autem m(*agist*)rá|tu(*um*) vicem ter et vicie(*ns*). (§)
(*Pr*)o conlegio xv virorum magis(*ter con*)|(*l*)e(*gi*)í
colleg(*a*) M. Agrippa (§) lud(*os s*)aecl(*are*)s C. Furnio

<hr>

1 quinquens (*sic*), quinquiens *Mon. Ant.*

<hr>

20 σαις τα(ῖς ἐν ᾿Ι)ταλί‖αι πολειτείαις καὶ ἀποικίαις
συνεχώρη(σ)α τὸ (πέμ)|πτον ὑπατεύων, καὶ ὕστερον
ὁσάκις (αὐτ)οκράτωρ·| προσηγορεύθην, τὰς εἰς τὸν
στέφανο(ν ἐ)παγγε|λίας οὐκ ἔλαβον ψηφιζομένων
τῶν π(ολειτει)ῶν | καὶ ἀποικιῶν μετὰ τῆς αὐτῆς
XII προθ(υμίας, κα)θ‖ά(περ καὶ ἐψήφι)σ(το π)ρό(τερον.) |

22. (Τρὶς μονο)μαχ(ίαν ἔδω)κα τῶι ἐμῶι ὀνόματι
καὶ | (πεντάκις τῶν υἱῶν μου ἢ υἱ)ωνῶν· ἐν αἷς
μονο|(μαχίαις ἐμαχέσαντο ἐ)ν(γὺς μύ)ρι(ο)ι. Δὶς
5 ἀθλητῶ(ν) παν‖τ(αχόθεν) με(ταπεμφθέντων γυμ-
νικο)ῦ ἀγῶνος θέαν | (τῶι δήμωι π)αρέσχον τ(ῶι
ἐ)μῶι ὀνόματι καὶ τρίτ(ον) | τ(οῦ υἱωνοῦ μου. Θέας
ἐπόη)σα δι᾿ ἐμοῦ τετράκ(ις,) | διὰ δὲ τῶν ἄλλων
ἀρχῶν ἐν μέρει τρὶς καὶ εἰκοσάκις. § | Ὑπὲρ τῶν
10 δεκαπέντε (ἀνδρ)ῶν, ἔχων συνάρχοντα ‖ Μᾶρκον
᾿Αγρίππ(αν, τὰς θ)έας (δ)ιὰ ἑκατὸν ἐτῶν γεινο|μένας

380

coronary gold [a] contributed by the municipia and the colonies of Italy, and thereafter, whenever I was saluted as imperator, I did not accept the coronary gold, although the municipia and colonies voted it in the same kindly spirit as before.

22. Three times in my own name I gave a show of gladiators, and five times in the name of my sons or grandsons ; in these shows there fought about ten thousand men.[b] Twice in my own name I furnished for the people an exhibition of athletes gathered from all parts of the world, and a third time in the name of my grandson.[c] Four times I gave games in my own name ; as representing other magistrates twenty-three times.[d] For the college of quindecemvirs, as master of that college and with Marcus Agrippa as my colleague, I con-

[a] The custom had grown up for cities affected by a victory to give crowns of gold to a triumphing imperator. These crowns seem later to have been commuted for cash which was called *coronarium aurum*. The amount named here, 35,000 pounds, corresponds to the number of the tribes and would seem to have come from them. The occasion was his triumph in 29 B.C.

[b] Of these eight gladiatorial shows, seven are mentioned in other sources : 29 B.C., on the occasion of the dedication of the temple of Julius ; 28 B.C. ; 16 B.C. ; 12 B.C., in honour of Gaius and Lucius ; 7 B.C. ; 2 B.C., at the dedication of the temple of Mars Ultor ; A.D. 6, in honour of the elder Drusus.

[c] Suet. *Aug.* 43, states that on one occasion (probably 28 B.C., *cf.* Dio, liii. 1) wooden seats for the spectators were erected in the Campus Martius. Which grandson, whether Germanicus or Drusus, is referred to in connexion with the third exhibition is not known.

[d] These were the usual games of the circus and theatre given by magistrates when entering upon their offices.

C. (*S*)ilano cos. (*feci*.) | (*C*)on(*sul* XIII) ludos Mar(*tia*)les
pr(*imus feci*), qu(*os*) p(*ost i*)d tempus deincep(*s*) |
ins(*equen*)ti(*bus ann*)is (*s. c. mecum*[1] *fecerunt co*)n(*su*)les.
⁴⁰ (§) (*Ven*)ati(*o*)n(*es*) best(*ia*)||rum Africanárum meo
nómine aut filio(*ru*)m meórum et nepotum in ci(*r*)|co
aut (*i*)n foro aut in amphitheatris popul(*o d*)edi
sexiens et viciens, quibus | confecta sunt bestiarum
circiter tria m(*ill*)ia et quingentae. |

23. Navalis proelí spectaclum populo de(*di tr*)ans
Tiberim, in quo loco | nunc nemus est Caesarum,
⁴⁵ cavato (*solo*) in longitudinem mille || et octingentós
pedés, (§) in látitudine(*m mille*) e(*t*) ducenti.[2] In quo
tri|ginta rostrátae náves trirémes a(*ut birem*)és, (§)

¹ s. c. mecum *supplied by Wirtz*.
² ducenti (*sic*).

ὸν(ομαζομένα)ς σ(αι)κλάρεις ἐπόησα Γαΐωι | Φουρ-
νίωι κ(αὶ) Γαΐωι Σε(ι)λανῶι ὑπάτοις. (§) Ὕπατος
τρισ|καιδέκατον (θέας Ἄρεως πρ)ῶτος ἐπόησα, ἃς
μετ' ἐ|κεῖνο(ν χ)ρόνον ἑξῆς (τοῖς μ)ετέπειτα ἐνιαυ-
¹⁵ τοῖς || δ(όγματι συνκλήτου σὺν ἐ)μοὶ ἐπόησαν οἱ
ὕπα|(τοι) . . . . ν . . . .
. . . . ης θηρίων ε |
. . . .
. . . .
. . . .
. . . .

23. Ν(αυμαχίας θέαν τῶι δήμωι ἔδω)κα πέ(ρ)αν
τοῦ Τι|(βέριδος, ἐν ὧι τόπωι ἐστὶ νῦ)ν ἄλσος
Καισά(ρω)ν, | ἐκκεχω(κὼς τὸ ἔδαφος) ε(ἰ)ς μῆκ(ο)ς
χειλίων ὀκτακο|σίων ποδ(ῶν, εἰς π)λάτ(ο)ς χιλίων
ᴄᴠ διακο(σ)ίων. Ἐν ἧι || τριάκο(ν)τα ναῦς ἔμβολα
ἔχουσαι τριήρεις ἢ δί|κροτ(οι, αἱ) δὲ ἥσσονες πλείους

ducted the Secular Games in the consulship of Gaius Furnius and Marcus Silanus.[a] In my thirteenth consulship I gave, for the first time, the games of Mars, which, since that time, the consuls by decree of the senate have given in successive years in conjunction with me.[b] In my own name, or that of my sons or grandsons, on twenty-six occasions I gave to the people, in the circus, in the forum, or in the amphitheatre, hunts of African wild beasts, in which about three thousand five hundred beasts were slain.

23. I gave the people the spectacle of a naval battle beyond the Tiber, at the place where now stands the grove of the Caesars, the ground having been excavated for a length of eighteen hundred and a breadth of twelve hundred feet.[c] In this spectacle thirty beaked ships, triremes or biremes,

[a] The fifth celebration of the secular games, June 1-3, 17 B.C. An inscription reporting this celebration of the end of the century was found in 1890, *C.I.L.* vi. 32,323. For an interesting account of it see Lanciani, *Pagan and Christian Rome*, p. 73.

[b] The *Ludi Martiales*, celebrated for the first time in 2 B.C., on the occasion of the dedication of the temple of Mars Ultor.

[c] The Naumachia Augusti was directly across the Tiber from the lower corner of the Aventine. The present church of S. Francesco a Ripa is located near one focus of the ellipse and that of S. Cosimato near the other. Remains have been found of the pavement and the travertine walls. The water was supplied by the Aqua Alsietina, 33 kilometres long, built by Augustus expressly for this purpose.

plures autem | minóres inter se conflixérunt. Q(*uibus*
in) classibus pugnave|runt praeter rémigés millia
ho(*minum tr*)ia circiter. § |
24. In templís omnium civitátium pr(*ovinci*)ae Asiae
50 victor orna||menta reposui, quae spoliátis tem(*plis is*)
cum quó bellum gesseram | privátim possederat.
§ Statuae (*mea*)e pedestrés et equestres et in | quad-
rigeis argenteae steterunt in urbe xxc circiter, quas
ipse | sustuli (§) exque eá pecuniá dona aurea in áede
Apol(*li*)nis meó nomi|ne et illórum, qui mihi statuá-
rum honórem habuerunt, posui. § ||
V   25. Mare pacávi á praedonibus. Eó bello servó-
rum, qui fugerant á dominis | suis et arma contrá
rem publicam céperant, triginta fere millia capta § |
dominis ad supplicium sumendum tradidi. § Iuravit

ἐναυμάχησαν. § | Ἐν τ(ούτωι) τῶι στόλωι ἠγωνί-
σαντο ἔξω τῶν ἐρετῶν | πρ⸌σπ(ο)υ ἄνδρες τρ(ι)σ-
χ(ε)ί(λ)ιοι. ||
5   24. (Ἐν ναοῖ)ς π(ασ)ῶν πόλεω(ν) τῆς (Ἀ)σί(α)ς
νεικήσας τὰ ἀναθέ|(ματα ἀπ)οκατέστησα, (ἃ εἶχεν)
ἰ(δίαι) ἱεροσυλήσας ὁ | ὑπ' (ἐμοῦ) δ(ι)αγωνισθεὶς
πολέ(μιος). Ἀνδριάντες πε|ζοί καὶ ἔφιπποί μου
καὶ ἐφ' ἅρμασιν ἀργυροῖ εἱστήκει|σαν ἐν τῆι πόλει
10 ἐγγὺς ὀγδοήκοντα, οὓς αὐτὸς ἦρα, || ἐκ τούτου τε
τοῦ χρήματος ἀναθέματα χρυσᾶ ἐν | τῶι ναῶι τοῦ
Ἀπόλλωνος τῶι τε ἐμῶι ὀνόματι καὶ | ἐκείνων,
οἵτινές με (τ)ούτοις τοῖς ἀνδριᾶσιν ἐτείμη|σαν,
ἀνέθηκα. |
25. Θάλασσα(ν) πειρατευομένην ὑπὸ ἀποστατῶν
15 δού||λων (εἰρήν)ευσα· ἐξ ὧν τρεῖς που μυριάδας
τοῖς | δε(σπόται)ς εἰς κόλασιν παρέδωκα. § Ὤμοσεν
384

and a large number of smaller vessels met in conflict. In these fleets there fought about three thousand men exclusive of the rowers.[a]

24. After my victory[b] I replaced in the temples in all the cities of the province of Asia the ornaments which my antagonist in the war,[c] when he despoiled the temples, had appropriated to his private use. Silver statues of me, on foot, on horseback, and in chariots were erected in the city to the number of about eighty ; these I myself removed, and from the money thus obtained I placed in the temple of Apollo golden offerings in my own name and in the name of those who had paid me the honour of a statue.[d]

25. I freed the sea from pirates. About thirty thousand slaves, captured in that war, who had run away from their masters and had taken up arms against the republic, I delivered to their masters for punishment.[e] The whole of Ita^ly voluntarily

[a] For this spectacle see Vell. ii. 100. The date was 2 B.C., on the occasion of the dedication of the temple of Mars Ultor. Dio, lv. 10, states that the fight represented a battle of Athenians and Persians, and that the former were victorious.

[b] At Actium in 31 B.C.

[c] Antony is never mentioned by name. He had robbed of their statues and ornaments various temples at Samos, Ephesus, Pergamos, and Rhoeteum in the province of Asia and had given them to Cleopatra. *Cf.* Dio, li. 17.

[d] For the melting up of these statues see Suet. *Aug.* 52, and Dio, liii. 52. Suetonius says that these golden offerings were tripods.

[e] He is referring to the war with Sextus Pompey, terminated in 36 B.C. Pompey's following was made up largely of runaway slaves, and his fleet, so manned, had cut off the grain fleets on their way to Rome. See Vell. ii. 73.

in mea verba tóta | Italia sponte suá et me be(*lli*),
quó víci ad Actium, ducem depoposcit. § Iura-‖
5 verunt in eadem ver(*ba próvi*)nciae Galliae Hispaniae
Africa Sicilia Sar|dinia. § Qui sub (*signis meis tum*)
militaverint, fuerunt senátóres plúres | quam DCC, in
ií(*s qui vel antea vel pos*)teá consules factí sunt ad eum
diem | quó scripta su(*nt haec*, LXXXIII, *sacerdo*)tés
ci(*rc*)iter CLXX. § |

26. Omnium próv(*inciarum populi Romani*), quibus
10 finitimae fuerunt ‖ gentés quae n(*on parerent imperio
nos*)tro, fines auxi. Gallias et Hispa|niás próviciá(*s*[1]
et Germaniam qua inclu)dit Óceanus a Gádibus ad
ósti|um Albis flúm(*inis pacavi*. *Alpes a re*)gióne eá,
quae proxima est Ha|driánó mari, (*ad Tuscum pacari*

¹ provicias (*sic*).

| (εἰς τοὺς ἐμοὺ)ς λόγους ἅπασα ἡ Ἰταλία ἑκοῦσα
κά|(μὲ πολέμου,) ὧι ἐπ' Ἀκτίωι ἐνε(ί)κησα, ἡγεμόνα
ἐξη‖(τήσατο. "Ω)μοσαν εἰς τοὺς (αὐτού)ς λόγους
20 ἐπα(ρ)‖χε(ῖαι Γαλα)τία Ἱσπανία Λιβύη Σι(κελία
Σαρ)δώ. Οἱ ὑπ' ἐ|μ(αῖς σημέαις τό)τε στρατευ-
(σάμενοι ἦσαν συνκλητι)‖(κοὶ πλείους ἑπτ)α(κοσί)ων·
(ἐ)ν (αὐτοῖς οἳ ἢ πρότερον ἢ) | (μετέπειτα) ἐγ(ένον)το
(ὕπ)α(τοι εἰς ἐκ)ε(ί)ν(ην τὴν ἡ)μέ|(ραν, ἐν ἧι ταῦτα
XIV γέγραπτα)ι, ὀ(γδοήκο)ντα τρε(ῖ)ς, ἱερ(εῖ)ς ‖ πρόσπου
ἑκατὸν ἑβδομή(κ)οντα. |

26. Πασῶν ἐπαρχειῶν δήμο(υ Ῥω)μαίων, αἷς
ὅμορα | ἦν ἔθνη τὰ μὴ ὑποτασσό(μ)ενα τῆι ἡμετέραι
ἡ|γεμονία, τοὺς ὅρους ἐπεύξ(ησ)α. (§) Γαλατίαν
5 καὶ Ἱσ‖πανίας, ὁμοίως δὲ καὶ Γερμανίαν καθὼς
Ὠκεα|νὸς περικλείει ἀπ(ὸ) Γαδε(ίρ)ων μέχρι στό-
ματος | Ἄλβιος ποταμο(ῦ ἐν) εἰρήνῃ κατέστησα.
Ἄλπης ἀπὸ | κλίματος τοῦ πλησίον Εἰονίου κόλπου

took oath of allegiance to me and demanded me as its leader in the war in which I was victorious at Actium. The provinces of the Spains, the Gauls, Africa, Sicily, and Sardinia took the same oath of allegiance.[a] Those who served under my standards at that time included more than 700 senators,[b] and among them eighty-three who had previously or have since been consuls up to the day on which these words were written, and about 170 have been priests.

26. I extended the boundaries [c] of all the provinces which were bordered by races not yet subject to our empire. The provinces of the Gauls, the Spains, and Germany, bounded by the ocean from Gades to the mouth of the Elbe, I reduced to a state of peace.[d] The Alps, from the region which lies nearest to the Adriatic as far as the Tuscan Sea, I

[a] In other words, all the provinces in the half of the Empire ruled by Octavianus.

[b] The number of senators at that time was about 1000.

[c] The extensions included : the temporary pushing forward of the German frontier from the Rhine to the Elbe; the creation of the new provinces of Pannonia and Moesia; the addition of the new provinces of Galatia and Paphlagonia in Asia Minor; the expedition of Aelius Gallus to Arabia Felix; and in Africa, in addition to the formal annexation of Egypt, some minor expeditions by the various pro-consuls.

[d] In the Gallic and Cantabrian expeditions of Augustus himself, 27-25 B.C., in that of Carrinas against the Morini, of Messala against the Aquitani, 27 B.C., and the numerous campaigns in Germany, particularly of Drusus and Tiberius. *Pacavi* could apply to Germany for a very brief period only.

fec)i nullí gentí bello per iniúriam | inláto. § Cla(*ssis mea per Oceanum*) ab óstio Rhéni ad sólis orientis
15 re‖gionem usque ad fi(*nes Cimbroru*)m navigavit, (§)
quó neque terra neque | mari quisquam Romanus
ante id tempus adít, § Cimbrique et Charydes | et
Semnones et eiusdem tractús alií Germánórum
popu(*l*)i per legátós amici|tiam meam et populi
Rómáni petierunt. § Meo iussú et auspicio ducti
sunt | (*duo*) exercitús eódem fere tempore in Aethio-
20 piam et in Ar(*a*)biam, quae appel‖(*latur*) eudaemón,
(*maxim*)aeque hos(*t*)ium gentís utr(*iu*)sque cop(*iae*) |
caesae sunt in acie et (*c*)om(*plur*)a oppida capta. In
Aethiopiam usque ad oppi|dum Nabata pervent(*um*)

μέχρι Τυρ|ρηνικῆς θαλάσσης εἰρηνεύεσθαι πεπόηκα,
10 (§) οὐδενὶ ‖ ἔθνει ἀδίκως ἐπενεχθέντος πολέμου.
(§) Στόλος | ἐμὸς διὰ Ὠκεανοῦ ἀπὸ στόματος
Ῥήνου ὡς πρὸς | ἀνατολὰς μέχρι ἔθνους Κίμβρων
διέπλευσεν, οὗ οὔ|τε κατὰ γῆν οὔτε κατὰ θάλασσαν
Ῥωμαίων τις πρὸ | τούτου τοῦ χρόνου προσῆλθεν·
15 καὶ Κίμβροι καὶ Χάλυ‖βες καὶ Σέμνονες ἄλλα τε
πολλὰ ἔθνη Γερμανῶν | διὰ πρεσβειῶν τὴν ἐμὴν
φιλίαν καὶ τὴν δήμου Ῥω|μαίων ἠτήσαντο. Ἐμῆι
ἐπιταγῆι καὶ οἰωνοῖς αἰσί|οις δύο στρατεύματα
ἐπέβη Αἰθιοπίαι καὶ Ἀραβίαι | τῆι εὐδαίμονι κα-
20 λουμένηι, μεγάλας τε τῶν πο‖λεμίων δυνάμεις κατ-
έκοψεν ἐν παρατάξει καὶ | πλείστας πόλεις δορι-
αλώτους ἔλαβεν καὶ προ|έβη ἐν Αἰθιοπίαι μέχρι
388

brought to a state of peace without waging on any tribe an unjust war.[a] My fleet sailed from the mouth of the Rhine eastward as far as the lands of the Cimbri to which, up to that time, no Roman had ever penetrated either by land or by sea, and the Cimbri and Charydes and Semnones and other peoples of the Germans of that same region through their envoys sought my friendship and that of the Roman people.[b] On my order and under my auspices two armies were led, at almost the same time, into Ethiopia and into Arabia which is called the " Happy," and very large forces of the enemy of both races were cut to pieces in battle and many towns were captured.[c] Ethiopia was penetrated as far as the town of Nabata,[d] which is next to Meroë.

[a] At Torbia (Tropaea Augusti), near Monaco, stood a monument, of which only fragments now exist, commemorating the subjugation of the Alpine peoples. Pliny, *N.H.* iii. 20. 136, has preserved the inscription: " The Senate and the Roman people to Caesar . . . Augustus . . . because under his leadership and auspices all the Alpine nations from the upper to the lower sea have been brought into subjection to the Roman people." There follows a list of forty-six peoples.

[b] For this naval expedition to the Elbe in A.D. 5 see Vell. ii. 106. The Cimbri inhabited the coast of Schleswig and Jutland, the Charudes (the Greek text gives " Chalybes ") were their close neighbours, and the Semnones were located between the Elbe and Weser.

[c] The Arabian expedition of Aelius Gallus, 25-24 B.C. The two other portions were called *Arabia petraea* and *Arabia deserta.*

[d] Queen Candace, taking advantage of the withdrawal of Egyptian garrisons for the Arabian expedition, captured some towns in upper Egypt. They were retaken by C. Petronius, 24-22 B.C. His punitive expedition penetrated Aethiopia.

est, cuí proxima est Meroé.   In Arabiam usque | ín
fínés Sabaeorum pro(cess)it exerc(it)us ad oppidum
Mariba. § |

27. Aegyptum imperio populi (Ro)mani adieci.
25 § Armeniam maiorem inter‖fecto rége eius Artaxe
§ c(u)m possem facere provinciam, málui maiórum |
nostrórum exemplo regn(u)m id Tigrani regis Arta-
vasdis filio, nepoti au|tem Tigránis regis, per T(i.
Ne)ronem trad(er)e, qui tum mihi priv(ig)nus erat. |
Et eandem gentem posteá d(esc)íscentem et rebel-
lantem domit(a)m per Gaium | filium meum regi
Ario(barz)ani regis Medorum Artaba(zi) filio regen-‖
30 dam tradidi (§) et post e(ius) mortem filio eius Arta-
vasdi.   (§) Quo (inte)rfecto (Tigra)|ne,[1] qui erat ex
régió genere Armeniorum oriundus, in id re(gnum)

[1] Read Tigranem.

πόλεως Ναβάτης, ἥτις ἐστὶν ἔγνιστα Μερόῃ, ἐν
'Αραβίαι δὲ μέχρι πόλε|ως Μαρίβας. ‖

xv   27. Αἴγυπτον δήμου 'Ρωμαίων ἡγεμονίαι προσ-
έθηκα. | 'Αρμενίαν τὴν μ(εί)ζονα ἀναιρεθέντος τοῦ
βασιλέ|ως δυνάμενος ἐπαρχείαν ποῆσαι μᾶλλον
ἐβου|λήθην κατὰ τὰ πάτρια ἡμῶν ἔθη βασιλείαν
5 Τιγρά‖νηι 'Αρταουάσδου υἱῶι, υἱωνῶι δὲ Τιγράνου
βασι|λέως δ(ο)ῦν(α)ι διὰ Τιβερίου Νέρωνος, ὃς τότ'
ἐμοῦ | πρόγονος ἦν· καὶ τὸ αὐτὸ ἔθνος ἀφιστά-
μενον καὶ | ἀναπολεμοῦν δαμασθὲν ὑπὸ Γαίου τοῦ
υἱοῦ | μου βασιλεῖ 'Αριοβαρζάνει, βασιλέως Μήδων
10 'Αρτα‖βάζου υἱῶι, παρέδωκα καὶ μετὰ τὸν ἐκείνου
θάνα|τον τῶι υἱῶι αὐτοῦ 'Αρταουάσδῃ· οὗ ἀναι-
ρεθέντος | Τιγράνην, ὃς ἦν ἐκ γένους 'Αρμενίου
βασιλικοῦ, εἰς | τὴν βασιλείαν ἔπεμψα. § 'Επ-
390

In Arabia the army advanced into the territories of the Sabaei *a* to the town of Mariba.

27. Egypt I added to the empire of the Roman people.*b* In the case of Greater Armenia, though I might have made it a province after the assassination of its King Artaxes, I preferred, following the precedent of our fathers, to hand that kingdom over to Tigranes, the son of King Artavasdes, and grandson of King Tigranes, through Tiberius Nero who was then my stepson.*c* And later, when the same people revolted and rebelled, and was subdued by my son Gaius,*d* I gave it over to King Ariobarzanes the son of Artabazus, King of the Medes, to rule, and after his death to his son Artavasdes. When he was murdered I sent into that kingdom Tigranes, who was sprung from the royal family of the

a In southern Arabia.

b In 30 B.C., after Actium. Before that time Egypt had been a nominally independent kingdom, though, in a sense, a Roman protectorate. Since 57 B.C., when Ptolemy Auletes was restored, a considerable Roman force had been maintained there. After Actium, Egypt, unlike other provinces was treated as the personal domain of the emperor. For the peculiar status of Egypt as a part of the empire see Arnold, *Roman Provincial Administration*, p. 113.

c In 20 B.C. See Vell. ii. 94.

d It was in the factional struggle which followed the setting up of Artavasdes that Gaius received the wound from which he died in February, 4 A.D.

mísí. § Pro|vincias omnís, quae trans Hadrianum mare
vergun(t a)d orien(te)m, Cyre|násque, iam ex parte
magná regibus eas possidentibus, e(t) antea Siciliam
et | Sardiniam occupatás bello servili reciperáví. § ||
35 28. Colonias in África Sicilia (M)acedoniá utráque
Hispániá Achai(a) Asia S(y)ria | Galliá Narbonensi
Pi(si)dia militum dedúxí. § Italia autem xxviii
(colo)ni|ás, quae vívo me celeberrimae et frequentis-
simae fuerunt, me(is auspicis) | deductas habet. |
29. Signa mílitaria complur(a per) aliós d(u)cés
40 ám(issa) devictí(s hostibu)s re(cipe)raví || ex Hispania
et (Gallia et a Dalm)ateis. § Parthos trium exercitum
Roman(o)|rum spolia et signa re(ddere) mihi supplices-
que amicitiam populí Romaní | petere coegi. § Ea

αρχείας ἁπάσας, ὅσαι | πέραν τοῦ Εἰονίου κόλπου
15 διατείνουσι πρὸς ἀνα||τολάς, καὶ Κυρήνην ἐκ μεί-
σζονος μέρους ὑπὸ βασι|λέων · κατεσχημένας καὶ
ἔμπροσθεν Σικελίαν καὶ Σαρ|δὼι προκατειλημένας
πολέμωι δουλικῶι ἀνέλαβον. |
28. Ἀποικίας ἐν Λιβύηι Σικελίαι Μακεδονίαι ἐν
ἑκατέ|ρα(sic) τε Ἰσπανίαι Ἀχαίαι Ἀσίαι Συρία(sic)
20 Γαλατίαι τῆι πε||ρὶ Νάρβωνα Πισιδίαι στρατιωτῶν
κατήγαγον. § Ἰτα|λία δὲ εἴκοσι ὀκτὼ ἀποικίας
ἔχει ὑπ' ἐμοῦ καταχθεί|σας, αἳ ἐμοῦ περιόντος πλη-
θύουσαι ἐτύγχανον. |
29. Σημέας στρατιωτικὰς (πλείστας ὑ)πὸ ἄλλων
ἡγεμό|νων ἀποβεβλημένας (νικῶν τού)ς πολεμίους ||
xvi ἀπέλαβον § ἐξ Ἰσπανίας καὶ Γαλατίας καὶ παρὰ |
Δαλματῶν. Πάρθους τριῶν στρατευμάτων Ῥω-
μαί|ων σκῦλα καὶ σημέας ἀποδοῦναι ἐμοὶ ἱκέτας τε
φι|λίαν δήμου Ῥωμαίων ἀξιῶσαι ἠνάγκασα. (§)
392

Armenians.[a] I recovered all the provinces extending eastward beyond the Adriatic Sea, and Cyrenae, which were then for the most part in possession of kings,[b] and, at an earlier time,[c] Sicily and Sardinia, which had been seized in the servile war.

28. I settled colonies of soldiers in Africa, Sicily, Macedonia, both Spains, Achaia, Asia, Syria, Gallia Narbonensis, Pisidia. Moreover, Italy has twenty-eight colonies founded under my auspices which have grown to be famous and populous during my lifetime.[d]

29. From Spain, Gaul, and the Dalmatians,[e] I recovered, after conquering the enemy, many military standards which had been lost by other generals. The Parthians I compelled to restore to me the spoils and standards of three Roman armies,[f] and to seek as suppliants the friendship of the Roman

[a] For the complicated question of the Armenian succession see Mommsen, *Res Gestae*, pp. 109–117.

[b] Antony had received by the treaty of Brundisium in 40 B.C. Macedonia, Achaia, Asia, Pontus, Bithynia, Cilicia, Cyprus, Syria, Crete, the Cyrenaica. The last five he had given over to foreign kings. These alienations of foreign territory were the occasion of the civil war which ended at Actium.

[c] By the defeat of Sextus Pompey in 36 B.C.

[d] For these colonies of Augustus see Mommsen, *Res Gestae*, pp. 119–222 ; also *Hermes*, xviii. 161 ff.

[e] The standards lost to the Dalmatians during the civil wars by Gabinius in 48 B.C., and Vatinius in 44 B.C., were restored to Augustus in 23 B.C. We have no account of the standards lost in Gaul. The loss of standards in Spain was during the wars with Pompey's sons, and the recovery must have occurred in the Cantabrian campaign of 25 B.C.

[f] Of Crassus at Carrhae in 53, of Antony in 40 and 36 B.C. The standards were restored by Phraates, the Parthian king, in 20 B.C.

autem si(*gn*)a in penetrálí, quod e(*s*)t ín templo
Martis Vltoris, | reposui. |

    30. Pannoniorum gentes, qua(*s a*)nte me principem
45 populi Romaní exercitus nun‖quam ad(*t*)t, devictas
per Ti. (*Ne*)ronem, qui tum erat privignus et
legátus meus, | ímperio populi Romani s(*ubie*)ci pro-
tulique finés Illyrici ad r(*ip*)am flúminis | Dan(*u*)i.
Citr(*a*) quod (*D*)a(*cor*)u(*m tr*)an(*s*)gressus exercitus
meis a(*u*)sp(*icis vict*)us profliga|tusque (*est, et*) pos(*teá
tran*)s Dan(*u*)vium ductus ex(*ercitus me*)u(*s*) Da(*cor*)um
| gentes im(*peria populi Romani perferre coegit.*) ‖

50   31. Ad me ex In(*dia regum legationes saepe missae
sunt, nunquam antea visae*) | apud qu(*em*)q(*uam*)
R(*omanorum du*)cem. § Nostram am(*icitiam petierunt*)
| per legat(*os*) B(*a*)starn(*ae Scythae*)que et Sarma-

---

5 Ταύτας ‖ δὲ τὰς σημέας ἐν τῶι ˮΑρεως τοῦ ᾿Αμύν-
τορος ναοῦ ἀ|δύτωι ἀπεθέμην. |

    30. Παννονίων ἔθνη, οἷς πρὸ ἐμοῦ ἡγεμόνος
στράτευ|μα ῾Ρωμαίων οὐκ ἤνγισεν, ἡσσηθέντα ὑπὸ
Τιβερίου | Νέρωνος ὃς τότ᾿ ἐμοῦ ἦν πρόγονος καὶ
10 πρεσβευτής, ‖ ἡγεμονίαι δήμου ῾Ρωμαίων ὑπέταξα
(§) τά τε ᾿Ιλλυρι|κοῦ ὅρια μέχρι ˮΙστρου ποταμοῦ
προήγαγον· οὗ ἐπεί|ταδε Δάκων διαβᾶσα πολλὴ
δύναμις ἐμοῖς αἰσίοις οἰω|νοῖς κατεκόπη. Καὶ
ὕστερον μεταχθὲν τὸ ἐμὸν στρά|τευμα πέραν
15 ˮΙστρου τὰ Δάκων ἔθνη προστάγματα ‖ δήμου
῾Ρωμαίων ὑπομένειν ἠνάγκασεν. |

    31. Πρὸς ἐμὲ ἐξ ᾿Ινδίας βασιλέων πρεσβεῖαι
πολλάκις ἀπε|στάλησαν, οὐδέποτε πρὸ τούτου
χρόνου ὀφθεῖσαι παρὰ | ῾Ρωμαίων ἡγεμόνι. § Τὴν
ἡμετέραν φιλίαν ἠξίωσαν | διὰ πρέσβεων § Βαστάρ-

394

people. These standards I deposited in the inner shrine which is in the Temple of Mars Ultor.[a]

30. The tribes of the Pannonians, to which no army of the Roman people had ever penetrated before my principate,[b] having been subdued by Tiberius Nero who was then my stepson and my legate,[c] I brought under the sovereignty of the Roman people, and I pushed forward the frontier of Illyricum as far as the bank of the river Danube. An army of Dacians which crossed to the south of that river was, under my auspices, defeated and crushed, and afterwards my own army was led across the Danube and compelled the tribes of the Dacians to submit to the orders of the Roman people.[d]

31. Embassies were often sent to me from the kings of India,[e] a thing never seen before in the camp of any general of the Romans. Our friendship was sought, through ambassadors, by the Bas-

[a] Only after its completion in A.D. 2. They were temporarily placed on the Capitol.

[b] Augustus had himself fought the Pannonians in 35-34 B.C. See Dio, xliv. 36-38.

[c] 12-9 B.C.

[d] The Dacians had invaded Roman territory many times during the late republic. Julius Caesar was about to make an expedition against them. Augustus, in 35 B.C., occupied Segesta on the Save as an outpost against their invasions. They figure in the civil war as allies of Antony. He is here referring probably to an invasion in 10 B.C. See Dio, liv. 36.

[e] Two such embassies are mentioned : the first, frequently referred to in Augustan literature, while Augustus was in Spain, 26-25 B.C. ; the second visited him at Samos, 20 B.C.

tarum q(*ui sunt citra flu*)men | Tanaim (*et*) ultrá reg(*es,
Alba*)norumque réx et Hibér(*orum et Medorum*). |

32. Ad mé supplices confug(*erunt*) regés Parthorum
VI Tírida(*tes et postea*) Phrát(*es*) ‖ regis Phrati(*s filius*) ;
(§) Medorum (*Artavasdes ; Adiabenorum A*)rtaxa|res ;
§ Britann(*o*)rum Dumnobellau(*nus*) et Tim......;
(*Sugambr*)orum | Maelo ; § Mar(*c*)omanórum Sue-
boru(*m.....rus*). (*Ad me rex*) Parthorum | Phrates
Orod(*i*)s filius filiós suós nepot(*esque omnes misit*) in
5 Italiam, non ‖ bello superátu(*s*), sed amicitiam
nostram per (*liberorum*) suorum pignora | petens.
§ Plúrimaeque aliae gentes exper(*tae sunt p. R.*) fidem
me prin|cipe, quibus anteá cum populo Roman(*o
nullum extitera*)t legationum | et amícitiae (*c*)om-
mercium. § |

20 ναὶ καὶ Σκύθαι καὶ Σαρμα‖τῶν οἱ ἐπιτάδε ὄντες
τοῦ Ταναίδος ποταμοῦ καὶ | οἱ πέραν δὲ βασιλεῖς,
καὶ ᾿Αλβανῶν δὲ καὶ ᾿Ιβήρων | καὶ Μήδων βασιλεῖς. |
32. Πρὸς ἐμὲ ἱκέται κατέφυγον βασιλεῖς Πάρθων
μὲν | Τειριδάτης καὶ μετέπειτα Φραάτης, βασιλέως
XVII § ‖ Φράτου (υἱός, Μ)ήδ(ων) δὲ ᾿Αρταο(υάσδ)ης,
᾿Αδιαβ(η)|νῶν (᾿Α)ρτα(ξάρης, Βριτα)ννῶν Δομ-
νοελλαῦνος | καὶ Τ(ιμ........, Σο)υ-
(γ)άμβρων (Μ)αίλων, Μαρκο|μάνων (Σουήβων
........)ρος. § (Πρὸ)ς ἐμὲ βασιλεὺς ‖
5 Πάρθων Φρα(άτης ᾿Ωρώδο)υ υἱὸ(ς υ)ἱοὺς (αὑτοῦ)
υἱω|νούς τε πάντας ἔπεμψεν εἰς ᾿Ιταλίαν, οὐ
πολέμωι | λειφθείς, ἀλλὰ τὴν ἡμ(ε)τέραν φιλίαν
ἀξιῶν ἐπὶ τέ|κνων ἐνεχύροις, πλεῖστά τε ἄλλα
ἔθνη πεῖραν ἔλ(α)βεν δήμου ῾Ρωμαίων πίστεως ἐπ᾿
10 ἐμοῦ ἡγεμόνος, ‖ οἷς τὸ πρὶν οὐδεμία ἦν πρὸς
δῆμον ῾Ρωμαίων π(ρε)σ|βειῶν καὶ φιλίας κοινωνία.|

tarnae and Scythians,^a and by the kings of the
Sarmatians who live on either side of the river
Tanais,^b and by the king of the Albani ^c and of the
Hiberi ^d and of the Medes.

32. Kings of the Parthians, Tiridates,^e and later
Phrates,^f the son of King Phrates, took refuge with
me as suppliants ; of the Medes, Artavasdes ; ^g of
the Adiabeni,^h Artaxares ; of the Britons, Dumno-
bellaunus ⁱ and Tim . . . . . . ; of the Sugambri,^j
Maelo ; of the Marcomanni and Suevi . . . . .rus.
Phrates, son of Orodes, king of the Parthians, sent
all his sons and grandsons to me in Italy, not because
he had been conquered in war, but rather seeking
our friendship by means of his own children as
pledges.^k And a large number of other nations
experienced the good faith of the Roman people
during my principate who never before had had
any interchange of embassies or of friendship with
the Roman people.

---

^a The Bastarnae were a Teutonic people then settled at
the mouth of the Danube. The Scythians lived in Southern
Russia.

^b The Don.   ^c On the Caspian Sea.

^d In what is now Georgia. ^e 26 B.C.

^f 20 B.C.   ^g 31-30 B.C.

^h An Assyrian people, mentioned here for the first time.

ⁱ Probably the same Dumnobellaunus whose coins have
been found in England. *Cf.* J. Evans, *Coins of the Ancient
Britons*.

^j The Sugambri, a German tribe living to the east of the
Rhine, were finally defeated in 8 B.C., and transferred to
the west bank.

^k It was really in order to get his legitimate sons out of
the way, so as to secure the succession for his illegitimate
son, Phraataces, whose mother was an Italian slave, a
present from Augustus. The date was 10 B.C.

33. A me gentés Parthórum et Médóru(*m per*
¹⁰ *legatos*) principes eárum gen‖tium régés pet(*i*)tós
accéperunt : Par(*thi Vononem regis Phr*)átis fílium, |
régis Oródis nepótem, § Médí Ar(*iobarzanem*), regis
Artavazdis fi|lium, regis Ariobarzanis nep(*otem*). |

34. In consulátú sexto et septimo, b(*ella ubi civil*)ia
exstinxeram | per consénsum úniversórum (*potitus*
¹⁵ *rerum omn*)ium, rem publicam ‖ ex meá potestáte (§)
in senát(*us populique Romani a*)rbitrium transtulí. |
Quó pro merito meó senatu(*s consulto Augustus
appe*)llátus sum et laureís | postés aedium meárum
v(*estiti publice coronaq*)ue civíca super | iánuam meam

33. Παρ' ἐμοῦ ἔθνη Πάρθων καὶ Μήδων διὰ
πρέσβεων τῶν | παρ' αὐτοῖς πρώτων βασιλεῖς
αἰτησάμενοι ἔλαβ(ον)· | Πάρθοι Οὐονώνην, βασιλέως
¹⁵ Φράτου υ(ἱ)όν, βασιλ(έω)ς ‖ 'Ωρώδου υἱωνόν,
Μῆδοι 'Αριοβαρζάνην, βα(σ)ιλέως | 'Αρταβάζου
υἱόν, βασιλέως 'Αριοβαρζάν(ου υἱω)νόν. |

34. 'Εν ὑπατείαι ἕκτηι καὶ ἑβδόμηι μετὰ τὸ
τοὺς ἐνφυ|λίους ζβέσαι με πολέμους (κ)ατὰ τὰς
εὐχὰς τῶν ἐ|μῶν πολε(ι)τῶν ἐνκρατὴς γενόμενος
²⁰ πάντων τῶν ‖ πραγμάτων, ἐκ τῆς ἐμῆς ἐξουσίας
εἰς τὴν τῆς συν|κλήτου καὶ τοῦ δήμου τῶν 'Ρω-
μαίων μετήνεγκα | κυρίαν. 'Εξ ἧς αἰτίας
δόγματι συνκλήτου Σεβαστὸς | προσ(ηγορε)ύθην
καὶ δάφναις δημοσίαι τὰ πρόπυ|λ(ά μου ἐστέ-
XVIII φθ)η, ὅ τε δρύινος στέφανος ὁ διδόμενος ‖ ἐπὶ
σωτηρίᾳ τῶν πολειτῶν ὑπερά(ν)ω τοῦ πυλῶ|νος
τῆς ἐμῆς οἰκίας ἀνετέθη, § ὅπ(λ)ον τε χρυ|σοῦν ἐν

ᵃ In 4-5 B.C. the Parthians asked that the throne, vacated
by the flight of Phraataces (see last note), be filled by

33. From me the peoples of the Parthians and of the Medes received the kings for whom they asked [a] through ambassadors, the chief men of those peoples ; the Parthians Vonones, son of King Phrates, grandson of King Orodes ; the Medes Ariobarzanes, the son of King Artavazdes, grandson of King Ariobarzanes.

34. In my sixth and seventh consulships,[b] when I had extinguished the flames of civil war, after receiving by universal consent the absolute control of affairs, I transferred the republic from my own control to the will of the senate and the Roman people. For this service on my part I was given the title of Augustus [c] by decree of the senate, and the doorposts of my house were covered with laurels by public act, and a civic crown was fixed above my door,[d] and a golden shield was placed in

[a] Vonones, the legitimate son of Phraates, then a hostage in Rome. For Ariobarzanes see Chap. 27.

[b] 28 and 27 B.C. In these and the following years he gradually divested himself of his extraordinary powers and contented himself with ordinary offices, but held in an extraordinary way, such as the *tribunicia potestas*, and the *imperium*. In form he restored the republic ; in substance the real power rested with him, perhaps, in view of the circumstances, unavoidably. The statement which he makes here is clearly the one which he wishes to be the view of posterity. At any rate, the revolutionary and extraordinary acts of the triumviral period ceased, by his own edict (Dio, liii. 2), with the expiration of 28 B.C.

[c] January 16, 27 B.C. The title was suggested by Munatius Plancus.

[d] This crown, or the laurels, or both, are represented upon coins. See Cohen, Nos. 43-48, 50, 207-212, 301, 356, 385, 426, 476-478, 482. Most of them have the inscription *Ob cives servatos*. The civic crown was the reward of the soldier who had saved the life of a citizen. It was given to Augustus because, by putting an end to the civil wars, and by his clemency, he had saved the lives of many citizens.

fīxa est (§) (*clupeusque aureu*)s in (*c*)úriá Iúliá posi|tus,
quem mihi senatum (*populumque Romanu*)m dare
20 virtutis cle‖m(*entia*)e iustitia(*e pietatis caussa testatum*)
est pe(*r e*)ius clúpei | (*inscription*)em.) § Post id
tem(*pus praestiti omnibus dignitate, potes*|*t*)atis au(*tem
n*)ihilo ampliu(*s habui quam qui fuerunt m*)ihi quo|que
in ma(*gis*)tra(*t*)u conlegae. |

35. Tertium dec(*i*)mum consulátu(*m cum gerebam,
25 senatus et equ*)ester ordo ‖ populusq(*ue*) Románus
úniversus (*appellavit me patrem p*)atriae idque | in
vestibu(*lo a*)edium meárum inscriben(*dum esse atque*[1]
in curia e)t in foró Aug. | sub quadrig(*i*)s, quae mihi
(*ex*) s. c. pos(*itae sunt, decrevit. Cum scri*)psi haec, |
annum agebam septuagensu(*mum sextum*). |

[1] atque *Wirtz*, et *Mommsen.*

τῶι βο(υ)λευτηρίωι ἀνατεθ(ὲ)ν ὑπό τε τῆς | συγ-
κλήτου καὶ τοῦ δήμου τῶν ʽΡω(μα)ίων διὰ τῆς ‖
5 ἐπιγραφῆς ἀρετὴν καὶ ἐπείκειαν κα(ὶ δ)ικαιοσύνην |
καὶ εὐσέβειαν ἐμοὶ μαρτυρεῖ. § ᾽Αξιώμ(α)τι (§)
πάντων | διήνεγκα, (§) ἐξουσίας δὲ οὐδέν τι πλεῖον
ἔσχον | τῶν συναρξάντων μοι. |

35. Τρισκαιδεκάτην ὑπατείαν ἄγοντός μου ἥ
10 τε σύν‖κλητος καὶ τὸ ἱππικὸν τάγμα ὅ τε σύνπας
δῆμος τῶν | ʽΡωμαίων προσηγόρευσέ με πατέρα
πατρίδος καὶ τοῦτο | ἐπὶ τοῦ προπύλου τῆς οἰκίας
μου καὶ ἐν τῶι βουλευτη|ρίωι καὶ ἐν τῆι ἀγορᾶι
τῆι Σεβαστῆι ὑπὸ τῶι ἄρματι, ὅ μοι | δόγματι
15 συνκλήτου ἀνετέθη, ἐπιγραφῆναι ἐψηφίσα‖το.
(§) ῞Οτε ἔγραφον ταῦτα, ἦγον ἔτος ἑβδομηκοστὸν |
ἔκτον. § |

the Curia Julia whose inscription testified that the senate and the Roman people gave me this in recognition of my valour, my clemency, my justice, and my piety.[a] After that time I took precedence of all in rank, but of power I possessed no more than those who were my colleagues in any magistracy.

35. While I was administering my thirteenth consulship the senate and the equestrian order and the entire Roman people gave me the title of Father of my Country,[b] and decreed that this title should be inscribed upon the vestibule of my house and in the senate-house and in the Forum Augustum beneath the quadriga erected in my honour by decree of the senate. At the time of writing this I was in my seventy-sixth year.[c]

[a] Not mentioned by ancient writers, but represented upon coins and inscriptions. *Cf. C.I.L.* ix. 5811, with two Victories supporting a shield and the words, " The Senate and Roman people have given to Augustus a shield on account of his valour, clemency, justice, and piety." Kornemann in *Klio*, vol. xv., points out that *virtus, iustitia, clementia,* and *pietas* are the subjects of the first four chapters of the *Mon. Anc.*

[b] Formally bestowed February 5, 2 B.C. Before that he had often been called *pater*, or *parens patriae* informally. Suetonius, *Augustus*, 58, gives part of the address of Messala including the actual salutation, " senatus te consentiens cum populo Romano consalutat patriae patrem."

[c] Augustus was seventy-six on September 23, A.D. 13. Chap. 8 of the *Mon. Anc.* refers to his third census which was completed one hundred days before his death. This would bring the date of writing to between May 11, A.D. 14, and his departure for Campania. Augustus died at Nola, August 19, in that year.

1. Summá pecún(*i*)ae, quam ded(*it in aerarium vel*
30 *plebei Romanae vel di*)mis‖sis militibus : denarium
se(*xi*)e(*ns milliens*). |

2. Opera fecit nova § aedem Martis, (*Iovis Tonantis
et Feretri, Apollinis,*) | díví Iúli, § Quirini, § Minervae,
(*Iunonis Reginae, Iovis Libertatis,*) | Larum, deum
Penátium, (§) Iuv(*entatis, Matris deum, Lupercal,
pulvina*)r | ad circum, (§) cúriam cum ch(*alcidico,*
35 *forum Augustum, basilica*)m ‖ Iuliam, theatrum
Marcelli, (§) (*p*)or(*ticus . . . ., nemus trans
T*)iberím | Caesarum. § |

3. Refécit Capito(*lium sacra*)sque aedes (*nu*)m(*ero
octoginta*) duas, thea(*t*)rum Pom|peí, aqu(*arum rivos,
vi*)am Flamin(*iam*). |

1. Συνκεφαλαίωσις (§) ἠριθμημένου χρήματος
εἰς τὸ αἰρά|ριον ἢ εἰς τὸν δῆμον τὸν ῾Ρω(μαί)ων ἢ
εἰς τοὺς ἀπολε|λυμένους στρατιώτας (§) : ἐξ
μυριάδες μυριάδων. § ‖
20 2. Ἔργα καινὰ ἐγένετο ὑπ' αὐτοῦ ναοὶ μὲν
Ἄρεως, Διὸς | Βροντησίου καὶ Τροπαιοφόρου,
Πανός, Ἀπόλλω|νος, (§) θεοῦ Ἰουλίου, Κυρείνου,
(§) Ἀ(θη)νᾶς, (§) Ἥρας βασιλί|δος, (§) Διὸς
Ἐλευθερίου, (§) ἡρώ(ων, θεῶν π)ατρίων, (§) Νε-|
ότητος, (§) Μητρὸς θεῶν, (§) β(ουλευτήριον) σὺν
XIX χαλκι‖δικῶι, (§) ἀγορᾶι Σεβαστῆι, (§) θέατρον
Μαρκέλλου, (§) β(α)σι|λικὴ Ἰουλία, (§) ἄλσος
Καισάρων, (§) στοαὶ ἐ(ν) Παλατ(ί)ωι, | στοὰ ἐν
ἱπποδρόμωι Φλαμινίωι.
3. § Ἐπεσκευάσθ(η τὸ Κα)|πιτώλιον, (§) ναοὶ
5 ὀγδοήκοντα δύο, (§) θέ(ατ)ρον Π(ομ)‖πηίου, (§)
ὁδὸς Φλαμινία, (§) ἀγωγοὶ ὑδάτων.

Summary [a]

1. The sum total of the money which he contributed to the treasury or to the Roman plebs or to discharged soldiers was 600,000,000 denarii.[b]

2. The new works which he built were : the temple of Mars, of Jupiter Tonans and Feretrius, of Apollo, of the Deified Julius, of Quirinus, of Minerva, of Juno the queen, of Jupiter Libertas, of the Lares, of the Di Penates, of Youth, of the Mother of the gods, the Lupercal, the state box at the circus, the senate-house with the Chalcidicum, the Augustan Forum, the Basilica Julia, the theatre of Marcellus, ... the grove of the Caesars beyond the Tiber.[c]

3. He restored the Capitol and sacred buildings to the number of eighty-two, the theatre of Pompey, the aqueducts, the Flaminian Way.[d]

[a] This summary, as Mommsen points out, is not by Tiberius, but apparently by one of the local magistrates of Ancyra.

[b] The total of the expenditures mentioned by Augustus in this connexion was 2,199,800,000 sesterces. The 600,000,000 denarii—2,400,000,000 sesterces—is accordingly a round sum. See Mommsen, *Res Gestae*, p. 157.

[c] A summary of Chapter 19 and part of 20. Temples are mentioned first to simplify grammatical construction, the other buildings at random. The Greek does not correspond with the Latin : there is no equivalent in the Greek version for *pulvinar ad circum*, nor exact equivalent in the Latin text for στοαὶ ἐν Παλατίῳ, στοὰ ἐν ἱπποδρόμῳ Φλαμινίῳ.

[d] A summary of Chap. 20.

4. Impensa p(*raestita in spect*)acul(*a scaenica et
munera*) gladiatorum at‖(*que athletas et venationes et
naum*)ach(*iam*) et donata pe(*c*)unia a (?) | . . . . . .
. . . . (*ter*)rae motu § in-
cendioque consum|pt(*is*) a(*ut viritim*) a(*micis sena-
t*)oribusque, quórum census explevit, | ín(*n*)umera-
(*bili*)s. § |

4. (Δαπ)άναι δὲ | εἰς θέας καὶ μονομάχους καὶ
ἀθλητὰς καὶ ναυμα|χίαν καὶ θηρομαχίαν δωρεαί
(τε) ἀποικίαις πόλεσιν | ἐν Ἰταλίαι, πόλεσιν ἐν
ἐπαρχείαις (§) σεισμῶι κα(ὶ) ἐνπυ|ρισμοῖς πεπο-
νηκυίαις ἢ κατ' ἄνδρα φίλοις καὶ συν‖κλητικοῖς,
ὧν τὰς τειμήσεις προσεξεπλήρωσεν : ἄ|πειρον
πλῆθος. |

4. The expenditures provided for theatrical shows, gladiatorial sports, for exhibitions of athletes, for hunts of wild beasts, and the naval combat,[a] and his gifts [to colonies in Italy, to cities in the provinces] which had been destroyed by earthquake or conflagration, or to individual friends and senators, whose property he raised to the required rating, are too numerous to be reckoned.[b]

[a] Summarizes Chaps. 22, 23.

[b] These donations to cities and to individuals are not covered by Augustus in his account. The names of some of the cities aided are supplied by the authors and inscriptions: in Italy, Venafrum in Campania (*C.I.L.* x. 4842), and Naples (Dio, lv. 10); in the provinces, Paphos in Cyprus, 15 B.C. (Dio, liv. 23), and several cities in Asia in 12 B.C. (Dio, liv. 30), and lastly Laodicea and Tralles (Strabo, xii. 8. 18 ; Suet. *Tib.* 8).

The census rating for a senator was raised from 800,000 sesterces to 1,200,000, and where senators were worthy, though poor, he raised their fortunes to that amount (Suet. *Aug.* 41).

INDEX

INDEX

INDEX

INDEX

409

INDEX

411

INDEX

412

INDEX

413

INDEX

415

INDEX

INDEX

417

INDEX

INDEX

419

INDEX

INDEX

INDEX

INDEX

INDEX

INDEX

429

INDEX

INDEX

431

INDEX